The Torrid Zone

The Carolina Lowcountry and the Atlantic World

Sponsored by the Program in the Carolina Lowcountry
and the Atlantic World of the College of Charleston

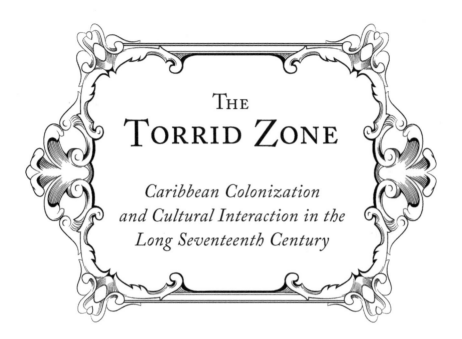

The
TORRID ZONE

Caribbean Colonization
and Cultural Interaction in the
Long Seventeenth Century

Edited by L. H. ROPER

The University of South Carolina Press

© 2018 University of South Carolina

Published by the University of South Carolina Press
Columbia, South Carolina 29208

www.sc.edu/uscpress

Manufactured in the United States of America

Library of Congress Cataloging-in-Publication Data
can be found at http://catalog.loc.gov/.

ISBN: 978-1-61117-890-6 (cloth)
ISBN: 978-1-61117-891-3 (ebook)

Contents

Acknowledgments

The idea for this volume germinated during a correspondence between Laurie Wood and I at the end of 2012, in which we noted the lack of a comprehensive historiographical treatment of the seventeenth-century Caribbean. As Laurie was then finishing up her Ph.D. at the University of Texas at Austin and entering the job market, we agreed that I would undertake the editorial work, take the lead in recruiting our contributors, and secure a publication venue while she would render such assistance as the pursuit of her career permitted. Happily, this plan worked: Laurie now teaches at Florida State University, and this book has seen the light of day. Whether the latter result has any merit is due entirely to the cooperation and professionalism of my colleagues, especially Laurie, who, in addition to the kind contributions of their own labors, patiently answered my questions and comments as well as critiqued the introduction, saving me from committing any number of howlers. I should also like to thank the other contributors, as well as Nikki Parker, for reviewing and critiquing the introduction, as well as the readers for the press for their scrutiny of the volume; of course, I bear responsibility for any and all remaining errors.

I also want to extend my thanks to Alex Moore, then acquisitions editor at the University of South Carolina Press, with whom I met at the 2013 meeting of the Southern Historical Association to discuss this project. His enthusiasm convinced the press to tender a contract, which naturally helped considerably in advancing the endeavor, and he also introduced Barry Stiefel to the project. Once USC Press had the manuscript, Alex having retired, Linda Fogle took charge of its production, and I should like to extend my profound gratitude to her as well for her attention and assistance.

Introduction

By the onset of the seventeenth century, the Caribbean Basin had been the scene of Spanish colonizing activities for over one hundred years. In 1600 the Spaniards claimed the region as their preserve, having established settlements on the islands of, most significantly, Hispaniola and Cuba, as well as Puerto Rico, Jamaica, and Trinidad, along with various locations on the neighboring "Spanish Main." These honeypots of American wealth proved an irresistible attraction to interlopers such as the Dutch "Sea Beggars," the English operators Francis Drake, John Hawkins, Sir Walter Ralegh, and smugglers from various nations who called at the Venezuelan salt pans. The Dutch Revolt against Habsburg rule (1568–1609, 1621–48), the French Wars of Religion (1562–98), and the furious English hostility to Roman Catholicism that manifested itself after the accession of Elizabeth I (November 1558) added religious fuel to the largely Protestant trading, plundering, and settlement ventures that sought to prey on "papist" shipping and duplicate the spectacular successes of the *conquistadores* in Mexico and Peru, as well as, perhaps more mundanely, create plantations of the sort that had emerged following those conquests and in Portuguese Brazil (also ruled by the Spanish Habsburgs from 1580 to 1630).

The accession of the ex-Huguenot Henri IV to the French throne (1598), the Anglo-Spanish Treaty of Westminster (1604), and the Twelve Years Truce that interrupted the Dutch Revolt (1609–21) stayed these politico-religious convulsions in Europe during the first decade of the 1600s. This fragile state of affairs famously did not extend "beyond the line" set by the Treaty of Tordesillas (1494) west of the Azores Islands and north of the Tropic of Capricorn, which purported to divide the world outside of Europe between Spain and Portugal. Accordingly, penetration of the "Spanish lake" continued apace after 1605, even with the departure from the scene of "El Draque" and some of his contemporaries. Ralegh never abandoned his quest for "El Dorado" in Guiana despite the official thaw in Anglo-Spanish relations, nor did his 1618 execution for violating royal orders against engaging the Spaniards by any means deter English investigations of the area between the

Amazon and the Orinoco Deltas. The Dutch and French likewise intensified their activities, while Danes began colonizing St. Thomas in the Virgin Islands in 1666. Competition among these interests made the Caribbean the scene of an unprecedented scale of overseas rivalry

Some of these ventures received formal authorization from governments, while others, notably piratical ones, lacked official imprimatur. Thus, political and economic conflict in the Greater Caribbean region continued to increase during the seventeenth century: between adventurers from the same "empire," between colonizers from different European states, and between Amerindians and Europeans. Non-Iberians took advantage of Spanish disinclination to perfect territorial claims, both on the mainland of South and North America and in the islands.

Thus, the English and French occupied parts of St. Christopher's (modern St. Kitts) as early as 1623–24. The English then assumed control of Barbados in 1627, followed by Nevis in 1628, Providence Island (located off the coast of modern Nicaragua but part of Colombia) at the very end of 1629, and Antigua and Montserrat (both settled in 1632), while the French secured Guadeloupe and Martinique in 1635 and Dutch West India Company forces seized Curacao in 1634. Even these efforts did not proceed without complication: the Kalinago contested the "French" islands, as their Carib counterparts did the Dutch presence in Suriname, and Tobago was the scene of endemic conflict between the Amerindians and Couronian, Dutch, English, and French colonists; meanwhile, the Spanish, in addition to repelling Ralegh's Orinoco incursion, overran the Providence Island colony in 1640 and defeated the Cromwellian "Western Design" against Santo Domingo in 1655. As several of the contributions to *The Torrid Zone* discuss, Jamaica, which the English wrested from Spain after five years of resistance (1655–60), constitutes the most famous case of seventeenth-century imperial enterprise in the Caribbean. Yet, Guiana, like Tobago, remained the fiercely disputed target of multiple European claims, with the Dutch displacing their English rivals along the Berbice and Suriname Rivers in 1667 and the French taking control of Cayenne in 1664.

This volume offers a different sort of consideration of these activities, as well as of the corresponding interactions among Africans, Amerindians, and Europeans and establishment of colonial societies, which occurred in the period prior to and including the time when staple agriculture and slavery became entrenched in the Caribbean. As a center of European commercial and colonizing activity, the "Torrid Zone" has always attracted scholarly attention. Only relatively recently, however, has the study of the region's early history elbowed its way into a comprehension of the European colonization of the Americas that remains focused on thirteen of the colonies that constituted British North America prior to 1783, since the development of the sugar industry and its notorious reliance on the labor of enslaved people of African descent around the Caribbean provide a natural point of comparison with developments on the mainland.

This newer seam of scholarship has continued to track the formation and character of the region's slave societies following the paths carved from an economic perspective by Richard Sheridan's classic analysis in *Sugar and Slavery*, from a social perspective by Richard Dunn's study of Barbados, and from an anthropological one by Jerome Handler and Sidney Mintz, arising from the earlier work of Eric Williams. These labors have certainly shed better light on the development of the Anglophone Caribbean, especially after 1713; the study of the parts of the region settled by non-English Europeans, however, has generated rather less attention, certainly in the English language, with the important exception of the work of Philip Boucher on the Francophone Caribbean. Even so, the importance of the region to a general understanding, even in comparative terms, of American colonization, certainly has yet to receive universal acknowledgment, notwithstanding the now-fashionable preference for an "Atlantic" perspective on the movement of people and commodities among Africa, the Americas, and Europe.[1]

The Torrid Zone invites readers to consider the "long" seventeenth-century Caribbean in an organic, transnational, holistic way that incorporates the diverse array of historical actors involved. In doing so, it includes considerations of relations among African, European, and Native people, as well as investigations of relations among Europeans of various stripes. It also claims a wide swath of territory on the mainland of both North and South America—from Carolina to Cayenne—for inclusion in the "Torrid Zone," since most of the economic and political rivalries that fostered European territorial expansion in the Caribbean in the wake of that expansion were generated by colonists. Thus, the aim is to provide a platform for considering such questions as these: What made the Caribbean the Caribbean? To what degree—and why—was the history of the Caribbean from circa 1580 (when non-Hispanic Europeans began arriving in the region in numbers) distinctive from that of other parts of the Americas?[2]

The approach here to these questions consists of three distinct, albeit integrated, parts. The first of these includes contributions by Tessa Murphy, Carolyn Arena, and Sarah Barber, who investigate indigenous and other seventeenth-century Caribbeans. Very little scholarship has concentrated on seventeenth-century Native-European relations in the Caribbean, especially in Native terms. Accordingly and most particularly, the enduring and significant territorial, diplomatic, and cultural influences of the indigenous people on the post-Columbian history of the Torrid Zone have faded from view. These essays, first of all, underscore the often-ignored reality that much of the region remained outside of European control even into the mid-eighteenth century, just as was the case on the North and South American mainlands.

Moreover, in restoring indigenous agency and perspective to the prominence these Indians had for Caribbean realities, the analyses offered by Murphy, Arena, and Barber provide a collective and salutary reminder that European domination of the Torrid Zone was, by no means, a foregone conclusion any more than it was elsewhere in the Americas. Thus, Murphy finds early French-Kalinago relations in Grenada, Guadeloupe, and Martinique to have been generally friendly, although, according to the missionary-chronicler Jean-Baptiste Du Tertre, an infusion of colonists soured matters as it did with the English elsewhere in the southern Caribbean. Even so, she contends, the Natives seem to have adapted relatively successfully to changing circumstances and indeed continued to impose their influence on their European neighbors into the eighteenth century.

Thus, in 1660 the Kalinago agreed to a formal treaty (the earliest known such accord in the Caribbean) with the English and French, whereby the Natives allowed the French to colonize Guadeloupe and Martinique and the English to possess Antigua, Montserrat, Nevis, and St. Christopher's. In return, the Indians retained Dominica and St. Vincent, from whence they had already driven European settlers, until the British captured the islands during the Seven Years War (1756–63). French efforts to extend this agreement to incorporate their claim to Grenada, though, ran into firm Indian resistance. At the same time French attempts to restrict access to Native-controlled territory by escaping slaves, as well as Native harboring of escapees, met with limited success, even in the early eighteenth century.

Moreover, as Arena demonstrates, the Caribs played as important a role as Europeans did in the history of Suriname. From the 1620s to the 1650s, the Natives, Dutch, and English engaged in a healthy commerce, including trading in tobacco and cotton, in the area between Virginia and Guiana. Yet, the "Indian trade" failed to flourish in 1640s Barbados, although it generated debts for the English involved in it, while Natives from neighboring islands conducted slave raids selling the Africans they seized in neighboring colonies. Even so, Amerindian-European commercial relationships provided the basis for Dutch and English attempts to settle the Wild Coast in the 1630s, although the survival of these plantations remained dependent on Native goodwill as, for instance, a 1643 English settlement in Suriname discovered to their cost.

These interactions continued, and the English finally planted a permanent colony on the South American mainland in 1650—which the Caribs permitted as they found prospective trade with it to be attractive. Yet, despite the Dutch eagerness to create a trading zone with Caribbean Natives from New Granada to Cayenne, they alienated the Amerindians following their acquisition of Suriname. Unfortunately, the Dutch position remained dependent on the English colonists they acquired, and many of these were unhappy at finding themselves under Dutch authority: serving as interpreters with the Caribs, the English encouraged those Indians to resist Dutch overtures, while their countrymen harassed the Arawaks, pre-existing trading partners of the Dutch. The nature of the resulting conflict, Arena observes, obliges us to consider Anglo-Dutch conflict in the Caribbean after 1664 as part of a wider conflict that involved Natives as well as Europeans and facilitated a Dutch commerce in Native slaves. This, in turn, generated fierce

Native outrage—and an alliance between erstwhile Arawak and Carib enemies—and a rebellion by Indian and African slaves. The ensuing ransacking of plantations, accompanied by the killing of slaves and the escape of many others into the interior became so devastating by 1684 that the colonial authorities were obliged to agree to terms with the Caribs (finalized in 1686) whereby the Dutch promised, among other things, to cease enslaving Indians. This tumultuous history of African-European-Native interaction also provided a firm grounding in reality for Aphra Behn's *Oroonoko,* an account, often dismissed as fanciful, which celebrated Indian and African leaders, condemned the Indian slave trade, and tracked the deleterious effects of slavery on Suriname while, of course, absolving many of the English of blame for these.

In a similar vein, the Kalinago commanded events in St. Christopher's, an island they shared with English and French colonists after 1624. As Barber discusses, fears of these "fierce Caribs," which arose from the heated Native-European encounters on the island, fueled French and English perceptions of Native people generally; indeed, the behavior of the Kalinago gave rise to the very conception of the Caribbean—the territory of the "cannibals"—itself. In both the French and English cases, European observers claimed to track a decline in relations. Du Tertre claimed that the first French to arrive on St. Christopher's allied with the Kalinago out of the mutual distrust and loathing of the Spanish. Likewise, when Thomas Warner, the founder of the English settlement, arrived on the island, he and his colonists also enjoyed cordial relations with the Indians. For reasons that remain hazy, however, a falling out, marked by the "Kalinago genocide" at Bloody Point in January 1626, occurred—Du Tertre blamed drink—between the three groups within three years: the English and French presence increased, while the Kalinago largely retreated to neighboring Dominica (also claimed by the Europeans).

Nevertheless, the Indians became embroiled in the subsequent hostilities between rival English claimants to Caribbean power and the French at Guadeloupe, which were punctuated by "massacres" of English settlers in Antigua and of Natives in Dominica. The unfolding of these events were accompanied by competing characterizations of the Kalinago as amiable by their European allies and as "treacherous" by the opponents of those allies. By the second half of the 1670s, though, the latter view held sway in English minds, as Sir William Stapleton, governor of the Leeward Islands, employed it to advantage in denigrating the careers of his opponents as he consolidated his political position in both the Caribbean and the metropolis.

These rivalries receive further treatment in the second part of *The Torrid Zone,* the contributions to which investigate the related phenomena of international conflict (including the agendas of Caribbean Natives and Africans) and sociopolitical development in Suriname, Jamaica, the Danish West Indies, and Saint-Domingue (modern Haiti). The nature of these disputes necessarily exerted an overarching influence in the configuration of imperial boundaries, especially in the cases of the acquisitions of Suriname by the Dutch and of Jamaica by the English, just as they did in the history of European colonization of the Americas more generally; this pair of imperial episodes has received a recent surge of scholarly attention. In a similar vein, subsequent attempts at imperial consolidation necessarily involved attempts by colonial authorities to bring people and landscapes under their control, efforts that yielded decidedly mixed results as they did throughout the Americas.

The theme of negotiation and conflict among Europeans and Natives, discussed by Jessica Vance Roitman as well as by Suze Zijlstra and Tom Weterings, continued on the South American mainland as Dutch, English, and Carib interests (often overlooked) competed intensively over Suriname. Roitman's contribution details the tribulations incurred by the Dutch in their various diverse attempts to settle the "Wild Coast" of South America. The rain and attendant mud of the climate, along with hostility from the Natives and the French, invariably spoiled food supplies and washed away crops, as they brought exhaustion, unfamiliar and devastating tropical diseases, and widespread death to the colonists rather than the prospects of prosperity advertised by the likes of William Usselincx, the Dutch counterpart to the English promoter of colonization, Richard Hakluyt.

Thus, good relations with Indian neighbors were required for survival, but as had happened, for instance, with the English on St. Christopher's, the Dutch felt free to help themselves to the Natives' food supplies, thereby generating enmity. A litany of Wild Coast failure ensued, notwithstanding a keen desire by the Dutch to create a second New Holland following the loss of Dutch Brazil to the Portuguese at the beginning of 1654 after a ten-year war. Suriname provided the only modicum of success out of all the Dutch "Wild Coast" ventures, and this colony owed its survival to the inheritance of a healthy infrastructure, including a reported five hundred sugar plantations in 1665, constructed by the English, along with good relations with the neighboring Caribs. Thus, Roitman observes, the English brought sugar to Suriname, thereby providing the basis for a successful Dutch colony. Even so, the continuing use of forced labor by enslaved Africans was required to make Suriname a going concern.

The Dutch finally secured their claim to the area by the peace that ended the Second Anglo-Dutch War (1665–67) following the capture of the English colony on the Suriname River (founded in 1650) by a Zeeland fleet. As Zijlstra and Weterings show, the new rulers of Suriname were aware of the record of dismal failure that Dutch efforts to colonize this part of the mainland had accumulated. In accordance, then, with the perennial American need from Boston to Bridgetown for successful colonists of whatever stripe, they declined to press the loyalty oath stipulated in the articles of capitulation on the defeated English planters. Rather, they hoped to encourage them to remain under Dutch authority and contribute their experience—and their plantations—to the growth of the colony despite the smoldering hostility between England and the Dutch Republic that would break into the Third Anglo-Dutch War (1672–74) five years later and the constant threat of French attack.

These hopes proved chimerical. The English planters refused to take the loyalty oath and resisted the attempts to enlist their support for the Dutch regime. Instead, a number of them agitated for a return to English rule to the extent that the ringleader of this effort, James Bannister, was sent to Zeeland in chains; and when an attack from the English Caribbean generated an alarm in 1672, the government imprisoned the English inhabitants as a precaution. Thus, while cases exist of seventeenth-century interimperial cooperation (including, ironically, English Suriname), especially with respect to Dutch shipping of English colonial goods as part of the Dutch promotion of "free trade," an examination of the experience of the Surinamese planters demonstrates that "European" wars often revealed the shallow nature of this cooperation, as colonists in the American theaters of these conflicts used them as opportunities to advance or protect local interests. The colonial effects of these wars also included the shoring-up of boundaries, both territorial and personal, on the mainland as well as on the islands.

Amanda Snyder and James Robertson consider the case of Jamaica (seized, like Suriname, during an imperial conflict), with Snyder focusing on the run-up to the Western Design. Despite the serious short-term consequences of the Design's failure to achieve its main goal, Jamaica nevertheless constituted the first overseas prize acquired by force of English arms. The acquisition of the island, then, provides a helpful illustration in microcosm of the increasing influence—haphazard, yet palpable—of the English state in imperial affairs and the increasing decline—also haphazard, yet palpable—of Spanish power in the Caribbean after 1630.

These coincidental patterns, as Snyder describes them, stemmed from the inattention of the Spanish government to the importance of Jamaica geographically and the attendant warnings it had received from colonial administrators as far back as the 1570s, an inattention that historians of Spanish Jamaica and of the Caribbean generally have since replicated. Despite containing no mines (despite enduring rumors of them, as Robertson's contribution discusses) or fabulously wealthy Indian empires, the centrality of the island and its location along the routes traversed by the treasure *flotas* on their way to Seville readily attracted pirates—many of whom were, of course, English—in such numbers as to generate the first alarms over the state of Jamaica's defenses in 1570.

Nevertheless, the Habsburg monarchy, as Snyder notes, failed either to devise a strategy for defending Jamaica more substantially or to provide a suitable navy for patrolling Caribbean waters, especially since it became embroiled increasingly in conflict in other parts of its vast dominions. Moreover, while Castilians generally shunned the sea as a means of social and political advancement, their English counterparts, especially impoverished ones, did become mariners, either as an option to reduced opportunities or via impressment, a manifestation of the relative determination of the government of the island state to defend itself (although this practice also alienated those it targeted). Possessing an unprecedentedly powerful military, the Commonwealth that emerged after the English Civil Wars (1642–51) found itself in a position to take advantage of eighty years of Spanish negligence and strike at the geographic, but neglected, heart of the ancient enemy's American empire. Even though this assault brought only partial short-term success, the retention of Jamaica enabled much more substantive long-term success, especially in terms of imperial dynamics.

Robertson then investigates how the English conquerors, as they endeavored to remold the island's social and physical landscapes after their takeover of Jamaica, adapted certain Spanish and Taíno agricultural and architectural practices while wiping away others and tried to come to terms with the activities of the population of free Africans (a number of whom had obtained terms as reward for assisting the English against the Spanish). Even as they pursued the cultivation of preexisting crops, including citrus fruit and especially cocoa (grown on the island from the early sixteenth century until a blight of 1670–71 killed most of the cocoa walks), the English experimented with new commodities—cotton, tobacco, and indigo—before sugar assumed its well-known precedence.

Imperial transition also had a profound effect on the interior of the island. The establishment of English rule after five years of fighting permitted the resumption of hunting, which had sustained earlier populations of buccaneers. It also invited the pursuit of mining initiatives. The most profound result, though, was deforestation, both to advance agriculture, as had happened on Barbados some twenty years earlier, and the grazing of livestock. Although dramatic in terms of its environmental results, this laborious clearing process, Robertson observes, took considerable time: the sugarcoated portrayals of the Jamaican landscape were the products of late-eighteenth-century artists. At the same time, as Spanish and Taíno influences on the island ebbed after 1660, African ones flowed to a degree sufficient to annoy colonial authorities: escaped slaves joined the communities maintained by the *cimmarones* who assisted the English invaders, who planted rice, medicinal herbs, and other crops according to African methods.

Erik Gøbel provides an account of the simultaneous expansion of Danish interests into the Caribbean. Danish pursuits included the establishment of colonies in the Virgin Islands, which are invariably excluded from considerations of the region but whose histories reveal a familiar scenario. Seventeenth-century Denmark, although it included modern Norway and, until 1658, the southern tip of Sweden, suffered from demographic and geographic handicaps in the pursuit of overseas commercial and colonizing opportunities. Even so, the course of the Danish Empire in the Torrid Zone followed the pattern of its Dutch, English, and French counterparts, albeit on a smaller scale. First, Danish interests were inextricably and deeply linked, practically from their inception in the

1640s, to opportunities in West Africa, where the Danes first came to trade in 1647, especially for slaves; the Guinea trade provided the impetus for—and then maintained—subsequent Danish endeavors in the Caribbean. Then, following several false starts, reminiscent of the experiences of other Europeans, a chartered proprietary company established a colony on St. Thomas in the Virgin Islands, an island still unoccupied by Europeans, in 1672.

Danish colonizers had the same problem recruiting European migrants as their counterparts did; indeed half of the free adults in St. Thomas in 1688 were Dutch. Then, as with, for instance, the case of the English and Barbados (for which, see Stiefel and Roper's contributions to this volume), St. Thomas provided a base for the expansion of the Danish presence in the Caribbean: in 1718 the island's government directed the occupation of nearby St. John, which had also remained unoccupied by Europeans (despite English and Spanish claims that had halted Danish attempts to settle the island as early as 1675), and St. Croix, purchased from France in 1733.

These Danish colonies readily adopted the Caribbean socioeconomic norm as the settlement of them coincided, perhaps not inadvertently, with the full-blown conversion of many of the region's economies to sugar production. This Danish presence, of course, never approached the scale of that of the English or French: indeed, the authorities in the Danish islands had to rely on foreign assistance in the event of slave rebellions, and a substantial number of Dutch planters found St. Thomas to be a conducive location. Moreover, the Danish islands suffered from mismanagement, including support for piracy. Slaves and sugar then provided a similar platform for a thriving transatlantic commerce after 1750 for Denmark, as they did for that kingdom's larger counterparts.

Piracy, of course, played an important role in Caribbean history, although Carla Gardina Pestana has recently argued that the significance of pirates in the history of the seventeenth-century English Caribbean, at least in the period between the anti-Spanish operations conducted by William Jackson in the 1640s and by Henry Morgan in the 1660s and 1670s, has been overstated. Nevertheless, the consistent importance of piratical activities to developments in the early history of the French islands remains apparent, as Giovanni Venegoni's essay attests. His contribution utilizes the *flibustiers* (freebooters) of Saint-Domingue as a case study for tracking the histories of early modern imperial administration and of colony building.

In 1707 a new governor, the Marquis de Choiseul-Beaupré, arrived in the colony with charges to build a new capital and to bring the *flibustiers,* who had operated on the island of Hispaniola since the 1620s, under his authority. Choiseul-Beaupré, who had experience with pirates during his service in the Mediterranean, set about clearing the administrative and physical infrastructures of the colony: his government issued a series of *ordonnances* that directed the construction of new ports to serve as *flibustier* bases, which reconfigured the administrative structure of the colony. He also oversaw the building of a hospital and of roads to connect the new ports, thereby facilitating commerce, and recommended the site for the new capital.

At the same time the resumption of peace in 1697 reenergized relations between intercolonial networks of Huguenot, Irish, and Jewish settlers, as well as sugar cultivation in Saint-Domingue. Indeed, the French colony, whose boundaries were confirmed under the terms of the treaty, found itself well placed to benefit in the aftermath of the War of the League of Augsburg (1689–97), during which participants in the Lesser Antilles, Brazil, Jamaica, and the Spanish Main had all incurred (and committed) depredations. The corresponding drop in supply spiked the price Europeans paid to cater to their collective sweet tooth, and relatively unscathed French planters and merchants quickly moved to increase slave imports and agricultural activity to unprecedented levels in Saint-Domingue.

To facilitate these operations, maintain the European population, and preserve domestic peace, Choiseul-Beaupré issued an amnesty for the freebooters, allowing them to serve as a coast guard even as they continued their smuggling operations in cooperation with their Jamaican counterparts—another manifestation of the importance of intercolonial migration, albeit temporary in this case, to Caribbean history. Not all reforms met with freebooter approval, however, especially the revisions made to the rate of compensation paid for prizes; meanwhile, perhaps paradoxically, imperial peace opened the blind eyes that colonial administrators had turned during the war on smuggling and other intercolonial activities. At the same time, the *flibustiers* created the designation of quartermaster who negotiated the extent of the privileges of the freebooters with the Saint-Domingue government that, accordingly, in Venegoni's terms, undertook to pursue a "guildisation" of the pirates, the first generation of whom had been left to their own devices between the 1620s and the 1660s and, accordingly, whose position in Saint-Domingue did not stabilize until French recolonization of western Hispaniola began in the 1680s. This nascent alliance came to an end, he argues, with the death of Choiseul-Beaupré and the end of the War of Spanish Succession (1702–13): this time peace brought an Anglo-French alliance against freebooting activity, the beginning of the end of the "golden age" of piracy, and the corresponding establishment of the *habitants* (planters) as the power in the colony in the 1730s.

The third part of this volume, consisting of essays by Laurie M. Wood, Barry L. Stiefel, and Lou Roper, examines the extension of the Torrid Zone in cultural, social, political, and temporal terms, which was generated by migration from and around the Caribbean Basin. These activities energized developments, networks, and cultural, social, and political sensibilities—ranging from religious toleration to the establishment and legal administration of the familiar plantation model— that moved with those who held them out of the Caribbean to acceptance by the wider world.

Just as the Francophone Caribbean constituted the scene of intensive Native-European economic and political interaction and of the effects of the environment on the sociopolitical development of European colonies, as illustrated by Murphy and Venegoni, it also provided a platform for the creation of a "global judicial elite." Wood tracks the history of this group, which emerged from a cadre of Martinicans with a military record, such as Michel de Clermont and Philippe de Courpon, who became the leading legal figures in that colony from the mid-seventeenth century. Their emergence, she notes, accompanied that of a plantation-based society in that island; the descendants of Clermont, de Courpon, and their cohort translated their legal ability, along with the elite Caribbean perspective that accompanied it, when they migrated to Saint-Domingue in the early eighteenth century.

Not coincidentally, Wood observes, this movement of people occurred at the same time that Saint-Domingue surpassed Martinique in population (especially the enslaved segment of the islands' demographics) and economic importance as sugar production became entrenched there. Also not coincidentally, the cadre of Martinican entrepreneurs, who had meshed their economic interests with social and political ambitions to join the magistracy and ultimately enter the nobility in the metropolis, dispatched their sons to Saint-Domingue with this formula for sociopolitical success in hand.

This group not only managed the rapid advancement of Saint-Domingue's plantation system in the period between the prevalence of the buccaneers in the mid-seventeenth century and the first part of the eighteenth century and thereby began filling the tinder box of the French Caribbean that caught fire with such dramatic effect after 1791, but it also meshed with its regional counterparts that appeared around the French colonial world, including the Indian Ocean, to form a global entity. This "global themistocracy," as Wood terms it, a network of legal experts grounded in the common pursuit of advancement via the legal profession, then served as the center for discussions on the nature of empire generally and the manufacturing of a legal framework for imperial administration under the *ancien regime*. Accordingly, in the French case, Wood contends, their careers illustrate the importance of this migration within the French Antilles, as well as the more familiar movement of people between the West Indies and France, to the success of those island colonies. They demonstrate, moreover, the significance of intercolonial migration for the incorporation of the sociopolitical plantation theme of European colonization throughout the French Caribbean.

As Stiefel discusses, Jews migrated to the Torrid Zone as their Christian contemporaries did. The commercial and colonizing activities of these migrants, as well as *conversos* residing, for instance, in Jamaica, then extended, especially after their expulsion from Dutch Brazil, to English colonies; having been encouraged to settle on the island by the Cromwellian Protectorate in 1655, notwithstanding their legal expulsion from England by Edward I (ruled 1272–1307), they received the right to settle in Barbados from the colony's assembly.

Jewish support for the Western Design and the persuasive arguments of Rabbi Menasseh ben Israel, helped convince Cromwell and then Charles II of the industry and loyalty of Jews. Thus, these governments readmitted Jews to England more than 350 years after they had been expelled and also approved their rights to settle in English colonies and to practice their faith despite the opposition of those ill disposed to extend such favor to these "aliens." This new toleration extended to Denmark and its colonies in the last quarter of the seventeenth century.

Suriname, as with most Caribbean colonies, came into existence as the result of territorial and commercial pursuits by colonial players. Carolina, Suriname's counterpart on the North American mainland, founded in 1663, famously constitutes another manifestation of the expansion of Barbadian interests; that island, equally famously (or notoriously), constituted the greatest demographic success of seventeenth-century English colonization, with a population reported to be in excess of fifty thousand people (over thirty thousand of whom were enslaved Africans) and its sugar economy well entrenched by 1676.

Yet, as Roper demonstrates, the creation of Carolina also involved expansionary initiatives from Massachusetts and Virginia as well as Barbados in a replication of the pattern of the colonization of Suriname in this part of the North American mainland. These colonial leaders, including the Virginia governor Sir William Berkeley and the prominent Barbados planter Sir John Colleton, appear to have worked their patronage connections in the metropolis to recruit the proprietors in order to provide a higher level of direction for these forays. Thus, the establishment of this colony on the North American mainland, as with all episodes of Anglo-American colonization, mandated the employment of networks that necessarily involved the cultivation of both political factions and estates by colonists from an array of backgrounds.

The interests of the metropolitan patrons of these colonial leaders centered on the transatlantic slave trade and hostility towards the Dutch, enemies of the English on a global scale for over a decade by 1663, and that republic's ally (after 1648), Spain, whose Florida colony could be threatened by a new, vigorous English presence in southeastern North America. They also constituted common economic ground for men who had backed different sides during the recently concluded Civil Wars and Interregnum. The Second Anglo-Dutch War, though, intervened shortly after the issuance of the Carolina charter and rendered these efforts moribund.

After that conflict ended, the Carolina proprietors, with the assistance of their secretary, John Locke, devised fundamental constitutions to guarantee the positions of European migrants to their colony. Still, the numbers of those migrants remained disappointing because of the meteorological and political climates of the place—environments that this North American mainland province shared with the islands. However, those Europeans who did arrive in Carolina ("North" Carolina did not exist officially until 1712 but did so in the breach practically from the issuance of the first Carolina patent) readily employed the customary blueprint for American success, as refined particularly in the Caribbean: slave labor and, after more than twenty years of experimentation, the cultivation of rice as a staple crop.

As with Suriname, involvement in slavery for white Carolinians also involved the enslavement of Natives. However, the scope of Carolina's Indian slave-trading ring far exceeded that of its South American counterpart, as it ranged from the Mississippi River to the Florida Keys; many of these slaves were sold in Barbados and other islands. This commerce, which the proprietors had banned, generated hostility among the Natives and, in another parallel with Suriname, threatened the colony's existence. Thus, many colonists opposed the perpetrators of the trade, who came from various parts of the English-speaking world, not solely from the Caribbean. The ensuing fight between the slave traders and their enemies, which sometimes involved connections in England, convulsed South Carolina for more than thirty years; a replication of the factional battles that convulsed Barbados and other colonies around the Americas. The early history of this colony, Roper suggests, illustrates that the question of a peculiar "Caribbean" political culture and socioeconomic worldview, generated by the region's particular reliance on slave labor, amounts to one of degree rather than of absolutes in comparison with English colonies in other regions.[3]

Although the limits of space prevent a wholly comprehensive treatment of the seventeenth-century Caribbean here, the contributions to this volume do incorporate extensive geographic, demographic, and thematic scopes. In providing a rare comparative treatment of seventeenth-century European activity in the region, their considerations of, among other things, the behavior of indigenous people, Jewish planters and traders, Maroons, the Anglo-Dutch Wars, the Western Design, and pirates enable a relatively wide examination of the "imperial" history of the Torrid Zone. This in turn sheds clear light on the socioeconomic character of the West Indies prior to and during the emergence and extension of the complex of sugar and slaves that came to define these colonies—and perhaps colonial America generally—following its entrenchment in Barbados after 1640. The goal, then, is to add to the understanding of the social, political, and economic sensibilities to which the operators in this "Torrid Zone" subscribed as well as to what they did, along with a better comprehension of the motives for their behavior and the consequences of that behavior. After all, the creation of the social framework entailed in the shift to staple agricultural production and slave labor was the most significant of those results, the ramifications of which continue to ripple into the present day.

Part I

Indigenous and Other Caribbeans

Kalinago Colonizers

Indigenous People and the Settlement of the Lesser Antilles

Tessa Murphy

In 1674 Jean-Charles de Baas Castelmore, governor-general of France's Caribbean colonies, sent a panicked letter to his superiors in the *Ministère de la Marine,* the branch of the French Navy responsible for overseeing colonial ventures. "The war that we have against the Dutch, against the Emperor, and against the Spanish causes a great deal of chagrin to the inhabitants of the islands," de Baas reported, "but they fear these three powers less than they do a war against the Caribs." The governor's letter sheds light on a lengthy contest that shaped the colonization of the seventeenth-century southern Caribbean, yet has remained largely overlooked by historians. Settlers in Guadeloupe, Martinique, and particularly Grenada were alert to the possibility of war with European rivals, the governor explained. But they were even more apprehensive of the prospect that their decades-long conflict with the islands' Amerindian populations, which originated soon after the arrival of French settlers in the region in the 1620s, would be reignited. War with the southern Caribbean's indigenous inhabitants "is of such a difficult nature that it is impossible for us to resist," observed de Baas, and the small number of French settlers in Grenada were "therefore obliged to be continually in arms." If peace could not be reached in Grenada, the governor warned, the French "must resign themselves to abandon" the infant colony.[1]

A close reading of accounts like that of Governor de Baas suggests that little-studied contests between European and Amerindian polities—not just between rival Europeans—continued to shape the colonization of the southern Caribbean throughout the seventeenth century. Narratives of the European destruction of the Caribbean's indigenous populations, beginning with the famously vivid sixteenth-century account of Bartolomé de las Casas, continue to color historical analyses of the region.[2] Moreover, demographic studies of the devastating effects of disease and enslavement on the indigenous inhabitants of Hispaniola are often extrapolated to the wider Caribbean, leading historians to conclude that Native peoples did not pose a significant challenge to European colonization elsewhere in the region.[3]

Yet recent research by archaeologists and historians suggests that the indigenous peoples of the smaller southern Caribbean islands, or Lesser Antilles, were not affected by Europeans in the same way as their counterparts to the north.[4] While the indigenous population of the Lesser Antilles was greatly reduced by epidemics, warfare, and Spanish slaving missions throughout the sixteenth century, surviving texts reveal that Amerindian residents of the region engaged settlers in lengthy diplomatic and military contests over territory, trade, and the expansion of slavery and plantation production throughout the seventeenth and early eighteenth centuries.[5]

Challenging characterizations of near-total indigenous extinction, this chapter focuses on the "island Caribs" of the Lesser Antilles—referred to here as Kalinago—as a polity that actively affected and even participated in the colonization of the region.[6] Recognizing the extent to which the Kalinago shaped European prospects for settlement, dominion, and the expansion of the plantation complex in the seventeenth-century Lesser Antilles affords new insight on the day-to-day realities of colonization and highlights the necessity of integrating indigenous peoples into studies of the colonial Caribbean to achieve a more comprehensive understanding of the region's history.

European contemporaries almost never referred to the people they encountered in the Lesser Antilles as "Kalinago." Missionaries, colonial officials, and settlers instead used the generic term "Indian" or signaled what they perceived to be inherent differences between themselves and their Amerindian neighbors by labeling them *"sauvage"*—wild, untamed, or savage beings. "Carib/Caribee"—a term Europeans used to distinguish the allegedly bellicose indigenous inhabitants of the Lesser Antilles from their purportedly peaceful Arawak neighbors in the Greater Antilles—originated during the voyages of Columbus and came into increasingly popular usage by the eighteenth century.[7] Yet, as Peter Hulme has noted, "the two names, Carib and Arawak, mark an *internal* division within European perceptions of the native Caribbean"; it is unclear whether the pre-Columbian inhabitants of the region would have actually recognized or espoused the group identities Europeans assigned to them.[8]

In eschewing these European labels in favor of a term by which the indigenous inhabitants of the Lesser Antilles described themselves, the use here of "Kalinago" seeks to privilege an Amerindian perspective on seventeenth-century Caribbean colonization.[9] Thus, rather than exploring European responses to the peoples they encountered in the Lesser Antilles, this chapter focuses on how the region's indigenous inhabitants drew on and experimented with a range of approaches to the arrival of new peoples. Referring to the Native peoples of the Lesser Antilles by terms they originated rather than those ascribed them by Europeans also seeks to place the Kalinago on an equal analytical footing with the French, English, and other Europeans with whom they engaged in trade, diplomacy, and war.[10]

An absence of primary sources by Kalinago authors naturally complicates the task of privileging their perspective on seventeenth-century Caribbean colonization but does not render it impossible. Firsthand accounts by Europeans who participated in initial attempts to colonize the Lesser Antilles primarily focus on the experiences and assumptions of their respective authors.[11] Yet surviving texts by missionaries Jean-Baptiste Du Tertre and Raymond Breton, as well as by an anonymous colonist in Grenada, can be mined for what they reveal about Kalinago impressions of and responses to these early interactions.[12] European correspondence offers another important and underutilized window on the role of Caribbean Amerindians in shaping the colonization of the Lesser Antilles: the letters of colonial officials are rife with complaints of attack by Kalinago forces, while frequent mention of attempts to broker peace with Kalinago representatives from different islands reveals that both Europeans and Amerindians deployed a variety of military and diplomatic tactics in an effort to achieve their respective goals.

One of the clearest illustrations of the extent to which indigenous people shaped the colonization of the seventeenth-century Caribbean can be found in the earliest extant written treaty between the Kalinago and Europeans. Signed in the French colony of Guadeloupe in March 1660 by Kalinago delegates from a number of islands and by representatives of the English and French Crowns, the treaty formally recognized Kalinago dominion over the islands of Dominica and St. Vincent. In exchange, the Kalinago agreed to allow European settlement in the nearby colonies of Guadeloupe, Martinique, and the Leeward Islands.

By engaging in a close reading of contemporary accounts and colonial correspondence, particularly the 1660 treaty, then, this chapter sheds light on how the Kalinago actively shaped and delimited the colonization of the Lesser Antilles. The decision to draw primarily on French accounts and correspondence reflects the particularly pronounced challenges that the Kalinago posed to French settlement of Guadeloupe, Martinique, and especially the southernmost colony of Grenada. In addition to counting thousands of Kalinago inhabitants when the French first claimed the islands in the first half of the seventeenth century, these colonies were in close proximity to Dominica, St. Lucia, and St. Vincent, all islands in which Kalinago driven from neighboring colonies had settled.[13] Highlighting the range of tactics that Kalinago adopted in an effort to retain their influence in the Lesser Antilles, this essay analyzes Caribbean Amerindians not as passive victims of relentless European expansion but as a polity that sought to counter foreign incursion through a combination of diplomacy and force. The treaty of 1660 provides particularly strong evidence that colonial officials recognized the necessity of sharing territory with the indigenous inhabitants of the Lesser Antilles and highlights the role of the Kalinago in shaping settlement, trade, and the expansion of the plantation complex in the southern Caribbean.

Early Kalinago-European Interactions

A number of works analyze European colonization of the Lesser Antilles.[14] Historians largely agree on the general course of events: although Spanish colonizing activity largely centered on the Greater Antilles and the American mainland, in the sixteenth century sailors made landfall in Lesser Antillean islands to take on water, provisions, and wood. As in the Greater Antilles, these corsairs, freebooters, and buccaneers sowed the seeds for subsequent colonization; their knowledge of the islands, as well as their trade with indigenous peoples, provided a basis for European settlement.[15]

Following Charles I's ascension to the throne of England in 1625 and the appointment of Cardinal Richelieu as Louis XIII's chief minister in 1624, England and France began to devote greater resources to Atlantic commerce and colonization. Thomas Warner successfully led an English colonizing mission to St. Christopher's in 1624, and French settlers arrived in the same island soon after. English colonies were established in Antigua, Barbados, and Nevis in the subsequent decade, and in 1635 France's *Compagnie des Iles de l'Amérique* sponsored the establishment of new settlements slightly farther south, in Guadeloupe and Martinique. French colonization of Grenada began fifteen years later, in 1650.[16]

Kalinago-European Military Contests

While histories of European expansion in the Caribbean chronicle territorial struggles between competing monarchies, they usually elide similar negotiations and contestations between European and indigenous polities. Events in St. Christopher's foreshadowed interactions on other islands throughout the region. Although St. Christopher's Amerindian inhabitants reportedly tolerated initial European settlement of the island, relations soon soured. As the number of settlers increased, competition for land and trade heightened tensions. In 1627 French and English colonists joined forces to launch what they described as a preemptive attack against the Kalinago, driving them from the island and dividing the land between the two European nations.

Despite these hostile beginnings in St. Christopher's, the earliest French subjects to settle in Martinique and Guadeloupe in 1635 did not seem to fear the Kalinago presence in the new colonies. Du Tertre, who participated in initial French colonization of these islands, credited the Kalinago with rescuing the first settlers from famine, writing that "the Savages never came to see the French empty handed, and as they saw them in need, they always brought them some provisions."[17] The missionary claimed that it was only when the French, "no longer content with areas abandoned by the Caribs, [made] new settlements, cut down the woods, and planted provisions and tobacco," that these initially promising relations gave way to rising tensions and reciprocal violence.[18]

Du Tertre might be thought of as a defender of the Lesser Antilles' indigenous inhabitants. His depiction of the Kalinago, whom he calls Carib, evolved significantly between the 1654 publication of his *Histoire générale des Isles* and his subsequent four-volume history of French colonization of the Caribbean, *Histoire générale des Antilles Habitées par les François,* first published in 1667. In the earlier work Kalinago people are not discussed in detail for the first four hundred pages. When they do appear, they are characterized as "the leftovers of the innumerable barbarians that the Spanish Christians exterminated"; Du Tertre hypothesizes that Kalinago reluctance to accept the presence of European settlers was due in part to the fact that "some of the oldest among them were eyewitnesses to the extreme cruelty that the Christians visited on them and on their fathers" during Spanish colonization of the Greater Antilles.[19] In addition to condemning Spanish barbarity, in his later publication Du Tertre also passes judgment on the French, whom he accuses of seeking "any occasion to commit acts of hostility against the Savages."[20] In both of Du Tertre's accounts, Kalinago attacks against French settlers were prompted by the latter's increasingly intrusive presence, as well as by French designs to incite violence in order to "have a pretext to seize" Kalinago territory and provisions.[21]

By assigning blame for the outbreak of violence to Europeans, Du Tertre depicts the indigenous inhabitants as peaceable people ripe for religious conversion. As an agent of evangelism, Du Tertre had ample motivation to portray the Kalinago as potential Christians, and the missionary sought to assure his readers that "the good treatment . . . that our missionaries give [the Kalinago] . . . could with time soften their barbarous nature."[22]

Du Tertre, though, was not the only seventeenth-century eyewitness to suggest that Kalinago violence against Europeans was a direct response to the newcomers' infringement on their increasingly circumscribed territory. The account of Breton, who spent several years attempting to convert the indigenous inhabitants of the island of Dominica to Christianity, confirms that the Kalinago turned to violence as a means of limiting the European presence in their territory.

Rather than directly narrating his experiences as one of the only Europeans to live in Dominica in the 1640s and 1650s, Breton sprinkles revealing anecdotes and explanations into his bilingual dictionary of the Kalinago language, which was first published in France in 1665.[23] Along with serving as a tool of translation intended to aid in the conversion of the indigenous population, the dictionary therefore acts as a detailed ethnographic source. For example, the entry for *canóoa,* the Kalinago dugout canoes later adopted by settlers throughout the Lesser Antilles, offers the insight that the Kalinago would use the watercraft to "go as far as Cayenne and Suriname to join the Galibis their allies, either to trade their goods . . . or to form an armed corps to go and attack the Arawak their enemies."[24]

Instead of a simple translation, however, Breton's explanation provides his readers with a glimpse of relations between different indigenous polities and illustrates that by the time of his writing in the mid-seventeenth century the Kalinago were accustomed to forming economic and diplomatic alliances and to coordinating military assaults. His entry for "Ouáitoucoubouli," the Kalinago name for the island of Dominica, thus lends further credence to Du Tertre's argument that Kalinago violence was motivated in part by their sense of dominion or sovereignty over specific territory; the entry notes that ten French settlers sent to establish a colony in the island were killed by "the savages."[25]

An anonymous account of French efforts to colonize Grenada beginning in 1649 further confirms that the island's Kalinago residents were determined to guard against foreign settlement. The French narrator demonizes the English, alleging that the Kalinago believed that English settlers "sought only to make war against them, to exterminate them and to seize their lands." Aware of their "weakness to resist such strong enemies," Amerindian residents of Grenada then reportedly sought and obtained an alliance with the French.[26] This promising initial interaction contrasts markedly with reported relations between French and Kalinago inhabitants of Grenada in the succeeding years. In their first exchange, the French allegedly took great pains to appease the Kalinago and assure them of their good intentions, promising that the French sought to protect the Kalinago against English incursion and to "live with them in good peace, good friends and good *compères*."[27] A seven-month period of peaceful cohabitation—during which time, the author stresses, the Kalinago and the French actively engaged in trade—was shattered by an attack on Grenada led by Kalinago combatants from neighboring islands.[28] According to the author, the attack had two principal motives: to prevent further French settlement in Grenada, which was a vital stopping-off point for Kalinago journeying by sea to the South American main, and to avenge a recent attack perpetrated by French forces from Martinique against the Kalinago of St. Vincent: "not being able to take vengeance on" the French in Martinique, who "were too strong and too far away," the Kalinago instead elected "to unleash their anger against those who had recently established themselves in Grenada while they were still weak."[29]

Unlike Du Tertre, the unnamed chronicler of French settlement in Grenada repeatedly sought to depict the island's indigenous inhabitants as "barbarians." Yet his account of Kalinago-European violence also illustrates the variety of military and diplomatic tactics that Caribbean Amerindians deployed in response to foreign incursions. In first seeking the aid of the French against the English, Kalinago residents of Grenada demonstrated an awareness of the ongoing contest between the two European polities. Their decision to forge an alliance with the French rather than with the English further suggests that they recognized differences in the respective practices of colonization of the two groups and perhaps found those of the French to be more amenable to their own goals.

Kalinago actions are also revealing of the relatively strong position that they continued to occupy in Grenada at mid-century. According to the anonymous author, Kalinago leaders informed French settlers that they "should content themselves with the area that they made available, without establishing themselves elsewhere" in the island.[30] This account reveals that as late as the 1650s, the indigenous inhabitants of the Lesser Antilles were in a position not just to influence but to attempt to dictate the terms of European settlement in the region.

Contemporary accounts also highlight another strategy the Kalinago used to delimit European settlement of the Lesser Antilles. Just as French and English colonists formed defensive alliances against Amerindian attack, Kalinago residents of different islands also united against foreign forces in their midst. In one particularly striking example, Du Tertre reported that in 1636 the Kalinago of Martinique, "not believing themselves strong enough . . . to entirely chase the French from the island . . . called to their aid those of Dominica, St. Vincent, and Guadeloupe, and having composed a corps of fifteen hundred men, presented themselves at the fort."[31] While this impressive show of military strength failed to dislodge the growing number of French settlers in Martinique, the experience likely influenced subsequent Kalinago responses to European colonization. By later joining forces to launch an attack on French settlers in Grenada "while they were still weak," Kalinago combatants sought to contain French expansion while they were still in a position to do so. Cognizant that they lacked the manpower or military technology to rout settlers from more well-established colonies, the Kalinago residing in various islands instead chose to work together to prevent further European colonization elsewhere in the Lesser Antilles.

Kalinago-European Diplomacy

While coordinated military attacks left the strongest impression in the writings of Europeans, they constituted only one of several strategies the Kalinago used to shape the colonization of the Lesser Antilles. By engaging in verbal negotiations with English and French officials, Kalinago leaders actively sought to restrict foreign settlement to specific islands or parts of islands, while reserving the remaining land for their continued use. Numerous verbal treaties concluded between European and Kalinago representatives from the 1630s through the 1650s laid the groundwork for the first written treaty between the three parties, which in 1660 divided the Lesser Antilles into mutually agreed-upon English, French, and Kalinago zones.

The treaty was motivated in part by the policies that guided French settlement of the Americas: early settlers were explicitly instructed not to initiate violence with the Caribbean's indigenous inhabitants. Officials in the *Compagnie des Iles de l'Amérique,* the charter company responsible for the initial settlement of Guadeloupe and Martinique, instead encouraged officials to seek accommodations. In 1639 the company ordered Governor du Parquet of Martinique "not to chase the savages from the island"; the governor was instead advised to "draw them closer and convince them to have better intentions in the future." By promising the

Kalinago "every assistance and good treatment," company officials hoped that Du Parquet could convince his indigenous neighbors "not to undertake any [attacks] against the French and even to inform [him] about what they could discover from the savages of other islands or the enemies of the French." Betraying the limited faith they had in these negotiations, the company also sent the governor an additional supply of "gunpowder . . . half for muskets and half for cannon."[32]

In 1640 "after many discussions of the sort that we can have with people who express themselves more by signs than by words, and who have no more reason than brutes," a verbal treaty was also concluded between Kalinago and French residents of Guadeloupe. According to Du Tertre, "promises were reciprocally made . . . to never again do each other any wrong, and to treat each other from this point forward as good friends."[33] News of peace had the ironic effect of attracting greater numbers of French settlers to the colony; the Kalinago responded by resuming their attacks on the growing settler population and by withdrawing to the neighboring island of Dominica.[34]

Given the short-lived nature of these verbal agreements, the nature of treaty making evolved as colonizers and Natives sought to broker more widespread and lasting peace in the Lesser Antilles. In 1657 negotiations in Grenada were attended by Kalinago residents of the French colony as well as by Kalinago representatives from the islands of St. Vincent and Dominica, which remained under their dominion. In recognition of their mutual pledge of peace, the French presented Kalinago leaders with "hatchets, blades, and knives," while the Kalinago brought the French "three beautiful turtles, a rich caret, and lizards." More than presents, these tokens were interpreted by the French as "signs of the acceptance and ratification of [peace by] *all the other Caribs and Galibis of all the adjacent islands.*"[35]

Arguing that the Kalinago "all dress the same way, wear the same colors, [speak] the same language [and] bear the same arms, have the same interests, live all together and are of the same intelligence," the anonymous French settler in Grenada reasoned that these commonalities rendered it impossible to broker peace with the inhabitants of only one island. The belief that "a peace could not be good if it is only with a few individuals" prompted English, French, and Kalinago representatives to attempt to reach an accord that would be respected by all parties.[36]

The need to ensure that a commitment to peace was shared by the Kalinago of different islands reflected evolving concerns that verbal treaties failed to satisfy. It is difficult to know whether the indigenous inhabitants of different islands or of different parts of the same island organized or thought of themselves as separate and distinct polities prior to the arrival of Europeans. What is clear is that as the rise of plantation production increased the number of settlers and slaves in the Lesser Antilles, as well as the amount of space they occupied, Kalinago leaders increasingly relied on interisland alliances to counter European colonization. By organizing as a broader polity, the Kalinago consciously attempted to preserve a degree of dominion, along with economic and military influence in a region increasingly subject to European control.

Sharing Space in the Lesser Antilles: The Treaty of 1660

The desire to ensure a general peace between Europeans and Amerindians in the Lesser Antilles gave rise to the first extant example of a written treaty between the two groups. The treaty was signed on March 31, 1660, by English, French, and Kalinago representatives assembled at the home of Charles Hoüel, governor of Guadeloupe. The French and English signatories were empowered by the governors of their respective colonies, while the Kalinago were represented by "fifteen of the most notable . . . of the Caribs" from the islands of Dominica, St. Vincent, and "those who formerly lived in the said island of Martinique."[37]

In addition to identifying more than a dozen Kalinago men afforded positions of authority within their respective communities, Hoüel sought to ensure that the promises of these representatives would be honored by all Native inhabitants of the Lesser Antilles. Through interpreter Jean Jardin, the governor "asked the said Caribs whether they had the power to treaty for themselves and in the name of all the other [Kalinago] of the said islands [of] St. Vincent and Dominica." The Kalinago representatives confirmed that "having spoken to the largest part of the said savages, who consented" to the terms of peace, they were in a position to speak for all Kalinago.[38] The three parties—English, French, and Kalinago—can therefore be argued to have engaged in this diplomatic negotiation as equals, with each group of signatories representing a broader polity animated by specific and clearly articulated concerns.

At least two copies of the 1660 treaty survive in France's colonial archives. The first is classified in the correspondence of Adrien Dyel de Vaudroque, who served as governor of Martinique from 1658 until 1662, and the second is described in the archives' inventory as having been "found in the papers of M. de Blénac" who served as governor-general of the *iles de l'Amérique* from 1677 until 1690. Curiously, however, neither copy appears to have been sent to France until years after the treaty was signed.

The text of both copies is identical, save for a brief note that explains when and why each document was sent to France. The copy archived among the correspondence of Governor Dyel dates from 1722 and is described in a note appended to the end of the document as a certified copy made from "a register belonging to Monsieur Le Marquis Hoüel," the governor who brokered the peace. The other copy, archived among the surviving papers of Governor de Blénac of Martinique, appears to have been forwarded to France in 1686 or 1687. The first page of the document, which is written in a different hand from the nine-page treaty that follows, is marked by two marginalia in the upper left corner: "sent in February 1687" and "23rd [November?] 1686." Both notes are struck through with a single line but remain easily readable, and seem to indicate that the first page of the document was appended by another writer in 1686 or 1687, more than twenty-five years after the treaty was drafted. The page briefly summarizes what were, at least for the French officials to whom it was sent, the most important elements of the treaty that followed. "Offensive and defensive treaty of union between the French and the English for the maintenance of *peace with the Caribs,* stipulating," announces the first line, "That all prisoners will be returned by one side and the other. That neither the French nor the English will ever possess the island of St. Vincent nor of Dominica, but that they will remain [the dominion of] the Caribs. And that these Savages are happy to be instructed by French missionaries and offer to receive them amongst them."[39]

The nine-page text that follows this brief list suggests a much more complicated and lengthy negotiation between three distinct polities seeking to cohabit a limited geographic space. Rather than simply stipulating the terms of the treaty, the document begins by narrating the multistage process by which peace was reached. In early March 1660 Governor Houel first met with unnamed "governors and inhabitants" of the English colonies of Antigua, Montserrat, and Nevis at St. Christopher's, which at the time was shared between the English and French. "Having happily brokered peace" between English and French representatives, Hoüel then invited a number of Kalinago leaders to his residence in Basseterre, Guadeloupe. In addition to the English, French, and Kalinago signatories, others who attended the treaty negotiations were Père Beaumont, a missionary who lived among the Kalinago, Père du Fontaine, head of the Jesuit order in France's Caribbean colonies, and translator Jardin.[40]

The specific terms of the treaty hint at the years of violence and failed diplomacy that motivated all three parties to broker a formal peace. After noting that "the said island of Martinique has been engaged in war with the savages for the last six years, which has caused great misfortunes by the murders fires and kidnapping of slaves committed by the said savages," the signatories mutually agreed that "the said French and English nations inhabitants of the said islands Monserrat, Antigua, and Nevis and the said Caribs of the said islands St. Vincent Dominica and those who formerly lived in the said island of Martinique will live in peace all acts of hostility ceasing."[41]

While this passage explicitly attributes the crimes of murder, arson, and kidnapping to the "savage" Kalinago, it also reveals that Europeans were far from blameless in the lengthy conflict to which the treaty refers. The mention that some of the Kalinago signatories "formerly lived in the said island of Martinique" hints at the considerable migration and resettlement that some Kalinago undertook in the wake of European colonization. While the European signatories were motivated to ratify the treaty because of fears of further Kalinago "murders fires and kidnappings," Kalinago representatives had their own concerns. Aware that they would not be able to return to their former settlements in rapidly developing French and English plantation colonies, the Kalinago assented to the treaty in an

Tessa Murphy

attempt to ensure that their communities in neighboring islands not settled by Europeans would remain undisturbed.

Other elements of the text allude to further aggressions on the part of Europeans. One of the Kalinago signatories—referred to only by the title "Baba," signifying his role as chief or "father" of his people—requested that his nephews, "who had been taken by one Billaudel" of Martinique, be returned to him. In granting his request, the English and French representatives relied on the advice of the missionaries who attended the negotiations. The Jesuits reasoned that "it was not only just but necessary to undertake the said restitution, as it would be a means to confirm and maintain the peace." The return of the Baba's nephews can therefore be interpreted as a sort of prisoner or hostage release intended to assure future goodwill between all parties.[42]

The missionaries also expressed their hope that the return of the "Baba's" nephews would help accomplish another goal outlined in the treaty: the conversion of the Kalinago into Christians. Once again, a closer reading suggests that Kalinago signatories had their own reasons for assenting to the proposal. Kalinago representatives from the islands of Dominica and St. Vincent were asked whether "they wished to learn how to pray to God like [the French] and allow the said missionary fathers to instruct them."[43] In agreeing that Father Beaumont could continue to reside among them in Dominica, Kalinago representatives stipulated that missionaries should be the *only* Europeans of "one or the other [English and French] nation to inhabit the two islands of St. Vincent and Dominica, which are all that remain for their retreat."[44]

While French officials interpreted this element of the agreement as a first step in the conversion of Kalinago into Christians—and perhaps subsequently into allies and trading partners—an analysis of the treaty from the perspective of Kalinago signatories suggests a far different goal. By conceding that a single foreigner could maintain his residence in Dominica, Kalinago representatives attempted to ensure their continued dominion over an island in which increasing numbers of their people now congregated. By agreeing to share space with Europeans, the Kalinago sought to preserve the islands of Dominica and St. Vincent as "all that remain for their retreat."

The Growth of the Plantation Complex and the Limits of Shared Space

Although it has been argued that this "first 'international' intra-Caribbean treaty" created a lasting balance of power in the Lesser Antilles, surviving French correspondence reveals that the agreement ultimately failed to defuse tensions between Amerindian and European populations in the region.[45] The strength of the Kalinago polities that formed in the islands of St. Vincent and Dominica as a result of the peace of 1660 posed problems that the treaty largely failed to anticipate. In the last decades of the seventeenth century, as the rise of plantation production in neighboring English and French colonies rapidly increased the number of enslaved Africans in the Lesser Antilles, Amerindians adopted a new tactic to counter settlers' influence in the region. By offering shelter and forming alliances with runaway slaves, Kalinago residents of St. Vincent and Dominica continued to delimit European possibilities for economic and territorial expansion in the southern Caribbean.

Although Kalinago signatories to the 1660 treaty claimed to speak for all indigenous inhabitants of St. Vincent and Dominica, their promise did not extend to Grenada. Attempts to increase settlement and production in France's southernmost Caribbean colony repeatedly reignited conflict with the island's Kalinago inhabitants, and Grenada's population remained anemic in comparison with that of other French colonies. By 1671 the most populous French Caribbean colony, Martinique, boasted 4,326 free inhabitants and 6,582 slaves; Grenada counted only 283 free people and 222 slaves.[46] Attempts to extend the reach of the 1660 treaty to Grenada met with limited success. In February 1678 the Comte de Blénac, who succeeded Jean-Charles de Baas Castelmore as governor-general of France's Caribbean colonies, concluded a separate written treaty with "Pierre Moigna et Ionana, two of the Caribs of the island of St. Vincent, on behalf of all of their nation." Among other conditions, the treaty stipulated that the Kalinago "could not go inhabit the island of Grenada"; in exchange, the governor ordered French colonists to allow the Kalinago of St. Vincent to circulate freely, "without any trouble or hindrance."[47]

The agreement brokered in 1678 hints at some of the ways that European-Kalinago relations evolved after the signing of the 1660 treaty. As the Kalinago concentrated their settlement in islands over which their dominion was formally recognized, Dominica and St. Vincent emerged as centers of Amerindian power in the colonial Caribbean. The existence of a non-European territory amid the rapidly expanding plantation societies of the Lesser Antilles provided an attractive refuge for escaping slaves, who absconded in dugout canoes from nearby colonies to seek refuge among the Kalinago.

Some Kalinago initially attempted to ally with European colonizers against escaped slaves (Maroons). In 1678 the Governor of Martinique reported that two canoes full of Kalinago had visited him and "proposed to make war against" escaped slaves in St. Vincent; the governor worried that "as long as the *negrerie* of St. Vincent endures, you will never see the end of the slaves' marronnage."[48] Yet Kalinago allegiances soon shifted. Just one year later, the same governor was imploring his superiors to order troops against the Kalinago of St. Vincent, "who along with the [escaped] slaves in the island cause us the most trouble, and who we cannot chase."[49] Perhaps recognizing that the presence of other persons or polities hostile to European colonization would strengthen both their numbers and their ability to defend themselves, in the last decades of the seventeenth century the Kalinago tolerated and even welcomed the increasing number of slaves who escaped to their territory in St. Vincent and Dominica.

By the turn of the eighteenth century, officials in Martinique were convinced that any attempt to capture slaves who had taken refuge in St. Vincent was doomed to fail. Although some Kalinago residents of the islands were reportedly concerned that their new neighbors, "multiplying themselves and increasing in number," might one day overwhelm them, others viewed the runaway slaves as potential allies with whom "they lived together in good intelligence." In a reversal of their earlier offer to form an alliance with the French in order to launch a war against the escapees, by 1700 Kalinago residents of St. Vincent were demonstrably unwilling to permit French soldiers to land in the island to recapture the slaves. French officials reported that the Kalinago "would rather see two thousand blacks established in their island, than to see disembark just 50 armed Frenchmen." Determined "not to let the French gain a foothold" in the island, by the end of the seventeenth century the Kalinago of St. Vincent increasingly treated the escaped slaves of neighboring colonies as potential allies against further European incursion.[50]

Conclusion: Kalinago Colonizers?

The colonization of the Caribbean is typically analyzed as a European endeavor in which settlers usurped indigenous lands. But a further definition of colonizing, "to appropriate a domain for one's own use," can also be applied to the region's indigenous inhabitants.[51] As they relocated to islands not claimed by European Crowns, "Kalinago colonizers" continued to draw on a range of diplomatic and military tactics to establish or maintain dominion over specific territories. By providing refuge to and forming alliances with runaway slaves, Kalinago inhabitants of Dominica and St. Vincent added to a corps of people who opposed the expansion of plantation production in the colonial Caribbean.

Although the Kalinago military threat, as well as their participation in diplomatic negotiations, waned as the number and strength of Europeans and Africans in the Caribbean increased, indigenous peoples continued to influence the geopolitics of the Lesser Antilles well into the eighteenth century. In a 1700 letter to his superiors in France, the governor-general of France's Caribbean colonies enclosed a brief excerpt of the 1660 treaty. "The said islands of St. Vincent and of Dominica will forever belong to the said savages; they cannot be settled by one or the other of the said [English and French] nations," the passage reminded officials in France.[52] The governor's decision to include this single clause of the treaty suggests that debates surrounding possession of the islands were far from settled by the turn of the century, as French settlers hungry for additional land jealously eyed nearby Kalinago territories. Yet the general terms of the 1660 treaty would be respected for more than one hundred years, until Dominica and St. Vincent were claimed by Great Britain in the wake of the Seven Years War in 1763.

Historians seeking to explain why several southern Caribbean islands remained outside the sphere of European colonial rule until the latter half of the eighteenth century must pay attention to decades of contestation and negotiation between

Europeans and Amerindians. Attention to the role of Kalinago warriors, diplomats, and colonizers highlights the practical difficulties encountered by European settlers in the Lesser Antilles during the long seventeenth century and complicates current understandings of the rise of slavery and plantation production in the early modern Americas.

Aphra Behn's *Oroonoko,* Indian Slavery, and the Anglo-Dutch Wars

Carolyn Arena

Scholars have long debated whether certain elements of Aphra Behn's *Oroonoko,* a novel about a rebelling slave in seventeenth-century English Suriname, were based on actual events.[1] *Oroonoko* narrates how a "Coromantee" African prince leads an exodus of slaves from their Suriname plantations. The other slaves ultimately abandon him in his revenge, and the title character is tortured, drawn, and quartered for his rebellion.[2] Yet, no recorded slave revolt occurred contemporaneously with Behn's supposed 1663–64 visit to Suriname nor indeed at any time during the colony's entire English period (1650–67). It has thus been easy to dismiss *Oroonoko* as entirely fictionalized or as an extended metaphor for domestic English politics, rather than colonial ones.[3]

This essay, however, argues that Behn drew upon actual historical conflicts involving not only African slaves but also Indian slaves under both the English and Dutch periods of rule. It also endorses the relatively recent view that encourages scholars to acknowledge that Suriname had always been a place of "cohabitation" between indigenous, African, Dutch, and English populations.[4] Aphra Behn, perhaps in her role as a spy in England, Suriname, and the Low Countries, knew this intrinsically. The narrator in *Oroonoko* explicitly references events of violence between Suriname's colonists and its Indian population in the wake of the Dutch takeover in 1667; she is afraid that the Indians "shou'd fall upon us, as they did immediately after my coming away; and that it was in the possession of the Dutch, who us'd 'em not so civilly as the English . . . this feud began while I was there."[5]

Indeed, after Behn left, there was a period of continual violence involving the Indians of the region and colonial factions between the Second Anglo-Dutch War (1665–67) and the Indian War against the Dutch of 1678–80; the Indian War culminated in the rebellion of both Indian and black slaves against the plantations of Suriname.[6] Laura Brown had previously noted similarities between Oroonoko's rebellion and "a group of escaped slaves led by a Koromantyn known as Jermes," who attacked local plantations. Brown, however, mistook this as an isolated incident that occurred while Behn was in Suriname rather than properly contextualizing it as having occurred under the Dutch.[7] This chapter explains how the characters and events in *Oroonoko* mirror historical people and situations in English and Dutch Suriname. Thus, this period of colonial violence constituted a war parallel to the Anglo-Dutch Wars but with a momentum derived from conflicts within Suriname itself over indigenous trade and military alliances, Indian enslavement, and African slavery.

Seventeenth-century European legal traditions considered resistant heathenism and war captivity legitimate conditions for the enslavement of both Native Americans and Africans.[8] Indian slavery was condemned because most nations that claimed territory in the New World did so on the basis of the conversion of the Native population to Christianity, and one "cou'd not make a Slave, because a Christian."[9] The first English adventurers to Guiana, Sir Walter Ralegh and his lieutenant Lawrence Keymis, arrived in 1595 and noticed that Spaniards, and Natives themselves, bought indigenous war captives. They then transported the captives to pearl fisheries such as Margarita Island, where Indian and African slaves had worked together since the early sixteenth century.[10] For their part, Ralegh and Keymis solidified friendly trading relations with the Yao and Carib nations, as these nations, in turn, solicited English and Dutch military aid against the Spaniards and Lokono Arawaks near the Orinoco River.[11]

Echoing Ralegh and Keymis, Behn opens *Oroonoko* by distancing the English from the practice of Indian enslavement, even while later acknowledging her own use of an Indian slave to row and translate for her along Suriname's rivers.[12] Literary scholar Derek Hughes notes that *Oroonoko* shares additional similarities to Ralegh's *Discoverie of Guiana* (1596), which mixes a detailed first-person account of his voyage with fictionalized conjectures about Amazon warrior women, acephalous men, and empires of gold in ways that resemble the romantic elements in *Oroonoko*.[13] Historians consider the *Discoverie* a primary source, although the narrative contains romantic and fictional elements. In a complementary fashion, we can view *Oroonoko*'s fictional plot and romantic elements as nevertheless containing historical truths about slavery in English and Dutch Suriname, informed by Behn's own intelligence from her espionage during the Anglo-Dutch Wars and, perhaps, even first-person observations.[14]

Oroonoko's narrator begins her story in Suriname, and the opening scene contains the first of a few allusions to a future Indian rebellion: "But before I give you the Story of this *Gallant Slave,* 'tis fit I tell you the manner of bringing them to these new *Colonies;* for those they make use of there, are not *Natives* of the place; for those we live with in perfect Amity, without daring to command 'em; but on the contrary, caress 'em with all the brotherly and friendly Affection in the World; trading with 'em for their Fish, Venison, Buffilo's, Skins, and little Rarities."[15] *Oroonoko*'s idyllic Indians and Indian-colonial relations drew from Montaigne and other hopeful New World literature.[16] But Behn's readership was primed to expect cruel treatment towards Indians as well, including enslavement;

otherwise, her need to dismiss the practice in her opening pages would seem jarring and unnecessary.

A contemporary English readership would have been confused and dismayed about their countrymen participating in Indian slavery, an activity marred by Spain's "Black Legend" of bloody conquest. They would have accepted and been familiar enough, however, with English participation in the African slave trade and the existence of African slaves through "exhibitions" in London, neither of which caused a general recoiling from the trade itself.[17] Behn's praise of Indian trading partners, her dismissal of Indian slavery under the English, and the general acceptability of the African slave trade each account for her choice to make her hero and rebel leader, Oroonoko, an African slave, even though both groups were enslaved in contemporary Suriname. For Behn, these factors ensured that the story would focus on the individual tragedy of a prince turned slave, rather than the tragedy of slavery itself. *Oroonoko* would not be embraced by abolitionists until the eighteenth century, when it was staged as a play.[18]

Behn and her contemporaries reserved their condemnation for enslavement that occurred under dubious circumstances, including stealing unsuspecting people or luring them away under false pretenses. Other forms of enslavement were legitimate to seventeenth-century audiences, such as when Oroonoko made slaves of enemy combatants as a military captain when still in Africa.[19] Behn contrasts this with the story of how Oroonoko and his wife, Imoinda, become slaves through the jealous, greedy, and treacherous actions of evil-minded men, which make Oroonoko's rebellion against his enslavement a righteous one. Imoinda is enslaved in a jealous rage, when the king, lusting after her, realizes that Oroonoko has already married her. The king considers slavery a fate worse than death for a person of elevated rank and station such as Imoinda. For this reason, he regrets enslaving her and decides to spare Oroonoko so he might continue his military career.[20]

Oroonoko's enslavement comes later, at the hand of a seemingly friendly and charming English ship captain, to whom Oroonoko has previously "sold abundance of his slaves."[21] The captain invites Oroonoko and other young nobles aboard to drink and dine. Then he claps them in irons. Serendipitously, though, both Imoinda's and Oroonoko's ships sail for Suriname. They reunite and conceive a child. Yet, Oroonoko, despite impressing his owner, Trefy, and the lieutenant governor, William Byam, cannot secure freedom for his family. Oroonoko decides to lead a group of runaway slaves into the forest and with them plans to attack the plantations. His fellow escapees abandon him, however, leading to both Oroonoko's and Imoinda's deaths.

Indians and the Foundation of English Suriname

Ralegh, Keymis, and Robert Harcourt promoted their voyages as the basis for a cooperative relationship between the English, the Dutch, and the many Indian nations of Guiana. Most of the attempts of the English, Dutch, and French to settle this region between the Orinoco and Amazon Rivers from 1595 and 1665, however, were unsuccessful. The Indians prevented the growth of European settlements by destroying their infrastructure and cutting them off from trade routes, although fighting between settlers and Indians created captives traded from Guiana to the Caribbean, especially Barbados.[22]

When Indians were amenable to settlement, however, their aid in driving a contraband tobacco trade towards Spanish Trinidad provided both security and income for English and Dutch colonists.[23] This commerce, which Governor Aert Adriaensz Groenewegen managed "w[i]th great secrecy," enabled the exceptional Dutch settlement on the Essequibo River that survived from 1616 until the Second Anglo-Dutch War. This colony also provided Barbados's first settlers with thirty Indians who were "fetched" to "instruct the English in planting Cottons, Tobacco, [and] Indigo."[24]

With the help of their Dutch connections, Barbados quickly became a successful nodal point in interimperial trade. In 1638 the Earl of Carlisle, then proprietor of the island, contracted with a merchant to send forty-three thousand pounds of tobacco to Amsterdam.[25] In 1642 another Barbados merchant agreed to send four hundred pounds of cotton annually to Dutch merchants, while in 1644 Dutch merchants promised to pay 1,311 guilders in exchange for any "good cleaned cotton, tobacco or indigoe."[26]

Anglo-Barbadian merchants were less successful in the "Indian Trade," an ambiguous term that may either mean trade *with* Indians or the trade *of* Indians. Since Barbados had no indigenous population itself, and these documents do not specify which Indian nations were trade partners or what goods were being exchanged, it seems likely that "Indian trade" might be shorthand for a trade in Indian slaves.[27] Either way, it was not a profitable venture. In 1639 Anglo-Barbadian Richard Cutt owed James Maxwell, his "coepartner of Indian trade," 7,500 pounds of cotton wool, and in the next year, he owed him 29,580 pounds of cotton.[28] Despite the debt-ridden "Indian trade" and their unsuccessful record with Indians in Guiana, Englishmen continued to be interested in settling the region south of Barbados throughout the 1640s.[29]

The English at Barbados most certainly relied on Dutch merchants for imports of African slaves, as well as generally maintaining a regular stream of basic foodstuffs and supplies.[30] The short-lived English Republic hoped to advance commercial and political relations with the Dutch (with the relationship to be dominated by London), guided by ostensibly shared principles of Protestantism and republicanism. The 1649 execution of Charles I, however, had cooled the Dutch on the idea of too-close relations with their English counterpart, and the 1651 effort to consummate an Anglo-Dutch union failed.[31]

In retaliation, Parliament passed the Navigation Acts to limit the shipment of enumerated goods, including slaves, to English ships, prompting the First Anglo-Dutch War (1652–54). Meanwhile, Francis, fifth Lord Willoughby of Parham, a

Royalist who had fled to Holland during the Civil Wars, accepted the commission of the would-be Charles II as governor of Barbados and the "Caribbee Isles." He did not care to uphold the trade restrictions, as they were especially antagonistic to the Dutch.[32] As it happens, Willoughby and Aphra Behn's foster brother, Thomas Colepepper, were members of a secret Royalist society called the Sealed Knot. Janet Todd considers Behn's association with the Sealed Knot to have been her first entrance into the world of espionage. While Behn was slipping messages between exiles in Holland, she met Willoughby and began a trusted association.[33]

During Willoughby's first year in Barbados, he and his council submitted a petition that complained about the new imperial restrictions on colonial commerce. The Barbadian colonists claimed had been imposed upon them, although they had "representatives" of their interests in Parliament. They wrote that the new laws would liken them to slaves, especially to the licensed dealers from whom they would now purchase actual slaves. The Barbadians argued that they had settled the land at their own expense and should receive the benefits of their own trade. Furthermore, the planters were entirely "beholding to the Dutch for their subsistence" and aid in the original settlement of Barbados.[34]

In 1650 Willoughby directed, or perhaps usurped, the settlement of one hundred English men from around the Caribbean led by Lieutenant Colonel Anthony Rous on the Suriname River.[35] "Willoughby Land" was to extend to the Marrowijne and Saramacca Rivers and incorporate the rivers of Coppename and Berbice.[36] The Barbadian voyagers "fortified it and furnished it with about 300 men," all at the expense of Willoughby. The colony would not have survived, however, without Rous making a "firme peace w[i]th the Indians," supposedly by invoking Ralegh's name and history with them.[37]

In 1652 Willoughby was removed from his governorship, but his council pleaded (in vain) to Sir George Ayscue, whose fleet reduced Barbados to parliamentary authority, that the ex-governor might keep the colony on the Suriname River. They wrote, "if taken under the protection of the Commonwealth, would, in seven years, appear far more considerable than Brazil." Ayscue was sensitive to the economic potential involved, as well Suriname's strategic position. The Barbados Council also assured Sir George that a major benefit would be the "conversion of the Indians."[38] The rhetoric of conversion might have been lip service to the English Republic's goals.[39] Neither the English nor the Dutch were to make concerted missionary efforts, but the will to conversion, rather than reduction, revealed their pressing concern with having the indigenous population on their side while dealing with rivals.

Meanwhile, during the First Anglo-Dutch War, many Dutch merchants decided to stay in Barbados. In 1652 Dutch ships, combating the Portuguese, were also allowed to take on supplies at the island. The Barbadians, though, also used the Navigation Acts to gain an advantage over the Dutch in their trade with Indians, seizing, "as lawful prizes," so they claimed, "Three Hollanders, merchant ships, for trading with the Indians."[40] The increased naval presence at Barbados forced many Dutch merchants to transition from large vessels to smaller ships to avoid their ships being taken as prizes.[41]

Contraction would work for some merchants, but Dutch planters had an eye on expansion. In the early 1650s, however, this expansion was stymied in Brazil, when the Portuguese inhabitants of New Holland rebelled against the Dutch West India Company. The expelled Dutch planters turned towards well-tested sugar islands, but land there was limited. Dutch proponents of colonization considered Guiana to be the best option to re-create Pernambuco-style sugar plantations and encouraged migration from the Netherlands to the region (only a few planters went directly from Brazil to the Suriname River).[42] The Dutch and Jewish planters who left Brazil amplified the "sugar boom" throughout the Caribbean with capital and technology, although the English had already established sugar production in Barbados.[43] The planters also brought Indian slaves with them to sugar-producing islands, along with the penumbra of legal and moral dubiousness that shrouded Native enslavement.[44] The directors of the Dutch West India Company had previously sent instructions during the original settlement of New Holland. These instructions prohibited colonists from turning Native inhabitants into slaves, most likely intending that Indian slavery be prohibited throughout the Dutch Atlantic.[45]

As the First Anglo-Dutch War ended, Suriname was still a location that the English and Dutch found amenable to trade and mutual settlement. The neighboring Indian populations also seemed receptive. Anthony Rous left the colony to William Byam, "in a flourishing Condicion and in p[er]fect Peace w[i]th the Indians."[46] Deeds held in the National Barbados Archives show just how substantial the investments in Suriname were in the years after the First Anglo-Dutch War. In 1654 merchant Tobias Frere and his partners John Arnett and John Egron sold one thousand acres of land to John Frere.[47] In 1659 a woman named Rebeccah Austen sold her family's remaining thirteen acres in Barbados so that she could join her husband and family in Suriname.[48] Deeds also show that within the first decade of settlement, the potential fertility of the region had attracted interest from London merchants. In 1659 Thomas Noell, from the preeminent Noell merchant family, sold two thousand acres in Suriname to two other London merchants.[49] The English foothold in Guiana allowed for an alliance and a necessary trade with the Caribs who lived around the Suriname River; the Natives received manufactures, while the European settlers gained forest products and dyes. Another item of trade was the Indian war captives of the Caribs, who would become slaves in Suriname. Carib allies were not only helpful in supplying slaves but also in recapturing slaves who had escaped from their plantations.[50]

Indian slaves were of limited interest to metropolitan authorities compared to African slaves, however. By 1660 the pursuit of the transatlantic slave trade had generated a population with an enslaved majority in Barbados.[51] In the same year, Charles II was restored to the English throne, and he appointed Willoughby as governor of the English Caribbean. Willoughby, though, voiced his disappointment with the effects of the Navigation Acts, including monopolies on the slave trade, citing them as the reason Anglo-Barbadian colonists defected to French and Dutch islands.[52]

Suriname, now more than ever, was an important location for English colonists who wanted to regain their centrality in sugar production vis-à-vis Dutch and French sugar planters. Despite the land grab among prominent men who would reside in the colony (notably George Marten, who would be positively characterized in *Oroonoko*), Willoughby himself would not come to the colony until 1664–65.[53] Todd considers that if Aphra Behn indeed visited Suriname, she did so as an agent of Willoughby. As the absentee Royalist proprietor of a politically factious colony, he would have needed someone with experience in espionage to report to him on his holdings.[54]

Willoughby was not the only observer who regarded the colony cautiously. With the influx of intruders, the Indians of the region took advantage of the natural barriers in Guiana, such as rivers and waterfalls, to separate themselves from the colonists. George Warren wrote of an occasion when the Indians "had been down, and kill'd an English Woman, and robb'd the house wherein she was" but the retaliating party of English colonists could not reach them because of the cataracts.[55] Behn (who probably used Warren as either a source or a memory aid while writing *Oroonoko*) writes that it takes eight days for a large party to reach the "Indian Towns." She and her party, like Warren, are apprehensive about ventures this far upriver, because of the "Disputes the English had with the Indians." Behn says that these disputes had become worse under the Dutch "who us'd 'em not so civilly as the English, so that they cut in pieces all they cou'd take, getting into Houses, and hanging up the Mother, and all her Children about her; and cut a Footman, I left behind me, all in Joynts, and nail'd him to Trees." She overcomes her apprehensions by taking Oroonoko with her as a bodyguard and finding "a Fisherman that liv'd at the Mouth of the River, who had been a long Inhabitant there, and oblig'd him to go with us: But because he was known to the Indians, as trading among 'em."

Behn's characterization of a small-time fisherman and trader as a cultural intermediary constituted historical reality in seventeenth-century Suriname. In *Oroonoko* this fisherman enables peaceful encounters between the English visitors and the Indians, whereby both parties are filled with "Wonder and Amazement" at their foreign dress.[56] In the historical Suriname, these Indian traders became liabilities to diplomatic relationships with the Indians when trade, especially the trade in slaves, went badly. Behn's journey along the river is facilitated by both the fisherman and "our Indian slaves, that Row'd us," contradicting her earlier assurances that the English dare not enslave Indians.[57] If Aphra Behn had never visited Suriname, it might have been easy to maintain the romantic framing device of *Oroonoko* wherein the Indians occupy "the first State of Innocence, before Man knew

to sin," and Behn could easily have denied their enslavement.[58] But her incon-
sistency, and the deviation from Warren's text in adding the fisherman character, contains the truth of an observation rather than the trope of a literary tradition. Suriname's plantations might have held a number approaching five hundred
Indian slaves in the 1660s, as it did by 1671.[59]

The relationship of English colonists towards the neighboring Carib thus
ranged from dependent, as trade and military allies, to abusive, as captive takers
and slaveholders. The colonists' mixed feelings of admiration, fear, reprehension,
and condescension appear throughout the travel narratives and ethnographies of
the mid-seventeenth century. Warren and Behn both expressed cautious curiosity
towards Suriname's indigenous population. Warren, in addition to repeating certain tropes from Walter Ralegh, also seems to have drawn on French ethnographer
Charles de Rochefort's *Histoire Naturelle et Morale des Iles Antilles* (1658). Missionary de Rochefort was explicit about English culpability in the Indian slave trade,
identifying the English as the "biggest enemies" of the Caribs.[60]

Warren's short chapter "of the Indians" in his *Description of Suriname* seems to
be a summary of de Rochefort's more extensive and detailed ethnographic descriptions, relating the handsome appearance of the women and their customs of painting themselves with annatto, a dye native to the area, and wearing whatever "Baw-
bles their Service can procure from the English."[61] Most ethnographers agreed that
Carib wives were overworked and "like slaves to their husbands," painting them
with annatto and oiling their hair, as well as carrying out such tasks as cooking,
planting, and weaving hammocks.[62] Warren also repeats this trope, saying that
Indian women "wait upon their husbands" like "the meannest servants amongst
us are to their Masters."[63]

Behn, more accustomed to the drudgery and expectations of women's work
in England, was less shocked. She wrote that Indian wives have a "Servitude easie
and respected" and that they are the only attendants to their husbands, "unless
they take Slaves in War."[64] Behn's narrator thus acknowledges various degrees of
freedom within Indian societies as well, showing the martial origins of the captive
trade in Suriname. Accordingly, she praises the War Captains among the Indians
they visit, writing that they have "a sort of Courage too Brutal to be applauded by
our Black Hero [Oroonoko]; nevertheless he express'd esteem of 'em." This passage
is perhaps an allusion to the future alliance of necessity between the free Indians'
military leaders and black slaves at the end of the 1678–80 Indian War.[65]

In *Oroonoko* Behn describes the Indian population of Suriname as very peaceful and friendly when apart from the colonial population, and then very violent
and gruesome when colonists encroach upon them. This duality is also evident in
the character of Oroonoko. Like the Indians, who "understand no vice, or Cun-
ning," Oroonoko "whose Honour was such as he never had violated a Word in his
Life . . . believ'd in an instant" that the slaver who shackled him, and his masters
in Suriname, would eventually let him go free.[66]

Carolyn Arena

Indigenous freedom, though, was constrained by settlement and trade that increasingly demanded more than they were willing to give, while black slaves were constrained by their meager living conditions and lack of political recourse. Warren wrote that slaves in English Suriname received few allowances: they had to use their free time to work their own provision gardens, and when masters gave them "rotten Salt-fish" or a dead cow or horse, it was considered to be a "great favour."[67] He further described the slaves as "not seldome [driven] to desperate attempts for the Recovery of their Liberty, endeavouring to escape, and, if like to be retaken, [they] sometimes lay violent hands upon themselves; or if they hope of Pardon bring them again alive into their Masters power, they'l manifest their fortitude, or rather obstinancy in suffering the most exquisite tortures [that] can be inflicted upon them, for a terrour and example to other without shrinking." The majority of slaves had come "out of Guiny in Africa to those parts, where they are sold like Goods, and no better esteem'd but for their Work." Behn must have been aware of the real connections between "Guiny" and Suriname, as there are indeed records of a slave ship arriving in Suriname from the Guinea coast in 1664, making the notion that she styled her Oroonoko character as an ethnically "Coromantee" slave who came from this region plausible.[68]

Behn's character would become the heroic epitome of the "fortitude" and "obstinence" that Warren described in Suriname's real-life slaves. Oroonoko, when rallying his fellow slaves to abandon the plantations, questions what possible justification or reason their owners could give to have them "Sold like apes, or Monkeys, to be the Sports of Women, Fools and Cowards and the Support of Rouges, Runagades, that have abandon'd their own Countries for Rapin, Murders, Thefts and Villanies." Slavery, for Oroonoko, mirrors the process of colonization itself—that is, the imposition of "the degenerate Race" of English settlers on the (presumed) guileless Indians and African slaves.[69] With this speech, Oroonoko rallies the rest of the slaves to run away with him, the plan being to "travel towards the Sea; Plant a New Colony, and Defend it by their Valour," as slaves during the Indian rebellion would later do.[70]

Unfortunately, their flight does not last, and Behn's villain, Lieutenant Governor Byam, appears with a militia. Oroonoko promises to surrender if Byam can guarantee his freedom in writing. Byam agrees but does not keep his word; he has Oroonoko whipped brutally and pepper rubbed into his wounds.[71] After recovering, Oroonoko vows revenge on Byam. Oroonoko kills Imoinda to spare her (and their future child) from suffering for his bloody-minded actions. When Oroonoko is caught again, he unflinchingly endures his dismemberment and death while smoking a pipe of tobacco.

Indian Allies and Captives in the Second Anglo-Dutch War

In 1664 Byam wrote to Sir Robert Harley, an absentee landlord who owned the St. John's Hill plantation where Behn stayed, that "Astrea" had left; Astrea was Behn's chosen code name.[72] Behn's narrative in *Oroonoko* seems to corroborate this date as her departure. For instance, Behn's narrator discusses trading with the local Indian population for a feathered headdress, which would eventually adorn the title character in the play *The Indian Queen*. Not only are feathered clothes typical of Surinamese-Carib craftwork,[73] but Howard and Dryden's play *The Indian Queen* was indeed written and first performed in 1664.[74]

For the material in the play that takes place after Behn's departure, the author may have used, in addition to Warren's *Description,* Byam's *Journal of Guiana 1665–1667.*[75] Furthermore, Behn's involvement with the Royalist secret society, the Sealed Knot, and Willoughby were only the beginning of her career in espionage. She would continue to gather information on Dutch military affairs during the Second Anglo-Dutch War as a spy in Antwerp. Behn's original mission was ascertaining the loyalties of the son of an English regicide, William Scot, whom Behn might have met in Suriname. By 1665 Scot was living in Holland, and Behn needed to travel to the Low Countries to rendezvous with him.[76] This might explain why Behn's interest in Suriname was sustained in the twenty years between her visit to the place and the publication of *Oroonoko* in 1688. It was during this period that Indian and African slaves would try to destroy Suriname's plantations, similar to the protest described in the play.

Indian slavery became a major boiling point immediately after the Second Anglo-Dutch War, which pitted the English and their Carib allies against the Dutch and their Arawak allies. The Caribbean theater of the war began in 1665, when Willoughby sent Major John Scott with a fleet to conquer Tobago and St. Christopher's from the Dutch. Scott was successful and then made his way towards Suriname to aid Byam in the colony's defense. Byam wrote that when the English briefly held the Essequibo colony, they made sure to conclude a peace with the "Arrowayes." Byam knew that they could only usurp Dutch control over the region through the Arawaks, the primary Dutch trade partners. Major Scott was confident that the peace between the English and Arawaks had worked and that "This Yeare the English could boast of the Possession of all that Part of Guiana, a butting on the Atlantick Ocean, from Cayan on the South east to Oronoque on the North West."[77]

After about two months, however, the "Indians" (ambiguous) were upset about the conditions of this agreement. Perhaps the real Byam, like his character in *Oroonoko,* did not follow through on his promises towards either indigenous or enslaved communities. Soon the Indians "withdrew all commerce from the English in the forts." The Dutch were allied with the French. Jewish settlers subsequently left for Martinique or St. Christopher's. Without the support of the Indians at Essequibo, the English surrendered the colony back to the Dutch. Byam, though, decided to retaliate and attempted to rescue the remaining Englishmen. He sent Captain Peter Wroth to attack the Dutch and Arawaks at the Approwaco River with "a hondred swifts to still the Indians that greatly destroyed our colonies." Later that year, Byam sent a subordinate to relieve those Englishmen left behind. His force "stormed two warehouses of the Arwacas," killing about thirty men and taking about seventy captives.[78]

Although Byam's journal acknowledges seeking revenge against Indians and taking them captive, he does not describe any brutality against African slaves. Scholars have debated why Behn would choose Byam, a fellow Royalist, as the antagonist for her story, especially considering that her contemporary George Warren gives a personal and positive reference to Byam as "too much of a Gentleman to be the Author of a Lye."[79] Behn's characterization of him brutally torturing Oroonoko might have arisen from a personal dislike, but there are certain parallels between Byam's ruthless pursuit of the retreating Indian force during the Approwaco River campaign and Behn's description of how Byam hunted the runaway slaves led by Oroonoko. Behn makes Byam cruel and pretentious, "a fellow whose character is not fit to be mention'd with the worst of the Slaves. This Fellow [Byam] wou'd lead his Army forth . . . or rather to persue him; most of their Arms were of those sort of cruel Whips . . . some had rusty useless Guns for show; other old Basket-hilts, whose Blades had never seen the Light in this Age."[80]

At the end of the Second Anglo-Dutch War, the actual Byam was terrified, waiting for "the invasion of the Arwaca Indians, who will effect such mischoice as will consequently produce the inevitable ruining of us all." In 1667 Zeeland admiral Abraham Crijnsen's large fleet took Suriname from the English and effectively ended the Caribbean phase of the conflict. Byam, as many English adventurers before him, wrote that he relied on African and Indian slaves to carry the English away safely: he took fourteen boats "in which were Christians and Jews 168 men old and young sick lame and sound, besides negroes and some Indians that paddled the boasts."[81] As they left, Byam also knew they were leaving behind their Carib allies and trade partners in the region. He would remember this when drafting the Articles of Capitulation between himself and Crijnsen: article 6 of the treaty stipulated that the English have "the Liberty of Fishing, and Turtleing upon the Bays as before, and to trade with the Indians is permitted provided they have permission from the Governour." Article 8 states "That wee [the English] shall be furnished with Indian Trade."[82]

Indian Slavery and Rebellion in Dutch Suriname, 1668–1681

Victor Enthoven and, more recently, Alison Games, have described Dutch officials' difficulties rebuilding the Suriname colony in the wake of the Second Anglo-Dutch War.[83] Games details the uncomfortable Dutch dependency on the remaining English colonists for their communication with slaves and resuming sugar production.[84] Raymond Buve has also described this period as a difficult one, primarily because the Dutch tried to take over the Caribs' trade network that the English had cultivated in the Suriname River region. The Caribs, however, were not pleased by this change. Their mistrust probably grew because of the Dutch dependency on English translators for communicating with them. The Dutch pushed forward with attempts to secure Carib trade and maintain trade with their Arawak allies, hoping that the Dutch control of the entire region from Cayenne to New Granada would usher in an era of peace.[85] Despite the war, a peaceful trade was gradually established. Governor Julius Lichtenbergh reported to the Zeeland Chamber that by 1670 the Caribs sustained Dutch colonists with manatee meat and fish.[86]

The remaining English, in addition to being unreliable translators, used their retrenched position in Barbados to harass the Arawaks. In 1668, only a year after Crijnsen and Byam drafted the Articles of Capitulation, the Dutch caught a band of twenty Englishmen from Barbados, dressed in military uniform and armed for war. Upon inspection of the English ship, the Dutch found that these soldiers had instructions to wage war against all the Indian nations of the Wild Coast except the Caribs. The English insisted that the war was against the Arawak alone, as retribution for their crimes during the Second-Anglo Dutch War. The Dutch governor recognized that an Anglo-Arawak war would necessarily involve the Dutch as well and put their hard-won colony at risk. Crijnsen wrote that, in addition to English intentions to kill all Indian tribes other than the Caribs, *another* English ship had just been spotted capturing an entire family of Arawaks with the help of Carib allies.[87] William Willoughby, who had succeeded his deceased brother as governor of Barbados, fervently denied knowing about this reported slave raid, but continued to justify his orders for the war against the Arawaks.[88] Crijnsen sent the captured English soldiers to the Netherlands for trial, charged with undermining the peace.[89]

The Carib and English wars against the Arawaks continued even after peace was concluded with the Dutch. These ongoing conflicts covered the illicit enslavement and trade of Indians, as seventeenth-century Englishmen considered slaves acquired this way to be "vanquish'd . . . nobly in Fight" and won "in Honourable Battel."[90] Captain Wroth, who had successfully attacked the Dutch and their Indian allies in 1666, had been commodifying Indian war captives since, if not before, the Anglo-Dutch Wars. In 1670 Wroth sold a group of slaves in Barbados that included "Cirus a man Negro, Hannah a woman Negro and Semo an Indian Woman."[91] Shortly after Semo's sale, in 1673, Wroth entered a deposition of his actions during the Third Anglo-Dutch War, in which he admitted to bringing Indians from the Main (Guiana) as well: "Of the Indians, brought . . . from the Main by Capt Wroth, some are dead, but the rest shall be returned according to his majesty's commands, a thing designed by him before that they may keep amity with those savages, the contrary having always been very pernicious especially to the smaller Leeward Islands."[92] The Indian slave trade to Barbados had always been morally questionable, and certainly the colonial government knew it put relationships with neighboring Indians at risk. It was compelled to appease Charles II, if only with assurances about this specific case, without actually declaring Wroth's actions to be illegal.

Carolyn Arena

The disapprobation of Indian slavery shown by Charles II, similar to the previous instructions of the WIC in Dutch Brazil, set precedents for the public disavowal of Indian slavery in the Caribbean, even while colonists privately kept Indian slaves. Evidence from Suriname has shown similar tensions between official reports and private documents. Nicholas Combe, secretary of the Governor's Council, wrote the States of Zeeland, which governed the colony, advising that Indian slaves served their plantation owners in a limited and necessary capacity as hunters, fishermen, and navigators.[93] Many historians have read these reports and concluded that Indian slavery was indeed limited to these skilled roles.[94] However, since free Indians in the region also exchanged meat and fish with colonists as trade partners, it seems unlikely that these were the sole occupations of the five hundred Indian slaves in Dutch Suriname. Unlike colonial officials, the planters themselves did not downplay their use of Indian slaves. The petition from the residents of Suriname mentioned the five hundred Indian slaves in the context of needing more supplies to rebuild the infrastructure of sugar production.[95]

This suggests that Indian slaves were integral to the plantations, rather than addenda to them. The planters' mention of the high number of Indian slaves might have also been a tactic to persuade the States of Zeeland to petition the WIC to send more African slaves to Suriname, since Indian enslavement would have undermined the WIC slave-trade monopoly in the Dutch colonies. Suriname's colonists might have wondered whether they were in contempt of the WIC when they participated in the regional Indian slave trade. In 1672 the colonists asked Lieutenant Governor Pieter Versterre whether it was in their rights to trade with Caribs upriver (closer to the interior) for more slaves. The governor and council decided that because of the considerable expense to each of the purchasers in obtaining his own slaves, they could keep the slaves themselves.[96]

The Caribs were not happy to see their former small-time English trade partners, such as the fisherman characterized in *Oroonoko,* exchanged for independent Dutch traders, called *swervers* or *bokkenruylers.* These traders, like Suriname itself, operated independently of the WIC. The *bokkenruylers* bought European goods at a high price, or on credit, from colonial merchants. Consequently, they were almost always poor and indebted. They needed to turn over their merchandise cheaply and quickly back to plantation owners. Despite the general distrust of the Caribs towards the new *bokkenruylers* as trade partners, their ongoing wars with the neighboring Arawak and Waros tribes created captives, and the *bokkenruylers* incentivized the Caribs to offload these captives in the general direction of Dutch plantations. The desperation of these traders to turn a quick profit, however, also tempted them into using alcohol and other coercive measures to take Indian slaves.[97]

In addition to the small-scale Indian slave trade of "fishermen" and *bokkenruylers,* English and Dutch privateers used the Third Anglo-Dutch War to capture large numbers of African and Indian slaves. Slaves on prizes were probably in high demand, as the 1672 monopoly of the English Royal African Company temporarily drove up prices for African slaves.[98]

It is difficult to ascertain whether this increased demand for Indian slaves, but the proportion of Indian slaves to African slaves on at least one prize ship was similar to the proportion then found in Suriname. On June 7, 1673, Dutch commander Cornelis Evertsen brought a ship to Curacao with 206 slaves captured on prizes and through raids; forty-six of these slaves were Indians.[99] Although the schedule on the ship is not specific, these Indians were most likely Kalinago or Carib military allies of the English and destined to leave Curacao to serve in plantations elsewhere in the Caribbean.[100]

This did not help the mutual suspicions of the Dutch and Caribs on the mainland. An English resident of Suriname reported to the Barbados Council in 1673: "There is great hatred between the Caribbee Indians and the Dutch." He encouraged the council to send ships to retake Suriname, since the Dutch were vulnerable as they lacked indigenous support. The Barbados Council considered it, postulating that about eight hundred well-armed men could probably retake Suriname. In the end, though, they decided against it, as they "cannot forsee what assistance the Dutch may have from the Arawaca Indians, their friends their own negroes, or the meaner sort of English planters."[101] The English and the Dutch were in no position to claim authority in Suriname without securing indigenous allies first.

Rather than trying to retake the colony through Indian allies, the leaders of the Anglo-Caribbean waited until peacetime to whittle down the colony through legal means: using the terms of the 1667 Articles of Capitulation, renewed in the 1674 Treaty of Westminster, to siphon off and relocate the English population of Suriname along with their slaves, both African and Indian. In 1675, as the English ships were about to leave, a group of free Indians complained to the Dutch governor Pieter Versterre that their kinsman were on the ship and the English "wanted to carry them off."[102] The English claimed that the Indians were domestic servants who *chose* to leave with their masters and would be upset to leave the English.[103]

Contemporary to the conflicts over Indian "servants" leaving with the English, Carib Indians in Guiana killed two Dutch *bokkenruylers* amid the growing disputes over buying and selling Indian slaves. One Carib leader warned that he would retaliate, and his own network of alliances eventually built up to become a unified front of various Indian groups against the Dutch. By 1678 the wronged Caribs had convinced allied groups, including Arawaks, from surrounding rivers to join them in their attacks against the colonists. Versterre died before this series of Indian alliances culminated in the rebellion. The new governor, Johannes Heinsius, attempted to convince their Arawak allies to help the Dutch defend themselves, but many were unwilling. At first, the rebelling Indians ransacked plantations and even killed slaves, but later they encouraged African slaves, already marooning plantations and the harsh conditions of slavery in Suriname, to join the fight.[104]

On October 26, 1679, Heinsius issued an Ordinance on the "Sale of Captured Indian Slaves" related to the Indian rebellion. The governor wrote, "as we ourselves find ourselves embroiled in a bloody, inhumane, and nearly irreconcilable war with the Indians, our barbaric enemies, who are unceasing and they pursue us with fire and brands and everything living they can to clear and massacre us, about which we can not sit idle . . . we have concluded that all of the slaves from this country should be transported with the first departing ship."[105] Heinsius had realized what his predecessors had not—that keeping an enslaved population with ready recourse to nearby political allies was a dangerous proposition.[106] By 1681 African slaves had taken leadership roles in the rebellion as well. It was then that a slave of African descent named Jermes or Gemmert commanded a fort of runaways and Indians on the nearby Para Creek. By the end of the rebellion, between seven hundred and eight hundred slaves of both Indian and African descent had run away.[107]

Indian slavery continued in Suriname after the rebellion, but the numbers of Indian slaves decreased substantially, from 500 in 1671 to just 106 in 1684. The Dutch and Indians did not agree to a formal peace until 1686, wherein the colonists agreed not to enslave neighboring Indian communities.[108] Although both sides had suffered greatly, Indian communities in Suriname would continue to leverage their military strength and the reliance of colonial populations on their strategic knowledge to maintain their independence throughout the colonial period.

Meanwhile, Aphra Behn was writing *Oroonoko,* a narrative of slavery in seventeenth-century Suriname that valorized the independence and honor of an African prince, using, perhaps, these real-life models of Indian and African rebels. Like the original explorers of Guiana, Behn initially rejected the notion that English colonists practiced Indian enslavement. However, her narrative betrays the historic reality of how both Indian slavery and Indian alliances were deeply woven into the fabric of the colony. The story investigates the consequences of colonists who betrayed seventeenth-century ideals of acquiring slaves through the "legitimate" means of just war. Behn structured her work in a way that showed how slavery in Suriname ought to be contextualized in an indigenous world and within the tensions between neighboring Indians and English and Dutch colonists. Thus, the Caribbean "front" of the "Anglo-Dutch Wars" incorporated a parallel war within Suriname, fought by colonists, Indian allies, Indian enemies, and African and Indian slaves, which continued despite the pauses and limitations that European treaties and authorities appeared to command.

Indigeneity and Authority in the Lesser Antilles

The Warners Revisited

Sarah Barber

Throughout most of the seventeenth century, authority over all the islands of the Lesser Antilles was claimed by the English state and administered by a motley of British actors under the proprietorship of James Hay, 1st Earl of Carlisle, the Scottish favorite of King James VI and I. His patent as lord proprietor of the Caribbees, or Province of Carliola or Carlisle, was notoriously ill-framed by persons unfamiliar with the geography of the region and deliberately vague so as to mask dissent and contest even among the British themselves.[1]

There are exceptions here that were included elsewhere. Trinidad was firmly under Spanish control, but Tobago was settled by several European groups, including the English. There is no mention of St. Croix: Carlisle's rival, James Ley, third Earl of Marlborough, attempted an English colony there in 1645, which was ceded to the French after five years. There is no mention of Dominica, but the reference to Martinique as "Mittalania" implies the sense of a midline division of the chain, north to south. While the catchall description was a means to quash divisions within the British nobility, Carlisle's claim was seldom made good in total, as it depended on the other European powers and indigenous peoples giving way. It relied on the English (sometimes British and Irish) laying claim to their superiority by dint of God's Providence, natural law, and often, natural right.

The division between the Leeward and Windward Islands was indeed to a large extent arbitrary, if the terms *leeward* and *windward* are taken to refer to the prevailing winds and the requirements of navigation, but the distinction was concentrated on the tiny island of Dominica. At stake was the nature of authority and whether it emerged organically and had local and vernacular purchase, or whether it was imposed by a power that became dominant because it was the possessor, or at least asserter, of right or might. While the English state affirmed and imposed its authority, settlers, especially if they were asserting their right to new land for the first time, claimed for themselves a right based on their pioneering. They laid claim to their own indigeneity, sometimes as first settlers and those who carried the vernacular with them and sometimes as those who were welcomed by and treated with indigenous people.

The dominant nation of these indigenous people, both on the mainland and Lesser Antilles, were the Kalinago. An early account of them in English appears in Richard Eden's translation of the descriptions of the Spanish landings in the West Indies made by Pietro Martire d'Anghiera (Peter Martyr) and their use of the term *Caribe* to portray fearsome warrior people who habitually consumed the bodies of the vanquished. Having been welcomed and aided by the "meke and humayne" Taíno, both Natives and newcomers were driven out by "the wylde and myscheuous people called *Canibales,* or *Caribes,* whiche were accustomed to eate mannes flesshe."[2]

English encounters with the Carib people of Guiana, where the English conducted regular forays in pursuit of commercial and planting opportunities in the late sixteenth century, were not characterized by fear or hostility. They produced no such gruesome accounts of the Guiana man-eaters. They noted that they took their name and gave their name to the region because of the tradition of cannibalism, but English descriptions remained observational anthropology.

Captain Thomas Warner's discovery of St. Christopher's occurred as a consequence of his voyage to Guiana. Warner arrived there on January 28, 1624, with fifteen men, including his son, Edward, having been sponsored by the London merchant, Ralph Merrifield, who testified in May 1626 that he had furnished two ships to the undertaking.[3] Captain John Smith recorded that there were three Frenchmen (as well as a Native population) living on the island when the English arrived and that they initially and unsuccessfully sought to turn the indigenous population against the newcomers. The English lived for one month with the Kalinago, after which they built a "Fort, and a house, and plant[ed] fruits"; and while they waited for the crop of tobacco, which was destroyed by a hurricane, they lived on "Cassada bread, Potatoes, Plantines, Pines, Turtels, Guanes, and fish plentie; for drinke wee had *Nicnobbie.*"[4]

Warner is therefore established as not only leader of the first English settlement in the West Indies but also one who had cordial and cooperative relations with those already settled there. On March 18, 1625, he was joined by four men from the *Hopewell* of London, commanded by Warner's Suffolk friend John Jeaffreson: they brought supplies to be traded for tobacco, and Warner accompanied the tobacco shipment back to England in September 1625, leaving son Edward in charge.[5] Thomas Warner was absent between September 1625 and August 4, 1626, when he returned with around a hundred settlers, and a commission from the new king, Charles I, that gave him full powers to treat, trade, and send people to strengthen the plantation.[6]

There was further English migration and shipping: the *Hopewell,* with William Smith master, returned on October 26, 1627, bringing ammunition; around the same time Captain Pelham arrived with thirty men in the *Plow;* and a small

Bristol ship brought Thomas Warner's wife and "six or seven women more." Captain Charles Saltonstall arrived on November 26, 1627, and sailed back and forth despite the crippling freight and dues charged on tobacco; in 1629 he sailed with Sir William Tufton, taking two hundred people to Barbados and "all manner of commodities fit for a plantation."[7]

Between January 1624 and the end of 1629, then, the formative history of English St. Christopher's was laid out. With each arrival and departure, there were also changing relations with the indigenous population and other migrating Kalinago, as well as changing relations with the French settlers and other French migrants. It is the very different interpretations of these "spaces," nearly all composed retrospectively, that molded the character of the English Antilles.

Different groups of English, French, and Kalinago settled or sought to settle St. Christopher's. The three Frenchmen there when Warner first arrived were suspected of fomenting unrest, but this was soon resolved; and in the first months the English established themselves with a lifestyle shaped by the indigeneity of the island. They had amicable relations with the indigenous people, lived on native plants, and were at the mercy of the hurricanes. So, like the Kalinago, when the climate was kind, they produced a crop of tobacco for trade, but after hurricanes— on September 19, 1624, and September 4, 1626, with possibly a third, which damaged Saltonstall's ship and goods—they were reliant on "what we could get in the wilde woods" and the arrival of the turtles to lay their eggs, which provided an easy food source while they replanted cassava and potatoes.

The dearth of food, however, strained relations between the English and French, who were reported having a far more unstable relationship with the Kalinago. During the time over the winter of 1625–26, when Thomas Warner was in England, a French pinnace arrived with news that Kalinago had killed some French settlers elsewhere in the islands and that they were heading for St. Christopher's. Between four hundred and five hundred arrived in six pirogues, and although the English asked them to leave, they raided the coasts throughout November and December, with the English and French joining together to repulse them. On November 25, 1627, "the *Indians* set upon the *French,* for some injury about their women": twenty-six French, five English, and three Natives were killed by reed arrows tipped with poisoned stingray tails. By Christmas 1629, when around thirty English, French, and Dutch ships had arrived at the island, "all of the *Indians* [had been] forced out of the Ile, for they had done much mischiefe amongst the *French,* in cutting their throats, burning their houses, and spoyling their Tobacco." Ralph Merrifield was said to have rescued the orphan child of the Kalinago chief and raised him in England as his own.[8]

An account of European-Kalinago relations from the French perspective was provided by Jean-Baptiste Du Tertre, whose *Histoire* of French activities in the West Indies was first published in 1654. Du Tertre concentrated on the French leader Pierre Belain D'Esnambuc who arrived on St. Christopher's at around the same time as Warner (rendered as Vvaërnard throughout), and they formed an alliance based on shared rough treatment at the hands of the Spanish. Du Tertre claimed "ces Barbares" began to challenge both, with their excessive drinking of wine persuading them they should massacre every foreigner on the island.[9] With the intercession of divine Providence, both the French and the English were alerted by one of the Kalinago, who out of what was described as a particular interest, had discovered the intended massacre. Both the English and French detested such a horrible conspiracy, and so that same night, they killed between 100 and 120 people while they slept, "except for some of the most beautiful women, who, to satisfy their brutal lust, they made their slaves."[10] Following this, the Europeans realized that they must "design" how they lived on the island and resolved a division of the land. But the more often cited edition of Du Tertre on this event was that published in 1667, in which he named the indigenous informer as Barbe, and the wording is quite different.[11]

There was therefore a tension between the reputation of Warner as a soldier-leader, but with amicable relations between the Kalinago, and the colonists being forced into a concern for their security, both internally and against raids on St. Christopher's. A later account described Warner as "a good Souldier & a man of extraordinary agillety of bodie of a good witt & one who was truly honnest & freindly to all men"; the author went out of his way to stress the excellent relationships Warner had with various Kalinago chiefs, including Tegreman, who gave him and his small band license to settle on the island between two rivers on the west coast near the chief's house. The author hints at the dissimulation of the English, but also at deceit by the Kalinago chief, who changed his mind and was "minded to cut y^m off."[12] Warner was warned of the impending attack by "an old Indian woman y^t did often freq^t amongst ye English, who it seems they had used courteously soe y^t she had taken great affeccon to y^m"; she explained the Kalinago custom of drinking for three or four days, which presaged an attack. But instead of sailing away as she advised, as a good soldier and a wise man, he took advantage of their drunken state and attacked the Kalinago, stabbing through their hammocks, including that of Tegreman. In this account the child who was spared was an English boy whom Warner had brought with him and for whom Tegreman had such affection that he slept with the chief.

The nature of the various accounts is confused and jumbled. There is mention of Indian raids while Warner is absent and when he is present; accounts of Indian attacks from within and without St. Christopher's; references to Anglo-French cooperation and contest; a sense—maybe tailored for an English audience, but even then it is an interesting distinction—that there was a history of poor Franco-Kalinago relations; a child rescued from one attack who may have been either Kalinago or English; and a reference to a tipoff of imminent indigenous attack that may have been evidence of wider Anglo-Kalinago concord against dissident or "foreign" elements or of a sympathetic individual who wished to avoid shedding the blood of people who had behaved honorably. While the harmonious relationship between the three cultures on St. Christopher's seems to have lasted a mere five years at most, the events of those years became conflated such that, despite some extremes of contestation, they defined both the internal development of the island but also the wider history of Anglo-French and indigenous relations throughout the West Indies. A single event is now referred to as the Massacre at Bloody Point and sometimes to the "Kalinago genocide," positioned at the end of January 1626. The more southerly of the rivers between which Tegreman and the English settlements fell was termed the Pelham River by the English. Having massacred the Kalinago as they slept in their hammocks, the Europeans were said to have piled the bodies up and thrown many into the river, causing it to run red for several days, and the place where the river emptied its gory witness into the sea was renamed Bloody Point. There are Kalinago petroglyphs picked out at the site, including the evil and portentous monkey god.

Du Tertre has the French returning in numbers to St. Christopher's in May 1627. In this account Warner, realizing that the French were not going to abandon the island, formed a company under "Milord Karley" (the Earl of Carlisle) and returned with four hundred people and a wealth of provisions, at which time the two European nations came to a formal truce.[13] This would explain the reference in the English account of the *Hopewell*'s second visit, under William Smith, at the end of October 1627, which brought weapons, powder, and shot from Carlisle, the newly patented lord proprietor of the Caribbees. This coincided with Du Tertre's account of the formal treaty of division of St. Christopher's: the English retained the Middle Quarter; the French settled on the northern and southern ends of the island. The treaty was made more likely by the relative weakness of the English military, both by land and sea, so Thomas Warner sent his son, presumably Edward, though Du Tertre merely has him as "a young, very well-born man" who was "very friendly towards the French," to secure the treaty.

That the massacre of the Kalinago was vital in securing the interests not of the settlers of St. Christopher's but of the central English authorities is illustrated by two key, surviving, almost contemporaneous documents. The first was dated April 3, 1628. It is an indenture for land issued to John Jeaffreson (and Edward Johnson, presumably his financial partner).[14] It is remarkable in several respects. It deviates from the usual format to articulate a particular reason why Jeaffreson had gained authority, sanctioned by London, to control land.[15] The indenture makes it clear that Jeaffreson was already possessed of land in St. Christopher's that he voluntarily gave up to the Crown and now had granted back to him through the proprietor, Carlisle. These were all those lands now in Jeaffreson's and Johnson's possession, "late beinge p[ar]cell of certain gardens late belonging to the Indians the Savage natives of that Island."

Further, they were to take control of more lands, amounting to a total of one thousand acres, but only assigning lots of one hundred acres at a time, as such

Sarah Barber

lands could be "implanted" or could be used and occupied. This was the grant of a feudal manor, for which one thousand acres seemed to be a customary measure in the smaller islands of the West Indies. He would pay rent on the lands, and thus held them in socage, as was the case with other indentures issued throughout the British West Indies. But Jeaffreson was also assuming "native right" because he was in occupation of "gardens," that is the provision of mixed native cultivation by indigenous people. And then, he had defended the land and the people of the island against attack, possibly during the period in which he was acting governor, in Warner's absence, and thus this is the only land indenture to make reference to tenure by "Knighte Service." Carlisle was therefore using the retrospective action at Bloody Point (or other Anglo-Kalinago conflicts) to claim his feudal authority over those settlers who had preexisting de facto tenure and position under Warner. Ironically, this indenture survives because it was used against the Earl of Carlisle in the 1650s as various planters took advantage of Interregnum reform of land tenure to (re)claim their debts against the earl. At this later date, Jeaffreson referred to himself as a "primitive" planter whose de facto action in establishing English people on the land took precedence over imposed feudal authority.[16]

It would be more than a year later before Carlisle confirmed Warner's position.[17] This was done for three reasons: first, because he was "descended Lineally of the worthy and ancient family of the Warners in the Counties of Suffolk and Essex"; second, because his personal commitment to founding the colony gave him de facto authority ("the Adventure of his person Life and Estate by Travaile and frequentation for many yeares in severall parts of the West Indies"); and third, because, having during his absence in England gained royal sanction for his settlement in St. Christopher's, he had laid the foundations for "a lasting and happye plantation."[18]

Carlisle expressed faith that Warner would continue "the perfecting and finall Establishing of the Colonie and Plantations soe happuly begun." For Carlisle this seemed to extend primarily or even solely to internal and external defense through military exercises, a good store of ammunition and the imposition of martial law where necessary. Warner, however, drew up a written code of conduct, of a type seemingly based on Sir Thomas Dale's *Lawes Divine, Morall and Martiall* in Virginia around fifteen years earlier. The "Orders" are not dated, but both civil and military clauses stressed the obligation to pay dues to or obey the authority of the Earl of Carlisle, so they must have been part of the mutual recognition and confirmation of authority. Among the lists of expenses incurred by the earl's creditors as he planned the settlement of his authority on Barbados in 1628 were luxury ceremonial carbines and swords to be "presented" to the governors of Barbados (Charles Wolverston) and St. Christopher's.[19] Warner differed from Dale in being briefer and in distinguishing thirteen civilian clauses ranging across religious observance, maintenance of families, and designating levels and types of planting provision for self-sufficiency.[20]

Described as general of the Caribbee islands and governor of St. Christopher's and praised for his martial exploits, Sir Thomas Warner died on March 10, 1649. Meanwhile, Dominica, lying at the midpoint of the chain of Lesser Antilles islands, became the center of Kalinago settlement as bands were driven from neighboring settlements. The majority of islands were divided up between the English and the French, despite the English claim to them all.

At the Restoration, the Crown made attempts to gather systematic information about its colonial claims, the degree to which they could be made good, and its servants in far-flung places. The Treaty of Breda (1667), which brought to an end the Second Anglo-Dutch War, enabled the English to regain control of Antigua and Montserrat from the French and to resume the partition of St. Christopher's between the two nations.[21] Nevertheless, Anglo-French relations were tainted in the longer term, as the English state, already uncertain of the extent and security of its Caribbean colonies, was further plagued by claims for compensation and restitution from displaced and incommoded settlers in the northern islands. Current and potential settlement on Dominica, between the French-held islands of Guadeloupe to the north and Martinique to the south, was a source of contention as the French and English struggled to build an accord.

The English lord proprietor of the Caribbees was now Francis, fifth Baron Willoughby of Parham, leasing his title from the Earls of Carlisle. Although based in Lincolnshire, the fact that his title was centered on Parham Hall, a stone's throw from Sir Thomas Warner's childhood home, may explain how he came to be involved in the Torrid Zone. It may also account for the preferment of a man referred to as Sir Thomas's son, also called Thomas Warner, created governor of Dominica.[22] Francis Willoughby died at sea in 1666 and was succeeded by his brother, William, but "the English colony at Dominica," having been "lately much annoyed by the French, his lordship resolved to visit that island in his way home [November 1668] with a sufficient force to redress the injuries which the inhabitants had sustained," which "vigorous measure produced the desired effect, and his lordship procured from the Caraibs a formal surrender of the island to his Britannic Majesty."[23]

The governor of the French Antilles was Joseph-Antoine le Fèbvre de la Barre. De la Barre's reading of the treaty was that the French had ceded Dominica to the Kalinago and were therefore bound to keep peace with them, and the English were barred thereby from settling there. "Captain [Thomas] Warner" was in French hands, and they would not return him to the island because he would begin a new war with those Kalinago the French had promised to support, despite the Frenchman's contention that Warner lived as a Kalinago, was never a Christian, and did not consider him covered by the terms of the peace.[24] Willoughby continued to support Warner, owning the latter to be a subject of King Charles and Dominica to be part of his authority and that therefore the French had no right to determine where an English subject might live. Warner's fate, according to Willoughby, had been determined by his "step-mother." It makes no mention of who the woman might be. Thomas may have left for Dominica after Sir Thomas's death, and therefore the stepmother who forced him out may have been Anne Russell; but Willoughby described Thomas Warner as Sir Thomas's "deputed" son, who had been raised by Sir Thomas until the age of thirty (had he been his natural son, he would have to have been born before 1618). He had taken the Oath of Allegiance and had a full commission from Francis Willoughby.[25] A month later, Willoughby ordered Major James Walker to take Warner back to Dominica, try to build an accord with the French and Kalinago, attack any hostile Kalinago settlements, rescue as many English and Kalinago as possible, and along with Warner take them to Barbados.[26] The notes made by Joseph Williamson, secretary to the Southern Department, presumably glossing William Willoughby's information, described Dominica as being under "Governor Warner, who married an Indian woman, and is son of the late Governor of St. Kitts."[27]

In the 1670s Williamson made some more notes about the English Torrid Zone: Barbados was now governed by Sir Jonathan Atkins, and the English-held islands of St. Christopher's, Nevis, Antigua, and Montserrat had been federated as the Leeward Islands under the leadership of an Irishman, Sir William Stapleton, who had crowned his dominance of the region by marrying in 1671 Anne, the youngest child of Randall Russell.[28] Stapleton's position became even stronger in 1673 with the death of William Willoughby, but the Council of Barbados had sent a commission to "Warner the Indian" to continue as governor of Dominica, as styled in his former commission from the Willoughbys. When Warner promised to fulfill this, it was noted that there had been no French presence in Dominica for the previous three months (March–May 1673).[29] Around six months later, Atkins was commissioned "Govern^r of Barbados, Sta Lucia, St Vincent, Dominico, and the rest of the Caribbee Islands to Windward of Guardaloope."[30]

English and French attitudes towards the Kalinago became tied to inter-British rivalry, particularly that between Atkins (Windwards) and Stapleton (Leewards). Stapleton's success in federating the Leeward Islands was based on a dual strategy of lobbying for English compensation claims in Antigua, St. Christopher's, and Nevis against the depredations of the French and a policy of fomenting terror of the Kalinago: he predicted an invading force of twenty-five hundred to three thousand.[31] The proprietorship of the Caribbees having been divided, the issues rolled together in the confused and conflated history of the person of "Warner the Indian."

Atkins informed the Crown that Philip Warner, the governor of Antigua, had launched an assault on the Kalinago in Dominica to avenge successive attacks on his island. Thomas Warner offered him assistance, commanding around sixty Kalinago in eight pirogues, and, having been successful, Philip Warner invited "Sixty or Seventy persons, Men, Women and Children, to an Entertainment of thanks for their good Service." He then deliberately "made the said Thomas Warner and his said Indians drunk with Rum and such other Liquors as they gave them." Atkins's informant, William Hamlyn, testified that on Philip Warner's signal, the English killed nearly all the Kalinago at a place on the west coast now known as Massacre.[32]

A bill was drawn up for the matter to be tried in London but instead was handed over to Atkins in Barbados. Sir Thomas Warner's widow, Anne Russell, now Lady March, petitioned the Crown on behalf of Philip Warner, denouncing Hamlyn's information as vengeful, because Philip had stopped him from trading tobacco with the Dutch, while Philip informed Atkins that Hamlyn's testimony was inconsistent but nevertheless believed by the multitude who now perceived him a "monster." Having described the pretext for Philip Warner's imprisonment in the Tower—"murdering his owne brother and destroying some Indians in freindshipp w^{t}h ye English"—she corrected herself that although he had not been guilty of these deaths, the worry of having displeased the king had made him dangerously ill, and besides, "ye person supposed to be his brother was an Indian Infidell; and who had murthered more of yor Majtyes Subiects (then all ye Indians of these partes)."[33]

Philip Warner described Thomas Warner as his "halfe-Brother an Indian" and a "young Lad," who lived on as a servant to a merchant called Crisp in Antigua, and said that rather than assist in the reduction of Dominica, he had left Philip Warner undersupplied with Kalinago to manage the eight pirogues. In November 1666 he had killed Governor Robert Carden of Antigua which had paved the way for the French invasion.[34] On the second page of his petition, Philip Warner uses the name by which Thomas Warner came to be known by posterity, and denied any blood relation: "That Indian Warner was not Brother to Coll: Philip Warner: but being Slave to Sr Thomas affected his Name as usually they doe." Like his (step?)mother he praised "his Father Old Sr Thomas Warner" whose enterprise and loyalty had settled all of these islands, and augmented the Crown's coffers, funding employment for thousands of families and multiplying shipping. Posthumously, it recast Sir Thomas Warner's reputation for amicable and cooperative relationship with the Kalinago at St. Christopher's.

Philip Warner called for the commission and witness statements ordered for his trial not to be held and taken in Barbados but that it be in Nevis, the closest Leeward Island to Dominica and home of Stapleton, and that an equal number of Leeward Islanders sit with Windwarders on the commission.[35] This did not happen, and instead, both Atkins and Stapleton sent a list of depositions. Atkins stressed the need to keep amity with the Kalinago now that the English were more bedeviled by the French. Not doing so had proven "pernitious," especially for Britons in the smaller Leeward Islands. Now, however, there had been a change of attitude and policy in the West Indies, and Atkins feared that Kalinago goodwill had been lost forever.[36] Philip Warner had acted without recourse to Atkins and had killed the only person "in all these parts that asserted the English interest . . .

his halfe Brother (for they had both one Father)." But this does not confirm that they were related by consanguinity, as Thomas could have been adopted into Sir Thomas's household. Regardless, William Hamlyn, commander of the sloop *Bettie,* swore that he had been ordered by Philip Warner in Antigua to carry letters to Stapleton in Nevis. From thence he received further orders to join a fleet, of which Philip Warner was part, to Dominica, where he was joined by Thomas Warner.[37]

The enemy in this engagement was described as the "Windward Indians." In response, Stapleton repeated Philip Warner's information: that "Indian Warner" had been Sir Thomas's slave and had been harboring those Kalinago whose crimes against the settlers of Antigua were so heinous that it cried out for vengeance, but the "son [who] p'tended to bee killed is att St Christophers."[38] Stapleton, meanwhile, had been building bridges with the French who were cooperating to restore the economies of the Leewards devastated by Kalinago raids. Stapleton sent a number of testimonies that would, despite the claim that Thomas Warner was a slave, prove "Indian Warner his ffraternity with Coll: Warner." Philip Warner's antipathy towards the Natives as a people was clear. Had he "destroyed all the Charibbee Indians" he would have done the best service conducive to English settlement, in case the peace broke down with his "potent Neighbours:" not the Kalinago, but the French.

Another deponent, Walter Carwardine, claimed to have come over with Sir Thomas Warner to St. Christopher's and to have served him for four years. His recollections were those of a sixty-year-old man who had been about fourteen when he emigrated.[39] Sir Thomas was depicted as a man who kept a household of indigenous slaves, within which "family" he had "a certaine male Child, which the Inhabitants Slaves had others comonly called Warner or Indian Warner." At their arrival, the baby was around six months old, was never baptized, "or looked upon any other person then An Slave or Nigroes child borne in any English family in America" and was never reputed to be Sir Thomas's child. Lieutenant Robert Choppin was a couple of years younger. And he too remembered that it was forty-six years before (1629) when Sir Thomas Warner called all of his slaves together: they were all Indians and there were "about twenty four." The first child born to his slaves, then about six months old, Sir Thomas called Warner. Later, conveniently, the child was "carried away by his Mother or some others to the number of about Twenty ffowre who run of from Sr Thomas Warners Plantation." Brought back, this "Warner" subsequently served Sir Thomas as a slave until the governor died and afterwards served Anne, his widow.[40] This last piece of evidence was supported by Choppin's wife, Sarah, ten years his junior; she had been a servant to Sir Thomas Warner when a Captain Fletcher sailed from Scotland to bring the slave back to his master and his lady.[41]

Stapleton's next witness was Randall Russell, Stapleton's deputy and father-in-law. Russell had also served in Sir Thomas's household since 1637 and had taken an "acco' of his family both of Indian Slaves and others, As also an acco' of his

Indians, several then run away" to Dominica. Russell had never heard Sir Thomas Warner refer to this man as anything other than a slave and unbaptized.[42] Sir Robert Southwell visited Philip Warner in the Tower and took from him an account of all English possessions in the West Indies; he found his testimony so useful to the Crown that the Lords of Trade wrote to Stapleton to require of him more maps and accounts of the defense and state of the Leeward Islands.[43] What Stapleton sent amounted to further (already prepared) corroboration of his anti-Kalinago version of the events of the previous fifty years.[44]

Stapleton's already mustered documentation was now resubmitted as a digest of the state of the Leewards. In Montserrat he constituted the council to take thirteen testimonies, at least eight of which were from elderly Irishmen, who swore to the terrible actions of the Kalinago over the years they had lived on the island.[45] He acquired three testimonies from St. Christopher's, taken before the governor, Abednego Mathew. One was from Gilbert Loxley, aged seventy-eight, who reported that from Sir Thomas Warner's first settlement on the island, he had several indigenous slaves, including a boy called Tom, who had an Indian wife. Kalinago, under the reputed leadership of Indian Warner, had raided Montserrat and killed Thomas Russell, and several testified to a Kalinago intention to extirpate the Russell and Ashton families.[46] In 1667, however, Loxley had been a signatory to a petition from St. Christopher's, which extolled the civilian rule of Sir Thomas Warner because of the great flexibility and liberality he had shown under the capacious umbrella of the Church of England.[47] Carwardine gave evidence again, from Nevis, and this island, home base of both the Russells and the Stapletons, sent addresses. Further testimonies came from Antigua, justifying the particular revenge mission against the Kalinago, but the most telling statement came from the address sent from St. Christopher's: "That from the first settlement of his Maties part of this Island It hath not been knowne by any of us that ever any Trade or commerce hath been held or Negotiated with the Canniballs Salvages or Indians inhabiting or dwelling att the neighbouring Islands of either Dominico, Sᵗᵃ Lucea or Sᵗ Vincent. . . . But on the contrary they have ever proved themselves Treacherous and perfidious Infidells."[48]

Thus, Stapleton had consolidated his power and confirmed the Leeward Islands as his fiefdom.[49] He had humbled Barbados, and that island's civilian governor, whose chosen strategy of alliance with the Kalinago to maintain the integrity of the whole Caribbee chain, had been defeated.

In rescuing Philip Warner, furthermore, Stapleton altered the reputation of the whole Warner family. He emphasized that Sir Thomas Warner's success was primarily martial, and in providing security for St. Christopher's, he had promoted secondary migration. But all these fledgling settlements had been destroyed by the Kalinago with Sir Thomas's reputation recast as that of a man who, having chosen to accept the service and loyalty of the Kalinago, was shown to be naïve. What were probably his indigenous servants, part of the household, were posthumously always referred to as his slaves. The incorporation of his household within one family now stretched to claims of paternity. But while few emerge with any honor, one thing that could be said of Sir Thomas Warner was that he was among the freest from hypocrisy. Within his moral commonwealth of St. Christopher's were clear instructions for the obligations of any "M^r of Familie or other Wise in Cheife" (one of the earliest references to "Masters of Families" to describe a household head), including the stipulation that "noe pson dare to medle or defile his bodye w^{t}h any women whatsoever be they Christians or Heathens (yt being a breach both of divine and humane lawes)." There was no mention of any except servants nor any delineation between white and indigenous service.[50]

Thus, "Indian Warner" could not have been any blood relation of Sir Thomas: the degree of the governor's hypocrisy would certainly have been exposed at the time. Had "Indian Warner" been a servant adopted into the household, the child must have had two indigenous parents, and it seems unlikely that such an adoption would have happened had Warner's household been enslaved. That Sir Thomas Warner's authority could be posthumously sullied by branding him a slave owner of Natives who all ran away, whose naïve trust was subsequently played out by perfidious people who so designed the eradication of English settlement that his household would tear itself apart, even to the point of brother against brother (adopted or blood), was a construction signaling that the fate of "Indian Warner" was a metaphor for the death of Native right, the triumph of the grandee-plantocracy, and its thrall to the dictates of Empire.

Part II

Empire, Settlement, and War in the Torrid Zone

The Cases of Suriname, Jamaica, Danish West Indies, and Saint-Domingue

Second Is Best

Dutch Colonization on the "Wild Coast"

Jessica Vance Roitman

The scene on the frosty dock of Texel's harbor a few weeks before Christmas of 1676 was chaotic but hopeful.[1] As one account noted, the dock was jammed with "entire families with women and children, furnishings and household goods, belongings in storage, horses, cattle, along with all sorts of farming implements."[2] Their departure had been delayed by a hard frost, but they were finally ready to board the waiting ships, cross the ocean, and start a new life. On December 14, a group of "75 sails" left to establish a colony on the Oyapock River, which today serves as the border between Brazil and French Guiana.[3] These ships had 350 colonists on board, including soldiers, families with male and female servants, a school teacher, and a vicar, all of whom were embarking on an adventure on the so-called "Wild Coast" of South America.

The settlers left cold North Holland with high hopes of arriving in "Guiana, an incredibly beautiful land full of gold."[4] At the end of February 1677, they reached their destination on the Oyapock. At first they were not disappointed. When they disembarked at the location where they intended to settle, they found a place that had "so pleasant a prospect and [was] so diverting to the eye that it was as though it was designed expressly to give pleasure. It was as if the land here was greener and better and gave more gratification to our people, though they are used to such land."[5] Yet quite quickly these pleasant prospects in the New World, which were "with care and expense and energy [to be] peopled, built up, strengthened, cleansed and planted," turned into a rain-drenched, muddy nightmare of sickness, dissent, and conquest.[6]

The construction of the colony went very slowly because of the tropical rains. Some colonists had already died on the voyage over, including Harman Hartman, the father of the diarist Elisabeth van der Woude and her sister Margarieta. Within a short time, sixty more colonists perished after being weakened by disease and exhaustion. Elisabeth herself was struck with some sort of tropical sickness and returned to the Dutch Republic on March 18, 1677, in the same ship upon which she had come, despite the governor's express prohibition against her leaving.[7] Those who stayed became involved in internecine conflicts that threatened to become deadly, and in the end, the French captured the colony in July 1677, less than half a year after the ill-fated Dutch colonists had set foot there. A few colonists made it to Suriname, but the majority returned to the Dutch Republic in 1678 after being imprisoned by the French in Cayenne and Martinique for months. As the expedition's other chronicler, Gerardus de Myst, narrated, "Within five months, lost, conquered, and humiliated: What is that if not wasted work?"[8]

The Dutch wasted a great deal of effort on the area between the Orinoco and Amazon Deltas in the seventeenth century. While various trading posts and forts did manage to survive, at least fifteen attempts at setting up colonies failed, and there may even have been more than these.[9] Thus, this dismal history resulted in only one successful Dutch plantation colony on the Wild Coast: Suriname, seized from England, which was modestly successful because the infrastructure for successful plantation agriculture had already been put in place by the English.[10] This infrastructure included not only the clearing of the land and the construction of houses, barns, sugar mills, and the laying of roads; it also meant that some sort of accommodation had been reached with the Amerindians. Lastly, it implied that there were enough "seasoned" colonists—settlers with the immunities to the endemic diseases, knowledge of the region, and experience in practicing agriculture in the area—to keep the colonies going.

The Land of Plenty ... and of Opportunity

Though this region that makes up present-day Guyana, French Guiana, and Suriname is now a largely forgotten economic and political backwater, in the seventeenth century it was the object of fierce competing imperial ambitions and a constantly shifting frontier, as the Spanish, Portuguese, Dutch, English, and French vied for control of the Wild Coast. Initially, after its "discovery" by the Spaniards in 1499, it did not seem to promise much. Guiana, a name derived from the Amerindian name meaning "land of water," was a muddy, difficult-to-reach coastal region full of mangrove swamps.

It would be nearly a century before there was any sort of concerted effort at European settlement in the area. This interest stemmed, at first, from greed for gold. Sir Walter Ralegh, the English courtier and explorer, claimed in his *The discoverie of the large, rich and bewtifull empire of Guiana,* published in 1596, that the fabled El Dorado, or "city of gold," could be found deep in the interior of Guiana. Ralegh's largely fanciful account was an early modern bestseller and was widely translated and distributed across Europe.[11] Lawrence Keymis, Ralegh's second in command, returned on his own and also wrote a rather fantastic narrative, which included the claim to have seen the mythical Lake Parime, reputedly the location of El Dorado.[12] Ralegh and Keymis described a paradise "overflowing with milk and honey" full of friendly Natives more than happy to help the visitors.

These narratives inspired others to follow in their wake, including the Amsterdam mapmaker, Jodocus Hondius, who returned from his sojourn to make a map of "Guiana, Land of Gold," which depicted the nonexistent Lake Parime. Adriaen ten Haeff, a merchant and local official from the city of Middelburg in the province of Zeeland asked for, and was granted, permission in 1598 to send several ships to the river where he believed El Dorado was located.[13] There followed several other requests to send ships to the area, all of which were granted.[14] Yet it soon became clear to these explorers that El Dorado was not going to be so easy to find, if it even existed at all. Adriaen Cabeliau's report on the journey he made in 1598 threw doubt on the existence of any gold mines in the region. He did find twenty-four rivers between the Amazon and the Orinoco that "have not been known in this land nor navigated."[15] Cabeliau also described how well disposed the Natives were to him and his men. Not only had they traded with him, but they also hoped to form an allegiance with these Dutch visitors against the Spaniards, with whom the Amerindians' relations had soured, adding that "the said coasts are as of yet unconquered."[16]

The prospects of both trade and the chance to undermine Iberian hegemony on the mainland of South America by allying with Amerindians against them were powerful incentives to continue exploration in the region. William Usselincx, the Flemish merchant who would later be one of the main advocates of forming a Dutch West India Company (WIC) as a way to thwart Iberian aims in the Atlantic, was a proponent of settlement and the establishment of plantations on the Wild Coast. It is possible that he did so as early as 1603 as the author of an anonymous petition received by the States General on the need to colonize "the province of Guiana."[17]

At any rate, Usselincx certainly saw Dutch colonies on the Wild Coast as vital to the Dutch Republic's objectives and sketched a particularly positive view of the area in his writings. Like Cabeliau, he assured readers that the Amerindians bore nothing but goodwill towards the Dutch, that there were many navigable rivers, that there was a good climate for tropical agriculture, and that there was an abundance of natural riches such as dyewood and other valuable types of wood.[18] He mentioned the possibility of gold but downplayed it in favor of the riches to be had from tropical goods.

Usselincx was not alone in describing the good life on the Wild Coast to be had for the taking. There were many pamphlets that described this fertile land and the friendliness of the Amerindians at length.[19] The Wild Coast was said to be one of "the most agreeable, pleasurable, fruitful and richest lands under the heavens": crops such as sugar cane, tobacco, cotton, ginger, cacao, indigo, gum, and dyewood were praised as "bringing great profits and benefits," while it was claimed that the sea and rivers were full of "the biggest, most beautiful and delectable fish of decorative sorts." These pamphlets went on to praise the most beautiful and most delicious birds that flew around the forests and the fields and meadows full of the tastiest wild animals. All sorts of fruits, the best in the world, grew in Guiana, as did peas, beans, spices, rice, and other grains. Settlers would have an abundance of food at their fingertips with little effort or work. Moreover, the animals they brought along would do better than at home. There would be no need for hay to feed them because they could graze upon the grass, of which there was plenty.[20]

That this land of plenty could provide tropical products in a proto-mercantilist fashion for the emergent Dutch Republic, while also forming a bulwark against Iberian dominion on the mainland of South America and thereby furthering Dutch geopolitical aims in the Atlantic, made it all the more attractive. The author of the above-mentioned 1603 petition to the States General, likely Usselincx, argued for the settlement and the establishment of plantations, writing that further exploitation of Guiana had to wait "until the said land has been populated and fortified with strong cities and fortresses lest any riches discovered be snatched by lustful neighboring nations."[21] It was not just Usselincx who was an advocate for a policy of colonization. Pieter de la Court, one of the most important economic thinkers in the Dutch Republic, urged that plantations be set up on the Wild Coast to cultivate tropical products.[22]

The interest in the Wild Coast among travel writers, merchants, and pamphleteers is in marked contrast to the rather tepid attention paid to New Netherland in North America. Otto Keye, who had served the WIC in Brazil as commander of a company of foot soldiers, wrote a pamphlet in which he contrasted the possibilities for colonization in both areas. Keye believed that although the possibilities in New Netherland were not bad, they were better in Guiana because of the climate. He thought that colonists on the Wild Coast could plant and harvest the whole year through. In addition, Keye opined that the cost of clothing and housing would be less in a warm place than in a cold one. Tepid, too, was Keye's zeal for converting the Amerindians to "God's Holy Word," which was only mentioned in passing in his pamphlet.[23] In this Keye was no different from most of the other authors writing about settlement on the Wild Coast at the time. Even the vicar Johannes Apricius, who initiated the ill-fated attempt to colonize the Oyapock mentioned above, made only one passing remark about the establishment of "the church of Jesus Christ" and the conversion of the Amerindians to the Christian faith in his pamphlet.[24]

Unending, Unmitigated Disaster: Dutch Attempts at Colonizing the Wild Coast

People listened to these calls to set up colonies on the Wild Coast. The first attempt was made by Paulus van Caerden under the auspices of the States General; he led six warships carrying construction materials, colonists, and soldiers for a colony on the Amazon. Despite these preparations, however, Van Caerden returned to the Dutch Republic in 1605, having failed to get the colony off the ground.[25]

That the States General took the initiative to found a colony, especially during the early part of the seventeenth century, was exceptional. Mostly it was individuals with permission from the directors of the WIC who proposed and carried out colonization projects. The Republic first attempted to farm out settlement in the colonies through private initiatives. Applicants were issued *patroons*—parcels of land grants—with the understanding that they would ensure its colonization with at least fifty colonists within three years' time. The applicants had administrative and judicial powers over their land. Later in the seventeenth century, these *patroonschappen* were converted to mixed chartered companies such as the Societiët van Suriname (Suriname Society), which was a joint venture between the WIC, the city of Amsterdam, and the Van Aerssen van Sommelsdijck family.[26] For instance, the second attempt at setting up a colony on the Wild Coast was made by Jan van Ryen who tried to plant tobacco and sugar at the Oyapock in 1620. But he found the "20 men" he had brought to be "too few folk to take the plantation in hand."[27] The WIC sent "20 adolescent boys" from Zeeland instead of the requested Africans.[28] Only a few survivors of this early colony managed to reach the Antilles.[29]

A group of Walloons under the leadership of Jesse de Forest, who had petitioned the WIC directors and "had enrolled several families desirous of settling in the said Indies," was next. Ten families left Texel in July 1623 for Guiana.[30] Once they had arrived on the Wild Coast, they made contact with an English settlement named "Tilletille" on the Okiari River.[31] From there the migrants went to the Oyapock, where upstream there was a suitable piece of land for the founding and settlement of a colony. From then on, the colonists faced disaster after disaster. De Forest died there, and some of his colonists became involved in a war between two Indian groups; the promised help from the Republic did not arrive; and part of the group left for an unknown destination—never to return. The remaining colonists decided in April 1625 to head for the coast on a self-built raft. There they were picked up by the ship the *Vliegende Draak* and taken to Suriname, where they transferred to the *Zwarte Arend*, which brought the straggling survivors to Vlissingen on November 11, 1625.[32]

Nevertheless, the Oyapock remained a popular destination for settlement. Nicolaes Oudaen had been kicked out of a fledgling colony on the Amazon by the Portuguese. Undeterred, he tried again, this time on the Oyapock in 1625, with between eighty and one hundred colonists.[33] By 1627, because of conflicts within the group, particularly between the presumptive leaders of the settlement, as well as because of Amerindian attacks, there were only three survivors discovered by Jan van Ryen when he arrived to attempt another colony, having also failed previously;[34] Van Ryen referred to these colonizers as "Captain Haudaen's people."[35] Van Ryen's second attempt, this time with thirty-six colonists, lasted less than a year. In 1628 Dutch sailors discovered four survivors from Van Ryen's colony who had fled to St. Vincent and Tobago.[36]

Also in 1628 the directors of the WIC set up regulations for private colonization in Brazil, Guiana, and parts of the Caribbean islands in the hope of stimulating more settlement after these fitful first attempts. The person who received such a concession was obliged to get a certain number of colonists, usually fifty, in the area within three years. In exchange, he (and it was always a he) would receive tax breaks and was able to run the colony, though with the help of a local council of colonists and in cooperation with the WIC.[37] Men like David Pietersz de Vries tried to take advantage of these concessions. De Vries was from Hoorn in North Holland. He left in July 1634 with his ship the *Coninck David* for Cayenne. On board the ship were thirty male planters "to make the beginnings of a colony." They were the trailblazers who were going to set up plantations for the production of cotton, tobacco, and dyewood. In the end, though, the men he left behind did not even wait out the harvest. They took over a Spanish slave ship that was stocking up on fresh water and killed the Spaniards. De Vries could not understand why these "villains" had abandoned such a rich colony."[38]

These failed colonization attempts took place in the early part of the seventeenth century. However, it is not particularly surprising that the majority of colonization attempts occurred in the second half of the century after the loss of Brazil. Many potential colonists had left Dutch Brazil just before or during its fall and hoped to build a new Brazil on the Wild Coast, where the production of sugar and other tropical products could compete with that of the Portuguese and with other countries' production. In reality, though, this would never come to pass.

A few projects were set up by Portuguese Jews from Amsterdam who wanted to go from Brazil to the Wild Coast.[39] One of the first of these Jewish settlements was founded in 1658 by David Nassy, who brought with him an unknown number of fellow Jews and their slaves to the Essequibo and Pomeroon Rivers. A few years of problems with the governing board led Nassy to decide to set up a colony on the Cayenne River farther south. The WIC directors gave him a charter in which the colonists were granted "freedom of conscience and public expression of their faith, with a synagogue and school."[40] In addition to Jews from Brazil, Jews from the Italian port of Livorno joined in this endeavor.[41] This colony, though, was not to have a long life, as it was an area in which the French had already founded colonies and therefore thought of as their own territory. In 1664 a French ship appeared and cleared out the Dutch settlement. Most of the colonists fled to Suriname.

The last colonization attempt in the seventeenth century was made by Jan Reeps, a merchant from Hoorn in North Holland. He received a permit from the States General in 1689 for the establishment of a colony between Kaap Oranje and the Amazon in today's French Guiana. He managed to get between forty to fifty colonists to sign up for the venture via promotional pamphlets and word of mouth. They left in September 1692 for the Wild Coast, where his ship, the *Amazone,* wrecked on the river after which it was named. After an adventurous journey via Cayenne and Suriname, seventeen survivors eventually returned to the Dutch Republic. Reeps

Jessica Vance Roitman

and his colonists never managed to get a plantation colony established.[42] The other failed colonies lasted between a few months to less than eight years.

Of course, not all attempts at colonization were complete disasters. The first settlements in Guiana that endured were on the Essequibo River. In 1616 Aert Adriaensz van Groenewegen, a merchant from Zeeland, built a fort called Fort Kijkoveral on the Essequibo River. But it was hardly a grand success either. In the 1630s the WIC directors even considered abandoning Essequibo, but after the loss of Dutch Brazil in 1654, the company hoped to make it into a prosperous plantation colony. The WIC lacked the resources, however, and the three Zeeland towns of Middelburg, Flushing, and Veere accepted control to develop the settlement; renamed Nova Zeelandia, it languished as a trading post until the eighteenth century.[43] Nevertheless, nothing described thus far about Dutch colonization on the Wild Coast would seem to contradict Bernard Bailyn's evocative description of the area as a "scene of devastation: squalid settlements, abandoned shelters, burnt-out forts, and ragged survivors of jungle raids and small battles seeking some kind of security."[44]

Paradise Lost—or Never Found: Why Colonies Fail

There are diverse reasons that these colonies failed: climate, disease, lack of settlers, agricultural conditions, competition from other European nations, and the local Amerindian population. Additionally, Henk den Heijer has argued that one of the major causes was the colonists' lack of preparation.[45] They had read pamphlets that described Guiana as a wonderful, temperate place full of game, fruits, and easy-to-cultivate land just waiting for their arrival. In reality and contrary to the opinion of Keye, the warmer climate was not better than the colder: heavy tropical rains hindered the construction of houses and spoiled the supplies of food and goods the colonists had brought along.

Gerardus de Myst described just such circumstances in his account of the doomed colony on the Oyapock River in 1677, when the colonists had the bad luck to arrive during the rainy season in February: "All the people set themselves to cultivating the land and went to work in the mornings. The most hindrance came from the continual rain that endured so long that there was almost no time in which it was dry. There fell so much rain that the goods, already wet from the ship, could not be dried." This unceasing rain led to chaos. As De Myst went on, "Everyone was to be found where there was a place to take shelter from the rain. Here lay chests and shelves, tables, and chairs in a pile."[46] The goods that had not been spoiled on the ship itself were soon rotted through on the shore.

The area's climate was devastating to nonacclimated Europeans and disease was endemic. Sicknesses to which the colonists had no immunities felled many or even most of these potential colonizers of the Wild Coast. The aforementioned De Forest died of what was likely a tropical fever within two weeks of arriving in the area, leaving the rest of his group literally and figuratively adrift. Even the promotional material that most lauded the region had to admit that new settlers would likely be sick. In George Warren's otherwise lyrical description of Suriname, he does acknowledge that newcomers would suffer from "fevers and agues . . . yaws . . . and dropsy."[47] At least sixty colonists of the settlement attempt on the Oyapock in 1677 died of disease. De Myst wrote that one of the first things the settlers had to do in the torrential rain was to set up a rudimentary hospital for all the sick.[48]

With every straggling group of survivors from these failed colonization attempts who returned to tell their sad tales, the Dutch became even less willing to venture across the ocean to these disease-ridden climes. This was especially the case for women. The directors of the WIC were aware of this problem. In 1627 they demanded that "households had to have at least three people" for the colony of Berbice to be founded by Abraham van Pere, a merchant from Vlissingen.[49] This was easier said than done.[50] Not many women were prepared to go, at least initially. The first group of colonists that sailed from Vlissingen in September 1627 had on board forty men and twenty boys.[51] That is not to say that there were no women involved in colonization efforts. Though exact numbers of women and children are unknown, De Forest and Nassy both managed to bring families along, as did Apricius's catastrophe-ridden colony on the Oyapock.

But even Dutch men had hardly been eager immigrants. The Dutch Republic was experiencing its "Golden Century" in the seventeenth century, and the economy was booming. Thus, there was little need for these prosperous people to move. Employment was so plentiful that the Dutch East and West India Companies depended upon immigrants from the neighboring German and Scandinavian lands to man their forces and fleets.[52] Moreover, there were not that many Dutch people. There were just under 1.9 million people in the Dutch Republic around 1650 and just over that figure in 1750.[53] Thus, the number of Dutch citizens crossing the Atlantic to settle elsewhere was modest, certainly in comparison to those settling in the Dutch East India Company orbit but also in comparison to the European population in other parts of the Atlantic. Around 1735 some five thousand Europeans were living in all the Dutch Atlantic colonies taken together, in 1750 perhaps around eighty-five hundred, and by about 1800 just over sixteen thousand.[54]

As if the climate and the illnesses that struck down the colonists were not bad enough, the settlers also had to contend with a land that was difficult to cultivate. Elisabeth van der Woude wrote, "The land was full of trees with heavy scrub forests, thick clay soil, and here and there morasses; there were many ants who took over whole areas of the ground with their nests that did much damage. Some of them were like here [the Dutch Republic] and others were half a finger long."[55] The only way to get rid of the huge ants was to burn the scrub forest that contained them. Moreover, the land was waterlogged. Turning this swampy ground into a viable place for plantation agriculture took enormous effort involving the implementation of complicated and labor-intensive hydraulic systems.[56] In fact, it would prove to be an almost impossible endeavor without the large-scale labor of enslaved Africans, a "resource" these early settlers did not have.

Thus, it was nearly impossible for these first waves of colonists to survive without the help of the local Amerindian groups, particularly the Galibi and Yao. This is something individual Dutchmen in America had been doing for several decades. In 1637 Spanish authorities on Trinidad reported that the "las Olandeses" posed a serious threat because marriage ties with locals enabled them to raise a significant force on the island and the mainland, explaining that "the said Hollanders marry the Cariba Indian women and the other nations."[57] The luckless colonists on the Oyapock heard of just such a "stray" Dutchman. Both Elisabeth van der Woude and De Myst noted in their diaries that the local Amerindians asked them about a colonist named Jacob, a Dutchman who lived in Guiana and who apparently had a plantation farther up the river.[58]

These same Amerindians, according to Elisabeth van der Woude, "came in canoes and boarded our ship and greeted us in a friendly way."[59] They pointed the hopeful colonists towards a place farther up the river where they could build their settlement. Yet despite this friendly beginning, they was afraid of the Amerindians. De Myst observed that only a week or so after this cordial encounter, the settlers placed men on double guard duty to look out for the Amerindians. He added that they could not rest in the evenings because "everything is in an uproar. In the meantime, a double watch is made by civilians acting as soldiers to protect the place against the Indians."[60]

The earlier attempted settlements were even more dependent on the Amerindians and, accordingly, as or more vulnerable because they had stumbled upon a particularly complex political situation among the Native groups.[61] Moreover, the Amerindians were often far less willing to accommodate the newcomers than these migrants had been led to believe. The Oudaen colony's demise, for example, came when the Amerindians tired of all these visitors and "decided to rid themselves of these guests." This decision was probably the result of attempts to take cassava from indigenous villages, likely because they were unable to feed themselves. The Amerindians took revenge, and in the end, only three men out of the original fifty were alive by the spring of 1627. The same fate befell the contemporaneous Van Ryen colonization attempt. After destroying the dwellings and sowed fields, the Amerindians allowed the people to build boats and depart.[62]

Other Europeans were neither overly adept in negotiating the complexities of the Amerindian political constellations, nor were they successful in securing long-term support from these groups. As Neil Whitehead has described it, "The French in their attempts to settle the Cayenne River region in the period 1620–1650 repeatedly ran afoul of these complexities. They were unable to maintain neutrality in conflicts between the Palikurs and Caribs, which they themselves also fomented." Whitehead cites the example of a colonization attempt made by the French on the Saramacca River in 1626 with some five hundred men and women from La Rochelle. It was deserted by 1629 because of sickness and "the Indians being troublesome."[63]

The French returned to the Saramacca with nearly four hundred people ten years later. They were able to hold on until 1642, when, eventually, "they grew careless, spread themselves to [the] Surinam [River] and Corentyn [River], had great differences with the Indians, and were all cut off in one day." It was not just the French or Dutch, however. Almost immediately after the annihilation of the French settlement on the Saramacca, the English arrived with three hundred families in 1643. These colonists settled on the Suriname, Saramacca, and Corantijn Rivers and "lived peaceably until the year 1645, at which time they espoused the quarrel of the French and were cut off by the natives." The French made one further attempt at settling the Saramacca, but they were expelled by the Caribs and Suppoyos in 1649.[64]

It is clear, then, that falling afoul of the local Amerindians spelled disaster for these European colonists. Once their support was withdrawn, the best the colonists could hope for would be to be allowed to leave quickly, as had been the case with the Van Ryen settlers. The worst-case scenario, however, was starvation or massacre. This vulnerability meant that colonists had little choice other than to become involved in the conflicts among the local Amerindian groups. A clear example was the De Forest settlement on the Oyapock. It was heavily dependent on the Yaos for food. They had to reciprocate by joining their hosts in conflicts with other groups.[65]

Yet even support from local Amerindians could not guarantee survival on the Wild Coast, as demonstrated by the De Vries colonization attempt described above. Landing at present-day Cayenne, they were welcomed by local Carib people. De Vries wrote, "The savages came on board of us when we were not yet anchored, bringing refreshments of bananas, pineapples (which is a fine fruit to eat) and other refreshment."[66] Nevertheless, the settlers wanted to leave and, as described above, hijacked a ship and fled. Clearly, the Wild Coast was not as wonderful as they had thought.

One reason it was not so wonderful was the competition from other European powers, and this was another cause for the colonies' failures. The ever-changing landscape of seventeenth-century European politics was mirrored on the Wild Coast. The Dutch were certainly not the only ones who wanted to set up plantation colonies. The English, French, Irish, Spanish, and Portuguese were all active in the region. As Bernard Bailyn described it, "The struggles were continuous, almost formless. Some involved groups of Indians loosely associated with Spanish and Portuguese soldiers bent on driving out the English, Dutch, and Irish; others consisted of ragtag English raiders attempting to beat off the Spanish, who were at the same time subject to assaults by the Dutch."[67] Elisabeth van der Woude had already returned to the Dutch Republic, but De Myst was still in the colony on the Oyapock when the French conquered it. Half a century before, the Oudaen

Jessica Vance Roitman

settlement was destroyed by the local Amerindians with the help of their Portuguese allies.[68] The constantly shifting alliances between European nations and their Native allies contributed to the pervasive instability in the region and helped insure the limited lifespan of most of colonies.

Sweet Success:
Settlement in Suriname

The one place on the Wild Coast in which the Dutch were successful in setting up a plantation colony in the seventeenth century was Suriname. Yet until 1626 central Suriname was not a favored site for colonization. The Oyapock, Cayenne, Maroni, Berbice, and Essequibo Rivers attracted the first Spanish, French, and English interlopers with varying results, as described above. Contemporary with these efforts at the settlement of Suriname was the intermittent establishment of Dutch trading posts on the Suriname River, possibly also entailing some clearances for sugar plantations on the Maroni and Commewijne Rivers, as also occurred on the Berbice River under the Van Pere family.[69]

The first real attempts to settle in the area known as Suriname by Europeans was in 1630, when English settlers led by a Captain Marshall attempted to found a colony. They cultivated tobacco but the venture failed financially. It would be another twenty years before European settlement began in earnest. In 1650 Major Anthony Rous set out from Barbados to settle Suriname. It is unclear whether Rous was sent by the later proprietor, Francis, Lord Willoughby of Parham, or whether Willoughby went to Suriname himself or had usurped Rous's settlement.[70]

Whatever the case may have been between Rous and Willoughby, it was Willoughby who provided the financial investment needed to keep the colony going. He sank £26,000 into the venture. He also rounded up three hundred settlers and supplied them with food and provisions.[71] Willoughby offered these settlers fifty acres freehold, plus a further acreage, depending on their gender, age, and status. Single people without the means to transport themselves would be transported, at Willoughby's expense, to become his personal servants and tenants. Willoughby also offered all the monies, slaves, foodstuffs, stock, and tools required to set up the colony for its first eight months.[72]

Willoughby, according to contemporaries, had "drawne in some Merchants of London, & great persons of Barbados to engage wth him" with "greater vigour then successe." Despite the fact that Suriname was an "unhealthy and inconvenyent" place, he created "one of the fertilest most spacious and beautifullest countreys," from which the English could expand northward and settle the Orinoco River and where Amerindians could be used as forced labor.[73] Thus, his fellow Royalists flocked to Suriname during the English Civil Wars; these settlement attempts had as much, or more, to do with the exhaustion of the land of the soil in Barbados, as well as the engrossment of the land by sugar planters, as they did with European politics.[74] In fact, Suriname was seen as "the first major Barbadian colonization project."[75] Displaced Barbadians, such as the ones Willoughby brought with him, settled in Suriname from the 1650s, bringing their slaves and their sugar-producing acumen with them. As Sarah Barber has argued, it was Willoughby's investments in money, settlers, and provisions that undoubtedly made the difference between a small, autonomous outpost and a viable limb of empire.[76]

For many years, it was thought that the Dutch had been key to the dissemination of knowledge of how to produce sugar throughout the Caribbean from their time in Brazil. Recently, however, the emphasis on the Dutch role in the Caribbean sugar revolution has been modified considerably.[77] In fact, it seems that know-how from Barbados was crucial to the progress of the English colony in Suriname and, ultimately, for the Dutch when they took over the colony. This experience with and skill in sugar production was soon evident. "Willoughby Land" reached its peak between 1660 and 1665. George Warren, an English visitor, reported that the colony had some five hundred plantations with forty to fifty sugar works around this time.[78] Willoughby Land's five hundred plantations and sugar works were owned or operated by around five thousand "present inhabitants."[79]

The English were able to build up so many plantations and have so many people in the colony not just because of the expertise in sugar cultivation they brought from Barbados, though this was certainly of prime importance. The English were also able to negotiate workable alliances with the Caribs, who traded with them and assisted them by retrieving runaway slaves; and as noted, without the help and support of the local Amerindian groups, European settlement attempts were doomed from the start. The English were able to negotiate these alliances because they treated the Natives with respect. Moreover, at least some of these early colonists took the time to learn the Amerindians' language. The first Dutch governor, Julius Lichtenbergh, realized how important these factors were: "It is of great importance for the security of the plantations that we have the Indians on our side, which we can accomplish by means of as much civility and politeness towards them as possible. To this end I shall do my best to learn their language, as should we all, because these are a people who can be led where we will if we but speak their language. This was a great advantage for the English and could be for us if our nation will but learn their speech."[80] In fact, the Amerindians "did not want their country to be governed by any nation other than the English."[81]

Thus, the English succeeded in building a workable and prosperous settlement on the Wild Coast. With the presence of these skilled English sugar planters, Suriname beckoned to the Dutch as a "second Brazil."[82] The flourishing sugar industry in Willoughby Land was attractive in and of itself, but especially as a way to recoup the Dutch losses in Brazil, which had fallen to the Portuguese in 1654. The Dutch wanted the English planters, their slaves, their mills, and their sugar-planting acumen. And they got it: in 1668 Abraham Crijnsen conquered the colony for the States of Zeeland.[83]

Jessica Vance Roitman

William Mogge, was given the task of surveying the new acquisition. As Alison Games has noted, Mogge's depiction of Suriname in the years immediately after the Dutch conquest show that, at least initially, the new Dutch arrivals adopted English land-use practices. Warren's pamphlet in its Dutch translation and a 1671 Dutch map reveal that English information about the colony and English agricultural practices shaped Dutch colonial knowledge and conduct after the conquest.[84] Perhaps most important for Dutch success in Suriname, however, certainly in the beginning, was keeping the English planters with their know-how in the colony. Even the English admitted that the Dutch offered generous terms of surrender because the Zeelanders realized that the experienced English planters were an asset to the colony.[85] All the English had to do to be granted the same rights as the Dutch colonists was to swear an oath of loyalty and they were guaranteed their possessions.[86] The Dutch also made a concerted effort to include the English in their newly minted administrative structures.[87]

At the same time Zeeland did its best to stimulate migration to its new colony waiving taxes for five years and even offering thirty guilders to pay for potential settlers' passage to the colony. The States of Zeeland also promised that all people, regardless of their "condition or religion" would be treated the same.[88] The Dutch went as far as to send ships to other parts of the Caribbean, such as Martinique and Guadeloupe, to pick up colonists.[89]

Yet despite these efforts, it proved to be incredibly difficult to attract settlers to the colony. Thus, when English settlers sought to leave in the 1670s, the Dutch went to great efforts to hinder their departure, although they had been guaranteed the right to leave at any time with their possessions, including their enslaved Africans, under the terms of surrender. They even invented rules to keep the English from leaving, to no avail.[90] The Dutch had greater success preventing the Jews who had come when the colony was under English control from leaving, arguing that the terms of surrender did not apply to Jews because they were not actually English.[91]

In the end, though, the Dutch were not able to keep these planters who were so vital to the functioning of the colony. Thereafter, the colony entered into a period of decline. Governor Pieter Versterre wrote in 1676 that the ships in the colony "are making slow progress because of the lack of sugar to load. There is not much sugar any more, it is hard to believe how much this colony has been weakened by the departure of the English."[92]

Conclusion

Despite these setbacks, in 1676 Suriname was the biggest Dutch settlement in Guiana. By way of comparison, neighboring Essequibo was hardly flourishing with a population of twenty-five WIC personnel and a few dozen planters and slaves; the settlement around Fort Kijkoveral was basically a trading post rather than a colony. The WIC had tried to set up new sugar plantations and get more people to settle in the area. But nothing helped. The number of plantations did not grow at all until the eighteenth century.[93] Even then, Essequibo had just 19 plantations, 60 Europeans, and 426 African slaves in 1700.[94] Exact figures for the number of plantations and inhabitants in Berbice are not known, but it is certain that the colony was much smaller than Essequibo.[95] Therefore, the 40 or 50 English families who remained in Suriname in 1675, the 240 "men of the Dutch nation," which included other European nationalities, and the 115 men of the garrison, plus their families, did not constitute a small group within the context of the Wild Coast.[96] The existence of this population suggests that there were enough "seasoned" colonists—settlers with immunities to the endemic diseases and knowledge of and experience in sugar cultivation in the area—to get the colony off the ground.

These numbers, though not small by regional standards, illustrate the fact that the Dutch were unable to attract, much less keep, settlers on the Wild Coast. As noted, the climate was less than favorable. Rain and mud literally and figuratively bogged down efforts to form sustainable settlements in the region. Food supplies brought from the Netherlands were spoiled within a few days of arrival; tropical diseases to which the would-be colonists had no resistance struck with alacrity; and the attempts at agriculture were impeded by the soil, which required huge amounts of effort to cultivate—labor the colonists could or would not provide. Moreover, the expectation that the Amerindians would supply this labor proved to be a naïve pipedream. In fact, the Amerindians were the fulcrum upon which survival balanced. Good relations with Amerindian neighbors were vital, but the Dutch all too frequently seemed to have failed to realize this fact. For example, stealing the Amerindians' food supplies led to the destruction of an entire settlement. Lastly, European conflicts were transplanted to the Americas, and the Dutch faced the constant encroachment of the French, who were also vying for a viable toehold on the South American mainland.

The Dutch finally secured such a toehold by the peace that ended the Second Anglo-Dutch War (1665–67). Suriname was hardly a great profit-making colony on the grand scale of the other nations' Caribbean sugar islands, such as Barbados, Jamaica, Cuba, and Martinique. Nevertheless, it was a modest success and the only one the Dutch would hold on to long-term in the Americas. Yet even this moderate prosperity was created only because the infrastructure for profitable plantation agriculture (the clearing of land; the construction of houses, barns, and sugar mills; and the laying of roads), as well as the basis of accommodation with the Amerindians, had already been put in place by the English. Even so, the continuing use of forced labor by enslaved Africans was required to make Suriname a going concern.

It is possible that this success in Suriname, albeit rather limited, bolstered initiatives like that of Johannes Apricius, who, perhaps not coincidentally, set off in 1676 from that frosty deck in Texel to try his luck on the Oyapock. After all, there was now an established colony in the area, and the time seemed ripe to continue colonizing this area. Although this attempt proved disastrous in the short term, the Dutch presence on the Wild Coast for the long term had been secured, ironically only because the English had laid the foundations for a successful colony in Suriname. All the other Dutch attempts at large-scale settlement in the Americas failed. New Netherland and New Holland were lost to geopolitical machinations and (re)conquest in the seventeenth century as were Essequibo and Demerara in the eighteenth. The Antilles were never profitable on any sort of large scale, though Curacao and St. Eustatius did function as lucrative free ports in the eighteenth century. Thus, it seems that the Dutch could only succeed if a viable blueprint borrowed from another European nation was employed in their American settlements.

Colonial Life in Times of War

The Impact of European Wars on Suriname

Suze Zijlstra and Tom Weterings

When the Dutch took Suriname from the English in 1667, they required the English planters who remained in the colony to swear an oath of loyalty that included a promise they would not undermine the Dutch authorities and would join the new government in any fight against its enemies.[1] Every colonist also had to pledge that, when an English fleet would attack the colony, they would "keep my selfe quiet, and neither directly nor indirectly assist them, and if it shall please the Governor render my selfe a Prisoner into his hands."[2] Most of the English planters refused to swear the oath, because they feared that those English colonists who actively opposed the Dutch would also turn against them. Yet, as late as 1669, the governor did not force them to take the oath, so long as they cohabited peacefully with the new Dutch inhabitants.[3]

The provision in the oath of loyalty about a possible invasion was not superfluous, as became clear in 1672 when the Third Anglo-Dutch War (1672–74) erupted. Although the war started in Europe, the planters in Suriname had to prepare themselves for an invasion by a fleet from one of the English Caribbean islands. The government summoned the Dutch and Jewish colonists and their slaves to the colony's town of Paramaribo to strengthen the defenses of the stronghold Fort Zeelandia. The English inhabitants of the colony, on the other hand, had to remain at their plantations. Whenever a rumor reached the colony that an English fleet was on its way to Suriname, the leaders of the English planters were even taken from their plantations and imprisoned in the fortress. While the government professed to take these measures because it feared that the English colonists would reinforce the English invasion forces, the wife of an English planter alleged that the Dutch did so to profit from the abandoned English plantations.[4]

The position of the English in Suriname in 1672 gives an impression of the problematic situation that could arise when people from various European countries lived together in an early modern colony. Recent scholarship has maintained that European colonists generally got along very well in the seventeenth-century Caribbean. Even though colonies changed hands multiple times, merchants and planters managed to continue trade with colonies governed by other European powers. Because of these transnational contacts, the Dutch could play a significant part in the development of an English Empire, as they assisted the English traders as middlemen. Moreover, when colonies changed hands, the incoming government often treated the resident colonists well: it did not want to lose valuable planters, regardless of their background, and therefore offered them profitable conditions of residence. This scholarship could give the impression that it hardly mattered which European power possessed a colony and that war only became significant for planters when an enemy swiftly took over. European wars had a great impact on colonists, however, even when they did not result in a change of government.[5]

In the 1670s the Dutch Republic was frequently at war. Two potential threats from abroad that the colonists in Suriname strongly anticipated in this decade shed particular light on the impact of war on their daily lives and on the position of non-Dutch inhabitants. Relations between the Dutch and the English, in particular in the context of the Third Anglo-Dutch War, as well as those between the Dutch and the French, who were anticipated to attack the colony in 1677, provide particular illumination not only because various government documents are preserved but also because private correspondence written in 1672 by the colonists themselves is available. This correspondence ended up in English archives after English privateers captured the ships that transported the letters.[6] Supplementing governmental documents with this personal correspondence from colonists living in Suriname will give a balanced view of their experiences during times of war.

An English Colony Conquered by the Dutch

War had been the natural state of affairs in Europe for centuries. It was no different in the colonies in the Torrid Zone; rather, war seemed even more endemic there. The second half of the seventeenth century was no exception as the Dutch Republic found itself at war with the English on three separate occasions from 1652, this rivalry ended in 1688 when the Dutch stadtholder William III of Orange seized the English throne from his father-in-law James II. Much has been made of the importance of these wars, finding their origins in rivalry over trade and eventually leading to England becoming the more prominent "empire." At the same time, Louis XIV's France was more belligerent than ever and actively sought an alliance against the Dutch Republic, leading to war in the "Disaster Year" *(Rampjaar)* of 1672, which would last until 1678.

Almost naturally, all this fighting spilled over to the various European colonies, in particular those in the Caribbean. After almost a century of nearly undisputed Spanish dominance over the region, the northwestern European powers first dipped their toes in these waters around the start of the seventeenth century. By the middle of the century, they had taken the plunge and were fighting both Spain and each other for dominance. Most colonies in the region changed hands at least once during this period. For example, Tobago successively became a Couronian, Dutch, English, and finally French colony between 1654 and 1678—a period of less than a quarter-century—and that does not include several failed attempts by these powers to (re)conquer the island.[7]

Suriname was no exception to this pattern. The colony was first established by the English in 1651 on the initiative of the Royalist governor of Barbados, Francis, fifth Lord Willoughby of Parham. Although Willoughby was forcibly removed the following year, he left behind a promising colony of about three hundred settlers. The first commonwealth governor proved very unpopular, and after he left in 1654, no new governor was appointed. Instead, the colonists were largely left to their own devices, with a General Assembly of Freeholders, led by an elected governor, governing the colony. During this period, the settlers traded extensively with the Dutch, who had nearby colonies at Berbice, Pomeroon, and Tobago. There is also evidence that a small number of Dutch settlers lived in the English colony. The 1660 Restoration ended the autonomy of the settlers, first when the previously elected governor, William Byam, ended elections in 1661 and then when Charles II made Willoughby, Lawrence Hyde, and their heirs the proprietors of the colony. Byam then effectively became Willoughby's representative in what was also called "Willoughby Land."[8]

The colony prospered under English rule as the settlers were experienced planters from Barbados. The territory along the Suriname River offered just the environment they were looking for: an abundance of land with a tropical climate that provided a fertile soil to plant the sugar cane that was in high demand in Europe. The English built a fortress near the mouth of the river and established their main town of Torarica in the south, some seventy kilometers upstream. While the colony steadily expanded until the early 1660s, in 1665 a severe epidemic raged through it, killing hundreds of settlers. In the following years the colony continued to be a dangerous place, as new settlers were especially prone to diseases. This left the colony vulnerable, particularly because there were soon few men left to defend it.

This vulnerability quickly became the downfall of English rule. Suriname had not been subject to attack during the First Anglo-Dutch War (1652–54), but towards the end of the Second Anglo-Dutch War (1665–67), a fleet raised by the Dutch province of Zeeland sailed up the Suriname River. Realizing the colony was virtually defenseless, the fleet swiftly conquered the colony, which thereby became the possession of this maritime province.[9] On March 6, 1667, fleet commander Abraham Crijnsen reached an agreement with Byam whereby any Englishman who wished to leave that same day or the day after would not be hindered. Moreover, they would be allowed to sell their possessions and take any property (including slaves) they wished with them; the incoming government would even help find a ship to aid them in doing so. Those who wanted to stay were guaranteed their possessions as well as freedom of religion.[10]

Suze Zijlstra and Tom Weterings

Dutch control at first seemed rather tenuous. Crijnsen's main task had been to harass English shipping along the North American coast, and rather than stay in Suriname, the majority of his fleet was compelled to continue with this mission. This once again left the colony poorly defended and made it a realistic possibility that it would yet again be captured, particularly since the Anglo-Dutch War was not yet concluded. Crijnsen had left Captain Maurice de Rame in charge.

No documents from Suriname in the first months after Crijnsen's departure are preserved. From the Dutch side there only remains a testimony written in early 1668, in which the colony's new secretary, Johan Treffry, complained about the capabilities—or rather the lack thereof—of the interim governor De Rame. The "dictator," as Treffry called him, had no problem considering himself a prince, and he lacked all characteristics that a good governor needed. This negative assessment may have arisen from De Rame's refusal to permit Treffry a vote in the colonial council, while Treffry claimed that the secretary was entitled to a vote. Apart from this personal feud, Treffry did not comment on the way the colonists were living right after the takeover. Presumably most lived as they did before, especially as new settlers from the Dutch Republic did not arrive immediately.[11]

It soon became clear that William Willoughby, who had succeeded his brother as governor of Barbados following the latter's death, was unwilling to leave Suriname in the hands of the Dutch. He sent his son Henry with a fleet to reclaim the mainland colony, which they did successfully in October 1667, transporting six hundred enslaved Africans to Barbados as spoils of victory. This recapture, though, violated the articles of the Peace of Breda that the English and Dutch signed in July 1667. During the peace negotiations the parties had agreed that they would keep the territories that were in their possession as of May 20, even though news of the peace had not yet reached the Caribbean in October 1667.[12]

Only after the English fleet had left for Barbados did the news of the Peace of Breda reach the Caribbean. In November 1667 six merchantmen and a frigate from Zeeland arrived in the Suriname River to trade with the colonists and bring them the news of the recently established peace. Yet, even after receiving this information, the English refused to abandon control of Suriname. When Governor Willoughby realized he could not hold on to the colony, he sent Henry to make sure the Dutch would benefit as little as possible from their new possession and that as many English as possible left with their belongings; this would make it infinitely more difficult for the Dutch to make a profit from the colony. The governor wanted these colonists to leave for Antigua, because he felt there they would contribute the most to English colonial endeavors. At the same time Willoughby urged the metropolitan government not to give up Suriname because he suspected that not all settlers would be willing to leave their property. He therefore also instructed Henry to delay the surrender of the colony as long as he could.[13]

In December 1667 the Dutch were unsuccessful in reclaiming Suriname, despite the peace treaty. The new government arrived with official documents, signed by the king of England, ordering the handover of the colony in the exact condition it was when they received the royal instructions. Instructed by his father, however, Henry Willoughby refused to hand over the colony, claiming that he could not surrender without personally receiving explicit instructions from either the king of England or the governor of Barbados, while pretending that he had not yet learned of the peace himself. The written protests of the Dutch could not change Willoughby's resolve. Although the Dutch mission had failed, the ship that brought them remained in the Suriname River to make sure that the English would not strip the colony of its valuable resources.[14]

While it was clear that Suriname would eventually return to Dutch control, most of the English chose to remain. Henry Willoughby nonetheless managed to persuade the "most principle and ancient" settlers to leave for the island in February 1668; a total of sixty-seven colonists left and took 412 slaves with them, as well as livestock and kettles for boiling sugar. Moreover, the departing English ransacked many plantations to make sure that the Dutch would not benefit from anything left behind. As the plantations depended on labor, tools, knowledge of sugar production, and a long-term investment in the development of land, this left the Dutch with a colony that had lost a considerable part of its value.[15]

Suriname finally returned to Dutch hands in April 1668, after Zeeland had dispatched another force to compel its handover. Yet again, Crijnsen headed the fleet, and this time he would remain to govern the colony as interim governor. The English leaders encouraged the planters to leave with them, and even threatened that they would lose their rights as Englishmen if they would remain in Suriname, but this was an empty threat as the king of England did not support it. In March 1668 Willoughby had campaigned to persuade the planters to join the first group in Antigua. The majority of the English planters chose to stay in the colony, where they would enjoy the same privileges as the Dutch inhabitants. If they would depart, they hoped to do so "with more of advantage & less of ruine."[16]

The 1667 and 1668 takeovers demonstrate how problematic European war could be for a seventeenth-century Caribbean colony. These conflicts brought great uncertainty to Torrid Zone settlers in various ways: the duration of a war, the results of peace negotiations in Europe, and of course the extent to which another power in the Caribbean itself would choose to turn against a colony. Even if a takeover did not result in a significant change of status for most inhabitants, especially as the Dutch were eager to promise English planters equal rights to ensure they would stay, European disputes could inflict severe damage upon a colony.

The English Threat to Dutch Suriname

Having failed to persuade most English settlers to leave, the Willoughbys then instructed Major James Bannister to look after the remaining English possessions and to continue the effort to induce the remaining English settlers to depart Suriname.[17] Bannister set about his task with vigor, first trying to obtain official

Suze Zijlstra and Tom Weterings

permission from Crijnsen for himself and others to leave along with their slaves and possessions. Crijnsen, however, had no intention of letting them go.[18] As this did not deter Bannister from stirring up unrest among the English population, Crijnsen became fed up and in the end had Bannister arrested and shipped off to Zeeland to be judged by the Provincial States.[19]

While Bannister was on his way to the Dutch Republic, Crijnsen organized an inquest into the mentality of the English population, concluding that most professed loyalty, although a few did more so out of fear of (retaliatory) violence than because of any true affection.[20] Willoughby, meanwhile, started to protest the treatment of both Bannister and the other English, accusing Crijnsen of breaking his own treaty.[21] Crijnsen and his successor Philip Julius Lichtenbergh contended that allowing the colonists to leave would ruin the colony. Some of the English settlers, including Bannister, had complained that they were governed arbitrarily, without any guarantee that their possessions would be kept safe. Lichtenbergh tried to counter these accusations, made by "malevolents," by instating some new laws to guarantee just that. He was convinced that the colony could turn peaceful, if only no further attempts "by the English king" to instill unrest were made. He therefore greeted the news that the States of Zeeland had banned Bannister from returning with enthusiasm.[22]

Only a few months later it appeared that his optimism had been rather premature. Charles II himself had intervened on behalf of Bannister, and the States were compelled to let him go. The increasing rumors that he was on his way brought considerable unrest, and Lichtenbergh even laid out some plans for defense in case Bannister arrived in the colony in force.[23] The news had a profound influence on the English settlers. Many seem to have been indecisive. On the one hand, Lichtenbergh remarked that Bannister's imminent return made it nearly impossible to receive any oath of loyalty from the English (many apparently feared being roughed up by Bannister and his troops upon their return if they did so). On the other, the longer it took for Bannister to arrive (the first rumors of his return dated from April 1669, but he was still not in Suriname by the end of August), the more settlers, even those who were Bannister's strongest supporters, decided to go ahead with work on their plantations, which, as a decidedly long-term investment would not have been undertaken if they expected to leave soon.[24] Accordingly, Lichtenbergh was actually fairly confident that hardly any settlers would be willing to leave, even if so ordered.[25]

In the end it took Bannister until January 1671 to return to Suriname. Despite earlier misgivings, a significant number of people still wanted to leave the colony. No fewer than ninety-eight people desired to go with Bannister, although Lichtenbergh reflected that there were only "three, who could be counted as decent persons, one of which is in possession of sugar works, the rest being only a troop of insignificant people, between sixty or seventy strong who had not even one negro between them, being a mangy rabble, who spent most of their time begging with the Indians."[26] Nevertheless, he tried to obstruct them in any way possible—for example, by demanding that all transactions be made in cash, making it difficult if not impossible for colonists to sell their possessions—but in the end to no avail.[27] Lichtenbergh was so disgusted by the entire affair that he left for Europe soon after.[28]

The remaining settlers noted that all this was detrimental to the development of the colony: they needed people, and especially Europeans, to keep Suriname viable and prosperous. By the second quarter of 1671, the population consisted of about eight hundred white settlers of different origins (English, Dutch, Jewish, and others), including women and children, as well as approximately twenty-five hundred African slaves and five hundred Indian slaves, spread between a few hundred plantations and the colony's few towns: Paramaribo, Torarica, and the Jewish settlement later known as "Jodensavanne."[29] Probably at least half of these eight hundred European settlers were English.[30]

Lichtenbergh's replacement, Pieter Versterre, noted in May 1671 that "more and more of the English nation are wanting to leave, to which end they expect the Major Bannister, who has promised them to return within eight months, with a powerful commission, so all who want can be transported to his majesty's dominions or elsewhere to their satisfaction."[31] Very few, he feared, would be planting new canes for sugar production, instead cutting valuable snakewood as a means of making quick money to settle their debts.[32] As it happened, though, they were out of luck: Bannister did not return within eight months, and the outbreak of the Third Anglo-Dutch War prevented his peaceful return altogether.

On March 23, 1672, the Dutch trade fleet returning from Smyrna was unexpectedly attacked and defeated by an English fleet. Some four days later, the English published a declaration of war. As many had feared, a French declaration of war followed on April 6.[33] Things then went downhill fast for the Dutch Republic. In June the armies of Louis XIV and his allies, the bishops of Münster and Cologne, had crossed the borders and moved deeper and deeper into the Republic's territory. By June 14 the French had reached Utrecht. After long deliberations by the States General, the Dutch army was ordered to retreat and defend the Water Line surrounding the central province of Holland, much to the chagrin of the Prince of Orange, the army's commander.[34] On June 19 the French took Naarden, only three hours from Amsterdam. Though the enemy's advance then stalled on the Water Line, the Republic was in a very precarious position, and its internal politics were crumbling just like its outer defenses. The de facto leader of the Dutch Republic, Grand Pensionary of Holland Johan de Witt, abdicated from his position after an attempt on his life. On August 20 De Witt and his brother were lynched by a mob in The Hague.[35]

The Suriname colonists had long been aware of troubling developments in Europe, and war with the French or, worse, with both the French and the English had been feared.[36] On June 6 the *Susanna*, sailing from Middelburg, arrived in Paramaribo. It had left on April 6, the very day on which Louis XIV declared war

Suze Zijlstra and Tom Weterings

on the Dutch Republic, carrying in addition to its normal cargo a company of sixty musketeers led by Lieutenant Dominique Potteij, sent by the States of Zeeland to reinforce the colony in case of an English or French attack.[37] This appears to have been a last-minute decision. Potteij noted to a friend attached to the garrison in Hulst that he had to leave in such a hurry that he had not had time to say goodbye or have some clothes made for the journey.[38] Not too far away from Zeeland, the *Susanna* managed to surprise an English trading vessel coming from Villefranche with a cargo of fruit, which, though its crew at first "laughed at us," had not counted on sixty musketeers being on board. Their journey proved otherwise uneventful.[39]

Unfortunately for the inhabitants of Suriname, the *Susanna* would prove to be the last ship arriving there for a long time; not until the arrival of the *Eendragt* in February 1673 would any further news or supplies from Europe reach the colony, as the war would soon make any journey by sea a very dangerous prospect.[40] The *Zeekoe* had been present earlier that year, but sailing back in the direction of Guiana from the Amazon River, it was apparently taken by the French, who shot one of its captains and captured the other.[41] The *Witte Zeepaard* was captured by the English on its way back to the Dutch Republic, as evidenced by the presence of the mail it had on board now found in the National Archives of Great Britain.

Understandably, the lack of news on the war was by itself more than enough to unsettle the colonists severely. How did the war in Europe go? Had there been any battles yet?[42] Was Suriname itself at risk of being attacked?[43] In particular, the fact that the Republic was at war with not just one, but two great powers at once was a source of great worry. As one colonist wrote, "with sadness [I] saw [that] the English and French published a declaration of war against us, there must have been hostilities already, 2 powerful enemies, [I] hope that God the Lord will help and aid us, because without the same it would be impossible that we could resist."[44] As evidenced by the course of the war in Europe during 1672, their worries were certainly justified. How long could the colony remain unaffected?[45]

The colonists feared not only for the state of the homeland and their relatives and friends still in Europe, but also for the position of the colony itself. Suriname had, after all, been invaded twice only a few years ago. The English were expected to attack from the direction of Jamaica or Barbados and, unsurprisingly, to be led by Governor Willoughby.[46] Preparations had to be made; the defense concentrated mostly on Fort Zeelandia, the fortress (still extant) near the main settlement, Paramaribo. Along with the modest garrison (which consisted of some thirty soldiers in 1671, reinforced by Potteij and his sixty musketeers), the male colonists (both Dutch and Jewish) were obliged to hold watch at the fort. They were summoned almost immediately upon receiving news from the *Susanna*, "so that immediately, all planters, merchants, and craftsmen, whatever their state or quality, were pressed to hold residence, everyone with their gun, at the fort."[47] For the rest of 1672, this militia, consisting of nearly all the male European colonists, was kept at the fort almost permanently.[48] The mobilization extended to ships and their crews present in the colony, and slaves were used to improve the fort itself.[49] It seems that these measures did inspire a modicum of confidence in the colony's leadership. Governor Versterre was certain that, because of all their preparations, the fortifications would withstand an attack.[50]

Despite all this work, the lack of contact with Europe had unfortunate consequences. Soon, the colonists were suffering from a lack of drink, food, and other supplies.[51] Besides that, all economic activity on the plantations had ground to a halt, as most planters and many of their slaves were busy at the fort. This meant that even if ships would again be able to come to and leave from Suriname, the next crop of sugar would certainly be disappointing, which would have dire consequences for the colony's future economic wellbeing.

Suriname's substantial English population was naturally suspect in case of an enemy attack. Indeed, the oath of loyalty specifically stipulated measures to be taken in that situation: while all other male settlers were ordered to the fort, the English were instead confined to their plantations, and eventually their leaders were confined in Fort Zeelandia.[52] However, there is not much evidence of suspicions of treasonous activity among the non-English settlers. Only one of them, Jean le Grand, spoke of this, even implying a connection with a possible Indian attack, as well as an attack from English Jamaica, "because we fear very much from inland of the Indians, and the English rapscallions that had remained here, as well as of the four ships that we expect every hour from Jamaica commanded by Lord Willoughby."[53] Le Grand continued ranting against the "treasonous English rascals, who are treaty breakers," but oddly enough he appeared to be the only settler who was explicit about suspicions concerning the English. It should be noted that Le Grand was a very recent arrival in the colony, so perhaps the older settlers were already too familiar with their English neighbors to harbor serious doubts about them.[54]

Meanwhile, the war continued into 1673, but the Dutch managed to regain the offensive. The French proved unable to cross the Water Line in the winter of 1673, and by then, the Dutch Republic had been joined by allies: the emperor, the elector of Brandenburg, and the king of Spain. Though his armies managed to conquer the major fortress city of Maastricht in July 1673, Louis XIV was forced to abandon his Dutch conquests. The English, meanwhile, were faring even worse. The Dutch, led by Admiral Michiel de Ruyter, managed to gain a strategic victory on sea after defeating the English and French fleets in Europe on three separate occasions, and the English suffered defeats elsewhere, too, losing New York (Dutch New Netherland until 1664) in July 1673 and suffering defeat in the East Indies. They were therefore no longer in a position to threaten the Dutch. The rising unpopularity of the war eventually forced Charles II to sue for peace, which both parties signed in January 1674.

The Suriname settlers had suffered much by this point. In particular, the garrison was in bad shape, lacking food and drink. Versterre had ordered planters to

Suze Zijlstra and Tom Weterings

provide both a sugar mill and cows for the use of the soldiery, as his men were "as thin as greyhounds."[55] The arrival of the *Eendragt* in February 1673 brought much-needed victuals but to the governor's dismay no more than three months' worth. The subsequent arrival of a small squadron of warships did bring relief in the form of reinforcements for the garrison,[56] as well as a number of slaves the squadron had acquired as "booty" on their way to the colony.[57] However, they brought little in the way of food. In January 1674 a settler noted that although "by [God's] mercy" they had remained unmolested by the enemy, they still lacked severely in the way of provisions.[58]

With the war over, attempts to encourage the English settlers to leave Suriname resumed. A commission was set up to check up on their condition and to arrange for their departure. The States of Zeeland agreed to the conditions set by the English and ordered Versterre to treat the commission with civility and to give them full assistance.[59] What the States probably did not know, however, were the views of the English Lords of the Admiralty, who were adamant that the colony should not be allowed to regain the prosperity it had under English rule, as that might disincline some to leave their possessions.[60]

Preliminary investigations made in early 1675 revealed that, of the 120 remaining English adult male settlers—a very conservative estimate made by Governor Versterre—about 100 were prepared to leave, among whom were three owners of sugar works. The remaining 20, according to Versterre, were almost all owners of sugar works and would only be prepared to leave (for England itself, with the rest destined for English colonies in the Caribbean) if they could sell their possessions for cash. In such impoverished conditions, however, it was very hard to find people willing to buy.[61] When the commission arrived in mid-June 1675, they quickly came to an agreement with Versterre and the other colonial representatives (despite the commission members not really getting along all that well with each other, apparently).[62] The departing English settlers would leave behind all their cattle, furniture, and horses, though they would be taking their slaves with them. In the end, the majority of the English (between 80 and 100 adult men) left, taking with them over 1,000 slaves. A number of Natives made it aboard the English ships, despite protestations by Versterre and others, and managed to leave the ailing colony as well.[63]

Still, the Dutch Republic was at war with France. Versterre was pleased to note, some months before the arrival of the English commission, that they could count on the English settlers in case of a French attack.[64] Thus, he was confident that the defensive measures taken would suffice against such an attack, even if the costs of the defense for the inhabitants of the colony seemed heavier than elsewhere. Nonetheless, it was felt to be worthwhile as the garrison in March 1675 seems to have numbered about 120 men, a far cry from the 30 in May 1671.[65] In 1672 Potteij had observed that the colony could become prosperous "if only they had peace." But was it to last?[66]

Preparing for a French Attack

Although the relationship between the English and the Dutch colonists forms a natural focus of attention when discussing the threats of invasion in the 1670s, studying Suriname at a time when the French threatened to invade the colony uncovers the influence of war on colonial life when various inhabitants did not share a complicated history. The French had established a colonial presence in the Caribbean since settling certain islands, most prominently Martinique, in the 1630s. Their presence along the Wild Coast was less substantial than their activities on the islands, but in 1664 they reclaimed the colony of Cayenne from the Dutch. The English planters noted at that time that the French were strengthening their position on the mainland. The colony's government was aware that these French could become a threat in the future.

After the takeover of Suriname, the Dutch also realized the French in Cayenne could become a threat. In 1669 Governor Lichtenbergh wrote to the States of Zeeland that the governor of Cayenne had proposed to establish free trade relations between the colonies. Lichtenbergh advised the States to refuse the offer and forbid all trade with Cayenne because this would prevent the weak colony from becoming stronger. Lichtenbergh mentioned that the French had already been hindering the English in Suriname when they were catching turtles, and the Dutch feared that the French would soon do likewise to them when they sent out an expedition for turtles themselves.[67]

It may have been a good decision to reject free trade. The French were unable to develop Cayenne profitably, and in 1675 Versterre received reports that the French were in a miserable state. He contemplated the possibilities of taking back a part of this colony with the help of indigenous allies. In 1676 a fleet from the Dutch Republic briefly took Cayenne, but the French managed to regain it that same year. Cayenne remained a threat as long as the Dutch were at war with the French.[68]

In contrast, in Suriname there was generally no hostility towards French settlers. Because the Dutch were eager for new colonists, they welcomed people from all European nations into the colony. They even tried to persuade people from the French Caribbean islands to move to Suriname.[69] The number of French settlers was nevertheless low in the 1670s, as a 1675 list of inhabitants shows. In this overview of the colony's male settlers, the government listed three groups of inhabitants: the departing English, the Dutch, and the Jews. Only in the accompanying letter did the governor mention that the second list also included French settlers.[70] After the departure of the majority of the English settlers in 1675, the available lists of inhabitants did not distinguish between Dutch or English anymore, even if some English settlers remained. Only the Jews are listed separately in overviews from the early 1680s. Nevertheless, one can find a few individuals with French names and even some Spaniards, which emphasizes the international nature of Suriname's population.[71]

Yet with these lists it is hard to establish the exact composition of the French population. French-speaking Walloons had moved to the Dutch Republic in the late sixteenth century, as religious strife motivated Protestants from the southern Netherlands to leave their country of origin. These Walloons rapidly established themselves within Dutch society. Bringing their skills and their contacts with them, they contributed to the spectacular growth of the Dutch economy in the early seventeenth century. Within a few generations they intermarried with people of Dutch origin and thus became an integral part of the society. While Suriname welcomed many Huguenots after the Revocation of the Edict of Nantes in 1685, in the 1670s most people with French names living in the colony were not recent religious refugees.[72]

Personal letters written by colonists of French or Walloon descent confirm their long-established connection to the Netherlands. The colonists Jean le Grand, Du Plessis du Bellay, Samuel Thierrij, and Nicolas Combe could all write in perfect Dutch. Except for Combe, the correspondents even wrote exclusively in Dutch and sent all their letters to people living in the Netherlands. Most of their recipients were Dutch as well, and they were an important part of a Dutch correspondence network. This could result from both business and family contacts. For instance, the merchant le Grand had various Dutch business contacts, while Thierrij had traveled to Suriname to join his Dutch uncle Isaac van Mildert. Combe, the colony's administrator (who arrived in Suriname in 1668), was an obvious exception but proves the rule: while he regularly wrote his more formal letters, such as his reports to the States of Zeeland, his superiors, in French, he used Dutch for his correspondence with other business contacts. His need to use some Dutch words even in his French letters suggests that he grew up in a Dutch environment.[73]

For people with an official function, such as the administrator but also the secretary of the colony, it was an advantage to be multilingual. People in Suriname were aware of the importance of these language skills. When Suriname's secretary Johan Bolle died in 1671, various people were eager to follow in his footsteps and claim this lucrative post. The recent arrival Johan d'Olijslager wrote to all the contacts he could think of in Zeeland to emphasize his desire to become secretary and explain why he was the best man for the job. One of the things he mentioned in several letters was his ability to speak both English and French, a testimony to the importance of both nations in and around the colony.[74] Around that time, the States of Zeeland also appointed a new minister for Suriname, François Chaillou, who was expected to deliver his sermons both in Dutch and in French.[75]

Though the Dutch inhabitants of Suriname did not comment on the presence of French colonists—in contrast with the way they sometimes mentioned the English—it becomes clear from the 1671–72 correspondence that the fear of invasion was not only inspired by war with the English. Even if the Dutch and French did not share the same complex history, various correspondents mentioned in early 1672 that they heard rumors of war, especially with the French. They emphasized how they longed for ships from the fatherland, because they longed to hear the latest news about the situation with France. The planter Samuel de Witt was already preparing for war with France in early 1672 when he instructed his mother about which goods she had to insure to protect him against possible losses due to the war. Another planter Willem Blaeu even explained that the possibility of war with France—and the threat of being taken by privateers— had led him to decide to stay in Suriname instead of returning with the ship with which he had intended to return; he considered the voyage too dangerous. Suriname's government also tried to prepare the colony for a French invasion, even if there were no direct threats. In May 1673 a commander from the Dutch Republic arrived, and he had to replace the eleven French soldiers in the garrison with as many Dutch soldiers.[76]

Although war did break out in 1672, seriously affecting the situation in the Dutch Republic, it only affected Suriname indirectly until 1677. The colony itself had weakened since the conclusion of the Third Anglo-Dutch War, particularly because a total of 250 English settlers—men, women, and children—had left for Jamaica in 1675, leaving only a few hundred Europeans—Dutch, English, French, and Jewish.[77] Thus, in his letters to the States of Zeeland, the governor emphasized how weak the colony had become after the departure of the English and stressed the need to send reinforcements and new settlers, but this did not have much effect.[78]

At the same time, the number of migrants to Suriname increased significantly, but the approximately sixty people sponsored by the States of Zeeland who moved to Suriname in 1675 were not enough to compensate for the departure of the English inhabitants. In addition, the colony struggled with its financial situation, as the costs of keeping a permanent defensive force were so high that the government had to increase taxes in 1675 and again in 1676. The government also established a day of fasting and prayer in that year to beg for the war to end, explicitly ordering Dutch, English, French, and even Jewish people to participate in this day of prayer.[79]

While the governors and colonists had considered the possibility of a French attack since the outbreak of war in 1672, reports reached the colony in November 1677 that a French fleet had set sail and an attack was imminent. It is impossible to determine how these rumors came to light, but the measures the government took show that they regarded it as a serious threat. Because the garrison was not considered strong enough, only consisting of forty men—many of the soldiers manning the fortress in 1675 must have died or left service—the three civil militias of the colony had to supply half a company each for fourteen days to help defend the fortress, after which the other half of their company had to take their place. The government also instituted another day of prayer, in which all inhabitants again had to participate.[80]

Suze Zijlstra and Tom Weterings

The similarities here with the preparations for an English invasion in 1672 are evident, especially when it comes to the government's attitude towards the colonists. After many deliberations, the political council and the war council decided on December 11 on a detailed plan that resolved to pair up all the French people living in the colony and handcuff them, according to the administrative division where they lived. This would enable the government to remove them from the colony if necessary. It was left to the discretion of masters, however, to decide whether their servants were trustworthy enough not to have to be handcuffed. In that case the masters had to vouch for them. Those Frenchmen who did not have a permanent residence had to be taken to the fortress, where they would be held in custody. The other civilians in the colony had to swear an oath of loyalty, promising to obey the government and the officers. Considering the capacity of the Dutch forces, the number of Frenchmen taken into custody was probably very low.[81]

Apart from these measures taken to ensure the loyalty of the colonists, the government took other practical measures. For instance, it prepared to undermine the armory, to blow it up in case it fell into the hands of the French. Then, those women who could leave the colony were allowed to sail with the bark of planter Samuel Nassy, which would be dispatched to Barbados and Tobago to inform them of the situation and inquire after the status of the French. Those women of Paramaribo who did not leave the colony were required to travel upriver to secure their safety. The government also bought all the available victuals in case a shortage should arise, so that they could evenly distribute the available food while all the administrative documents were transported upriver.

It also ordered ships staying in Suriname that sailed to other parts for trade to leave twenty men each in Paramaribo to defend the colony, and a few weeks later it decided to commence construction of a new fortress north of the mouth of the Commewijne River, which was closer to the ocean than Fort Zeelandia. Several prominent colonists had to provide the materials for this fortress, and the colonists had to send fifty male slaves with their tools and provisions, which would last a month. Moreover, the planters had to provide fifty men for three months to defend the colony. Finally, the government decided to go through its records to see who still owed the colony money so that they could raise the fifty thousand pounds of sugar that were necessary to prepare the colony for an invasion.[82] As the government minutes of 1672 had not been this elaborate, it remains unclear whether the 1677 preparations were more extensive than those of five years previously. The 1677 preparations may have been more extensive, as the garrison was much smaller and the possibility of a defeat therefore even higher than in 1672.

In spite of the government's expectations, the French attack did not materialize. The attention of the government soon had to be directed elsewhere, as some twenty Africans escaped from Nassy's plantation in January 1678. In September of that year the Dutch Republic and France ended their war.[83] Yet again, it took some time for this news to reach the colony, so when new rumors reached the colony in November 1678 that the French were approaching, the government had to take measures again, although the threat was not as significant and the measures taken were accordingly modest. It only decided to station a ship at the Commewijne River and one near Fort Zeelandia.[84] No significant hostilities took place, however, and the news of the peace finally ended the colonists' anxiety.

While neither the French nor the English attacked Suriname in the 1670s, the planters were displeased with the way the war affected their lives, especially as increased taxes made running a plantation much more difficult. In 1678 they sent an urgent dispatch to the States of Zeeland with eleven requests, some of which resulted from their frustrations with the war effort. They asked whether the States could send one hundred European laborers who would sign a contract to work for three to five years, explaining that they needed these laborers to send in their stead "in times of alarm," so as to continue to run their plantations themselves and not have their property ruined by Amerindians and escaped slaves.[85] They also requested that one hundred soldiers garrison Fort Zeelandia during wartime; the planters offered to pay for this force as long as they were allowed freedom from taxes during wartime. Finally, they asked permission for the construction of the new fortress near the Commewijne River. While their requests did not yield many results, as the States only granted the last one without restriction, they show how the wars of the 1670s directly influenced the planters' agenda.[86]

Conclusion

Even if a hostile takeover never took place in the 1670s, European wars severely disrupted the lives of the colonists of Suriname, especially when a direct attack was rumored to take place imminently. In the cases of both English and French threats, the government required potentially hostile planters to stay on their plantations or to surrender themselves. Also, the colonists had to contribute to the colony's defenses personally and send slaves to reinforce the fortress. This caused the colony's sugar production to stagnate.

At the same time, the number of ships arriving in the colony declined substantially, leaving the planters with a pressing shortage of supplies, and those supplies had to support the increased number of soldiers as well as the colonists. Moreover, the planters had trouble shouldering the colony's increasing tax burden. As a result, Zeeland did not make as much profit from the colony as it had anticipated. The province was forced to sell Suriname to the Dutch West India Company at the beginning of 1683.

Even more pressing than these material burdens was the impact war had on the colonists' private lives. Particularly following the various transfers of the colony in 1667–68, all colonists were well aware of the potential harm a takeover could do. They continually waited for news from Europe to assess their own situations properly; the uncertainty caused them great unrest with the sporadic arrival of news making matters even more unpredictable.

Suze Zijlstra and Tom Weterings

Personal relations in the colony were strained as well, as government orders that distinguished between English and other colonists, and later on between the French and the others, emphasized the severity of the situation and the fact that neighbors could easily join the enemy. Nevertheless, the personal correspondence that remains reveals a consistent fear of the enemy without: the fleet of the English or the French that might arrive, rather than any threat from their neighbors in the colony itself. In the French case, the importance of personal relations at times of war becomes particularly clear. French inhabitants with masters who were willing to vouch for them were not imprisoned.

When comparing the Suriname government's response to the English and French threats, then, one thing stands out in particular: while the number of Englishmen living in the colony dwarfed the number of Frenchmen, the measures taken to defend the colony remained similar throughout the 1670s. Yet, even though most of the English had to remain on their plantations whenever an attack threatened to materialize, they generally were not imprisoned, just as the French could remain free once their masters vouched for them. This demonstrates the level of trust that had been forged between the inhabitants of the colony. The real defense measures were taken to protect the colony from a hostile takeover initiated by a fleet manned by unfamiliar persons. Most of those living in the colony were trusted not to turn against their neighbors; personal feelings aside, this would most likely not be in their own interest. After the chaos of the takeovers in the late 1660s, the inhabitants craved peace and quiet to conduct their own business above anything else, regardless of their own backgrounds.

This proved to be difficult as European warfare continued to affect the Torrid Zone either through conquest and reconquest or from the threats of invasion or piracy and the ensuing disruption of colonial life. In the case of Suriname, the threat of an English conquest did subside after the Third Anglo-Dutch War. Only in the late eighteenth century did a new conflict with the English lead to the takeover of some Dutch Caribbean possessions such as St. Eustatius and Berbice, Demerara, and Essequibo, although the conquered colonies returned to Dutch hands after the war ended in 1784. The French, however, continued to influence the development of the Dutch Caribbean well into the eighteenth century. The privateer Jacques Cassard caused the most havoc in 1712 with an attack on Suriname and Berbice. While Cassard eventually left, the colonists had to pay a substantial sum to be rid of him. The bigger threat the planters faced, though, came in the form of resistance of the enslaved Africans and those who had managed to escape slavery.[87]

Reassessing Jamayca Española

Spanish Fortifications and English Designs in Jamaica

Amanda J. Snyder

Notwithstanding the importance of Jamaica, scholars have largely overlooked the period prior to the English Western Design (1654–55), which wrested the island from Spain, in their treatments of the imperial significance of the island. Spanish historians portray Jamaica as a backwater of little importance. For historians writing in English, the Design generally constitutes a failure. Archival research shows the need for a reevaluation of these traditional arguments.[1]

Some scholars argue that Jamaica's role in the Spanish empire dwindled after the conquest of Mexico as settlers did not establish a large-scale *encomienda* system on the island as they did in many other colonies.[2] Even so, Jamaica sat at a vital point along the transatlantic ligaments that connected Spain and America. Accordingly, despite being habitually overlooked by contemporaries as well as by historians, the Spanish archives contain a steady stream of warnings from colonial officials and settlers to the metropolitan government over the need for its greater defense. Locals cited as one danger the large number of pirates operating on Jamaica's coastline. Besides pointing out personal financial losses, these reports emphasized how detrimental the loss of the island would be for the whole of Spain's American empire.[3]

Yet, for over a century, Spain's imperial administration failed to respond to these tocsins, and the English ultimately capitalized on that neglect. The failure of the Spanish government to secure Jamaica opened the door for a revolutionary English leader to take hold of the island and begin a new phase of English expansion and, ultimately, empire—much to the detriment of Spanish power both at home and abroad. The Western Design may not have achieved its main objective of acquiring Hispaniola; it did, however, manage to capture Jamaica. Though some English historians regard Cromwell as a "backwoods country squire"[4] with little head for foreign policy, work by such scholars as Charles Korr and Timothy Venning, coupled with a reexamination of the extensive and accessible Thurloe State Papers and Interregnum State Papers, show that Cromwell and his government do not deserve their overwhelmingly negative reputation in modern historiography—at least with respect to naval and foreign policy.[5]

Cromwell's advisors, especially Secretary of State John Thurloe, remained well informed of Spain's struggles and Caribbean finances. Thus, his government successfully played the diplomatic game to gain more information about their opponents, toy with various alliances, and play a waiting game as well as Elizabeth I did. These machinations and diplomatic maneuverings even earned the Protectorate's first international recognition from the Spanish Crown itself.

By the summer of 1654, Cromwell and Thurloe felt the time was right—a view encouraged by certain merchants—for an expedition intended to strike at the heart of Spanish American trade and establish a dominant English presence in the Caribbean. This endeavor included the recruitment of some five thousand "unruly" inhabitants of the English Caribbean.[6]

These men largely came from rover communities that became established in the Caribbean following James I's reversal of Elizabethan privateering policies.[7] Regretting his predecessor's encouragement of the "surprising and taking" of Spanish ships at sea, "Rex Pacificus," much more eager for peace with Spain, gave English seamen one month to uphold his new peace treaty with Spain and to "stop going warlike to sea." Any mariner not heeding James's proclamations faced "being reputed and taken as Pirates," having their goods and lands confiscated, and risking a death sentence. The language of this proclamation differed greatly from early Elizabethan "letter-transfer" legislation under which seamen need only switch out their licenses for a Tudor seal.[8]

Mariners ignored these proclamations as they enjoyed the living they had made under the late queen; privateering had become an occupation. Accordingly, as the Habsburg ambassador to the Dutch Republic related, they resented the king's attempts to curb prize acquisition and his pursuit of peace with Spain.[9]

Facing increasing numbers of "rogues" and "incorrigible" attacks at home and abroad, James thus decided to expand his earlier decrees and to curb this resentment through punishment. Within a year of the king's accession, the High Court of Admiralty executed more men for piracy than it had for almost four decades. Mariners who continued their predations could also be sentenced to banishment to Newfoundland or to the East or West Indies.[10] Spain, of course, applauded James's new policies and the new peace, and it expected to pick up the pieces left as England stepped up its prosecution of pirates. Officials expected to buy confiscated ships, as well as seize more English ships coming into Spanish ports, and thereby expected its rival's navy to diminish in size and power.[11] But through the pursuit of this policy, James unwittingly increased the scale of piracy.[12]

Offered little alternative but punishment for pursuing their livelihoods, many mariners took their skills to the Caribbean and the Mediterranean. A number of them operated as true pirates not beholden to any one Crown and preying indiscriminately. Others still gained letters of marque and merchant licenses from various foreign princes generally in the Italian or Ottoman states despite repeated proclamations from James prohibiting these practices.[13]

In response, James increased piracy punishments for the first time in almost a century and openly encouraged impressment of his own subjects, instructing port officials and naval officers to press into service any seamen found committing piracy or in the service of any prince but the king of England.[14] This policy, of course, did not help the loyalty issues already rampant between the king and his mariners, resulting in the continued exodus of seamen from English shores.

Meanwhile, Spain's inability to mount an effective defense against English marauders and England's growing wealth and power from such attacks allowed English interests to nibble at the periphery of Spanish claims in the New World, and the coastlines of Jamaica served as a refuge for English mariners, pirates, and exiles, operating in and around the traditionally Spanish island during the reigns of the early Stuarts.[15]

Though many scholars have denounced the exaggeration of the "Black Legend" of Spanish imperial history, the case of Jamaica, unfortunately, feeds the legend. Discovered by Columbus on his second voyage to the New World, Jamaica proved a crucial possession for further Spanish voyages into Mexico and north into Cuba and La Florida. In 1514 King Ferdinand V (ruled 1474–1516) allowed settlers to the island to possess their own ships and trading vessels for use throughout the Caribbean. Several colonists wrote that Jamaica held numerous stores of livestock and other resources useful to the colonization efforts in nearby territories. Francisco de Garay, the second governor of the island, informed the king of the abundance of produce as well, claiming that "the colonization of Terra Firma will not cease because of a shortage of supplies" to come from his island.[16] If the island had no other significance to the Crown, it did at least provide a steady supply of food and resources for the conquering armies of the New World. These supplies had also been "essential" for Vasco Nuñez de Balboa on his expedition to discover the South Sea.[17]

Occasionally, the government did recognize the importance of promoting the settlement of Jamaica. One of these few promotional policies occurred in 1521 when the Spanish Crown waived custom duties on personal goods for any Spaniards who chose to settle there.[18] The scale of encouragement for such policy, though, remained minimal until the English took the island over a century later.

By the beginning of the seventeenth century, despite its location and the scale of resources reported there, only one working fort existed on Jamaica. Especially considering the regular crossings of the Vera Cruz Plate Fleets between Cuba and Jamaica, the island needed greater fortification. Admiral Ménez de Avilés and the abbot Don Francisco Márquez de Villalobos informed the king once more of the island's deficient security. Numerous other accounts outline these fears. Some of them speak to great loss of resources and trade security, and more still relate the constant appearance of *piratas* and *corsarios*. Letters to the Spanish ambassador in London, Don Gerau Despes, reiterated this fact by relating news of *bienes robados* (stolen goods or stealing of goods) by the English in 1570.[19] Other letters to Despes related how pirates waited at the harbors to trade slaves and attack the "five good ships" defending the island.[20] Governor Licado also warned the king of the dangers of losing Jamaica.[21]

Some of the problems in constructing forts on the island stemmed from the mismanaged government there. Columbus and his descendants had received numerous rights to Jamaica resulting in an almost carte blanche management of the island. Over the course of Jamaica's history, these Columbus descendants, the king himself, various *audiencias* (courts), and still more governors or admirals gained charge of the island. Jamaica rarely had one efficient or effective hierarchy of government for any extended period of time, which led to the Crown's continued

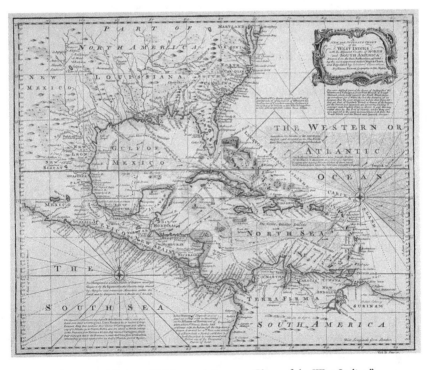

Emmanuel Bowen, "A New and Accurate Chart of the West Indies."
Found in John Harris, *Navigantium atque Itinerantium Bibliotheca*
[A Complete Collection of Voyages and Travels], 1748. Courtesy of
the Norman B. Leventhal Map Center at the Boston Public Library.

disregard of the island.[22] In his requests for increased defensive measures, Licado also called for an end to the negligent rule of the Columbian descendants.[23]

As Jamaican inhabitants knew all too well, its location, central to practically all Spanish-American trade, created an environment ripe for piracy. A steady flow of contraband trade existed during most of the island's history, involving settlers, pirates, and government officials alike, from Jamaica's earliest Spanish settling until long after the English takeover. Correspondence dating back to 1571 warned of "pirates lying in wait" and the foreign navies that prowled the open waters.[24] The amount of traffic encircling the island further attested to its strategic importance. A glance at the accompanying map makes clear that the island lay directly in the path of Spain's Plate Fleet routes from Vera Cruz, New Spain, past Santo Domingo or Havana, before continuing on to Seville.

At the start of the seventeenth century, Governor Fernando Melgarejo Córdoba did actively address the importance of defending Jamaica's coastline. He made plans to construct new forts and to create a small naval fleet to remain in the island. Spanish officials first conceived of the *Armada de la Guardia* after Francis Drake's continued raids throughout the Caribbean prompted some of the first official recognition of need for a protective fleet in the Indies. Coupled with the ever-increasing number of pirates, Drake's incursions underscored the vulnerability of Spanish naval forces abroad. In response, in 1595, the Council of the Indies pleaded for the creation of a permanent Caribbean fleet. Alternately called the *Armada del Mar del Sur* or the *Armada de Barlovento,* the proposed fleet would prevent the English marauders from maintaining their own bases in the Carolinas, from which they could more easily attack the trade of the Spanish islands.[25] Much of the plans for this new Caribbean fleet drew from the creation of the Armada of Flanders created to defend the interests of the Spanish Netherlands in the English Channel.[26]

The experiences of the Armada of Flanders and the war with Elizabethan England demonstrated to the Spanish the need for a restructuring of the traditional Spanish Armada. Dutch ships and sailing expertise quickly proved a serious threat to Spanish control around the world. The "Invincible Armada" that set out against England in 1588 had failed miserably, motivating Philip to listen more intently to his shipbuilders' advice. Pedro López de Soto, one such builder and inspector of the Lisbon fleet, warned Philip of the need for a completely redesigned fleet to keep up with the English. López told the king that English superiority rested "solely" in the "speed and good design" of their ships, coupled with their "efficient artillery and marksmen."[27]

As too often happened, these plans never fully materialized. In the middle of Philip III's reign, in 1610, the number of Spanish vessels in the Caribbean dropped below twenty though it did increase to fifty in the following two decades.[28] This dearth dramatically affected Spain's ability to hold overseas territories. Don Diego Sarmiento de Acuña, Count Gondomar, the Spanish ambassador in London

Amanda J. Snyder

from 1613 to 1622, expressed his concerns to Philip over the continued growth of the English fleet, reminding his sovereign that only mastery on the seas secured mastery on land and that Spain lagged far behind the competition.[29] As further proof of this deficiency, in 1621 English *piratas* once again skirted Spanish defenses and attacked Cartagena. One of many continued attacks, the "well-armed" pirates absconded with one thousand bushels of maize and more than six million pesos in gold and silver, while causing much damage to the ports and merchants operating there.[30]

The damage done by such attacks continued to aid English naval plans while hampering Spain's. Unlike James I, Charles I (ruled 1625–49) did implement some shipbuilding programs that moved his kingdom towards a more professional navy and constructed larger warships than England had traditionally employed. Charles's plans, though, paled in comparison to those of the ensuing Interregnum governments (1649–60).

At the start of the Interregnum, the English navy consisted of fifty warships and some smaller vessels.[31] Smaller vessels had been the staple of the English naval force for almost a century, but Charles I had continued to build larger ships, much as the Spanish had done. When Parliament assumed control of the navy in 1643, some of its first plans included building twenty-five new ships of a more agile and versatile design.[32] The new English Republic planned to add thirty more such ships by 1652,[33] making its fleet the rival of any contemporary.[34]

Spain, on the other hand, did not take note of many of the contemporary changes to ship design, technology, and naval practices. For one, these changes and retooling of the navy would require a great expenditure on an already thin budget. Even after the government implemented the *Armada de la Guardia de la carrera de las Indias,* the fleet sailed as protection to the Plate Fleets only, performing only a fraction of its originally intended purpose. The *Armada de la Guardia*'s plans made no considerations for defending coastal forts in the Caribbean islands. Melgarejo, more than the Crown, realized the deficiencies in this arrangement, claiming that coastal forts meant little if the sea remained open, free, and unpoliced.[35]

Although Melgarejo wrote up these plans, he never put them into motion. Generally acknowledged as one of the more corrupt of a number of corrupt Jamaican governors, Melgarejo constantly undermined his own efforts. Colonists reported how the governor sold gunpowder to passing ships no matter their nationality because of the inflated profit he could earn. Melgarejo also dismissed the island's official arms maker, depriving the island of a resident manufacturer of munitions.[36] Therefore, even if the governor had followed through on his ambitious defensive plans, the ships and forts had no readily available firepower.

Further stressing the necessity of reinforcing the island, Spanish ambassadors complained that every English ship left its port armed. Prepared for attack on every league of the journey, these ships stood ready to overwhelm poorly armed Jamaican residents quickly. As other nations, especially the English, recognized this situation, piracy steadily increased with supply bases beginning to turn up in places such as Barbados and the Carolina coast. While other extra-national bands of maritime predators also closed in on the island, England began to make official plans to add Jamaica to its growing New World empire.

Yet, after Melgarejo's dismissal of the island's armorer, the Crown never assigned a replacement. While the militia suffered from the resulting lack or arms, the Jamaican *cabildo* (Spanish colonial administrative council) tried to convince themselves that at least the majority of settlers could help defend the island, citing the hunting experience of the settlers: "skilled shots of such caliber that when flint pieces, gunlocks, and cocks were lacking, with gun barrel and stock in one hand, and a length of fuse in the other, they were [still] able to fire those arms."[37] When the English landed just a few years later, though, these "skilled shots" fell short.

The increase in piratical attacks during the end of Melgarejo's term prompted Phillip III to take some sort of action, and the king sent out a galleon fleet in 1608 that did little to stem the growing tide of piracy.[38] The 1620s saw steady attacks by the English and Dutch primarily. Some sources total the losses of this period at around seven hundred thousand ducats. In response, Philip IV (ruled 1621–65) gave orders in 1627 for the creation of another fleet to sail to Jamaica and Santo Domingo. This proclamation, though, seems to have had no effect and certainly did not constitute a deviation from the general lack of Spanish imperial consideration given to Jamaica.[39]

While the English government had some success in bringing armed forces under state control starting in the sixteenth century, Spain did not. In numerous instances, the Council of Seville actually rejected plans for an armed fleet to secure regular Atlantic trade. The Councils of State and of the Indies objected to this dismissal, pointing out the defensive deficiencies of the ships making these voyages.[40] The vulnerable convoy system remained the council's preferred method of transport. Occasionally, armed ships accompanied trade fleets, but this did not constitute standard practice at the time.[41]

Moreover, despite the intricate bureaucracy of its government, Spain lacked an effective naval strategy or control over many of its own ships. In the early years Elizabeth rented out her dilapidated ships, but Philip had very few ships of his own or that belonged directly to the Crown. According to some figures, nearly two-thirds of Spain's Mediterranean galleys belonged to private owners in the mid-sixteenth century.[42] The government did own some ships, but other countries and princes owned the majority of ships in Spanish fleets. According to Venetian reports, the Mediterranean squadron had eight large ships and six galleons from Spain. As for the rest of the fleet, twenty-six galleons came from Naples and Sicily, and eighteen from other Italian states.[43]

If the government had no official warships, it stands to reason that there was no official navy—simply soldiers serving on ships and slaves in the galleys that transported goods and monies to and from the colonies. Because of their size and generally outdated technology, these vessels were not readily equipped for the combat awaiting them at the hands of pirates. Moreover, for much of the sixteenth century, they had little protection, all of which meant continued threats on the sea. At the same time, Spanish kings relied too heavily on outdated papal edicts and the sheer right of settlement to keep their many overseas possessions. Either that, or the kings believed that the treasures of the Americas would always fund the hiring of ships from private owners. While the government did take in significant revenue from taxing merchant trade to the Atlantic, it did not see the advantages of state versus private trade to the Indies.

As has been noted numerous times, Spaniards constantly lamented the presence of pirates in the Caribbean. Armed men first sailed with merchant convoys there in the 1520s, but again, private merchants conducted this policy. Forty years later, the Spanish government took strides to make this sort of armament standard for the Armada of New Spain. The *Armada de la guardia de la carrera de las Indias,* according to official communication, generally consisted of eight galleons and three smaller *pataches* (dispatch ships). Approximately one thousand seamen and nine hundred soldiers served aboard these ships.[44] Official plans did not always translate into effective deployment, however.

The navy occupied a very different place in the Spanish political strategy than it did for other European nations. Naval service in England under the Tudors and Cromwell offered men of lower social status an opportunity for wealth and advancement. Spanish men could find fame and prestige in the army, but a naval commission did not hold the same prestige.[45] Castilians, especially, simply did not see the need for naval service when the navy already employed so many pilots and mariners who came from the various Spanish territories.[46]

As Spain proper found itself in more conflict with its provinces, this fact became a crippling weakness for its empire. Philip II (ruled 1556–98) did develop some maritime policies in regards to galley schedules and trade, including the system of the twice-a-year Plate Fleet crossings to the New World. The problem still remained that many of these pilots did not come from Spain itself, besides the Basques. Many Belgians and Portuguese, also subjects of the Spanish Habsburgs after 1580, served aboard these fleets.[47] Castilian pilots knew the Mediterranean well, but according to contemporaries, they had practically no knowledge of the western seas, even when they deigned to serve in the navy in the first place: when the Great Armada sailed for England, Spain had to recruit French pilots because they could not even find suitable Portuguese pilots.[48] Spain certainly needed knowledgeable pilots; however, they also needed pilots who were loyal to Spain. Should the Luso-Spanish union end (as it did in 1640), Spain had no guarantee of these pilots' allegiance.

Then, Spanish sailors considered New World sailing posts as a means to an end rather than as an inroad to a naval career. Once in the New World, large numbers of sailors deserted, hoping to establish themselves as farmers or merchants. The same could easily be said of men of most nations. Spain, however, offered its men less incentive to see the navy as an adequate career choice since the government did not even see the fleet as something permanent in the early years, as evidenced by the scant attention it devoted to naval construction. Occupation as a sailor was also more open to men of varying social and even racial backgrounds. Crews supplemented their numbers with second sons, poor jobless men, and the occasional drunk. Many a young or ruined man could find employment and "an earthly paradise . . . [at] the ends of the earth" when he stepped aboard a ship.[49]

Sailor, merchant, and Captain General of the Navy and Fleet of New Spain (1595) Juan de Escalante de Mendoza (1529–1596) described the two sorts of men who took to the sea. The first included those second sons and poorer men who had neither the means nor ability for other careers. "Restlessness" and a desire to do "something else" rather than stay the course their fathers may have set for them inspired the second class of sailors.[50] While some scholars argue that shipboard discipline was particularly harsh, this was not always the case. In the official galleons, the government sentenced criminals to work the ships' galleys. Such policies upheld this idea of particularly rigid order onboard. For other ships, and especially merchant vessels, discipline and working conditions relaxed as the distance widened between the ship and metropole.[51] Galleon fleets did not necessarily constitute a fleet—at least not a sustained naval force. Galleons used for transporting New World goods were occasionally equipped for battle, but Spain did not have a permanent naval fleet. Without a permanent fleet, coastal fortifications became increasingly important.

When Philip IV finally sent a military engineer, Juan Bautista Antonelli, to Jamaica in the 1630s, the latter reported that it had too small a harbor for bigger ships and was therefore not likely to be as coveted an island, though much of the contemporary correspondence shows evidence to the contrary.[52] Antonelli, however, did not address the existence of the smaller, lighter ships of the English pirates, which navigated such harbors much more easily than Spanish galleons. Nevertheless, an internal rivalry between the Cuban and Jamaican governors made moot any of Antonelli's plans and further consideration of Jamaica's defenses. Desiring the completion of his own new fort, the Cuban governor, Lorenzo de Cabrera y Corbera, detained Antonelli.[53] Without the supervision of one of Spain's chief military engineers, little to nothing changed with respect to the defense of Jamaica for the next two decades.

Losing the trade routes that encircled the island would have devastating consequences for Spanish America, and once lost, Jamaica would be practically impossible to recover.[54] Don Carlos de Ybarras, appointed captain of the *Armada de la guardia de la carrera de las Indias* in 1634, related the scope of trade to the island. Frigates brought three to four hundred people to Jamaica in that year alone; within a year, he estimated, this population would produce a revenue of at least ten thousand pesos. Since the enemy recognized the island as "an island of many provisions," Ybarras entreated the king to recognize the need for protection

Amanda J. Snyder

of this wealth, referencing the continued need for an *Armada de Barlovento* to guard the island.[55]

Also in 1634 the Marquis de Cadereita tried to convince the king of the fertility of Jamaica's sugar and tobacco crops, which naturally enticed other nations to make attempts against the island.[56] Citing the ease in which enemies came and went from Negril Harbor, the marquis asked again for protection of the island and its valuable resources, especially wood, which enemies acquired with impunity.[57] Letters to the king in 1638 became more concerned about the lack of protection afforded Jamaica. Claiming that the government had done nothing to protect the island for two and a half years, colonial authorities reported how it "would easily be overrun" if fortification plans did not proceed quickly.[58] On various occasions the Spanish Crown sent out directives to Cuba, Hispaniola, and other nearby islands to send supplies and support to Jamaica. Rarely, though, did the governors of these places actually follow such orders, and rarely did the Crown enforce them.

The governors of Santiago de Cuba, especially, showed an intense animosity towards their Jamaican neighbors, creating a "friction . . . [that] was one of the most outstanding features" of seventeenth-century Caribbean governance.[59] By the mid-seventeenth century, as the fragility of Jamaican defenses became a ticking bomb for Spanish power in the Caribbean, the king sent orders that the Greater Antilles turn all their attention and efforts towards Jamaica. The Cuban governor, for one, flatly refused.[60] These disagreements only added to or amplified the powerlessness of the Crown in the Caribbean. The viceroy of New Spain wrote in 1658 that the governors of Jamaica did not help themselves either, calling them "more absolutist and [with] greater freedom of action than [even] the nobles of Venice."[61]

In 1635 Antonelli had tried to reassure Philip IV that the island had adequate artillery for defense with its eight large cannons. The engineer, however, had scarcely even had the opportunity to see the Jamaican defenses, as the Cuban governor kept him detained with Cuban fortification projects. Contradicting Antonelli's reports, Captain Juan de Arencibia noted in 1643 that only one of these eight cannons fully functioned. The Duke de Veragua supported the captain's findings, adding that the island had very few and "ill-preserved" muskets and cannons with little gunpowder to even use in them. The duke resorted to ordering Captain Jacinto Sedeño and Captain Albornoz to travel to Cartagena or Santo Domingo to purchase as much ammunition as possible but reminded the king that gunpowder was "quite expensive." As the duke's predecessors noted, Jamaica's lack of defensive capability meant that pirates constantly interfered in the island's trade and supplies, forcing inhabitants to resort to bartering among themselves. Luckily, settlers found abundant fruit, fleeces, and meat to help sustain them despite their poverty of currency. Veragua petitioned for a number of ships to police the surrounding waters regularly, citing the "well known need to preserve this island," its importance for Spanish colonial navigation, and the damage that would result in the event of its loss.[62]

Jamaica thus occupied a significant place within the Spanish Caribbean, but misinformation and slow progress constantly plagued the matter of its defense. If the Crown questioned the importance of the island, the reports it received also repeatedly described the quantity of foodstuffs and goods available there. Simply because the government was preoccupied with other wars or favored islands such as Cuba and Hispaniola did not make Jamaica any less important to the supplying of those colonies; nor did it make Jamaica any less strategically placed amid Spanish trade and therefore increasingly desirable to pirates and expanding English territorial and commercial interests (as well as to Dutch and French sailors looking to expand their own trade and influence). Already, in 1640 enemies of Spain occupied San Christobal, Dominica, and other places within easy striking distance of Jamaica. Officials, as always, wrote about the "known risk of losing the island," with the enemy ever closer and better armed than many of Jamaica's settlers.[63] The king did approve requests to send ships to Jamaica with war supplies in 1644. By 1651, however, the original petitioner, Veragua, had not even received one ship.[64]

The lack of defense of Jamaica, or its conquest by the English, thus had less to do with the "worthlessness" of the island than with the inefficient governance and supply of the island by the Spanish government. As in the case of the famed armada three-quarters of a century before the Western Design, the Spanish government remained mired in its own bureaucracy.

In the 1650s the Caribbean played a significant role in Anglo-Spanish politics and Jamaica stood at the forefront of this renewed focus. In 1653 Cromwell's supporters overthrew the republic that had come to power following the execution of Charles I in 1649. As the leader of a new regime, especially a revolutionary one, Cromwell knew he had to find a way to establish his new government's authority and earn the official recognition of the European powers to make his revolution permanent. With this goal in mind, Cromwell crafted his Western Design to found a colony in the lucrative Caribbean while also striking at the heart of the mighty Spanish Empire, thus extending England's newly forceful martial reputation to the New World after the convulsions of the Civil Wars.

Having solidified his position with the crushing of Royalist forces at Worcester and Dunbar (1651), followed by the subjugation of Ireland (completed 1653), the ejection of the Rump Parliament (December 1653), and the defeat of the Dutch in the First Anglo-Dutch War (1652–54), Cromwell turned his sights across the Atlantic. Colonists felt the effects of these events, although modern accounts of the Civil Wars and Interregnum periods have generally remained Eurocentric, rarely mentioning how the war affected the colonies.[65] Only recently have scholars begun to explore the dissemination of pamphlets abroad and colonists' reactions to them,[66] despite the fact that only six of the twenty-four English colonies—Antigua, Barbados, Bermuda, Maryland, Newfoundland, and

Virginia—declared for the king and rebelled against the republican government created after the regicide.

Most Anglo-American colonies, being so far detached from the mainland and so reliant on their neighbors in the smaller, tougher environment of colonial life, tempered their opinions about the Civil Wars. The most vehemently Royalist, Virginia, submitted to the Commonwealth by the end of 1649.[67] In Barbados during 1649–50, there existed a "Treaty of Turkey and Roast Pig" meant to keep peace among the settlers. The treaty stated that "whosoever named the word *Roundhead* or *Cavalier,* should give to those that heard him a shot [young hog] and a turkey . . . to be eaten at his house who made the forfeiture . . . that they might enjoy the company of one another."[68] Though Barbados had a population with a majority of exiled Royalists, many of these hesitated to declare for the king, favoring the "Treaty of Turkey and Roast Pig" for as long as it lasted. Barbados, like Jamaica, welcomed exiles from either side of the fight.[69] Even as divisions in the colony grew, Cavaliers and Roundheads alike continued to engage in friendly communication and cooperation for the sake of the colony's success.[70] Any resistance to the Interregnum regime seemed to dissipate by 1652, when the Commonwealth established control over all the Caribbean islands when it dispatched Sir George Ayscue's fleet to the region.[71]

The Interregnum governments understood the importance of America better than their predecessors did. Whereas the early Stuart monarchs saw colonial possession more as their right in the expansion of their kingdom, the Interregnum governments, particularly that of Cromwell, better understood the economic and political necessity of gaining control of the colonies. Accordingly, an "Oath of Engagement" was required of all Englishmen departing for the Americas to ensure, at least nominally, the support of Englishmen in every corner of the realm.[72]

Especially following the execution of Charles I, the English government monitored colonial correspondence and publications as much as possible, as a united England meant further proof of the Commonwealth's legitimacy to the rest of the world.[73] The scheme worked as Spain officially recognized the "Republic of England" in 1650.[74] France remained more skeptical of the new regime, and chief minister Mazarin continued engagement in the Dutch War until 1654 to avoid the issue, using the time to devise a scheme to prevent an Anglo-Spanish alliance by emphasizing the wealth of the West Indies to Cromwell.[75]

Having already recognized the importance of the Caribbean, Cromwell began preparations to attack the Spanish presence there, both for the wealth he expected from prizes and for the respect he expected to earn from other European governments. By April 1654 Cromwell and his army had disbanded the Rump, and Cromwell had taken the title of "Lord Protector." Some of his councilors proposed attacking Spain proper, but Cromwell preferred to attack the Americas first and foremost. He believed that a Caribbean island "of substantial size," won under the name of the Commonwealth, "would come in more useful than Barbados where Royalists had previously been sent."[76] In the same vein of thinking as Elizabeth's, Cromwell believed that striking at Spanish colonies in the Americas would help his new regime acquire necessary financial gains, while he believed that Spain remained too distracted elsewhere to retaliate effectively against an island attack (although one of his top generals, John Lambert, thought otherwise).[77]

In the Caribbean, Cromwell recycled Elizabethan privateering policies and diplomatic justifications for such endeavors and gained the Atlantic colony he saw as crucial to the establishment of his new political rule. Having kept the support of the navy throughout the Civil War, Cromwell had the full force of naval power at his disposal.[78] During Christmas 1654 the Western Design fleet sailed for Barbados with sixty ships and four thousand soldiers; there it picked up a dozen more ships and at least five thousand more soldiers from among the settlers, local militia, and the "unruly set" of exiled mariners that operated in the surrounding waters.[79] General Robert Venables recruited more "unruly" men in St. Christopher's.

After failing to secure Hispaniola, the fleet found success in Jamaica, thanks in part to the continued recruitment of exiles and pirates. On November 28, 1655, Cromwell issued a charter for the establishment of an English city at Port Royal, to be the capital of the new Commonwealth colony. He further declared, "Within the tropics where there is never Peace, and without the tropics where Peace yet is, there shall now be War with Spain. . . . We will maintain Jamaica, send reinforcement after reinforcement to it; we will try yet for the Spanish Plate Fleets . . . and have no peace with Spain."[80] With this expedition, and with the help of Caribbean pirates and exiles, Cromwell gained recognition and peace with France, proved his might against the Spanish foe, and set out to plant the foundations of what became one of England's most lucrative colonies.

The loss of the strategic ports and fertile land of Jamaica, on the other hand, certainly contributed to the decline of the Spanish Empire after 1660. Government officials could hardly ignore the "importance and vulnerability" of nearby colonies after the Western Design since the island, situated within the most lucrative trade routes of the Caribbean, served as an ideal base for potential attacks on Cuba, Hispaniola, Panama, and Mexico. Rivals, such as the French watching from Saint-Domingue, took note of diminishing Spanish power. Spain thus found itself facing threats in Tortuga and Hispaniola, prompting further strains on its treasuries and resources. In fact, the financial constraints under which the empire now operated, exacerbated by these attacks and the need to prepare against future threats, forced Spain to withdraw from the former island in 1660 despite having to repel a French attack on that island.[81]

Amanda J. Snyder

Making Jamaica English

Priorities and Processes

James Robertson

What was involved in establishing an English "colony of settlement" in the West Indies?[1] How far could pursuing such goals overlap with a newly conquered territory's ongoing transformation from a beleaguered military garrison into a slave-based "colony of exploitation"?[2] Contradictory priorities were a part of the wider experience of "reformulating Englishness" in many new colonies, but the clash between Oliver Cromwell's initial intentions for establishing a new English settlement in the Caribbean and its actual practice under Cromwell and the restored Stuart kings proved particularly conspicuous in Jamaica.[3] There the reconstruction of the island's society as an English colony began as a military occupation after its inadvertent conquest, seized by the "Western Design" that Cromwell sent to the Caribbean in December 1654 that had only diverted to Jamaica in May 1655 after its effort to conquer Hispaniola failed.[4] Then, as food supplies ran short, the expedition's soldiers faced an alternative of plant or starve.[5]

Initially the limited areas the English controlled were "run as a conquered territory administered by army officers," with the soldiers assigned to garrison duties required to spend two hours every morning and another two each evening in cultivating the land.[6] Despite the colony's military origins, its tropical climate, and its unfamiliar vegetation, along with the subsequent introduction of a plantation-based economy, the original goals of establishing a society based on English culture, with its essentially civilian structures of common law and limited representative government, remained persuasive. These were instituted, and when sugar and smuggling generated local fortunes, the beneficiaries chose to display their new wealth through importing English luxuries—including carriages and unsuitable London fashions—along with commissioning a strongly English-influenced creole architecture.[7]

The military imprint was prominent because retaining Jamaica remained uncertain in the face of persistent external threats and weak social bonds. The Western Design's unforeseen success in seizing the island had managed to fulfill one of the expedition's initial goals: establishing a base for English trading into and raiding against Spain's mainland American empire. The other side of this achievement was persistent fears that either Spanish reinforcements would arrive from its neighboring colonies or else the escorts from the next outward-bound Spanish fleet would make a detour and land invading troops. During its first five years— and, indeed, up to Spain's final cession of Jamaica in 1670 in the second Treaty of Madrid—the new colony faced an imminent "specter of Spain."[8]

Meanwhile the dogged resistance sustained by some persistent Spanish settlers not only destabilized English efforts at settlement but meant that an experienced set of local guides was available to lead any Spanish troops who landed on the island's south coast to attack the invaders' main settlements. Given the English army's misadventures during its own invasion of Hispaniola, many of which were because of their commander, Robert Venables, and his officers wandering without guides, this was a significant potential asset.[9] Fortunately for the English, the Spanish governor in St. Jago de Cuba, a professional soldier who had sought to command the campaign to recapture the island, knew better than to listen to the recommendations from the local resistance's Jamaican-born commander, Cristóbal Arnoldo Ysassi. Accordingly, he directed the reinforcements raised in 1657 in the other Spanish islands and again in 1658, those sent from Mexico, to land on Jamaica's north coast—more convenient for shipping from Cuba but on the wrong side of the island's rugged central mountains for an assault on the English population centers.[10] Afterwards Philip IV assigned greater importance to preserving the warships necessary to escort the annual fleets and their cargoes of American silver back to Spain in order to sustain his many European wars, so no Spanish squadron tried to fight its way into today's Kingston harbor or land experienced troops to attack the English garrison.[11]

Rather, the English spent much of their initial years in Jamaica fighting a tenacious Spanish settler resistance and preparing for Spanish invasions. As a result, the new settlement maintained a military organization and devoted a significant proportion of its resources into erecting batteries to command the entry into the harbor—in striking contrast to their Spanish predecessors, who had provided Jamaica with negligible funds for upgrading its defenses because the island had been the Columbus family's personal territory since 1536. In 1661 the new English strongpoint became Fort Cromwell, which was tactfully renamed Fort Charles after the restoration of the monarchy.[12] The English also laid out further defenses for their inland command center at the Spaniards' former principal settlement, a place the English knew as "the Town," "the Spanish Town," or "St. Jago de la Vega."[13]

This meant that the new settlers' efforts to secure Jamaica proved an unexpectedly protracted conquest. Despite the island's Spanish-born governor signing a surrender and departing within six weeks of the English landing, some island-born Spanish settlers still managed to hold out for five years. The prospects for either side winning had remained open up to 1660. It was only then that a band of African Jamaicans led by Juan de Bolas allied with the English.[14] This

James Robertson

prolonged campaigning not only led to the destruction of most of the Spanish colony's infrastructure and provided several years for bush to cover abandoned farms, fields, and pastures but also meant that the island continued to be run as a military operation. As a contemporary commented in 1657, "as yet Jamaica looks only like a great garrison," to be characterized "rather as an Army than a Collonie." This memorandum's author had therefore urged Lord Protector Cromwell to seek a "Convinceing way" to "declare that you will encourage, enforce, and protect planting," so that merchants in England would be persuaded the island was being settled and therefore a good enough credit risk to consign goods there, while experienced planters who settled elsewhere would choose to "speedily transplant, and repair thither." Such goals had already provided a rationalization for an ingenious proposal to order the Council in Scotland to identify Highlanders and other "troublemakers" who could be shipped off to Jamaica, where they would be equipped, given a hammock and issued firelock muskets for around seven pounds per head—inclusive of their passage out. Afterwards they would be transferred to island's treasurer, who would assign them a value of ten pounds each and then grant them to military officers, in lieu of the officers' accumulated back pay.[15]

This scheme to conscript Scots went no further, as Lord Broghill, lord president of the Protectorate Council for Scotland and an experienced Anglo-Irish politician, had already pointed out that if news circulated in Scotland of plans by Cromwell's regime "to press men for that service, it will put the whole country in a flame."[16] Other projects along similar lines still continued to circulate, however, with a proposal floated in October 1655 to ship out Irish girls and young women as brides for the English soldier-settlers sent on to the Irish military command for consideration.[17] Although that plan also went no further, the English government's long established policy of "shovelling out dissidents" meant involuntary Celtic emigrants were still consigned to the new colony, with "The Dirge of Ireland," a Gaelic-language poem from the late 1650s, incorporating a single English phrase, "Transport, Transplant go to Jamaica."[18]

Returning, however, to the original rationale for recommending such a radical proposal: although the Cromwellian government's efforts to line up enforced migrants were daunting for those caught up in them, the early migration and settlement of Cromwellian Jamaica remained insufficient to attract additional merchant-investors or for planters to consider the possibility of relocating to Jamaica.[19] With the introduction of such proposals into the discussions of Jamaica's development in London, the initial intentions for the Western Design to establish a godly civilian settlement in the Caribbean territory that it was to seize were subordinated to the pressing military need to protect the tentative foothold the English had secured on the island.

The Western Design's original social goals had led Cromwell to impose a complicated joint-command structure with civilians in the majority on the expedition's

Council of Commissioners. There were some early civilian settlements: early in 1656 one group of settlers relocating from Nevis disembarked at Yallahs to the east of the main harbor, where a fifth of them quickly died of fevers. Even this group soon needed to be supplemented by disbanded soldiers to prevent damage to the new colony's image if these civilians were attacked.[20] Then, as a thriving port with merchants and tradesmen, Cagway—later Port Royal—also began to house a civilian population by the late 1650s.[21] Even so, until the arrival of Charles II's newly appointed lieutenant governor in 1662, the island's government remained dominated by the army.

Turning this beleaguered garrison into a civil society was a challenge, but the invasion's officer corps included some of the more enthusiastic proponents of making these changes. Grants of land were issued early. When Admiral William Penn, Venables's co-commander, left for England in June 1655, he carried a bundle of land grants with him, presumably assigning slices of prime land to himself and those of his fellow senior officers who were returning with him. These have not survived, probably because the army's Council of War, reflecting the opinions of the officers remaining in Jamaica, passed a resolution after Penn's departure declaring that grants made to persistent absentees would lapse.[22]

Yet, the prospect of securing grants of land in a newly conquered territory was an attraction. Officers from the original expedition who remained after Venables departed in July could consider taking their accumulated back pay in land and foresee becoming civilian landowners. Before the English invaders had been on the island for a year, Colonel Francis Barrington's "resolutions [were] fixed for some years stay here."[23]

Making this decision work proved more difficult because capital would be needed, and as Barrington was only a cadet member of an English gentry family, he would either have had to use the still-unpaid arrears he was owed for his wartime service in Ireland or else tap his kinfolk for assistance. In the latter case he could make a persuasive pitch, as "the island is very promising, and great estates may be raysed by such as have good stocks to begin with."[24]

By 1657 Barrington's regiment was assigned to the Guanaboa Vale, "a pleasant and I hope fruitful place," near where the Columbus family had established substantial cocoa walks in the 1640s. In July he could report that "in this little time" he had "brought a plantation into handsome Condition" and was ready to expand on these foundations when the involuntary potential servants to be sent by Cromwell arrived—some of whom, Barrington had been informed, had been assigned to him, although he already had "a good stock of Cattle & Sheep, sufficient to undertake a Sugar work, were my purse so able, my stock of horses hath done me good service of late in bringing me meat from my hunters, & were they in Barbados would yield the best part of £1000 sterling, yet here did not cost me £30 sterling, therefore I can say that this Island is as hopefull a place for a new settler as any in this part of the world."[25]

His hopes still failed. Colonel Barrington was shot by a sentry while making the rounds of his troops, and no Barrington dynasty established itself in Jamaica. Other officers' families, however, did become successful dynasts. Some, particularly those descended from regicides or senior Cromwellian officials, so whose surnames made them unlikely to receive political advancement or peerages in Stuart or Hanoverian England no matter how wealthy they might become, remained in Jamaica into the twentieth and twenty-first centuries. As landowners these officers-turned-planters became some of the most fervent defenders of civilian power and local political rights, because they would not want further incoming officials either telling them and their descendants what to do or casting any legal doubts on the land tenures they had secured. They included men like ex-lieutenant Samuel Long, the former secretary to the Council of Commissioners, who as the Speaker of Jamaica's House of Assembly in 1678–81, would offer staunch defenses of the liberties of the colonists as Englishmen and of their legal rights, first in the old wooden Spanish *audiencia* building in Spanish Town, where the Assembly of Jamaica met, and then in Whitehall Palace before Charles II and his Privy Council.[26]

The island's future remained uncertain for two years after Cromwell's death, when reinforcements and supplies from England dried up and the warships stationed in Jamaica became increasingly unseaworthy. Jamaica remained cut off from English affairs, so that even after proclaiming Charles II's Restoration, Edward D'Oyley, the island's military commander, still delayed using the new king's regnal years—which dated from his father's execution in January 1649—in his official journal for a further sixteen months.[27] During this prolonged transition, Ysassi, the leader of the Spanish resistance whom Philip IV had appointed governor of Jamaica, cherished hopes that D'Oyley could be bribed to order an English withdrawal.[28] English settlers commented that D'Oyley himself believed it likely that the government in England would return Jamaica to Spain whenever a peace was negotiated and "hindered those that were willing to plant, by telling them they would all be called off."[29]

Thus, the process of transformation from garrison command to civilian rule was only accomplished by Charles II's government after it decided to retain Jamaica. Demobilization of the remaining Cromwellian troops, who were paid off with land grants and cash raised through the duties levied on imported brandy, was accompanied by a royal proclamation offering English rights, along with the king's new governor establishing an assembly and extending the concessionary trade duties Cromwell had offered to the new colony—all adjuncts of English status that would encourage prospective settlers. Order would be maintained over those former Cromwellian veterans who did not choose to ship aboard the buccaneers, turtle hunters, and smugglers operating out of Port Royal by a militia led by the island's landowners and by a local government system transferred from England, which was based on the vestries of a newly established branch of the English state church.[30] Since the underpopulated and newly Royalist island remained more vulnerable than other English colonies in the Eastern Caribbean, there was a de facto religious toleration, with Jews arriving from England. And, in striking contrast to Barbados, Quaker settlers were left untroubled: there are no entries of Jamaican persecutions in the "Books of Sufferings" kept by the Society of Friends in England, and when George Fox visited Jamaica, he was invited to dinner by the governor.[31] This might not be how things were being managed in the rest of Charles II's dominions, but they constituted efforts to persuade minority groups to migrate from England to royal Jamaica.

This colony that new settlers encountered after 1660 had changed abruptly since the English invasion. First, a prolonged war saw the erasure of much of the landscape constructed by 160 years of Spanish rule and, indeed, several hundred years of Taíno residence too. Afterwards, a new civilian colonial society had to be reconstructed on foundations laid during the military occupation. The resulting overlay was certainly framed on English usages, which included the common law and a consultative element in the island's government. From the first, however, the new settlement also reflected practices—most conspicuously including slave-holding and plantation agriculture—developed over the previous twenty years of English settlement and sugar boom in the Eastern Caribbean.[32] The introduction of the buccaneer culture that had also developed in the Eastern Caribbean during the mid-seventeenth century offered a further alternative to transplanted English usages, as many ex-soldiers and then indentured laborers out of their terms of service preferred hunting in the interior or maritime ventures against the Spaniards to the continued grind of clearing newly regrown bush, hewing fields out of tropical forests, or even overseeing the newly landed indentured Europeans or enslaved Africans who undertook these tasks.

The island's English settlers acknowledged that this had been a long-settled place. The stories they told to newcomers invoked Spanish ghosts processing in St. Mary's Parish on the island's north side, riding around Spanish Town's old streets and squares, or as ever, concealing treasure in mountain caves.[33] But, once the English successfully seized Jamaica and then finally ousted their predecessors, what alternatives were there for its development, and how were these projects overlaid onto what was already in place?

Here John Rashford's researches have reaffirmed the continued presence of agricultural transplants from both the Taíno and the Spanish periods, with the Taínos' cassava remaining a staple.[34] Gardens housed oranges, both bitter and sweet, along with lemons and limes, pomegranates and figs, all acknowledged as Spanish imports; palm trees, transferred in an extension of the "Columbian Exchange" from the Indian Ocean via Portuguese galleons and the Cape Verde Islands, were already naturalized, as were bananas, which had arrived via the Canary Islands.[35] A "Guava walk" and a "Plum Walk" were both cited in early land grants, while tamarind trees, themselves testifying to earlier wayfarers' nibbling, shaded some rural crossroads.[36] Many of these legacies were long lasting, with

Victorian visitors remarking at the surviving avenues of ancient tamarinds they saw in Spanish Town and at another rural site near the Bog Walk Gorge.[37] Later English residents also noted Annotto as another Spanish transplant.[38] We can see this varied botanical legacy taken still further in the prominence assigned to the pineapple, itself a Taíno introduction, in the coat of arms designed in London for the new royal colony in 1662. Imaginations at the royal court were captured by a fruit that had only recently been introduced into English glasshouses.

In the wider English society, a further Spanish-era introduction, cocoa, made an even larger impact on the island's development after 1660. The cocoa walks of the Columbus family in Guanaboa, north of Spanish Town, comprised twelve thousand trees rented out at one silver peso a year. These were taken over by the English garrison stationed there, for whom the "Sixteen Mile Walk" provided an early landmark. Officers soon began shipping cocoa beans back to England, and if some of these sacks were loot from raids on Spanish territories and shipping, others were Jamaican-grown.[39] Chocolate soon became a fashionable drink, its virtues "hyperbolize'd upon every post in *London*."[40]

Under Charles II, court gallants turned to chocolate as a morning pick-me-up, while in 1661 the newly appointed physician to the first royal governor of Jamaica, Thomas, Lord Windsor, used his time while Windsor's fleet was delayed in London to compile a monograph on how to prepare chocolate. A long discussion on the merits of using either a marble or a heatable cast-iron table to grind chocolate cakes demonstrates the seriousness applied to this tasty drink that was becoming established in London as an alternative to the equally newly arrived coffee.[41]

At this juncture it could be proposed that Jamaica would complement the flourishing colony of Barbados, with Barbados producing the sugar while Jamaica produced the cocoa. This optimistic future was not to be. In 1670–71 a blight wiped out most of the cocoa walks on the southern side of the island, and the Spaniards refused to allow the English to import replacement saplings from Venezuela. Afterwards Charles's metropolitan subjects would flock to coffee houses, to talk politics and drink Turkish-grown coffee while planters in Jamaica turned to growing sugar. By 1687 Port Royal had a coffee house too.[42]

In Jamaica the place names from the seventeenth-century expansion of sugar cultivation still survive today, while most of the place names from cocoa's landscape, which had included such evocative early names as "Hutt hill" and "the Labyrinth" are long gone.[43] Until the blight struck, however, cocoa walks, with the tender saplings sheltered between lines of plantains, appeared to promise the highest returning investments for improving the value of an estate. Thus an agreement for splitting the revenues on an estate in St. Catherine's Parish promised a sharecropping deal on the existing cocoa plants, with the tenant receiving a tenth of the revenues so long as he kept them alive and free of weeds while, to encourage further planting, he was to "receive for every hundred cocoa trees he soe plant which shall stand one year after they are planted the sum of three shillings Current money" in order to promote "his Extraordinary care and pains." Such efforts had sought to make the Rio Magno estate, with its Spanish-sounding name, into a profit center for its well-connected grantee's family.[44] It would take an unforeseen plant disease to forestall such hopeful plans.

Whatever crops were to be grown, the most conspicuous impact of English rule was the clearing of the island's woods to extend the amount of land under sugar cultivation. For the next century, then, ringing and burning Jamaica's primeval forest cover absorbed massive efforts. The expansion of agricultural holdings proceeded unevenly and not just because well-connected courtiers or the cronies of successive governors secured massive blocks of land that then remained undeveloped but also because settlers rarely applied for grants of blocks of solid forest. Instead, edge territories were particularly sought. These would include woodland that offered the prospect of richer soils for sugar once it was cleared, but they would also incorporate savanna land, where cattle or sheep could be grazed in the meantime, along with the oxen required to turn the sugar mills. Hence, in St. Catherine's Parish, a string of early surveys and land grants were sited near the former Spanish-era defensive works "the Half Moon," where the road up from Passage Fort to Spanish Town left the coastal forest and entered the savanna.[45] Here experienced residents could recognize the ebony growing "everywhere" on the savannas, which had "a yellow flower like English broom, and, after it rains, puts forth its flowers making the savannas look like English broom-fields."[46] Meanwhile, new settlers wrote home claiming to "more & more . . . love the Countrey for to see how bravely the canes grow & how the negroes goe tumbling down the trees."[47]

Such a radical transformation of hardwood tropical forest demanded brutally hard work and necessarily proceeded very slowly. Inventories generally list hatchets, crowbars, wedges, and crosscut saws among the equipment for farms, but the acreages available to grow sugar remained limited: in a seventeenth-century lease for an estate of eight hundred or a thousand acres, perhaps thirty or thirty-five were planted with canes.[48] This newly cleared land, however, was fresh, and even these ratios would still appear profitable with tenants committing themselves to pay substantial rents. The same inventories also list livestock, which occupied a far more prominent place in this landscape in transition. They help explain the prickly hedges, be they of limes or else of the "Barbados Flower Fence . . . so called from their fencing in their plantations with this shrub, which is full of short strong prickles; . . . commonly called in Jamaica *doodledoes*."[49] Such small hedged-in fields are a long way from the open, cane-dominated landscapes that visiting artists and local land surveyors sketched and planned in the late eighteenth and early nineteenth century.[50]

If the botanical carryover from Spanish Jamaica was substantial, most nonbotanical imprints from either the Taíno or the Spanish presence were overlaid fairly rapidly. English settlers did not continue to use many Spanish-era houses. Within a generation the old houses that remained standing on Spanish Town's streets and at the town's edge appeared "very rustic" and remarkable survivors; a survey conducted there as early as 1663 cited "an old Ruined Street."[51] There might be another old Spanish house used as a tavern in Yallas and a large house at Ligonea, but other examples of reused properties soon became scarce.[52]

The prolonged guerrilla war where the English had destroyed many Spanish settlements proved harsh on the building stock of a poor colony. Even if individual English settlers took over Spanish-era estates, they tended to build anew instead of reusing older structures. A lease that Colonel Thomas Lynch, the colony's provost marshal, signed in 1664 described his thousand-acre seat, which included a "ruined plantation about Six acres" alongside a "new shingled Mill House and Mill frames," in addition to a boiling house, curing house, and still house, all characterized as "new" also, and his two-story dwelling house. This indeed contained "A Gilded Spanish Bed Head," a "Large Spanish Chest," and even a forty- or fifty-pound bell "unhung"; but the estate remained an English space.[53]

The main Spanish roads remained in use, while land grants and local maps still noted old Spanish paths, too; however, outside Spanish Town most of the buildings left behind by Jamaica's former inhabitants were soon demolished or else submerged beneath swiftly spreading tropical bush.[54] As the landscape was transformed, older common pastures and rights of access became increasingly vulnerable to encroachment by larger planters.[55] By 1684 the colony's assembly had to pass a law "For keeping open old Paths to Publick Watering-places," which established a procedure for local juries to testify to the existence of older routes that had been blocked within the previous seven years.[56]

The island's economy correspondingly underwent a rapid period of change. First, the prolonged guerrilla war wiped out most of the herds of semi-wild cattle on the southern side of the island, which had been central to the Spanish economy. Some cattle survived on the northern coastal plain and herds were driven south, to be sold and butchered near Spanish Town, where their meat fed both townspeople and the ships putting into Port Royal, which drew on the markets around the enclosed bay that became Kingston harbor for provisions.[57]

Mostly, however, the new royal colony grew tropical crops for export: sugar, yes, but also tobacco and cocoa, which were all cited in the first meeting of the Governor's Council of the new royal colony in a price-per-pound listing that aimed to establish official rates of exchange to allow the use of merchantable produce as currency.[58] A month later, cotton and indigo were added to the list.[59] Merchants soon objected to the quality of the island's tobacco, and within two years it ceased to be accepted as currency despite all the claims made for the superlative quality of Jamaica-grown tobacco in the briefing sheets written to encourage Charles II to retain this Cromwellian-conquered island. A comparable rapid decline hit tobacco exports from late seventeenth-century Guadeloupe, too, as "the weed" glutted metropolitan markets.[60]

Nor did cotton prove particularly profitable: not only did very few planta-tions remain in operation, but also the first slave revolt on the southern side of the island occurred at one Mrs. Grey's cotton plantation in 1682.[61] Indigo remained in production longer, and John Taylor, a minor gentleman from England who visited the island in 1687 with the intention of settling, made extensive notes describing its potential cash crops, taking considerable pains to note all the details on how this blue dye was produced. Yet, another knowledgeable contemporary's comment that "the way of making indigo is so difficult, that many planters never obtain it" suggests how inexperience, or the loss of a key specialist worker, would result in a far worse return for an investment than sugar promised. In its day, though, the crop flourished, and stray descendants of cultivated indigo plants continue to grow wild in the Yallahs Valley floodplain.[62]

Nor, once we move away from the coastal plains, was the hinterland left untouched. To begin with, its wild pigs and feral cattle offered a resource for the hunters. For a short while, at least, the cattle-killing economy that had sustained the first buccaneers on the north side of Hispaniola was adopted in Jamaica to try to feed the starving army. During the last years of military rule on the island, when supplies ran short, hunting parties contributed significant additional sup-plies. Most of the surviving licenses were issued to army officers, whose hunting parties were ordered to collect meat and not just hides. However, one early grant in 1659 to "Claude le Februs and Isaac Mansch Frenchmen to hunt and kill hoggs and beife provided they . . . come not within six miles of any [of] the officers hunting by the generall's order already," suggests that the officers' grants operated alongside individual buccaneers from Hispaniola recruited as hunters.[63] "The Frenchman's Station" that still provided a landmark in St. James Parish into the mid-1680s potentially recalled this period.[64] Englishmen had cabins, too, with "a place called Bagnalls hutt" a landmark in Palmetto Valley, St. Mary, in 1671.[65] Further early descriptions suggest how far hunting, along with game trails, had already helped define local landscapes: a land grant in the 1670s in St. Andrews was bounded "on a hunting path leading to Yallahs Mountain," while early land grants in St. Elizabeth Parish were bisected by "a hunting path" or else lay "near the hunters station."[66] Some of these routes ran along mountain ridge tops, as in the "Orange Ridge path" that ran parallel to part of the Wag Water Valley.[67]

After the guerrilla war eased off, hunting appeared even more appealing. Among the first laws the planter-dominated assembly passed were regulations to restrict the ownership of "gangs of dogs" to licensed freeholders with at least five acres, albeit with a few further licenses granted to individual worthy veterans, sug-gesting that ranging the forests offered an all-too-tempting alternative to free poor whites and indentured laborers. In discouraging such options, even planters were constrained, forbidden from keeping packs of hounds for their servants' use.[68]

The impact of the English settlement then extended farther inland still. Another law, which forbade the use of dogwood tree bark to poison fish in streams or ponds, offered a pioneering exercise in local ecological legislation although, like another law seeking to protect the island's carrion crows, it may indicate what continued to occur instead of halting an irresponsible process.[69] Meanwhile, lumbering and land clearance both had a wider impact in transforming the island: a law included among the island's 1683 laws for clearing "the River called *Rio Cobre,* or the Town River that passeth by St. *Jago* De *La Vega*" noted that the river had already "wholly lost its old Channel by means of the extraordinary Floods, and by the abundance of Trees and great quantities of Rubbish that hath been fallen above the said River, and upon other small Rivers and Gullies that fall into the same." Accordingly, several plantations were already vulnerable to flooding "upon small Floods," and it appeared evident that if nothing was done, "all the settlements and Sugar-works thereabouts will be altogether lost, and what is good Manurable Land now will be turned into mere Bog and Morass." These threats prompted the assembly to assign extensive powers to a new drainage commission to clear, dredge, and if necessary redirect the river's course.[70]

The continuing repercussions of land clearances were still not recognized for what they were. John Taylor's eager verdict in 1687 on the natural fertility of Jamaica, claiming "that the Plantations, are as much improved after the great rains, as our European Corn field are by Soyling with dung," probably says more about erosion upstream than all "the rotting trees and dung driven by the Violent rains from off the Mountains thither" that he invoked.[71] Instead, the level of erosion became even worse: in September 1708 the Long family's by then long-held estate at Lucky Valley in Clarendon Parish was subject to ferocious flooding, which not only pushed down walls but then buried the trenches in its cane fields "3 foot deep in Gravil & sand."[72] The list of potential developments continued with various attempts to prospect for minerals—if not gold, then silver or copper. These projects found investors, and even if the one group of indentured mineralogists sent out to search for all these treasures chose "under pretence of searching for Mines," to go "to Planters Houses, & get Drunk," instead of digging test pits to enrich the shareholders, they and their successors' efforts left further scars.[73] Such endeavors failed to deliver any profits but demonstrate that early Jamaica was never considered a purely agricultural colony.

The English settlers and their activities in reshaping the island's landscape remain well represented in the surviving records. Such settlers, however, were not the island's only residents during this period. The ex-*cimmarones,* particularly, remained a further distinct presence, although the English colonists consistently downplayed the military role of the "Spanish Negroes," the former members of Juan de Bolas's band, whose leader had negotiated terms for his people, including land grants upriver from Spanish Town.[74] Their settlement remained a presence for a generation, especially as they maintained at least one "Gate" across the king's highway, which presumably enabled them to take tolls from travelers.[75]

Nor was this all: some free African-Caribbean groups in the colony retained distinct skills. During a botanizing trip across Jamaica in 1687–88, Dr. Hans Sloane noticed rice planted "by some Negroes, on their own Plantations," where it thrived, but because it remained an unfamiliar crop for English farmers, requiring "much beating, and a particular Art to separate the Grain from the Husk . . . most Planters" ignored it as "too troublesome."[76]

Similarly, in his botanical explorations, Sloane found a wide range of unfamiliar herbs and vegetables cultivated in the garden plots of African-Caribbean and Amerindian farmers, free and enslaved.[77] The African names applied to plants used by local physicians testify to the intermediary experience of African-born plant collectors, whose hard-won knowledge could be bartered with European physicians or used as cures for the many illnesses of hard labor in a tropical climate.[78]

From the very start of the English colony, the preexisting African-Caribbean population retained an independent place in the landscape. During the late seventeenth century, particularly after the disastrous 1692 earthquake destroyed most of the English houses on the island, marronage became a greater problem for the colonial government. The *cimmarone* groups at the northeast of the island who refused terms in the 1660s were subsequently joined by other groups incorporating individual runaways, by survivors from a wrecked slave ship and, indeed, by slaves from several plantations who had rebelled successfully.[79] When the perceived threat of attacks by the Leeward Maroons meant that individual settlers became liable to arrest and taking on a bond for twenty pounds if they traveled farther than two miles from their home without carrying a loaded pistol or light musket, then the governor and his council, who issued this order, recognized that Jamaica's woods and mountains were indeed inhabited.[80] The Jamaican landscape beyond the plantation perimeters was never empty.

Then, despite the Spanish ceding their claims to Jamaica in 1670, from the late 1670s the island's domestic threats were increasingly supplemented by fears of external assaults. A French flotilla prompted alarms in 1679.[81] Then, in the aftermath of the great 1692 earthquake which not only destroyed most of Port Royal but also leveled thirty years of brick construction across the island, Jamaica appeared increasingly vulnerable to raids from the French in Saint-Domingue.[82] In 1694 a major raid led by Governor Jean-Baptiste du Casse incorporated a substantial contingent of *flibustiers,* who destroyed the English settlements along the coastal parishes of southeastern Jamaica. Afterwards the colony's white settlers had further foci for their nightmares, while Jamaica became a base for English attacks on Saint-Domingue.[83]

Within a very few years, English-ruled Jamaica was already very different from the Spanish colony that the Western Design had first seized and then just managed to hold onto. In addition to the secular institutions established under the Stuart

James Robertson

monarchs, including elements of the common law and, in its House of Assembly, of Westminster-style constitutional practice, the colony adopted the Church of England. The rectors of these churches were well paid, and even if few attended their sermons, they still earned substantial fees from conducting funerals.[84]

These were all the adjuncts of an "English" colony. Yet, while exports could pay for imported English cloth and other markers of prosperity, while houses that deliberately reproduced aspects of fashionable English building styles provided settings in Port Royal for colonists' displays of "worldly vanity . . . second only to London," maintaining a white population that could deliver the men necessary to oversee the enslaved workers and fill the ranks of the militia who constituted the core of the vulnerable colony's defenses was always difficult—even before yellow fever became endemic later in the century.[85]

White immigrants continued to be welcomed and could hope for land grants, most conspicuously the contingent of experienced English sugar planters who left Suriname in 1671. They obtained grants in "the Surinam Quarters" near the coast on what was then the island's western frontier. By then most of the Jamaican families who subsequently became enormously wealthy had already established themselves, although James Bannister, the refugees' leader whom Charles II had promoted from major to major general, would buck that trend, receiving grants amounting to almost three thousand acres and a seat on the island's council. Although he was murdered in 1672, his family flourished, with his widow accumulating grants to a further thirty-six hundred acres. In 1694 Bannister's son, also named James, became the first island-born "Creolian" appointed to the colony's council.[86]

In Jamaica's still only partially anglicized landscape, the settlers soon began polishing stories to reaffirm their shared English past, selecting from the Western Design's actions to highlight the remaining colonists' achievements in overcoming the Spaniards. They then sought to fit their settlement's origins into the contentious narratives of history and politics roiling Charles II's England. The king and his courtiers never forgot that Jamaica was one of Cromwell's conquests, quite soon the only one of the Protectorate's territorial acquisitions that the king had not alienated. Charles's Jamaican subjects still sought to reaffirm the common culture they shared as Englishmen and English women who had chosen to relocate to Jamaica.[87] Being "English" in late-seventeenth-century Jamaica was often as much a goal as an achievement; it remained a goal that the island's local leaders desperately sought to achieve.

The Danish West Indies, 1660s–1750s

Formative Years

Erik Gøbel

The Danish West Indies were made up of the three islands of St. Thomas, St. John, and St. Croix, colonized in 1672, 1718, and 1735, respectively. The islands are part of the Virgin Islands, located just east of Puerto Rico, and today they are the United States Virgin Islands. The former Danish islands are not very big; together they comprise 134 square miles. St. Thomas and St. John are rather alike, as they are mountainous and almost without any flat surfaces suitable for agriculture. St. Croix, on the other hand, benefited from a large and fertile plain, which makes up about half of the island and which turned out to be well suited for growing sugar cane. A problem on all three islands, however, was that the rainfall, while certainly sufficient, was much too irregular.

When it came to harbors, St. Croix was handicapped because its only harbor was at the town of Christiansted, but its coral reefs made landing there difficult. At the only other town on the island, Frederiksted, was just an open roadstead. On St. John, in contrast, there existed a good natural harbor with practically no traffic, while St. Thomas was favored with one of the best natural harbors in the Caribbean, the large protected bay at the town of Charlotte Amalie. These natural conditions meant that the economy of the islands developed rather differently through the centuries, even until today. On St. Thomas the most important activities had to do with shipping and trade—local, regional, and international—whereas St. Croix developed into an agricultural island, dominated first and foremost by the growing of sugar cane. Little St. John was for most of the time very quiet, and the island was considered more or less just an appendix to St. Thomas.[1]

Shipping to Guinea under the Danish flag commenced in 1647 by the Danish king's subjects in Glückstadt on the Elbe River,[2] but such sailings were not institutionalized until a Guinea trading company was established in Copenhagen in 1656 and a corresponding company in Glückstadt in 1659. Navigation was sporadic, but the Glückstadters succeeded in getting hold of Fort Frederiksberg on the Gold Coast.[3] Shipping to the Caribbean was begun from Copenhagen in 1652 by a successful expedition under the command of Erik Nielsen Smith. More sailings were accomplished over the next years, and in 1665 an expedition was sent out to colonize St. Thomas. In spite of the fine natural harbor, no other Europeans had settled that island. England had for a long time claimed sovereignty over St. Thomas, but as they did not want to settle the island themselves, they accepted the Danish initiative. Also Spain, in spite of its principal claim over the entire American world, put up with the Danish presence. Nevertheless, the attempt was in vain and had to be abandoned, as the few colonists suffered because of the lack of resources and insufficient support from home.

To strengthen the efforts, the Danish state established in 1671 a chartered trading company in Copenhagen, which would raise necessary capital and be in charge of navigation, colonization, and trade to St. Thomas. After 1674, it also took over responsibility of the Danish activities in Guinea—and consequently became the royal chartered Danish West India and Guinea Company. Nevertheless, the Caribbean became the main area of interest for the company, which existed until 1754.[4]

The first company vessel arrived after a prolonged and difficult voyage from Denmark to St. Thomas on May 25, 1672. Accompanying Governor Jørgen Iversen were 104 settlers, who started immediately to clear land for cultivation of provision crops such as cassava, millet, yams, potatoes, and beans. Construction of a fortification, Fort Christian, was also begun at once so that the settlers could defend themselves if necessary. The West India and Guinea Company managed to provide a fairly regular navigation, and a small European colonial society developed on St. Thomas, from which colonial products such as tobacco, indigo, ginger, and cotton were exported; as time went on, even the coveted raw sugar was shipped to Denmark. In 1674 a proud Governor Iversen shipped thirteen pounds of raw sugar, "being the first sugar, which has been produced at the Company's plantation, in a small keg."[5] Nonetheless, many of the colonial products that were shipped home during the early period originated from foreign islands in the Caribbean, where the Danes had purchased them in exchange for foodstuffs and other necessities sent out from Denmark.

It was difficult to attract or compel enough of the king's subjects to emigrate from Denmark to the West Indies, even though both indentured workers and prisoners were sent out. Instead, all Europeans from other Caribbean islands were welcomed if they wished to settle on St. Thomas. Consequently the white population became very cosmopolitan. The first census was taken in 1688.[6] At this time, only forty persons lived in the town of Charlotte Amalie next to Fort Christian; the remaining 690 inhabitants lived on plantations around the island, and in addition there were a few soldiers and company employees. On St. Thomas were 338 free inhabitants, 13 indentured laborers, 375 African slaves, and 4 Indian slaves. Half of the free adults were Dutchmen, while only every seventh was a Dane. In this settler society the planter and his family often worked hard side by side with the few slaves they owned. The planter often even had to supplement his earnings by doing other kinds of work—for instance, fishing.

Plantation culture peaked on St. Thomas in the middle of the 1720s, when there were 167 plantations under cultivation, of which 77 grew sugar cane, 74 grew cotton, and 9 grew provision crops, while the rest grew a mixture of crops. The population had risen to 4,814 persons, of whom 93 percent were enslaved; on average each plantation had 26 slaves at its disposal. Thereafter the population declined drastically; in 1754 there lived only 228 free persons and 3,481 enslaved persons on the island.

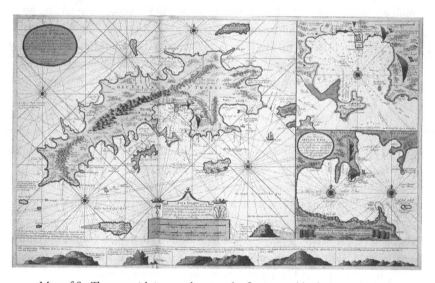

Map of St. Thomas with inserts showing the fine natural harbors at Charlotte Amalie (top right) and Coral Bay on the east end of St. John (bottom right). Both harbors were protected by fortifications—Fort Christian on St. Thomas and the small fort on St. John, where the slave rebellion was started in 1733. This map was made in 1718 and published in Gerard van Keulen's *De groote Nieuwe Vermeerde Zee-Atlas*, vol. 4 (Amsterdam, 1734). Courtesy of the Danish National Archives.

On St. Thomas shipping and trade soon became the most important source of income and remained so during all the Danish times. During the early period, relations with the neighboring islands—French St. Croix, English Tortola, and Spanish Puerto Rico—played an important role. After 1673 Jørgen Iversen, for instance, supplied St. Croix with European commodities such as clothing, food-stuffs, brandy, and gunpowder, for which he received in return, first and fore-most, raw sugar and tobacco.[7] On Puerto Rico the Danes exchanged slaves and European produce for tobacco, sugar, indigo, hides, and tortoiseshell. Also,

Erik Gøbel

close trading connections with the North American continent were established. So, when Governor Iversen examined the economic situation in 1676, the West India and Guinea Company had outstanding claims amounting to two hundred thousand pounds of sugar on other islands, particularly St. Croix.[8] (Sugar was the unit of accounting, as there was no cash economy on St. Thomas during the early years.)

The most essential traffic, however, went across the Atlantic to and from Denmark and Guinea. Shipping sailed either directly to St. Thomas or along the triangular route via Africa.[9] Early cargoes consisted typically of foodstuffs, manufactures, military equipment, and clothing.[10] In addition to a few necessary supplies to maintain the Danes on the African coast, cargoes from Denmark to Guinea consisted of commodities for the slave trade, above all East Indian cotton textiles, firearms, cowries, corals, and brandy, as well as various metal goods. From Guinea to the Caribbean, the holds were crowded with enslaved Africans and small quantities of gold and ivory. From around 1690, raw sugar became the most important product shipped from the Caribbean to Denmark; later it became totally dominant among colonial commodities.

When Fort Christian on St. Thomas was finished in 1680 and the colony was going well, Jørgen Iversen returned to Denmark. Unfortunately, his successors turned out not to be equal to the task of colonial administration. They conspired often with interlopers and, for example, granted a safe conduct to prominent pirates such as Bartholomew Sharp and William Kidd, which brought the island a notorious reputation.[11] Furthermore, the West India and Guinea Company had problems with maintaining sufficient shipping from Denmark, notwithstanding its monopoly on buying and exporting the produce of the island.

Consequently, the company tentatively entrusted its obligations to the Norwegian (Bergen) trader Jørgen Thormøhlen in 1690, but he also soon ran into problems with the profits, so he withdraw from this West India business in 1694. Between 1689 and 1697, the company likewise leased out its commercial and shipping rights to Guinea to Nicolai Jansen Arff, a Copenhagen-based ship owner. Against a recognition of two percent of the value of the slaves, which he shipped to the West Indies, he also agreed to pay the expenses for keeping the Danish forts and factories on the Gold Coast. Here Fort Christiansborg was the Danish headquarters after 1685.[12]

The West India and Guinea Company had already in 1685 signed a treaty with the newly established Brandenburg Africa Company, which was allowed to found a trading station on St. Thomas just outside Charlotte Amalie and to maintain it for thirty years. The Brandenburgers only had to pay a modest tribute. They established a plantation and started trading slaves from Africa to the Spanish colonies. Until 1699 they played a certain role with regard to the growth of the Danish colony and its economic life, even though there was a good deal of friction between the two parties.[13]

Friction was also inevitable between the monopoly company and the planters, who longed for looser reins and better profits. In 1706 and again in 1715, they sent delegations to the authorities in Denmark and demanded free trade (against the interests of the company, of course), reduction of taxes and dues, and local influence on the local government. Especially during the War of the Spanish Succession (1702–13), it was possible to make high profits under the neutral Danish flag.[14] The king ordered the company to comply with a number of the wishes; the planters were allowed, for instance, to export their produce to all places in Europe and America, except for Denmark and Norway.

St. Thomas was eventually brought fully under cultivation and the Danes wanted to expand their colony. Close by and to the east lay St. John, which the Danes had had to abandon as early as 1675, as both Spaniards and Englishmen protested their presence indignantly. But on March 25, 1718, Governor Erik Bredahl simply landed on St. John and planted the Danish flag. A handful of settlers and their slaves started immediately to establish a fortification on Fortsberg. Soon, also, planters from St. Thomas and foreign islands began to arrive to enjoy the offer of free land and seven years of exemption from taxation, in addition to permission to take as much timber and chalk as they needed to erect buildings on their plantations. In return they were obliged to have a white man on their plantations and to build sugar works within five years.

The result was that, starting in 1721, some plantations on St. John were able to generate a profit, and in 1729 St. John was almost totally cultivated with one hundred plantations, which grew sugar cane and cotton as well as small quantities of tobacco, indigo, and provision crops. A typical plantation of 150 acres would have a workforce that consisted of a manager and half a dozen slaves, but parts of the ground were often left as bush. The total population of St. John increased in 1733 to 208 free persons and 1,087 slaves. The vast majority of planters preferred to live on St. Thomas instead of a more or less isolated plantation on St. John. Almost half of the owners were Dutch. Surveying and development happened gradually as newcomers arrived; plantations were most often situated by the coast, where it was easy to have supplies of building materials and later to export sugar and other colonial products.

St. John had been totally cultivated by the mid-1720s, and the economy was going well, when suddenly everything was upset in 1733.[15] On November 23 of that year a rebellion broke out among the slaves on the small island. Led by Amina warriors of the Akwamu nation, the slaves captured the fort on the east end of St. John and soon after gained control over the whole island. The white colonists were either killed or managed to escape to nearby St. Thomas, or they defended themselves, assisted by a few nonparticipating slaves on an outer point belonging to Pieter Duurloe's plantation. Soldiers were immediately sent from St. Thomas to counter the rebels but without success; the rebels, fighting like guerrillas, succeeded in keeping their dominion over the island. Relief forces from other islands

Erik Gøbel

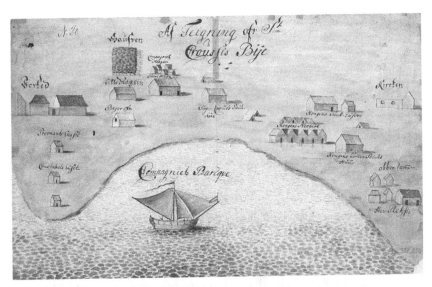

Map of St. Croix by Jens Michelsen Beck, 1754, showing the nine quarters and the many regular plantation grounds of the island. At this time there were ninety-four horse mills and twenty windmills, used primarily for crushing sugar cane. At the top are shown the town plans for Frederiksted (left) and Christiansted. Courtesy of the Danish National Archives.

were sent, but it was not until May–June 1734 that a French detachment succeeded in suppressing the last of the rebels. So, the revolt was one of the longest lasting in the history of the Caribbean. It must be remembered, however, that not all slaves in St. John participated in the rebellion; some did not believe in possible success, while others took the opportunity to run maroon and seek their own fortune in the wilderness. Yet, the plantation economy on St. John recovered after the rebellion with amazing rapidity. By 1739 the number of slaves had risen to 1,414, whereas the number of Europeans was even fewer than before the rebellion.

A new extension of the colony took place when St. Croix was purchased from France in 1733. This island is situated around forty miles to the south of St. Thomas and St. John, and it is somewhat larger than the other two. Sovereignty of St. Croix had been disputed, but since 1650 it had been under control of the French. They left it, nonetheless, practically uninhabited by 1695 and were willing to sell it to the Danish West India and Guinea Company; its acquisition by friendly Danes prevented France's enemy, the English, from acquiring the island.[16]

Taken over by the Danes in January 1735, St. Croix was quickly and efficiently surveyed and developed into plantation grounds; two thousand by three thousand feet was the standard size. Furthermore, the town of Christiansted was founded on the northern coast with a fort, church, squares, warehouses, and a grid of regular streets.[17] A large proportion of the planters coming to St. Croix were foreigners, in particular Englishmen, Scotsmen, and Frenchmen—as well as, of course, the many enslaved Africans who made up by far the largest portion of the population.

By the mid-1740s around 250 plantations were in full operation on the island, and in 1751 Governor Jens Hansen reported to the board of directors in Copenhagen that practically all arable land had been brought under cultivation. Ten years later, there were 134 sugar plantations (on the most fertile ground), 34 cotton plantations (on the poorest soil), and 207 plantations with mixed crops on St. Croix. The slave population on the island amounted at that time to 8,500 persons, while the Europeans numbered a mere 1,300, of whom two-thirds were English. In 1752 the town of Frederiksted was founded on the west end of the island. The plantation economy on St. Croix was increasing heavily by the middle of the century, while it had decreased since the 1720s on St. Thomas and St. John, where only 154 and 72 plantations, respectively, were run by 3,500 and 2,000 slaves.[18]

The plantations in the Danish West Indies were, just as in other Caribbean colonies, run by African slaves, and ships under the Danish flag participated in the transatlantic slave trade. It was, however, not until the second half of the eighteenth century that the Danish slave trade reached considerable dimensions, and Denmark became the seventh largest slave-trading nation, transporting an estimated 111,000 slaves across the Atlantic from the 1660s to 1806.[19]

Before 1755 the Danes shipped 39,000 enslaved Africans, approximately 2 percent of the total transatlantic slave trade to the Caribbean during that period from 1657 to 1755.[20] Such Danish-transported human cargoes were most frequent between 1690–1701 and 1747–55. Danish ships disembarked their slaves first and foremost in the Danish West Indies (35,000 slaves), but during the years 1679–95, more than 3,000 enslaved Africans were shipped directly to the Dutch Caribbean islands. Part of the cargoes of slaves that were imported to the Danish West Indies were re-exported immediately to other nations' islands, but the amount of this trade is not known. In addition to the trade of Danish ships, around 7,000 slaves were imported from Africa to the Danish West Indies under foreign flags, by far the most under the Dutch colors during the War of Spanish Succession.

The Danish trade on the Gold Coast and especially Danish involvement in the terrible transport along the Middle Passage across the Atlantic are discussed elsewhere.[21] It has been demonstrated that conditions of the Danish slave trade and on board the slave ships were very much similar to those conducted by other slave-trading Europeans, when it came to sailing routes, duration of voyages, mortality, and so on. For instance, the mortality on a handful of the earliest Danish voyages, sent out between 1698 and 1704, was extremely high: 60 percent.[22] The average mortality rate during those twenty-four voyages before 1754, of which we know the mortality, was 23 percent. When it comes to shipping, however, it must be remembered that in addition to this traffic there was direct shipping from Denmark; most of the well over two hundred ships sailed directly to the Danish West Indies and back home.

Administration of the Danish West Indies was the responsibility of the West India and Guinea Company under its charters.[23] From its headquarters in Copenhagen, general and principal instructions were issued either by the king or by the company's board of directors. In the islands themselves, a number of officials were employed who implemented the instructions from Denmark and took care of all aspects of the daily administration. In addition to the civilians, the company sent out soldiers to defend the colony from attack.

The upper civil and military authority on the three islands was always in the hands of the governor.[24] During the first decade on St. Thomas, it was difficult to speak of an administration, as to all appearances Governor Jørgen Iversen took care of practically everything himself. Yet, he took the opinion of a kind of popular assembly of planters, which in 1675 was replaced by a burgher council comprising twelve inhabitants, preferably civil servants, appointed by the governor. The council was to investigate all cases concerning the island and its inhabitants.[25]

Under Governor Christopher Heins in 1686, a secret council was established, consisting of four prominent planters, a little later supplemented by the company's merchant and bookkeeper. This council was the law court of the island and decided all substantial cases, primarily with relevance to trade. The governor, however, was not obliged to act upon the decisions of the majority of the council. Besides the governor, the most important officials were the merchant, the bookkeeper, and the treasurer. In addition to these was a Lutheran pastor sent from Denmark.

This arrangement worked satisfactory until 1702, when it was decided in Copenhagen that the secret council should constitute the upper authority of the colony and consist of the governor, the merchant, the bookkeeper, the treasurer, and the secretary. Neither planters nor any other social group had representatives on this revamped institution. There was, on the other hand, a tight community of interests between the members of the council and the other inhabitants, because the councilors often owned plantations themselves, carried out private trade, and were married into the local planter or trade families. While the secret council was the upper agency, subordinate officials were the fiscal, who was some kind of public prosecutor, and the sheriff, who served as police authority, administrator of estates, and land surveyor. Next came a series of smaller officials.

After the settlement of St. John, this island was also administered from St. Thomas. One of the prominent officials in Charlotte Amalie was appointed vice-governor of St. John and had as such a special responsibility to safeguard the small island's interests. On St. Croix a burgher council existed from the very beginning of the colony in 1735, representing both traders and planters. As agriculture and economy of the new island soon looked very promising, it received its own secret council in 1744, and three years later St. Croix had a vice-governor, though subordinate to the governor and secret council on St. Thomas, where all accounting also took place. In 1754, however, the government headquarters moved to Christiansted on St. Croix.

Finally, the judicial system of the Danish West Indies generally had the lower court (*byting* in Danish) as court of first instance; this was opened by the sheriff several times a week. Its sentences could be appealed to the upper court, which assembled every month, the governor presiding. Furthermore there was a special company court in Copenhagen for the company's employees.

The administration of the Danish West Indies was mostly of a very poor quality, as many of the officials were simply incompetent; in addition to their copious consumption of alcohol, their accounting particularly left much to be desired. For decades the administrators did not try to grapple with the colonial books; the result was that many planters, tradesmen, and company employees worked up considerable debts with the West India and Guinea Company. Finally, in 1725 the administration managed to determine that that the total debt to the company amounted to no less than 181,897 *rix-dollars*. Some of the debts dated back to 1707. The colonial society, though, profited to a substantial degree from credits, a large proportion of which came from moneylenders in the Netherlands.

The West India and Guinea Company was administered by a board of directors, whereas daily businesses were carried out by a number of employees. The headquarters in the center of Copenhagen included an elegant building for the administration, a large sugar refinery, and a shipyard. The fact that the management

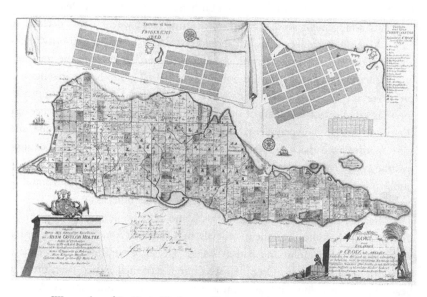

Watercolor of St. Croix Harbor at Christiansted shortly after the Danes took possession of the island in 1735. To the left is Fort Christiansværn ("Forted"), to the left is the church ("Kircken"), and in between are warehouses, workshops, and slave huts. The West India and Guinea Company's sloop is lying at anchor sin the harbor. Courtesy of the Danish National Archives.

Erik Gøbel

of the West India and Guinea Company in Denmark lacked thorough knowledge of the real circumstances in the Caribbean, however, resulted often in discussion and protest when the board of directors' armchair decisions were confronted with realities in the tropical society. Regulations of relations between slave owners and slaves were, of course, a special matter that was of the utmost importance to the local government. All the same, the Danish authorities never succeeded in making a proper slave law, which regulated all aspects of slavery.[26]

Philip Gardelin, however, made an attempt as soon as he took up the post of governor of St. Thomas in 1733. He was experienced in the civil service of the colony and worked out a so-called "Negro ordinance" on September 5, 1733, which has become notorious to posterity because of its severe regulations.[27] Leaders of escapees were to be pinched three times with red-hot irons and then hanged. Slaves found guilty of conspiracy were to lose a leg unless their owners requested leniency, when the sentence could be reduced to 150 lashes and the loss of the slaves' ears. An escapee who was caught within two weeks would receive 150 lashes or more in punishment; one who had been maroon for twelve weeks would lose a leg; and one who stayed away for six months would lose his life. A slave meeting a white person on horseback or on foot was to step aside and with all submissiveness stand still until the white had passed by; if he did not, he could expect a sound thrashing from the white.

Gardelin's ordinance took up nineteen such articles that governed relations between blacks and whites, maintenance of order, and so on. Its severity reflected the tensions that existed in the society. The ordinance had to be read aloud to the slaves three times a year; a slave owner could pick up a free copy with the clerk in the fort in Charlotte Amalie. The text was in Dutch, which was the official language of the colony in addition to Danish.

The numerous provisions for severe punishment of slaves were not executed in all cases, however. One reason for this was that the slave owner did not want to have his valuable property, his slaves, killed or mutilated; as a rule he wanted to keep them capable for work after the offence. Another reason was that the governor often mitigated the harsh punishment that had been sentenced according to the ordinance. A slave code was subsequently enacted in 1755 by the Danish Crown, heavily inspired by the French Code Noir of 1685; it reiterated the severe regulations, though in a somewhat milder form, but this law was never explicitly brought into operation in the Danish West Indies. Nevertheless, it formed the basis of a number of slave regulations, so-called placards, passed locally over the following decades.

A small group of inhabitants, known as the "Free Coloreds," found themselves in a challenging position in society between the free whites and the black slaves.[28] They were explicitly mentioned in Gardelin's ordinance, in Article 15, which laid down that "in case a free Negro provides for maroon slaves, handles and hides stolen goods, or is knowledgeable about any evil undertakings by the

Negroes to the harm of their masters and does not disclose it to a white, he shall have forfeited all his rights, his property shall be confiscated by the Company, he shall be flogged and chased out of the colony."[29]

In spite of their difficult position quite a few free blacks managed rather well. Mingo Tamerynd of St. Thomas, for example, was appointed captain of the Freedman Company in 1721, a militia manned by Free Coloreds to maintain order in town and countryside.[30] During the slave rebellion in St. John of 1733–34, Tamerynd went to that island as a leader of a group of Free Coloreds to locate and defeat slave rebels. Several branches of the Tamerynd family lived in Charlotte Amalie in the neighborhood assigned to the Free Coloreds by the authorities and where the Tamerynds achieved a kind of leadership by submitting loyally to the conditions established by the white rulers.

Even some slaves were successful in society in the same way. An example was Domingo Gesoe, who in early-eighteenth-century St. Thomas rose to a position of assistant plantation manager while still a slave. He became a missionary and preacher in the newly established Moravian community, entered into personal and familial relationship with his master, and traveled to Denmark on his own to attend to the plantation's business affairs.[31]

During the 1740s an enterprising and self-conscious class of merchants and ship owners emerged in Denmark. These wealthy people wanted to invest and participate with their own ships in the West India trade. To comply with the critique of its monopoly, the West India and Guinea Company in 1747 increased its share capital substantially and in this way simply incorporated the private interests into the company. There were constant disagreements between the company and traders and planters of the islands with regard to taxes, customs, the company's mismanagement of the colony, the insufficient shipping, the unfavorable trading conditions, and so on—in short, the company's monopoly. These disagreements caused the colonists to send another delegation, which arrived in Copenhagen in 1749. This time they wanted the Crown simply to take over the colony to get rid of the company, which to a substantial degree favored its own shareholders at the expense of the islanders. This precarious state of affairs ended when the Crown dissolved the West India and Guinea Company in 1754 by paying off all shares, and the Danish West Indies (and Guinea) thus became a Crown colony. Now all ships under the Danish flag could trade legally in the colonies and pay duties and other taxes.

The second half of the eighteenth century heralded a golden economic era for the Danish West Indies. As Denmark remained uninvolved in the many wars that were fought in this period, its colonies benefited from the demand of the combatants who sought neutral tonnage and goods. Traffic through St. Thomas flourished and sugar production on St. Croix boomed. Nevertheless, in 1792 Denmark decided to become the first European nation to end its participation in the transatlantic slave trade, which began in 1803. The motives behind this decision were humanitarian, economic, and political.[32] The humanitarian argument, of course, centered on the horrors of the slave trade in Africa and on the Middle Passage. The economic argument was that the slave trade was insignificant to Denmark's shipping and trade, while costing many sailors their lives; also, the upkeep of forts, factories, and garrisons on the Gold Coast was very expensive. Politically, the Danish government, first and foremost Minister of Finance Ernst Schimmelmann, was convinced in 1790 that Great Britain and perhaps France would very soon abolish the slave trade and that they might even agree to assert pressure on the smaller slave-trading nations to do the same. Given these circumstances, Denmark decided to move fast and become the first nation to abolish its slave trade.

From 1801 to 1802 and again from 1807 to 1815, the three Danish West Indian islands were occupied by the British. After the occupation the colony never recovered economically. Emancipation of the slaves took place in 1848. From the middle of the nineteenth century, decreasing world market prices of sugar meant that the production on St. Croix experienced heavy competition and hard times, while the harbor of St. Thomas suffered little by little from a decrease in the number of ships calling and the volume of trade. Urgent social problems in the islands resulted in 1878 in a rebellion on St. Croix among the black workers, who were bloodily suppressed by military force. After much discussion of the many problems of the colony, after several vain attempts at sale, and after rather halfhearted reform work, Denmark finally sold the impoverished colony to the United States. Transfer took place on March 31, 1917. Since then the three islands have been named the United States Virgin Islands.

By way of conclusion—and as an evaluation of the West India and Guinea Company and the Danish West Indies until 1755—one may quote Adam Smith, who wrote this about the Danish West Indies and the West India and Guinea Company in his famous book *The Wealth of Nations:* "Of all the expedients that can well be contrived to stunt the natural growth of a new colony, that of an exclusive company is undoubtedly the most effectual. . . . This too was the policy of Denmark." Smith elaborated on his criticism by pointing out that the small islands of St. Thomas and St. Croix were the only places in the New World to have been possessed by the Danes.[33]

These little settlements, too, were under the government of an exclusive company, which had the sole right both of purchasing the surplus produce of the colonists and of supplying them with such goods of other countries as they wanted. Therefore, both in its purchases and sales, had not only the power of oppressing the inhabitants but the greatest temptation to do so. The government of an exclusive company of merchants is, perhaps, the worst of all governments for any country. While it did not stop altogether the progress of these colonies, it rendered that progress more slow and languid. Ultimately the king dissolved this company, and subsequently the prosperity of the colonies greatly improved.

Thus Smith's verdict on the Danish case is withering. He was right in saying that the West India and Guinea Company was not successful in generating economic results. Narrow shareholder interests often stood in the way of developing the colony in the Caribbean (and Guinea). The state of affairs, however, was difficult for Denmark, which was just a relatively small and weak colonial power, one that allowed a non-government player—that is, the company—to act on behalf of the state face to face with great empires such as the Spanish, the English, and the French. Compared to these establishments, the Danish colony was small; it was provided with very limited resources; and there were only a few Danes on the islands. But in many ways the colony resembled those of the great powers, only on a smaller scale. Even though the period before the middle of the eighteenth century was not an unambiguous success for the Danish West Indies, the Danes had nevertheless acquired, by relatively modest investments, very useful experiences and thereby created an excellent starting point for the trade and shipping that flourished so extensively during the second half of the eighteenth century, activity that was of immense importance for Denmark, first and foremost with regard to economics.[34]

The Danish colonial experience resembled more and more, as time went on, that of the larger colonizing players, albeit on a smaller scale. After a couple of failed attempts to colonize St. Thomas, the Danish king, as befit Europe's most absolute monarch, declared that a chartered trading company should be established and ordered government officers and noblemen to participate as stockholders.

Thus, the West India and Guinea Company pursued colonization in the Caribbean, assumed the administration, defense, navigation, and provisioning of colonies, and had to purchase and transport the islands' produce as its Dutch and French counterparts did. Accordingly, the company enjoyed chartered privileges, such as a monopoly of the colonial trade as well as freedom from paying customs duties, and it oversaw all matters concerning the Danish West Indies until 1754, when it was dissolved and private interests took over shipping and trade, with the Crown taking over colonial administration.

Various circumstances, though, compelled the West India and Guinea Company to adopt strategies that contravened the Crown's mercantilist economic policy. First, a considerable portion of the produce that was shipped to Europe originated in Caribbean islands that belonged to foreign powers. Furthermore, the company was temporarily forced by its own straitened circumstances to delegate responsibility for conducting its trade to other Danish merchants and ship owners, and it allowed Brandenburgers to settle and participate in the transatlantic slave trade. On the other hand, Danish weakness was a substantial reason why the great powers, such as England, Spain, and France, accepted the Danish presence in the Caribbean since a small neutral colony might become both convenient and profitable to the combatants in case of war: they could sell their produce in the Danish West Indies or find tonnage there under the neutral Danish flag in order to ship cargoes safely to Europe or to American ports.

Erik Gøbel

A closing note: the company's activities in Denmark, on the Gold Coast, and in the West Indies resulted in a set of comprehensive archival materials that today are kept in the Danish National Archives.[35] The research potential of these materials with regard to the company's organization, trade, shipping, and more or less all aspects of the Danish colonies (including demography, administration, economy, agriculture, trade, slavery, living conditions, and social and cultural matters) is so great that UNESCO has added the West India and Guinea Company archives—together with those of other Danish tropical trading companies—to its prestigious Memory of the World Register.

Creating a Caribbean Colony in the Long Seventeenth Century

Saint-Domingue and the Pirates

Giovanni Venegoni

The administration of François-Joseph, Comte de Choiseul, Marquis de Beaupré, third governor of Saint-Domingue, constitutes a pivotal period in the histories of what came to be France's most important Caribbean colony and of the imperial character of the Torrid Zone more generally. Between the 1620s and 1660s, Saint-Domingue had constituted a frontier of European colonization of the Americas, whose first settlers included sailors, deserters, and escaped slaves, although the arrival of the first French governors in the mid-1660s necessarily entailed an attempt at imperial control and a sort of sociopolitical stability.

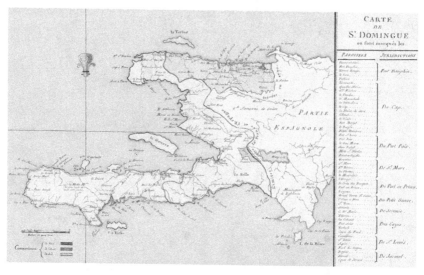

François-Pierre Le Moyne, *Plan d'une partie de l'Isle St. Domingue*, 1751. Bibliothèque nationale de France, Division 2 du portefeuille 146 du Service hydrographique de la marine consacrée à l'Ouest de Saint-Domingue; courtesy of The John Carter Brown Library at Brown University.

France had finally obtained official control of the western third of the island of Hispaniola (Spain retaining the eastern two-thirds) at the Peace of Ryswick (1697) after more than half a century of informal administration. Choiseul-Beaupré arrived in Saint-Domingue in 1707 in the midst of the War of Spanish Succession (1702–13), charged with creating a new capital city and with maintaining good relations with the crews of *flibustiers* (freebooters) who used the colony's ports as bases for their operations. With the help of Jean-Jacques Mithon, Saint-Domingue's first intendant, and a group of veteran officers, including Jean-Joseph de Paty, the new governor's management of the colony and his policies with respect to the *flibustiers* established a period of relative tranquility that enabled the colony's economic and social development.[1]

Choiseul-Beaupré, having acquired a good knowledge of his colony after leading it for almost four years, wrote a letter in June 1710, which could be considered a summary of his policies. First, he pointed out the necessity of increasing the number of missionaries, which was absolutely insufficient to manage the growing population of the colony, although he praised the work the religious orders had performed among both white colonists and slaves. Thus, he proposed the establishment of a new monastery as part of a larger administrative project, in accordance with the creation of the new capital, Léogane, which had received official recognition just a few weeks earlier.

The location of this new political center would also meet the need for a new port on the western coast of the Gulf of Gonâve, which would serve as the location of both a new fort, Saint-Louis du Sud (which would have been the biggest defense structure of the *bande du sud*), and a new hospital for soldiers and freebooters. The idea for the hospital had recurred in Choiseul-Beaupré's reports to his superiors as it constituted the cornerstone of the governor's plan to formalize the relationship between the colonial administration and the *flibustiers,* whom he regarded as important military auxiliaries whose usefulness would increase if they could be attached to the colonial society more securely.[2]

Defining Saint-Domingue's Landscapes

Choiseul-Beaupré wrote his letter after a long period during which he and Mithon had promulgated orders that would have defined the shape of the French colonization of Saint-Domingue had they come to fruition. In 1706, the year before the governor arrived, the colonial administration published the *Règlement du Conseil de Léogane, contenant la Détermination d'une Echelle de Distances, pour les Transports et Significations* ("Regulation of the Superior Council of Léogane, concerning the Determination of a Scale of Distance for Transportations and Notifications"), the first administrative manifestation of a comprehension of the geographical dimension of the colony. It did so, first of all, by formally calculating the distance between Le Cap and Port-de-Paix on the northern peninsula and the proposed new municipality on the southern peninsula, which also provided the legal dimension of the territory under French authority. Moreover, the report cleared the uncertainty of Saint-Domingue's dimensions. In other words, it officially asserted governmental cultural and legal knowledge of this part of the Americas, which would help determine its significance within the European colonization of the Caribbean.[3]

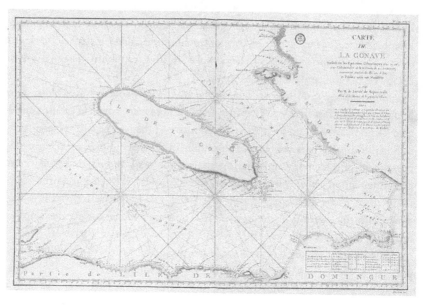

Pruvost, *Situation de l'île de la Gonâve par rapport aux côtes de Saint-Domingue*, 1790. Bibliothèque nationale de France, département Cartes et plans, GE SH 18 PF 151 DIV 2 P 7 D; courtesy of The John Carter Brown Library at Brown University.

Between the fall of 1709 and the summer of 1710, Choiseul-Beaupré and Mithon oversaw a set of *ordonnances* that would have further defined the shape of the French colonization of the territory surrounding the Gulf of Gonâve (the *"bande de l'Ouest"*). In late October 1709, the administration published the *Règlement concernant l'entretien des routes* ("Regulation concerning road management"), the first legal directive concerning the road system of the colony, which was intended to improve the terrestrial connections among the ports of the northern peninsula and between Saint-Domingue's two major peninsulas. This campaign of road building would have involved the Crown as the main financier of a large operation of public constructions; Choiseul-Beaupré and Mithon envisioned a transportation network that would have extended governmental engagement in the colony by following the roads and transcending the boundaries of cities and ports. Their defining of the administrative and commercial structure of the colony, which designated the capital of the *bande du Nord* at Le Cap and of the *bande de l'Ouest* at

Giovanni Venegoni

Léogane/Petit-Goave, fixed the position of two of the most important ports of the colony and thus established the main junctions between local transportation and Atlantic trade routes.[4]

In devising his solution to the vexing issue of a new capital city, Choiseul-Beaupré proposed the strategically and geographically well-positioned area between L'Ester and Petite-Rivière, which, situated on a large promontory between the two main peninsulas, offered all the necessary elements (water, plains, a bay, a hospital) for success. Located south of the pass that crosses the northern mountains midway between Le Cap and the *bande du Sud* and with an arch of hills that separated it from Spanish territory, this area was safer than the northern and southern plains, which were open to Spanish attacks. Moreover, its projected harbor was located in a relatively protected bay in the Gulf of Gonâve.

Founding a new capital addressed both metropolitan government requests and the colony's desire for a resolution to its demographic, economic, and political imbalances. But instead of using European measures to define colonial dimensions, the administrators used their knowledge of Saint-Domingue's climate and geopolitical situation to consolidate the French position on Hispaniola by promulgating *ordonnances* intended to set up the geographical disposition of roads, ports, and various civil and military infrastructures in accordance with local geographical circumstances. Thus, they fit French establishments into the geopolitical theater of the Caribbean and unconsciously "Americanized" the west coast of the island.[5]

Knowing Saint-Domingue's People

To improve colonial authority, Choiseul-Beaupré firmly believed that it was crucial to fit the *flibustiers* more securely into colonial political and social life, as well as necessary to fix the administrative structure of Saint-Domingue by plotting new geopolitical power centers on the colony's map.[6] In June 1710 the governor ordered the construction of a hospital to attend to the "relief" of the colony's troops and the freebooters, who would be the prime beneficiaries, as one of the main elements of an elaborate new military and political organization of the southern capital, Petit-Goave. Thus, in addition to bolstering the military organization of the colony by creating a space for sick and injured soldiers, this state-managed facility would be independent from religious interference and would provide the means for the government to cement its relation with the *flibustiers*.[7]

The choice of Petit-Goave was not accidental, and the following year, De Paty, governor of the *bande du Sud*, confirmed its importance for the crews.[8] The project thus included the creation of a fund for the construction, based on the "lots" that the *flibustiers* would have inherited from companions who had died at sea and that would have been deposited at the local hospital. Moreover, to support expenses associated with the construction of the facility, Choiseul-Beaupré proposed to use the "lot of Cartagena," seized by freebooters in 1697 and not yet shared.[9]

An institution in which regular interaction between the administration and the *flibustiers* would take place required rules to govern that interaction. Accordingly, Choiseul-Beaupré proposed that notaries intervene in the codes of the freebooters and buccaneers (such as the *chasse-parties*), thereby binding the colonial legislative and legal structures to the semi-informal system that existed among the freebooters. Finally, at the base of this relationship, the governor sought to create a solid but neutral link with the crews by dealing directly with them, thereby engaging the freebooters in a political, structured project; by asking the *flibustiers* to contribute to the construction of the hospital, he was soliciting their participation in the colony's military system.

Flibustiers were already used to giving part of their booty to the admiral or the king, but this was an obligation connected with the "commissions" the Crown gave to the crews to fight in its name. In some ways this was the price the crews had to pay to be considered an ally rather than an enemy of the state. Yet, the money that Choiseul-Beaupré was asking of the *flibustiers* also constituted recognition of their legal role in the colony: while everyone had to pay the *dîme de l'amiral* ("the admiral's tithe"), a tax on every prize taken by French vessels in time of war, the request for a contribution for the hospital of Petit-Goave was addressed especially to the *flibuste dominguoise*.

The Complex Relationship between the Government of Saint-Domingue and the *Flibustiers*

The Early Regularization of French Freebooters

To understand better Choiseul-Beaupré's thinking, it is necessary to analyze the legal and juridical situation of the *flibustiers* in the early eighteenth century. The late seventeenth century saw a series of changes in the metropolitan and colonial policy. On the diplomatic front, the changes began with the Truce of Regensburg (1684) and the Treaty of Whitehall (1686) and were consolidated in 1697 with the Peace of Ryswick. The Spanish cession of the western third of Hispaniola to France, together with the creation of the Franco-Spanish alliance between Louis XIV (ruled 1661–1714) and Charles II (ruled 1665–1701), gave the colony unprecedented military security. Good relations with English Jamaica, which had been complicated by nine years of war (1688–97), resumed through the resumption of commercial activities and networks of Huguenot, Irish, and Jewish colonists. Gradually, then, the "amity lines" between the Saint-Domingue government and the *flibustiers* disappeared as the diplomatic and political structure that had insured the latter's existence—the "space of uncertainty" of international relations between the colonies and cities—weakened. The effects of diplomatic change became rapidly evident in the French colony. From 1684 to 1700 the number of slaves increased by 400 percent, and the wealth of planters rose to unprecedented levels, along with the development of sugar plantations fueled by resources that had been pillaged by freebooters from Jamaica and Cartagena.

Supported by companies established in the late seventeenth century, the development of the French trading system placed Saint-Domingue in the center of a vast transatlantic trading network. And, as noted by Frostin, despite the conflict of 1690s and 1710s, the advent of the colony's sugar economy benefited from exceptionally favorable circumstances, particularly the decline of competitors in the Lesser Antilles (damaged by the attacks of buccaneers and European fleets) and Brazil. Now, the interest of the great families of the merchants of Paris and the French Atlantic coast (the so-called "Ponant" ports) aroused renewed attention to the prosperity and maintenance of traffic to and from Saint-Domingue.

The change also affected *flibustier* "spaces" as the consolidation of the plantation economy changed the needs of the settlers. Moreover, metropolitan commercial elites were pushing for the restriction of freebooters and the protection of trade routes to the Americas, as had happened in the English case, in which the growth of Jamaican sugar production generated a series of restrictions that dramatically circumscribed the activities of Jamaican freebooters between 1681 and 1696.[10]

Amnesties and Hangings: Regulating Relationships in Saint-Domingue

The Saint-Domingue government, though, continued to support the *flibustiers* as the extinction of the freebooters was not an economically viable option. On the one hand, fighting these groups meant turning a part of the colony's population into enemies, ones that were well organized militarily. On the other hand, *flibustiers'* prizes represented a significant infusion of resources for the settlers and the Saint-Domingue market, especially when war isolated the colony from other French establishments. Thus, with the Peace of Ryswick, Superior Councils approved an amnesty to attract freebooters from all nations before the resumption of hostilities that was looming. At the beginning of the War of Spanish Succession, the urgent military requirements of the colonial government subsequently strengthened the relationship between government and freebooters; in 1703 Governor Auger, after discovering the presence of many Spanish *flibustiers* in the colony, conceded new commissions to plunder the coast of New Spain.[11]

Choiseul-Beaupré maintained this good understanding with the crews. In 1708 he obtained from the Superior Council of Le Cap the recognition of a general amnesty that was extended to "all the Freebooters . . . of the French Islands of America . . . who, having been captured, had served on English and Dutch vessels to gain their freedom."[12] As the war continued, support for privateering was maintained. The conflict required the commitment of all available forces to the defense of the colony and the support of its economy, which had been stifled by British military superiority. As De Pry and Mithon observed to Versailles in 1711, the "faults" of the freebooters were bearable because the war had provided profitable opportunities for crews and administrators.[13]

The ability of the *flibustiers* to relate to different Caribbean circumstances enabled them to offer themselves to the Crown as a strategically important resource beyond Saint-Domingue. Moreover, the global dimension of the war offered several opportunities for *flibustier* involvement. As informers, the freebooters could count on their links with former adventurers in Jamaica and in the neutral islands of St. Thomas and Curacao to gain valuable information. Also, as a coastguard, although they were engaged in smuggling, they received the charge of destroying contraband trade with British and Dutch colonies. The results were limited, but in some cases were significant.

For instance, as part of the naval militia, they could move from one of the war's theaters to another; in Acadia, Captain Pierre Morpain intervened by supplying the isolated French forces for several months. His intervention, which contributed to the defense of Port-Royal, was highly praised by the Governor Daniel d'Auger de Subrecase. Although the French government was not able to take full advantage of this contribution, the usefulness of buccaneering found a new dimension: militarily, the *flibustiers* demonstrated their ability to act on a broad front.[14]

Not all actions that the administrators undertook toward the freebooters were accepted by adventurers, however, particularly during the last months of the war and following its conclusion. At the end of 1713, Mithon asked the French government for permission to compensate sailors who had been injured during the fighting. The year after, he was authorized to compensate injured *flibustiers,* following the code promulgated by Choiseul-Beaupré in 1710; they, however, revolted against this order as it imposed new reimbursement tariffs that were not satisfactory in the eyes of the crews.[15]

The least tolerated aspect of reimbursement was the system of repayments, which would have been paid with the introduction of a new taxation model for prizes. The ten percent of the value of pirate seizures reserved for the administration would have been assessed on the weight of the goods, not their value (as it was before). Although this system did not stop crews from cheating, it encouraged them to declare expensive (and relatively lighter) items that entered legal market as prizes. Moreover, the cessation of hostilities caused other problems related to the reduction of commissions and limitation of eligible prizes, while the relative impunity permitted during the late seventeenth century had been replaced by a growing government control. The severity of the punishment of François Jardif, an *aventurier* and "vagabond" hanged as a British spy, was not an isolated case and signaled the end of tolerance for illegal actions, as well as free movement between and connections with foreign islands, as crews quickly perceived. Thus, a new agreement had to be made between the *flibustiers* and administrators.[16]

The consequences of this shift soon became apparent in Saint-Domingue. In mid-August 1715, the new governor, Louis de Courbon, Count de Blénac, and

Giovanni Venegoni

intendant Mithon applied the new policy: a Spanish ship, which had on board some French *flibustiers* condemned to a French galley, had to stop in Le Cap where the prisoners asked for a new trial. "We decided not to proceed," wrote Courbon and Mithon to their superiors, "since the procedure was not well prepared and does not have strong enough evidences. We would have been obliged to absolve them, which would have had some dangerous consequences in these seas where there are still four or five French pirates [*forbans*]. My Lord, we are sending them to France since there are not enough evidences, but it will be less dangerous to find them innocent so far. The news of their exoneration, that here would have led the others in their exercise of the piracy, will not be rapidly renowned." The governor refused a direct petition from former *flibustiers,* even if he knew that the trial had been poorly managed. It was a clear sign that no more "faults" would be tolerated.[17]

From the perspective of the colonial government, the end of the War of Spanish Succession had significantly reduced, as had happened after 1697, the need to maintain an alliance with the *flibustiers*. Their priority became the consolidation of good trade relations with the neighboring colonies, to enjoy the peace and the new opportunities it offered. In addition, administrators had to reach agreements with the new planter elite (the so-called *grands-blancs*), which demonstrated their leading role in the hierarchy of the colony during the *affaire de l'octroi* (1713–15). Thus, while the *flibustiers* of Saint-Domingue had been valuable contributors to French success in the Caribbean prior to 1715, twenty years later they were forced to flee "pirate hunters" and seek new bases in East Africa and Madagascar. The relationship between the colonial administration and the *flibustiers* was now altered, either from the outside because of the interference of politics in Paris and Versailles or from the inside through the changes that were taking place in colonial society.[18]

Their disappearance marked a crucial reduction in the flexibility and in the permeability of the sociopolitical arrangement that had operated in the colony since the 1660s and 1670s. After the decline of the buccaneers, weakened by the expansion of the plantation system and the reduction of wild cattle since the 1680s, the *flibustiers* remained the only representative of this informal society. Although another kind of nebula were forming on the horizon (the smugglers who would play a central role in the economic and social development of the eighteenth-century Caribbean), a key period in the history of the New World disappeared with the freebooters.[19]

Quartermasters and Hospitals: The Americanization of Freebooting

Other changes within Saint-Domingue contributed to the demise of the *flibustiers,* most particularly the emergence of a new figure in the agreements between the pirates and colonial governments, the quartermaster. This office first appears in the records in 1688 when Mathurin Desmaretz on the *Sainte-Rose* signed the charter party, probably represented the entire crew, and was proposed as the mediator between the captain and the sailors on the vessel.[20] According to De Paty, "The *quartier mestre* . . . is a kind of attorney among [the *flibustiers*] who rules their accounts." A decade later, Charles Johnson provided a similar description of the "duty" (role) of the quartermaster among crews: "there is a principal Officer among the Pyrates, called the Quarter-Master, . . . who acts as a sort of a civil Magistrate on Board a Pyrate Ship."[21] On the advice of Captain Johnson, the quartermaster played the role of an intermediary between the captain and crew. In a context of the limited operability of European laws and without the possibility of recourse to the intervention of a hierarchical order, it was necessary for crews like the one of the *Sainte-Rose* to have a figure that could help resolve disputes and maintain the relationship between the captain and the sailors.

At the time, though, the definition of quartermaster did not follow that given by De Paty.[22] According to the *Dictionnaire Universel* of Furetière, the "quartermaster" was the sailor in charge of cordage, pumps, and anchors. It is obvious that the two definitions differ greatly.[23] In Saint-Domingue, the quartermaster was an entity who, in crossing the Atlantic and adapting to the Caribbean context, turned into something new.

Because of the lack of documentation, it is not possible to know exactly when this new figure began to emerge. In 1686, during a famous trial against a *flibustier* ship, *La Subtile,* the principal officers identified included "quartier maistre Pierre Beaudecorps."[24] The division of authority between the captain and the quartermaster on board the freebooters' ships is apparent in the accounts of Raveneau de Lussan, whose adventures dated from 1684 to 1685, and Captain Johnson.[25] So it was probably in the early 1680s that the role of this figure crystallized in Saint-Domingue. According to Marcus Rediker, who has extensively studied the crews of pirates of the 1710s–20s, the captain was the military commander while the "quartermaster was elected to represent and protect the interest of the crew."[26] And indeed it was as a representative of the rights of *flibustiers* that quartermasters appear in the historical record of Saint-Domingue.

In 1699 Jacques Hélin said that Sansoucy, "quartier maistre de l'*Europe*," had asked Governor Galiffet to be reimbursed for the nineteen hundred *livres* taken by the Sieur de Pontoise, who had accused the crew of the *Europe* of looting one of his ships.[27] In doing so, Hélin manifested a further development of the figure of the quartermaster. After becoming a point of reference in the *chasse-parties* and, therefore, in island "micro-societies," the quartermaster became the intermediary between the officers of the colonial administration and its crew. From then on, every time a *flibustier*'s ship had to deal with the government, quartermasters were required to act as "attorneys" for the crew.

Another example of this evolution of the role of the quartermasters in Saint-Domingue was the negotiation between La Grave, serving on the *Intrepid,* and the interim governor at the time, Jean-Pierre Casamajor de Charritte, in 1708. In this case La Grave played a crucial role, since its captain, Pierre Morpain, had accused the governor of abusing his authority to obtain favorable pricing (9,900 *livres*) in the purchase of twenty-two slaves who had been seized from the *Intrepid*. La Grave was the crew member in charge for the commercial transaction. Finally, the survey conducted by the commissioners of the Governor Blénac demonstrated fraud, and Charritte had to pay 712 *livres* as reimbursement. Without being in any way equivalent to the compensation given to the crew of the *Intrepid,* the amount was sufficient to suggest that the administration supported the requests of the *flibustiers*.[28]

In his letter of June 1710, Choiseul-Beaupré described a dispute between the *Compagnie de l'Asiente* and the freebooters. The crew, who had been forced to pay for permission to sell slaves captured in Jamaica, asked for the intervention of the governor through their attorney. The Superior Council, under the governor's scrutiny, decreed that the money had to be returned to the *flibustiers*. Choiseul-Beaupré added: "You can not believe, My Lord, how this little affair angered the *flibustiers*."[29]

This letter disclosed an important precedent. A crew returning from an attack asked and obtained permission to sell the slaves they had captured in the British colony, despite the opposition of the *Compagnie de l'Asiente*. Aided by the traditional acrimony between the inhabitants of Saint-Domingue (and then the counselors called to express their position) and French trading companies, the *flibustiers* obtained a considerable political victory. A few months later, this legal opinion led the lieutenant of the *bande de l'Ouest,* De Paty, to defend a crew who had been threatened and whose captain and the quartermaster had been imprisoned by the governor of Grenada, Darguen, so that he could seize slaves from the ship's cargo.[30] De Paty, in his letter, called for "Justice" for the *flibustiers,* against this administrative "violence." Together with Choiseul-Beaupré's letter of June 1710, these communications pointed out that the government felt it had to intervene to defend the privileges of the freebooters against abuses of authority.

The "Guildisation" of the Flibustiers

Flibustier partnership agreements (the *"matelotage"* contracts") helped preserve the property of the parties, but they also provided a basis for the development of their enterprise since the profits generated by their maritime activities enabled them to become indigo cultivators or sugar planters rather than husbandmen of livestock. These arrangements included *chasse-parties,* contracts signed by the sailors before leaving for a raid whereby the crew fixed the rules for the division of booty, with the sum to be given to injured sailors, and division of responsibility among the members of the party. Alexandre-Olivier Exquemelin, in his famous account, gave an example, and another survives from 1688 that was written from the coast of the Ile-à-Vache, along the southern peninsula of Saint-Domingue, by the crew of the *Sainte Rose*.[31] The most evident difference between the two descriptions is the role of the quartermaster: in Exquemelin's version it is absent, although some "delegates" appear in the account, while Desmaretz, serving as quartermaster, signed the *Sainte-Rose* letter.

In the late seventeenth century, the appearance of quartermasters was a reaction to the need for intermediary figures between merchant-vessel owners, captains, and colonial administrators. In response to the deployment of the economic, political, and social powers emanating from Europe, freebooters proposed a figure who, by posing as delegate for their interests, enjoyed a contractual capacity that no other officer or sailor had and guaranteed the privileges and rights of *flibustiers*.

Although thousands of miles away from Europe, French colonies in the Torrid Zone were an integral part of, and integrated into, the juridical, legal, and customary systems of *ancien régime* France. Early modern society was divided into several bodies, within which existed a multitude of guilds, orders, and political and social entities. This "plural legal order" was based on the union of all the constituent parts of the monarchy under the figure of the king and on the special relationship that each of those parts had with the Crown. Each privilege granted or recognized by the monarchy generated different relationships with other entities in the kingdom. For French officers in both America and France, "bodies" and "estates," including their institutionalized subdivisions, constituted the regular framework of society.[32]

It was on this basis that after the 1690s, with the appearance of the quartermasters, the *flibuste dominguoise* began a journey that could have led to its effective institutionalization, turning an informal group into a more formal entity, comparable to European guilds. The beginning of the process was related to quartermasters and their gradual acceptance in the French institutional and legal colonial context. Recognizing their function as crews' "attorneys," governors, judges, and Superior Councils fitted quartermasters into the colonial system. The cases of Desmaretz of the *Sainte-Rose* (1688), Sansoucy of the *Europe* (1699), and La Grave of the *Intrepid* (1708) were signals of the progressive incorporation of the role of the quartermasters in Saint-Domingue. This development underscored a profound transformation in the perception of the *flibuste dominguoise* by the colonial administration and furthered the "process of Americanization" of the *flibustiers*.

The *chasse-parties* followed a parallel story: born among the crews of privateers and the *flibuste ponantaise,* they were adapted to the interests and customs of the freebooters. The *chasse-partie* described by Exquemelin differed in almost every point from the one of the *Sainte Rose,* excepting its provision for "six hundred pieces of eight" as compensation to disabled freebooters. This was the same price that Choiseul-Beaupré and Mithon settled for in 1707 by offering payments to sailors wounded in combat. Of course, the origin of this estimate may have been a simple maritime custom, but the redundancy seems significant: by creating a legal channel for reimbursement through an ordinance, colonial administration formalized the existing relation between the *flibustiers* and the colonial government.[33]

Giovanni Venegoni

While Choiseul-Beaupré's plan to build a hospital in Petit-Goave was abandoned after the departure of the governor, the reimbursements he organized for the *flibustiers* remained. In 1713, towards the end of the war, the problem of disabled mariners returned to the agenda because of the proposed change of the rules of prize taxation. The metropolitan government wanted to raise to four *soldes* (the amount of money to pay for every ton of goods) as compensation for expenses supported by the Crown in defense of the colony. When Governor Paul-François de la Grange, Comte d'Arquian, tried to obtain the money from a crew of Saint-Domingue freebooters, they responded that "following their *chasse-partie*, this money was due to crippled sailors."[34]

What then was the significance of the actions taken by Choiseul-Beaupré towards the *flibustiers*? Apparently his acts barely differed from those of his predecessors, although he supported the freebooters no more than they had done and the results he obtained were not better or more impressive. Indeed, under his command, the *flibuste dominguoise* did not achieve any significant results; the 1697 sack of Cartagena remained the most important military action conducted by the Saint-Domingue freebooters.

Nevertheless, Choiseul-Beaupré did do something new and, in some ways, distinctive. When the governor arrived in Saint-Domingue in 1707, the context in which he was operating was quite different from the Caribbean into which his predecessors had sent freebooters. The west coast of Hispaniola was no longer a temporary French establishment on a Spanish island but had become part of the French *domination* in the Americas. The perspectives of government, both in Le Cap and Versailles, had changed with the evolution of the diplomatic and political theater. If seventeenth-century governors had proposed to extend the colony toward more salubrious places, Choiseul-Beaupré never entertained such a notion. The mission he had from the French government was to consolidate the establishment and to improve its socioeconomic situation. When he fixed the official positioning of Le Cap and Léogane and when he proposed to move the Superior Council to Petit-Goave and to found a new city on the Gulf of Gonâve, he was advancing the intention of the French to remain in this part of the Greater Antilles and to do whatever would be necessary to improve the condition of the colony; the "frontier era" of the French Caribbean was closing.

On the continent and on most of Hispaniola, this "space of uncertainty and negotiation," following Philip Boucher's interpretation, separated Europeans and Natives, masters and slaves, and the various colonial empires.[35] Serge Gruzinski and others have broadly analyzed the many different facets of the meeting of different cultures in the Americas. More important, they have shown how these encounters invariably generated a new "product" originated by a form of hybridization. The *"cultures metisses et metissées"* that Gruzinski studied in sixteenth-century Mexico were, at the same time, entangled in millenarian cultures and an expression of something new. In eighteenth-century Saint-Domingue,

Natives were still present but did not represent a substantial element of colonial society. After having been exploited during the Spanish colonization, under French government the last survivors of the Taínos were accounted among the *metisses et négres libres* ("persons of mixed race and free blacks"). On the other hand, the rapidly growing African population was already deeply influencing cultural formation in the colony even if it was heavily exploited.[36]

The policies employed by Choiseul-Beaupré also entailed a process that tracked the "domestication of governors."[37] In this case, no elites were involved. Rather Choiseul-Beaupré attempted a sort of "guildisation" of the *flibuste dominguoise,* which tried to mold the crews into a structured group with which he would be able to deal more readily.

How did Choiseul-Beaupré encourage the sailors to become part of the society from which they had parted, voluntarily or perforce? In addition to proposing the hospital for Petit-Goave, Choiseul-Beaupré, by recognizing the roles of both the quartermasters and the *chasse-parties* among the crews, as "attorneys" or as "codes," created de facto precedents upon which it became possible to create customs and practices and, finally, to define the privileges of the *flibustiers.* Thus, when the Superior Council declared in favor of the *flibustiers* and against the *Compagnie de l'Asiente,* it supported the freebooters' right to ignore a rule of one of the main trading companies in a manner that was unusual in America, although common in Europe, where guilds had their own set of privileges.

The project of "guildisation" that appeared in Saint-Domingue was not the first in the history of the French freebooters. In 1695 the lieutenant general Sébastien Le Prestre de Vauban developed a similar project, *Mémoire concernant la caprerie,* in which he proposed the creation of a new class of sailors. The Peace of Ryswick, however, ended governmental interest in this project as it no longer had any practical application.[38]

Probably, Choiseul-Beaupré had a similar idea, albeit in a different military and social context. The *flibustiers* had always used their mobility to advantage, which made them formidable opponents for European navies, although at the same time it encouraged their depletion and dispersion. By enlisting Michel de Granmont, Laurens de Graaf, and other captains in the colony's military hierarchies, the governor hoped to centralize freebooter activity gradually; by controlling the most important leaders of the crews, the administrators hoped to control all the sailors. Eventually, though, this plan failed, mainly because of the deaths of Granmont and de Graaf (in 1686 and 1704, respectively).

The result of the Choiseul-Beaupré's attempt to domesticate the *flibuste dominguoise* was the short-lived "Americanization" of colonial policy, which in Saint-Domingue meant that, while trying to tie the *flibustiers* permanently to colonial policy, the governor infected local justice administration with metropolitan influence. Even so, Choiseul-Beaupré never had the opportunity to completely develop this plan, as his departure and death (1711) and the end of the War of

Spanish Succession finally erased the opportunity for a colony-*flibustiers* alliance. This period also marked the process of "guildisation": the declining number of prizes, the new alliance with Britain, and the antipiracy actions launched by the European powers crushed a social phenomenon that had existed for nearly two centuries in the seas of America as the subjects of transformation disappeared. Probably Georges Pollet was right when he said that the *flibuste dominguoise* began to wane in 1711.[39]

Conclusion: The Dissolution of the Nebula of Saint-Domingue

After a period of almost forty years (1620s–1660s), the west coast of Saint-Domingue was incorporated into the process of "colony-building." The population of the colony during this time constituted a "social nebula," a set of individuals whose hierarchical and social positions varied according to different situations and occasions. In the midst of this informal entity, still unstable, three groups emerged (buccaneers, *habitants,* and *flibustiers*); and in a sort of star formation, each group began to define its boundaries, structures, and characteristics, eventually becoming the main actors in a new process of exploitation and evaluation of the colony.

Buccaneers were the first group whose structure had a firm but tenuous balance: they were hunters, traders of smoked meat and *cuir vert* (leather), and sometimes members of privateering or pirate crews. They thrived in the savannahs of Hispaniola, and their role in colonial society crystallized during the first phase of the colonization of the west coast of Saint-Domingue. Their "star" shone for more than half a century before fading in the 1680s, when the agricultural, economic, and administrative evolution of the island (with the attendant expansion of plantation and cultivated areas) forced them to change their habits.

The *habitants* had the closest relationship with the colony and understood its physical space as they depended completely on the environment they occupied to survive. In fact, the term *habitant* was used to define those who were primarily engaged in agriculture and plantations.[40] Unlike the *flibustiers,* they chose stability instead of mobility. Their star was occasionally obscured by metropolitan attempts to impose rules on colonial production and trade. But the resilience of the *habitants* (who resisted attacks, flooding, and tornadoes before they finally flourished) and their capacity to attract and absorb some of the other two groups enabled their star to brighten: between 1730 and 1740, they came to occupy the Saint-Domingue sociopolitical firmament by themselves.

The *flibustiers,* however, proved unable to maintain their own star. In addition to the considerable time they spent on board ship, freebooters followed singular trajectories, and their social history rather resembles a set of shooting stars. During certain periods, especially in times of war, their brightness seemed to obscure the rest of the sky, but peace intervened to render this preeminence fleeting. Prior to 1713 it seemed possible that these shooting stars might remain suspended in the firmament. The conclusion of the hostilities, though, finally brought them back into the nebula, where the freebooters' brightness was dissolved by new forces that were rapidly emerging. Incapable of adapting to the new economic, geopolitical, and social scenario, the influence of Saint-Domingue's freebooters declined after 1713 in accordance with their decreasing value as military and economic instruments in peacetime. Therefore, the interest of the authorities in establishing a sustainable and culturally acceptable relationship dwindled. No other governors would bother to systematize the freebooters' role in colonial society, and within a few years the star of the *flibustiers* had vanished from the blue sky of the Caribbean.

Part III

Extending the Torrid Zone

The Martinican Model

Colonial Magistrates and the Origins of a Global Judicial Elite

Laurie M. Wood

The frontispiece to Jean-Baptiste Du Tertre's seventeenth-century history of the Antilles inhabited by the French contains many pieces of stock imagery from that era. Floating cherubs ensconce the book's title, while Europeans and Native peoples populate each side of the image and, in the background, participate in a gift exchange. Towards its lower center, however, one notices a striking gap in the illustration: while a map clearly delineates the Antilles, the islands appear only as outlines against a white background signifying the sea. While Du Tertre's *History* is inhabited, its subject, the Antilles, remains mysterious and perhaps even empty. All of the material substance—indigenous Kalinago, floral and faunal produce in the form of gifts, European newcomers—has been pulled out and put into the

Frontispiece, Jean-Baptiste
Du Tertre, *Histoire générale
des Antilles habitées par les
François, 1667–1671* (Paris,
1667–1671). Courtesy of the
John Carter Brown Library
at Brown University.

larger frame. Those objects of Antillean origin that appear in the frontispiece also appear without specific reference to their origin. From which island, exactly, did this Native come? Whence his gifts and where did he meet French subjects? How did the French come to inhabit the Antilles and what did their presence mean as it changed over time?[1]

Though other contributions to this volume, especially by Tessa Murphy and Sarah Barber, address the former two questions, this essay seeks to answer the third question. It does so by investigating how a global judicial elite emerged out of a small group of families with military backgrounds in the French West Indies, especially Martinique. This approach enables the rendition of trans-Caribbean pathways that are obscured in studies that focus solely on indigenous-European relations. A diachronic exploration of a Caribbean-generated judicial elite also recasts the long seventeenth century Caribbean as a site of social and political origination that reverberated both within and beyond this region.[2] Exploring the seventeenth-century origins of the French Caribbean across this region thus reveals the interconnections that bound it into a recognizable social and political space, as in Du Tertre's blank map.

In the early decades of French colonial ventures in the Torrid Zone, socially and economically aspirant adventurers, such as the De Goursolas and Courpon families, advanced their careers via military service attached to nascent legal forums, such as the *conseils supérieurs*. Accompanying colonial entrepreneurs, including Pierre Belain D'Esnambuc, a founder of the colony on Saint-Christophe, they skirmished with competing English and Dutch imperial forces and pirates, building defensive forts and local militias along the Antillean chain. Settling, and sometimes retiring, in colonies like Martinique, they invested in newly booming endeavors, including plantation agriculture. There, they leveraged their economic interests with political aims by becoming magistrates in law courts, especially Martinique's *conseil supérieur,* and sent their sons to found newer ventures in the new colony of Saint-Domingue.[3]

In doing so, they latched onto France's legal infrastructure as a means to secure economic and political privileges (including noble status). Over time they formed a Caribbean regional *themistocracy,* or class of legal experts, that first created and then transferred this legal expertise from Martinique to Saint-Domingue. This themistocracy grew to intersect with other regional themistocracies, as in the Indian Ocean, that together formed a global network of legal professionals. Eventually, this mobility allowed them to use France's imperial legal regime as a vehicle through which to guarantee assets on both sides of the Atlantic, such as plantations in the colonies and trading firms in metropolitan France, and to participate in empire-wide debates about law and legality.

This essay thus uncovers the origins of Saint-Domingue, Martinique, and the French West Indian colonies more broadly, between the early era of buccaneers in the mid-to-late seventeenth century and the period of Parisian and noble planters

Laurie M. Wood

that signaled the rise of a plantation slavery economy in the first decades of the eighteenth century. This period constitutes a significant lacuna in the literature and remains a crucial area of inquiry for understanding the difficult, protracted, and highly distinctive development of Saint-Domingue's plantation complex, the dissolution of which has been amply documented and debated but whose origins remain little understood.[4]

This tilt is reinforced by histories that focus on the era in which the slave systems of the French Caribbean were at their most sophisticated, intensive, and deadly—at a pinnacle underscored by the revolutionary tumult that unfolded immediately thereafter with the 1791 spark of the Haitian Revolution. Historians thus recognize two complex and successive periods, that of the build-up of the slave system and of the revolution itself, but by limiting the first period to the era of roughly 1740 to 1790, they paint a picture of a unidirectional and ineffable tidal wave. John Garrigus and Malick Ghachem have widened this lens to explore the long eighteenth century in Saint-Domingue, but their aim is still to explain the coming of the Haitian Revolution rather than the seventeenth-century origins and logic that created such a volatile society in the first place.[5] By widening the perspective to a longer Caribbean chronology that stretches from the seventeenth into the mid-eighteenth century, this research avoids a model of colonial development that by necessity ends in revolution, no matter the originating causes, and rather opens up a new framework for understanding the pathways that Antillean actors first forged accidentally, then transformed into political rhetoric and ideology.

This essay also frames the French Caribbean as a region with many internal networks to recast this imperial zone as a coherent, if not always cohesive, unit. The relationship between metropoles and colonies is a perennial and necessary dynamic within imperial histories, but too strong a focus on this binary can occlude the often-tangential movements of historical actors within, rather than across, regions such as the Torrid Zone that are often characterized as "peripheral."[6] Migration *within* the French West Indies, not just between the Caribbean and metropolitan France, was a significant, though often ignored, dynamic that shaped the successive development of the Antillean colonies: Martinique and Guadeloupe, and Saint-Domingue. Recent work by Richard Dunn points to the possibilities of comparative scholarship, exploring early mainland America and the West Indies through the same analytic for the later eighteenth and early nineteenth centuries to explore how the plantation complex differed across space and time.[7] This comparative dynamic, however, should in fact be a hallmark of Caribbean scholarship and especially for the seventeenth century, when Europeans often settled for brief periods in several places around the circum-Caribbean along transient zigzags that often initially defied (as with pirates) and then later frequently defined (as with themistocrats) imperial contours.

This perspective, in turn, decenters Paris as the locus of the creation of legal knowledge and emphasizes local innovation and initiative at the developing edges of France's early modern empire in the new and internally coherent Caribbean system. Scholars from Richard Mowery Andrews to Michel Foucault have plumbed early modern conceptions of legality and social-network formation but they have ignored the extent to which France's Antillean colonies developed their own internal dynamics, which were largely pushed by families who used their legal careers and local law courts as anchors for transcolonial networks of knowledge and power. While these dynamics eventually formed transatlantic conversations about the nature of empire, they maintained a local and regional logic that worked within the Caribbean as well as beyond it.[8]

Martinican Origins

The term themistocracy derives from Andrews's work on Parisian legal elites, whom he describes as "a blend, or hybrid, of disparate, even contradictory social elements" in early modern France's *ancien régime,* which formed "a technically savant, vocational, and even modernistic governing class." Andrews's themistocrats devised their rulings from knowledge gained within the social matrix of *parlement* membership that was strengthened (and often accessed) through family ties.[9]

The Caribbean themistocracy can best be understood as a social phenomenon that changed over time, particularly through their migrations within the Torrid Zone, employing sociologist Sida Liu's "processual theory" for understanding the legal profession. In contrast to approaches that conceive of the legal profession as "a social structure, a market monopoly, or a political entity," he instead proposes legal practitioners as members of a "social process that changes over space and time." Liu's process contains four key components: "(1) diagnostic struggles over professional expertise; (2) boundary work over professional jurisdictions; (3) migration across geographical areas and status hierarchies; and (4) exchange between professions and the state."[10] Though Caribbean themistocrats displayed all these traits, their migration across geographical areas and status hierarchies has been the most obscure to historians, so it is this feature this research seeks to uncover in detail.[11]

Martinique, though not the first successful French colony, exerted a profound influence on the French Caribbean's development as it fostered a cohort of families who were both deeply enmeshed with each other and whose later migrations to Saint-Domingue and other colonies created a wide area of legal-knowledge transfer and personal connection. This colony became a political model for two reasons. First, it was the site of concentrated and ongoing settlement efforts by military officers, planters, and indentured servants who were eventually supplemented by large numbers of African slaves. The Martinican pattern of steady settlement beginning officially in 1635 thus contrasts with Saint-Christophe's steady change-over to English control and Saint-Domingue's eventual and violent divorce from France's early modern empire in the revolutionary era. Martinique also stands out against other examples, such as Louisiana and Cayenne, which sat at the northwest and southeast Caribbean peripheries, where they frequently became isolated from both Atlantic and Antillean migration patterns and imperial attention. Louisiana only became a hub of French West Indian migration in the wake of the Haitian Revolution, while Cayenne was first the site of several resettlement projects and then became a penal colony.[12]

Second, Martinican themistocrats self-consciously wrote their own histories, often framed in legal terms, from the earliest days of the island's settlement—a heritage of collective autobiography that continues to the present. The Jesuit Jacques Bouton published an account of Martinique's settlement in 1640 (five years after the colony was officially established), while more recently Martinican archivists have launched a multimedia website that documents the island's history from its earliest habitation to the present.[13] In between these bookends, prominent Martinicans wrote dozens of legal histories that documented the island's development through the lens of law.[14]

Martinique itself is quite small, especially given this lasting influence: the island comprises only about 436 square miles, or less than half the size of Rhode Island. It was claimed as a French possession and became part of the *Compagnie des Îles de l'Amérique,* populated by an overflow from neighboring Saint-Christophe under the leadership of d'Esnambuc, in 1635. Along with Guadeloupe, it was integrated into the Company of the Western Indies in 1664 and came under royal control in 1674. In 1714 a new government of the Leeward Islands *(Îles sous le Vent)* was established in Saint-Domingue, so Martinique became the seat of the general government of the Windward Islands *(Îles du Vent)* that included Guadeloupe, Grenada, and other neighboring islands. Guadeloupe was governed separately from 1763 to 1768 and from 1775 onward.

Eighteenth-century commentator Martinican Thibault de Chanvalon noted that settlers from the northwest French region of Normandy dominated the island, but early communities also included a surprising number of Dutch, Jewish, and Portuguese colonists.[15] By the early eighteenth century, the Abraham Gradis family (of Portuguese Jewish origin), had set up an extensive pan-Caribbean trading network in Martinique with ties by marriage to the Bordeaux Parlement. Among other members, David Gradis and his son were colonial agents in Bordeaux, while David's nephew and his wife resided in Saint-Domingue.[16] By the mid-eighteenth century, Chanvalon himself could claim to represent the fourth generation of Thibaults to be born in Martinique, a family with ties to the Petit family, another dominant family of themistocrats, and whose wealth was built through the sugar trade. Like most creole (that is, Caribbean-born) sons, he studied in France (at Bordeaux) and returned to Martinique to serve on the *conseil supérieur* and help run the family business.[17]

Families such as Chanvalon's exerted profound influence on the French circum-Caribbean, even in comparison with the diversified financial and political interests of the Gradis family. Those families who had moved to Martinique in the initial period of settlement from around 1627 to 1635 did so because of the cramped conditions on nearby Saint-Christophe. These families had thus worked together and shared governing responsibilities from the initial decades of the French colonization of the Torrid Zone, and by the 1670s their children had built tightly knit social and economic networks through intermarriage. The de Goursolas family, of Dutch extraction but French citizenship, was one of these families. Mederic Roole served as a major and lieutenant-general for Martinique in the middle of the seventeenth century and in the latter role served as a *conseiller* on the island's *conseil supérieur.* This service had significant enough merit for Mederic's widow, Jeanne Hurault (of another major Martinican and Guadeloupean family still dominant today), to request a continuation of tax exemptions for herself, her minor children, and her slaves in 1664.[18]

The granting of this exemption—especially for her slaves—signaled both wealth and status achieved through the means of legal services rendered in the *conseil.* Guillaume Dorange similarly constructed a legal argument for tax exemptions and other privileges based on the "hazards" faced by his family against Kalinago, unspecified local "rebels," and of course the English. His family's service in defense of the French kingdom in Saint-Christophe and Martinique since 1628 and their success in Martinique as a numerous (and by implication prosperous) family had qualified them for special recognition.[19]

With the replacement of company rule by direct royal rule under Colbert's 1674 reforms, however, these nascent colonial elites continued to turn to careers in law as vehicles that supplemented planting interests. In 1680 the Martinican *conseiller* (magistrate) de La Calle requested *lettres patentes* for approval to build a plantation on the island. Colonial magistrates such as de La Calle combined political and agricultural vocations to take advantage of France's dual imperial aims in the Caribbean: to garner geopolitical dominance by countering other European empires in the region and to profit from plantation-produced cash crops, especially sugar. At one time an agent for the *Compagnie d'Occident* in the French West Indies, de La Calle's company experience complemented his newer interests and signaled a shift in interest among colonial residents from primarily company-oriented trade to a more robust, imperially protected agricultural economy.[20] Necessary for this transition, however, were legal experts such as de La Calle who could serve on legal institutions like the *conseil* and employ their experience in trade and agriculture as magistrates.

Economic ventures such as de La Calle's plantation did not always succeed, however, so having a judicial career offered early European inhabitants of the Antilles a second livelihood with the added benefit of access to state resources. Michel de Clermont had a career that spanned the law courts of Martinique and Guadeloupe: he began as a *lieutenant de juge* in Martinique in 1691, advanced to judge in Guadeloupe, and finally achieved the rank of *conseiller* in Martinique's *conseil supérieur* in 1707. However, in 1690 the English took a French ship as a prize off the coast of Saint-Christophe. Clermont personally lost more than 40,000 *écus* (equivalent to 120,000 *livres*), a sizable sum that could purchase a large plantation, a disaster compounded by the fact that he had a large family. For unspecified reasons connected with this loss, Clermont's judicial position was revoked in 1700. At this nadir, having lost both economic and political means, Clermont begged the navy secretary for recompense to cover his decade of judicial service and asked for a vacant position on either the Guadeloupe or Martinique law courts. With the aid of recommendation letters and his judicial track record, Clermont succeeded and was restored to the Antillean magistrature. Economic ventures such as plantations and shipping could be won and lost easily, but judicial careers proved to be more resilient.[21]

Over time Caribbean elites recognized the durability of judicial careers and increasingly incorporated arguments about judicial service into their claims for economic privileges. By the end of the eighteenth century, requests for tax exemptions and investment approval articulated by Hurault and de La Calle had become well-rehearsed applications for noble status that reiterated family contributions to Caribbean colonial success but with a more explicit concentration on judicial service. Grandval de La Vigne wrote to the regional governors of France's Caribbean possessions in 1775 in the midst of his own ongoing application to the nobility. The core of his case had two dimensions. First, like Hurault and Dorange a century earlier, Grandval de La Vigne could point to an ancestor, Grandval Pierre Joziau, as among the founding members of Martinique as a colony from as early as 1656. However, this founding generation served primarily as the root of a more important distinction in his family: extensive and ongoing service on the magistracy (among other prominent roles). As the governors pointed out in their reply, genealogy reports were not sufficient to establish noble status.[22] Instead, careers in the Caribbean law courts became essential for securing familial and political status that could be recognized both at home and by administrators in metropolitan France.

Antillean Migrations

As Clermont's career demonstrates, judicial trajectories could span several colonies. The lives of several members of the Courpon family expose the basic pattern of migration and legal activity within the early modern Caribbean that followed initial family establishments. Philippe de Courpon began as a *conseiller* on Saint-Christophe's *conseil* sometime before 1682, when he received a letter reproaching him for issuing ordinances under his own authority (and an unspecified higher authority) without going through the *conseil* as a deliberative and legislative body that acted on the king's command. Despite this overstretch, however, by 1696 he had achieved the role of *conseiller* on Martinique's *conseil* and later served as a royal lieutenant back in Saint-Christophe as well as in Martinican and Guadeloupean postings until his death in 1709.[23]

By the first part of the eighteenth century, Courpon's descendants continued this career of royal lieutenancy with judicial stints, but began to work more
frequently in the newer colony of Saint-Domingue, especially in lucrative plantation regions like the central Artibonite plain. One of his relatives, most likely
his son, appears as a captain in Saint-Domingue as early as 1708, where he earned
promotions through major and royal lieutenant in various military stations
until he finally retired in 1739. These postings took a great physical toll, as the
king granted him leave to return to Paris to restore his health in 1737 before his
ultimate retirement.[24]

By the 1720s several branches of the Courpon family appear simultaneously in several Caribbean locales and some members openly acknowledged these
long-standing personal ties between Martinique and Saint-Domingue. In a letter dated May 9, 1748, the Martinican militia captain Courpon de La Vernade,
whose son was stationed as an infantry ensign in Saint-Domingue but who was
an English prisoner of war at this time, explained that, while he and his son had
no relatives in France itself, their family was based in both Martinique and Saint-
Domingue. Courpon de La Vernade *père*'s status as a militia captain reflected a
well-respected military status that had carried on from Philippe de Courpon's
original military-judicial vocation.[25] Though he does not appear in these documents as a legal practitioner, militia captains often performed multiple social and
political functions: those who held this rank usually were usually members of the
planter elite for whom military service could provide a practical means of protection from rebel slaves and foreign armies. These roles also often corresponded with
experience in law courts such as the *conseils*, as well as in lower jurisdictions like
courts of first instance, as witnesses, litigants, and magistrates.[26]

Courpon de La Vernade *père* cited these functions in his letter, emphasizing
his family's contributions to French West Indian interests "since the foundation
of the colonies" and continuing up to the present, citing his shared interest with
his son in at least one Saint-Dominguan plantation. Courpon de La Vernade *père*'s
own father (most likely Philippe, discussed above) had been made a *chevalier
de Saint-Louis,* a high military honor, and served as a royal lieutenant in Saint-
Christophe. His brother, de Pourpon, had achieved the same honors in Saint-
Domingue, while he himself had ranked as a grenadier captain for the last thirty-
three years (out of a military career of over fifty years thus far). In addition, his
own experiences comprised a *Saint-Louis* award for five campaigns against pirates
(forbans), the defense of both Guadeloupe and Saint-Christophe in 1703 and yet
more military achievements around the Antilles.[27]

Saint-Dominguan Transformations

Despite these critical movements of Martinicans to Saint-Dominguan outposts,
the most critical grant from the older to the newer colony lay in the realm of
the ideas that these migrants carried with them. Two trends emerge from an

examination of Saint-Domingue's formative years in light of its Martinican connections. First, Saint-Domingue relied upon Martinican ideas about colonial governance even though it developed a larger and more varied population. Second, Saint-Domingue families who participated in superior councils and wrote legal commentary nearly always had a Martinican background, so the lines of knowledge transfer from Martinique to Saint-Domingue can be best drawn through families across several generations.

As Saint-Domingue's population surpassed Martinique's around 1715, its sugar economy rapidly expanded, creating a need for guides to colonial governance both to ensure the French state's profits and maintain control over the majority slave colony.[28] Colonial administrators sought to present a clear vision of good colonial governance (sometimes citing Montesquieu, John Locke,[29] or Francis Bacon[30] as authorities), though this vision varied depending on the author's loyalties to local or metropolitan interests.[31] Many of the best-known colonial legal commentators of the late eighteenth century—Moreau de Saint-Méry[32] being the most famous—were residents of Saint-Domingue with Martinican roots. The Petit family included prominent council members from families with strong ties to Martinique and Saint-Domingue, who also commented extensively on colonial law, though some of his family was based in Dijon. Emilien Petit was born in Saint-Domingue[33] and served on the Superior Council of Léogane[34] in southern Saint-Domingue and then as a deputy to the Superior Council of Colonies in Paris. He published a survey of colonial law in 1771, *Droit public; ou, Gouvernement des colonies françoises d'après les loix faites pour ces pays* (*Public law; or, Government of the French colonies according to the laws made for these provinces*).

In this volume, Petit traced the history of French colonization in the Caribbean from the first settlements on Saint-Christophe to Saint-Domingue's plantation society, even including transcripts of charters and other founding documents. One example is a compilation of council records and laws by the Martinican council member Jean Assier. Petit complimented Assier's "choice of subjects" and explanations for his logic, which, according to Petit, "prov[ed] as well the intelligence of this officer as well as [his] zeal for the good of the colony." By citing these documents, Petit established a historical chain of political events that informed later rules and institutions that governed Saint-Domingue in the 1770s.[35]

While not born in the islands, another relative, Jacques Petit de Viévigne, married into a prosperous Martinican family. He was *sénéchal* (mid-level court officer) of Saint-Pierre, Martinique, and edited a 1767 edition of Martinique's legal code.[36] As with Emilien Petit's later volume, Petit de Viévigne intended his work to serve an educational purpose, informing colonial residents of colonial laws and ensuring their enforcement.[37] A chronological index of edicts and laws showed how colonial governance had changed over time, from the substance of laws on topics like passenger boats and runaway slaves to the structure and roles of Martinique's council and its members. This project underscored the local expertise of Petit de Viévigne, which drew on his practical experience and also offered an example of colonial governance that his readers could follow.

The participation of family members in an intercolonial discussion about local laws indicates that Caribbean colonies were governed on a regional level by parties interested in the experiences of those who had held their positions in the past. While military administrators often moved among colonies on different assignments, council members and Caribbean families used their own influence and connections to share knowledge about the past and present institutions while debating the future direction of colonial governance.

The case of council member Jean-Jacques Faure de Lussac illustrates the transfer of knowledge from Martinique to Saint-Domingue though physical movement. He transferred from Martinique's council to the Cap-Français, Saint-Domingue *conseil,* in the late 1770s. Like Petit, Faure de Lussac came from a well-established Martinican family with extensive ties to the island's Superior Council. His father had been born in Martinique in 1705 of Bordelais parents and served as a council member from the 1740s to the 1770s. Faure de Lussac was the eldest of eight children, and several of his siblings married into other prominent families with ties to Martinique's council and plantations in Saint-Domingue. He was nominated to the Martinican Superior Council on March 5, 1775, but requested a transfer to Saint-Domingue a few years later to join the wealthy plantations of his brother-in-law, Duval Monville. As Duval Monville became prosperous, Faure de Lussac sought to capitalize on this relationship by moving to Saint-Domingue.[38]

Faure de Lussac relied on other relatives in addition to Duval Monville in planning his move to Saint-Domingue. A man who identified himself as Faure de Lussac's son-in-law wrote a letter of recommendation to Saint-Domingue's governor, the Comte d'Ennery, in November 1775 requesting that his father-in-law receive the council position recently vacated by a Sieur Ruotte. The letter lauded Faure de Lussac as the son of a former council member, a good subject, and parent of the writer's wife, but acknowledged that he was *"assez pauvre"*—poor enough.[39] This last comment explains why Faure de Lussac wanted to join his brother-in-law's prosperous plantations even though he already held political power as a Martinican council member: he needed money. Another letter of nomination makes Faure de Lussac's poverty even starker, describing his attempt to transfer "the debris of his fortune" to Saint-Domingue.[40]

This coincidence of financial problems and reliance on family members highlights the necessity of family ties between colonies as a means of arranging alternative employment. Faure de Lussac's poverty thus reveals the economic—and, therefore, political—vulnerability that colonial elites could face, while his family ties—especially his connections to Superior Councils—offered a way out by enabling him to move from one council to another. Later records indicate that this strategy worked: by 1784, Faure de Lussac was receiving twenty-four hundred *livres* per annum as a council member.[41]

The career of the Faure family also illustrates a common pattern of movement for elite Martinicans: originating in Bordeaux and settling in Martinique, with later generations fanning out to other colonies. Most Martinican council members were native to the island, while Saint-Domingue's councils counted more members who came directly from France. Out of 109 Martinican council members nominated between 1675 and 1831, 70 were creoles, 2 had creole mothers, and 37 were native to metropolitan France (but 24 of them married creole women).[42] By contrast, many Saint-Domingue council members were only one or two generations removed from relatives either in other colonies (especially Martinique) or France, as the lives of the Petit family illustrate.

Not all *conseil* members moved from Martinique to Saint-Domingue while maintaining council membership. Instead, younger sons—such as Duval Monville—tended to move to Saint-Domingue, presumably as a means of establishing their own fortunes, whereas their fathers were content to manage their existing political and economic interests. However, colonial elites who survived the commercial and physical risks of Caribbean settlement to establish wealth and political clout could thus dominate the composition of local institutions across several islands as their families expanded. Faure de Lussac's career reflects how knowledge continued to be transferred directly between colonies through the movement of individuals. Later examples such as the Petits show how knowledge can be disseminated in several directions at once through the means of printed legal guides: from Martinique to Saint-Domingue and back again.[43]

Global Connections

As French legal experts recognized the opportunities afforded by careers in Caribbean law courts, they increasingly sought employment in the *conseils*. Some Europeans even obtained naturalization to establish their credentials. Martin Hussey, an Irishman, had assumed a post as an attorney *(avocat)* in Martinique's *conseil* in the early eighteenth century through his previous experience as an attorney for the Bordeaux Parlement. In 1727 he emphasized his legal education in France and Catholic faith, as well as his long residence in Martinique, including marriage four years previously, to request naturalization from the island's chief administrators, which they granted.[44] Later, his likely descendant, Walter Hussey, who lived in Guadeloupe, similarly sought naturalization by citing his longtime establishment on that island and obtained a recommendation that underscored his "honest conduct" and potential, based on his previous material success, for becoming a "useful citizen" of the colony."[45]

Both of the Husseys gathered strong evidence that they had contributed to the financial and social wellbeing of the French Antilles, but Martin Hussey's more detailed case brought up two issues that enhanced his argument. First, by acknowledging his Catholic faith (however sincere or compulsory), he contradicted any concerns that his loyalty might lean towards Protestant England and instead lined up his political and religious attachments to the king of France and, by extension, the legal framework over which he held authority. Second, Martin's purposeful mention of legal education in France conveyed a legal pedigree that connected his current practice in Martinique with an origin point that matched this French legal tradition and left no question of his legal integrity.[46] In between, his stint in the Bordeaux Parlement conveyed experience in one of the leading law courts of France in one of the leading Atlantic port cities. By the end of the eighteenth century, the continued presence of the Hussey family name in the Antilles signaled that this strategy had worked and had likely even allowed Martin's heirs to further their economic, as well as political, interests in the region.

Though not all Martinican themistocrats managed to maintain or expand their positions to the end of the eighteenth century, the fact that a substantial number did underscores this strategy as a successful one. As themistocrats gained seats on *conseils* throughout the Caribbean and simultaneously leveraged their economic interests in plantation agriculture and Atlantic trade, they were able to anchor themselves and their families in a tempestuous Atlantic World system and sometimes to thrive there. As themistocrats sought intermarriage, transcolonial careers, and political patronage, they further built these once-local livelihoods into a regional, then global, network of legal experts whose shared knowledge enabled France's early modern empire to work somewhat cohesively.

By the last decades of the eighteenth century, a themistocracy that had previously concentrated on the Caribbean merged with another regional themistocracy that was centered on the Indian Ocean. This latter themistocracy had developed from a much more consciously trade-oriented network of families and institutions that transported such luxury goods as spices and textiles from Asia to Europe via the Mascarene Islands and the Cape of Good Hope. Though each themistocracy retained some distinct regional traits, with the Caribbean themistocrats more intensely focused on agriculture in the Antilles and the Indian Ocean, a much more scattered trade network, some people did manage to transcend these regional centers through global careers. The wealthy and numerous Barbé de Marbois family was based in Saint-Domingue, where François Barbé de Marbois served as the intendant of the colony, but his brother Nicolas François worked as a *lieutenant de juge* in Île de France (modern Mauritius) in the Indian Ocean.[47] François Millon, too, served as a *sénéchal* and judge in a lower court in Saint-Marc, Saint-Domingue, but later became an attorney general *(procureur général)* in the *conseil supérieur* of Île Bourbon (now La Réunion), adjacent to Île de France.[48]

An Emerging Imperial Themistocracy

The primary settings for these contestations were law courts known as *conseils supérieurs,* which were established in each of France's overseas colonies as well as in new territories, such as Alsace, in Europe.[49] As the primary judicial forum in each colony, the *conseils supérieurs* were responsible for resolving local disputes

Laurie M. Wood

and hearing a wide range of cases, from smuggling to accusations of slave mis-treatment. They were also required to add new laws to the *conseil greffes* (regis-ters), a crucial means of transferring legal knowledge from the imperial center in Paris to colonial capitals. Across the Caribbean, the general organization of *conseils supérieurs* looked much like Martinique's, which had been founded in 1664, making it the second-oldest colonial *conseil* (younger than Québec's by merely a year)[50] and the same age as Guadeloupe's. A governor-general who managed several islands in the Antilles oversaw the *conseil* and worked with another governor who was solely responsible for Martinique, in addition to the colonial intendant, who oversaw financial and legal matters. Together, they were assisted by around twelve magistrates *(conseillers)* who heard and decided ca-ses argued by a prosecutor, who was occasionally assisted by attorneys *(avocats)* with evidence and arguments submitted by lower-level attorneys *(procureurs)*. Saint-Domingue contained two such *conseils* with similar personnel, one at the capital, Léogane (later moved to Port-au-Prince), in the middle of the colony and the other at Cap-François, the commercial center.[51] Together, these judicial personnel formed a Caribbean themistocracy, or a community of legal experts, who interfaced with a much more widespread French themistocracy that encom-passed all the *conseillers, avocats, procureurs,* and other legal practitioners who worked in a variety of law courts that spanned France's early modern empire from its European provinces to newer territories such as Pondichéry in South Asia and the Antillean colonies.

The stories of themistocrats like the Chanvalons, the Courpons, and the Petits emerge gradually from a wide range of archival sources that have been cross-referenced to reveal families, family and legal networks, and migration patterns.[52] By focusing, though, on legal knowledge and legal institutional membership held among Caribbean families, this essay accomplishes two distinct purposes that move beyond these forms of family history.[53] First, it identifies a specific variety of expertise, legal knowledge, which was carried within and beyond the Caribbean by members of similar family networks. Understandings of judicial process were con-structed in thin layers as jurists, like Clermont, moved from one judicial position to the next. Over time and especially over generations, jurists' experience coalesced through the repetition of work in colonial courtrooms. More explicitly, Caribbean themistocrats articulated self-understandings of their role within France's *ancien régime* empire by describing genealogies of family service in applications for noble status and law codes written to metropolitan audiences. This line of analysis thus seeks to move beyond the genre of collective biography and genealogy towards a more analytical and directional approach to family networks. Second, it under-scores the insights to be gained about pathways of knowledge transfer, especially for understanding the kinds of path dependencies that decisions made by early colonial participants created for future inhabitants, whether planter, slave, or administrator, both within the Torrid Zone and beyond.

Experimenting with Acceptance, Caribbean-Style

Jews as Aliens in the Anglophone Torrid Zone

Barry L. Stiefel

At the onset of the seventeenth century, the Caribbean was a Spanish lake, barred to all non-Catholic Europeans by the Alhambra decree of 1492, which expelled the Jews from all the Crown's domains, as well as the subsequent forced conversions and expulsions of Muslims, which took place in phases during the early sixteenth century. Protestants were also forbidden in Spanish dominions since they were considered heretics from the perspective of Catholicism at the time. The permanent settlement of English and French colonies on St. Christopher's in 1624, the Dutch on Curacao in 1634, and the Danes following on St. Thomas in 1665, however, caused this situation to change. During the early seventeenth century, Spain's imperial rivals—the European powers just mentioned—shifted their hostility from privateering to colony building and, of course, brought their differences in culture and faith with them.

Only in the Dutch Republic, during this initial period of colonization of the West Indies by Protestant nations, were Jews permitted to observe their religion. In contrast, while nonconformist Protestantism existed in England and France, in the 1620s the practice of Judaism was still illegal because of their prior expulsions from these kingdoms during the late thirteenth and fourteenth centuries. Therefore, Jews who identified themselves as such were aliens in the Caribbean during the seventeenth century, not only in a religious sense but also in civil (secular) terms. Moreover, the republic would not officially defend its Jewish residents in international matters until 1658. But by 1740, considered to be after the "long seventeenth century" (1598–1720), the situation had changed: Jews gradually became adopted into more host countries and their Caribbean colonies, specifically those where a form of Protestantism was the established faith.[1]

So what happened that enabled Jews to shed (at least some of) their alien status in the English Caribbean and in the British Isles, most particularly during the long seventeenth century? Since Jews had no loyalties to the Papacy, the Church of England, Luther, or Calvin, they were, in many respects, stateless. Was not having a loyalty to a nation-state with an established official religion an advantage or disadvantage, or both at one and the same time? The economic success of seventeenth-century Caribbean Jews lay in their economic resourcefulness, based on a co-ethnic trade network that transcended geopolitical borders. Their "tribalism" allowed Jews to extend credit (an incredibly valuable commodity in the cash-poor Atlantic World during this period) to their co-ethnic merchants, across vast distances and borders, which provided an important advantage in commerce. How these factors played out in relation to the Caribbean will also be part of the analysis.

Jews and Caribbean Colonization
at the Sunset of the Sixteenth Century

While Judaism was banned in the Spanish Caribbean, Iberian descendants of converted Jews (conversos, pl.) and secret Judaizers did make their way to the region, though this was also illegal. The earliest and perhaps most significant instance of this was Luis de Torres, the interpreter on Christopher Columbus's first voyage of discovery, which left Spain in August 1492, literally days after the Alhambra decree came into effect. During the fifteenth century and earlier, Iberian Jews along with Christian and Muslim colleagues had participated in the polyglot enterprise of translating ancient texts, many of them scientific treatises, into vernacular languages and Latin. Prior to Columbus's voyage, de Torres had participated in such projects. Other Jews would follow de Torres's precedent in providing linguistic assistance to the European colonial powers, notably Samuel Cohen, who was needed for his knowledge of Spanish in the capture of Curacao by Dutch West India Company (WIC) forces in 1634.[2] So, depending on the circumstances, *alienness* could make Jews a problematic "other" because their presence was a reminder of nonconformity (from the perspective of intolerant rulers in Iberia) or a useful "other" because they had skills and abilities difficult to find within the nation-state, such as the Dutch Republic, and in trade.

Of the seventeenth-century European colonial powers, the Dutch were the first to permit Jews residence and the opportunity to practice their faith, at least discreetly, beginning in 1603, although Jews had never formerly been expelled from the Netherlands. The practice of Judaism had been prohibited in France since 1394, although Henri II (ruled 1547–59) allowed Portuguese *conversos* to settle in Bordeaux in 1550 so long as they maintained a Catholic façade.[3]

In late-sixteenth-century England, we see the dichotomy in the simultaneous perception of Jews as desirable and undesirable aliens, though England had not yet ventured into the Caribbean, having just lost its colony at Roanoke in present-day North Carolina. The first document of analysis is a memorandum from the trial of Roger Lopez (1517–1594) in 1594, a crypto-Jew and physician, accused of attempting to assassinate Elizabeth I. Within the document Lopez is identified as "confess[ing] he is a Jew, though now a false Christian" and that "Lopez was convicted of the highest and most detestable treason that can be imagined."[4] While other evidence suggests that Lopez was likely framed for the charge of attempted assassination, what is significant here is the beginning emphasis that he was Jewish (thus an inherently untrustworthy alien) and not Spanish, with whom England was involved in the undeclared Anglo-Spanish War. Interestingly, Lopez also served as an interpreter between the pretender to the Portuguese throne, Don Antonio (1531–1595), and Robert Devereux, second Earl of Essex (1565–1601) and favorite of the queen, when they met in 1593. Matters did not go well during this discussion, resulting in Devereux's humiliation, creating speculation regarding whether he may have been behind the framing of Lopez.[5]

At approximately the same time, "Queen Elizabeth also received Fatim, a Jew; sent from Constantinople to England by his master Salomon [Cormano] (whom Murad III had made Duke of Metilli; and who settled the Jews at Tiberias) to know whether Qu. Elizabeth would assist the Emperor against the Turks, or not."[6] In this instance Fatim, and by extension, Salomon Cormano, were not only first identified as Jewish aliens—and not of another nationality—but were well received as foreigners providing a service to the English Crown. The English ended up allying with the Turks because of the family ties between the Holy Roman Emperor Rudolf II (1552–1612), and Philip II (ruled 1556–98) of Spain, both Habsburgs.[7] In both instances we see that Jews, while not English, were playing important supportive roles in both domestic and foreign affairs.

An archetypical example of Jews as aliens during this empire-religion-nation-state building was perhaps Samuel Pallache (1550–1614), whom his biographers Mercedes García-Arenal and Gerard Albert Wiegers call "A Man of Three Worlds." Born in Fez into a Jewish family that had fled to Morocco following the Alhambra decree, he became a merchant, diplomat, and sometimes Barbary pirate. In 1608–10 he was part of an embassy that sought to establish an alliance between the Moroccan Sultanate and the Dutch Republic against their common enemy, Spain. As part of this process he met with Sultan Zidan al-Nasir and the Dutch *stadhouder* Maurice of Nassau. During this process he encountered Spanish agents who also contracted for Pallache's services; thus he became a double agent. Pallache therefore not only shared Dutch and Moroccan secrets with Spain but important information about Spain with the Netherlands and Morocco.[8] His actions eventually caught the ire of some of his associates when he was forced to stop in Stuart England on December 23, 1614, because of a storm at sea. Maurice of Nassau intervened on Pallache's behalf, eventually enabling him to seek asylum in the Netherlands, though by this time he had lost his material wealth and health, dying in The Hague in 1616.[9]

It is significant here that Pallache is identified twice as "Jew," rather than as from Barbary or Morocco, or Spanish, or Dutch, even though he was acting as a go-between for these enemy countries, all of whom employed his services. Though this case involving a North African sultanate, Spain, the Dutch Republic, and England took place in Europe, during the following decade encounters between Jews and European powers would be transferred to the Caribbean because of English, French, and Dutch incursions there, with Jews playing an intriguing role as third-party aliens. In short, the torrid experience of Jews in the seventeenth-century Caribbean was a continuation of what had been occurring for more than a century prior in Western Europe.

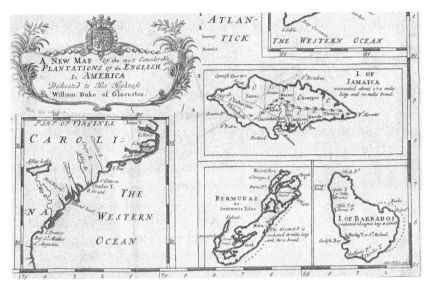

A detail of *A new map of the most considerable plantations of the English in America,* by Sutton Nicholls (London, 1700). Depicted here are the key English Caribbean colonies at the end of the seventeenth century. At this time Jewish colonists are known to have inhabited Barbados, Jamaica, and Carolina. Courtesy of the Library of Congress Geography and Map Division.

The Settlement of Jews as Aliens

After decades of rivalry between Spain with England, France, and what would become the Netherlands, Spain's competitors eventually broke into the Caribbean. The first attempts were by the French and English, including Charlesfort in present-day South Carolina in 1562 and Fort Caroline in present-day Florida in 1564 by France, along with Roanoke by the English in 1585. All three attempts ended in failure, but what is significant is that France and England both pursued early colonial experiments in these locations specifically because of their close proximity to the Caribbean Sea and Gulf of Mexico, where the center of Spanish activity was taking place. France and England were not yet ready to confront the power of the Spanish Habsburgs directly in the Americas. Indeed, as Lou Roper discusses in his contribution to this volume, the continued political and economic connections between the Carolinas and English Lesser Antilles during the seventeenth century brought the colonies from these two parts of the empire very close.

Jews were present at England's earliest colonial experiment in the Americas, on Roanoke Island. Joachim Gaunse, an Ashkenazi Jewish miner originally from (Habsburg) Prague, had settled in England in the early 1580s along with other foreigners invited to improve mining technology and techniques for the Royal Mining Company. Gaunse was instrumental in advancing England's copper-smelting techniques, which were required for preparing England's military readiness against enemies such as Spain and which proved valuable against the Spanish Armada in 1588. Copper, as well as being an ingredient in bronze, was paramount for the use of sixteenth-century guns and artillery.

In 1585 Gaunse was invited to join Sir Walter Ralegh's expedition to the Roanoke Colony. In the twentieth century, archaeological excavations conducted at Roanoke Island found lumps of smelted copper and a goldsmith's crucible among the ruins of the site, which have been attributed to Gaunse. The following year Gaunse returned to England with several other colonists when Sir Francis Drake's fleet passed by Roanoke. In 1589 Gaunse's Jewish identity was discovered while he was in the midst of providing Hebrew lessons to English gentlemen. During one of the lessons, he inadvertently made a blasphemous statement about Jesus Christ. He was brought to trial, but since he had never been baptized a Christian, whether Protestant or Catholic, he could not be accused of heresy—only of being an infidel. Unfortunately, the trial records are incomplete and Gaunse's ultimate fate is unknown. It is believed, though, that because of his connections on Elizabeth I's Privy Council and his expertise as a metallurgist, Gaunse was too valuable for England to lose, and the matter was dropped.[10]

Besides Gaunse, other Portuguese names are listed in relation to the settlement of Roanoke. Simon Ferdinando is identified as serving as a mariner and ship's pilot, exploring the inlets along the North Carolina coast. He, like Gaunse, was also fortunate in choosing to return to England, where he took up a career of piracy, preying on Spanish ships in the Caribbean.[11] While it cannot be substantiated whether these Portuguese at Roanoke had Jewish ancestry or practiced crypto-Judaism, the presence of these individuals there is a testament to how dispersed Iberian expatriate activity was within the English-speaking world, and the important roles that this diaspora played in England's earliest attempts at colonization.

Following the successful settlements of Tadoussac in 1600 and Québec in 1608 by France in what is now Canada, as well as Jamestown, Virginia, in 1607 by England, these rivals became bolder in their Caribbean exploits, bypassing the Carolinas for the Lesser Antilles and first occupying the small island of St. Christopher's in 1624. The Dutch followed suit with their own Caribbean acquisition in 1634, capturing Curacao. These competitors subsequently claimed larger territories on the mainland of North and South America in locations where the Spanish were not well entrenched. The Dutch also briefly held parts of Brazil, including Bahia (1624–25) and Pernambuco (1630–54). England and France would also go on to capture Jamaica (1655–60) and the western part of Hispaniola (Saint-Domingue, 1660s), respectively.

In response to the capitulation of Pernambuco to the Portuguese in 1654, the Dutch began to protect the interests of their Jewish colonists, realizing that if they continued to treat Jews as aliens living in their midst, they would not so eagerly participate in the very risky endeavor of colonial economic development, especially regarding the sugar trade and merchant shipping, where they had been helpful. That Jews had proven themselves to be economically important to Dutch exploits in the New World was not lost on their colonial rivals. A profound example is the official presence of Jews in French colonies, which came to an end in 1685 with the Code Noir ordering their expulsion from these territories, which, in conjunction with the Edict of Fontainebleau the same year (revoking the Edict of Nantes), effectively made the French Empire a homogenous Catholic nation, similar to Spain and Portugal.[12] Yet, governors of the French colonies of Martinique, Guadeloupe, Cayenne, and Louisiana on occasion turned a blind eye to the letter of the law, permitting economically useful Jews to settle in these colonies during the eighteenth century because of the economic benefit they brought, though they were still maintained as alien-foreigners. Moreover, France never established an Inquisition to root out Judaizing, unlike Spain and Portugal.

The assistance of Jews in the Dutch economic success of Pernambuco was not lost on the English either. Many Sephardic Jews had established themselves as successful merchants in the Dutch commercial system. Dutch Jews were also interested in expanding their economic opportunities to English territory. Their success came about because of an extensive network they established among themselves that transcended international borders and included means for extending credit, loans and other capital, business contacts, and insider information—an advantage the Dutch, and soon the English, recognized.

The loss of Pernambuco, however, sent many former Jewish colonists into an economic tailspin, exacerbated by England's Navigation Acts of 1651, which had the simultaneous purpose of bolstering English mercantile trade and harming foreign competition—primarily Dutch. The solution for Dutch Jews was to extend their network into England by establishing a family member or other business associate there. Indeed, in 1653 the merchant Jacob Carolos (also known as Jacob Pallache) from The Hague, the son of Samuel discussed previously, had his goods confiscated, demonstrating the problem of his "alienhood" through his identification as "a subject not of Holland [since this would not happen until 1658] but of the King of Morocco, where his ancestors have been for ages, and is a Jew."[13]

This is in contrast to the New Christian network of Spain, Portugal, and France, where *conversos* were accustomed to the hostility of these kingdoms. Because Jews in the Netherlands had enjoyed unofficial toleration since 1603, they desired similar privileges in England.[14] Dutch Jewish economic interest in

England and its colonies came with the aspiration for open tolerance of Jews there as well. It is also for similar reasons that the Danish Crown invited Jews to settle in Frederica and Copenhagen in Denmark, as well as the Danish Caribbean colony of St. Thomas, during the 1680s and 1690s.[15]

Looking beyond England's shores we find that crypto-Jews trickled into English Barbados, especially after 1654 with refugees coming from the Portuguese reconquest of Dutch Brazil.[16] England and its colonies were also in a state of political turmoil during the Cromwellian period (1653–58). Indeed, the Barbados Assembly granted permission for Jews to reside on the island before Oliver Cromwell allowed their readmission to England in December 1655.[17] Though the status of Jews was only that of unofficially tolerated aliens, how could the Barbados Assembly pass such an ordinance, which was in direct conflict with an established law (Edward I's expulsion order of 1290 was still in effect), or without permission from imperial authorities in London overriding the previous edict? During this period, which entailed the English Civil Wars (1642–51), Barbados was playing both sides of the conflict between the Royalists and Parliamentarians. Political exiles and refugees from the Civil Wars also sought asylum on Barbados. This impartiality, as well as their remote location from London-based authorities, enabled Barbados to retain a measure of autonomy in internal governance, enabling it to admit Jews extra-officially. Moreover, commerce with Dutch merchant shipping, which included Jews, reinforced Barbadian self-determination.[18]

The position of Dutch Jews as neutral aliens in the Royalist-Parliamentarian conflict was advantageous. So how did authorities in London respond to the permitted presence of Jews in Barbados without his authorization? Instead of challenging the actions of the wayward colonial assembly, Cromwell's government implemented its own trial by allowing two Jews, Abraham Mercado and Raphael de Mercado, to reside on the island in April 1655, eight months prior to his decision for the rest of the English Empire.[19]

The Mercados were useful colonists for developing Barbados's infant sugar industry, owing to their experiences in Dutch Brazil. Moreover, both Cromwell as well as the Barbados Assembly used Jews in this initial experiment as a colonist-commodity, similar to what Jessica Roitman discusses in her contribution to this volume. In contrast to the Wild Coast, however, the colonial assemblies of Barbados and Jamaica passed anti-Semitic laws when perceptions of Jews as undesirable aliens became widespread because of perceived economic competition—a topic that will be revisited below.

Meanwhile, in December 1654 Cromwell had sent a force under William Penn (1621–1670) and Robert Venables (c.1613–1687) to invade Spanish Caribbean territory, with the intended target of Santo Domingo. The English were defeated there but had better success in Jamaica, where the invasion party landed in May 1655, a month after permission was granted for the Mercados to reside on Barbados. A number of *conversos* were already residing on Jamaica, including Simon de

Caceres and Captain Campoe Sabbatha, who assisted Penn and Venables, enabling additional Jewish settlement after the conquest of the island was completed.[20]

The first half of the seventeenth century was an era of messianic fervor among Protestants, Catholics, and Jews, which had implications on European colonial societies in the Caribbean. Among many Europeans there was also a popularly held belief that Jews through their diaspora had an important role in the messianic redemption. This was complicated after 1492, when European explorers and colonists began speculating on the origins of the indigenous people of the Americas. Some theorists, including Rabbi Menasseh ben Israel (1604–1657), looked to the Bible for answers—proposing the possibility that the Ten Lost Tribes of Israel had perhaps made their way to the Americas in ancient times.

Rabbi ben Israel also observed the increasing potential of England and its Caribbean Empire as a prospective new land for Jewish settlement. Born into a crypto-Jewish family in the Portuguese Madeira Islands, he was well aware, from a young age, how geographically alienated the world was to those who observed Judaism. Besides excelling in theological studies, ben Israel also founded Amsterdam's first Jewish printing press in 1622. In 1650 he published, with the assistance of his son Samuel, one of his more influential books, translated into English as *Hope of Israel,* which was also published in Spanish, Dutch, and Latin, in which he argued that at least some of the Ten Lost Tribes were to be found in the Americas and that the messianic redemption could only come about once Jews were scattered to each corner of the earth. A significant corner lacking Jews, argued ben Israel, was England and its new colonial possessions.

Hope of Israel was directed towards Oliver Cromwell and other religiously fervent Parliamentarians.[21] The belief that at least some of the indigenous peoples in the Americas were descendants of the Ten Lost Tribes was shared by many seventeenth-century Protestants, Catholics, and Jews, the only difference being that Christians believed that the scattering of the Jews was required for the messiah's second coming, with Jesus Christ having been the first. So, besides economic rationalization, religious motives influenced Cromwell's decision to cease enforcement of Edward I's expulsion edict of 1290. Cromwell and his Puritan supporters could rationalize that the conversion of Jews to their "True Religion" could occur more successfully if Jews were exposed to it by being allowed on English soil, thus enabling the millennium to begin more swiftly.

An additional connection between ben Israel, Cromwell, and the Caribbean regarding the readmission of Jews into England and its colonies were ben Israel's in-laws, through his wife Rachel Abrabanel. David Abrabanel Dormido, ben Israel's brother-in-law and a crypto-Jewish merchant residing in England, had been an investor in Dutch Brazil. The Portuguese reconquest coupled with the Navigation Acts caused Dormido significant financial hardship. In England, Dormido assisted ben Israel in obtaining an audience with Cromwell, which eventually resulted in a conference at Whitehall to discuss the matter with advisers in December 1655.[22] Thus, one can see that multiple parties, both Protestant and Jewish, as well in Europe and in the Caribbean, where working together—though sometimes unknowingly—towards the task of promoting Judaism in England and its colonies. The petition ben Israel submitted in November 1655 included these provisions:

1. To take us as citizens under your protection; and for our greater security, to order your chiefs and generals-at-arms to defend us on all occasions.
2. To allow us public synagogues in England and other places under your power, and the exercise of our religion.
3. To give us a cemetery out of town, for quiet interment of our dead.
4. To allow us to trade freely as others in all sorts of merchandize.
5. To elect a person of quality to receive our passports, and oblige us to swear fidelity, in order that those who come in may live without prejudice or scandal.
6. That we may not trouble the justices of peace with our contests, to license the chief of the synagogue, with 2 almoners, to reconcile differences according to the Mosaic law, with right of appeal to the civil law, first depositing the sum in which the party has been condemned.
7. To revoke all laws against the Jewish nation, that we may live in greater security.[23]

At a special conference at Whitehall, Cromwell and his advisers considered the matter of readmitting Jews, per ben Israel's petition, on a broader basis than had been earlier employed in Barbados. A unilateral decision was made in December 1655 not to enforce Edward I's expulsion edict; however, the readmission of Jews was not legally sanctioned, since no law was ever enacted because of political opposition. Moreover, an edict of return was never issued either, and Cromwell's status as Protector at the time was insufficient to support a declaration of readmission as a proclamation. Therefore, most significantly, items 1 and 7 of ben Israel's petition were not addressed: the crypto-Jews residing in England, Barbados, and Jamaica were allowed to remain and to practice Judaism, though only privately at first, and they legally remained aliens—not denizens.

In April 1656 one encounters the earliest recorded test case of Jewish residency in the English Empire, which involved Antonio Rodrigues Robles (1620–1688), a Portuguese Jew living as a merchant in England, whose property had been seized without a hearing.[24] Despite his alien status Robles successfully asserted that he was a Portuguese Jew, not Spanish, and his property was returned. In 1675 Robles received denization following a lengthy and expensive petition process.[25] Though denization did not give him full citizenship, it enabled him and, by virtue of precedent, other Jews to acquire legal protection as resident aliens, on an individual basis, to engage in trade and other economic endeavors. In 1661 David Raphael de Mercado was still in Barbados purchasing his denization.[26]

Notwithstanding these incremental changes in the status of Jews in England, at the restoration of Charles II to the English Crown in 1660, Royalist opponents of the new presence of Jews in England petitioned the king to enforce the expulsion edict of his thirteenth-century predecessor regarding the "English Jews," who "renewed their usurious and fraudulent practices, and flourish so much that they endeavoured to buy St. Paul's for a synagogue in the late usurper's time."[27] Besides the trumped-up accusations of usury and fraud against them, there was, in this first officially recorded documented instance since 1290, the use of "English Jews"—not Portuguese, Spanish, Dutch, or another nationality. Jews, even in the sight of their enemies in England, could thus be *English*.

In the event, Charles II did not reinstitute the expulsion edict, at least for the time being. In 1661 Charles issued the Windsor Proclamation, which offered incentives for Europeans from non-English nationalities to settle in Jamaica.[28] Jews are not specifically mentioned in the proclamation, but corresponding with this moment was the petition of Jacob Jeosua Bueno Enriques from Jamaica "to naturalize me and my brothers Josef and Moise Enriques so we can use our [Jewish] law and to have synagogues confirmed by Parliament."[29] Then, in 1664 the Jews were granted a royal statement of toleration, which was reiterated in 1674, when Charles II granted them permission to assemble for worship.[30] A year later, the governor of English Suriname extended a formal invitation to the "Hebrew nation" to come and settle in his colony with liberal privileges for the free exercise of Judaism,[31] while in 1669 John Locke and Anthony Ashley Cooper, first Earl of Shaftesbury (1621–1683), coauthored the Fundamental Constitutions of Carolina, which declared that "that Jews, heathens, and other dissenters from the purity of Christian religion" had the right to practice their faith and form a congregation. Though the presence of Jews would not be recorded in South Carolina until the 1690s, this was a very forward-thinking document for a colony that was culturally and economically tied to the Caribbean.[32]

South Carolina also differed from the Dutch Caribbean, where the West India Company was actively involved in sugar production and export industry, and Jews played a significant part within this sector on many levels. Sugar was not commercially grown in South Carolina since its climate was not amenable to it; instead the economy relied on the export cash crops of rice, indigo, and cotton, of which only a few Jews owned plantations. Thus, Jews primarily participated in South Carolina's economy as merchants and shopkeepers. Then, because of the WIC's interest in Jews, they were key economic players in Pernambuco, Suriname, Cayenne, and elsewhere in the Dutch Wild Coast; and thus special accommodations were made for them, as described in Suze Zijlstra's, Tom Weterings's, and Jessica Vance Roitman's contributions to this volume. This was not the case for

South Carolina, where not only was there no sugar and no WIC, but the colony's proprietary founders also acted differently by simply allowing religious tolerance to be an incentive in and of itself for settlement. It was hoped that this might improve the overall fortunes of the initially struggling colony, which just so happened to include Jews.

By the mid-1660s Caribbean Jews were becoming more comfortable with the English Empire as a place of habitation. From 1666 one finds the "Petition of Jean d'Illan, Jew of Amsterdam, to the King, for a pass for a Holland ship to transport himself and 50 families of Jews from Amsterdam to Palestine."[33] The petition was initially presented in French, which suggests that Jean d'Illan may have been one and the same person as João de Yllan, the first Dutch Sephardic Jew to lead a contingent of Jewish colonists to Curacao in 1651. De Yllan also engaged in trade between Curacao and North America for a time, before returning to the Netherlands in 1655.[34] Moreover, De Yllan concluded his petition to Charles II with, "God has at length begun to gather in his scattered people, having raised up a prophet for them; they will pray for His Majesty when they arrive at Jerusalem," revealing that by 1666, he had likely become a follower of the false Jewish messiah Sabbatai Zevi (1626–1676), who had recently postulated that he would begin the messianic redemption in that year.[35]

It is not known what happened to De Yllan/d'Illan following his petition to Charles II, though it is intriguing to see that the travels of this wandering Jew—an outsider wherever he went—may have spanned nearly half the globe, from the Caribbean to the Holy Land. This was an episode in mid-seventeenth-century Jewish life that many religious leaders sought to suppress because of the challenges to authority Zevi and his followers caused, adding further fuel to this torrid period.

Another follower of the pseudo-messiah Zevi, and contemporary of De Yllan, was the Dutch Jewish poet, Daniel Levi de Barrios (1635–1701).[36] In one of De Barrios's poems, composed more than two decades after the Zevi debacle (dating from 1688), he provided an illuminating constellation on the locations of late-seventeenth-century English Jewry: "Now, in six English cities, are known six sacred lights of Israel: three in Nevis, London, Jamaica; the fourth and fifth in two parts of Barbados; [and] the sixth is verified in Madras Patân."[37]

At this time the Jewish communities of the English-speaking world were relatively small. Besides the one in London and with the exception of the English East India Company trading factory at Madras, India, English Jewry was clearly concentrated in the Caribbean. De Barrios, though, inadvertently left out New York City, though this is understandable considering the peripheral role New York's small Jewish community played during this period. Indeed, this puts into perspective the role of New York in the seventeenth century in the Treaty of Westminster, which ended the Third Anglo-Dutch War (1672–74), under the terms of which the English kept New Netherland and the Dutch kept Suriname.[38] The latter became

Barry L. Stiefel

one of the WIC's most successful Caribbean plantation colonies, in which many Jewish colonists were at the forefront, operating in Jodensavanne and Paramaribo.

For the Dutch, too, the Caribbean played a pivotal place of settlement for Sephardic Jews, though Ashkenazim in the United Provinces preferred towns in the metropolis. Besides Suriname and Curacao, already mentioned, Jews during the seventeenth century established themselves for a time in Berbice, Essequibo, and Demerara, as well as in Tucacas and St. Eustatius.[39] The difference in their status, however, as mentioned, is that by 1658 Jewish colonists in WIC territories were naturalized. Since English Jewish colonists in the Caribbean remained as resident aliens, this created difficulties and problems.

Shifting from Alien Status to Naturalization

On June 7, 1692, Port Royal, Jamaica, was rocked by a massive earthquake that caused part of the town to sink into the sea, resulting in the immediate death of thousands, and thousands more in the following days died of injuries and worsening living conditions. The economy of the pirate enclave and port city was ruined, taking many years to recover. Thus, on August 30, 1692, "Isaac Fernandez Dias, Isaac Motes Baruch, Isaac Nunes, and other Jews, late of Jamaica, merchants" petitioned King William and Queen Mary "to be made free denizens of England" because "they were inhabitants, for several years, of Jamaica, and by the earthquake . . . they have lost all they had."[40] Since 1681 Jews and Catholics in Jamaica had been discriminated against through a local law that required one to be a property-owning Protestant freeholder to vote or hold public office. This local law defied the Windsor Proclamation, from which Jews and others had the right to own property. The situation for Jews became worse in 1695 when a special tax was levied by the colonial government specifically on them, for purposes of funding defense. Jamaica's House of Assembly subsequently passed additional economic and political debilitating laws directed towards Jews into the eighteenth century.[41]

Beginning in 1668 and continuing into the eighteenth century, similar anti-Semitic laws were passed in Barbados. Bermuda also passed discriminatory legislation against Jews, though the island never had a permanent Jewish population.[42] Anti-Semitism climaxed in Barbados in 1739, when, following a confrontation between Jewish and non-Jewish Barbadians, an angry mob retaliated by destroying the synagogue in Speightstown—the only instance of such an act ever occurring against Jews in the Caribbean.[43]

In the instances of such legal restrictions, colonial governors and the Board of Trade in London gave orders to nullify such laws, which fell on deaf years, sometimes into the nineteenth century. With the passage of the Naturalization Act of 1740, sometimes called the Plantations Act, Jews and alien Protestants in the colonies achieved naturalized status as British subjects; this was not always enforced, however, in the way it was intended by magistrates in Jamaica and Barbados. Considering the relatively small number and lack of influence of Jewish colonists on the opposite side of the Atlantic, however, it was not worth elevating the issue, in the view of the Board of Trade, into an open conflict, when compliance on other important matters from London were more pressing. The anti-Semitic treatment of Barbadian and Jamaican Jews was largely fueled by economic jealousy from rival English merchant-colonists, who were a powerful lobby in local politics and who sought to gradually undermine their Jewish competitors.

Jews in England remained in a similarly precarious position. Not until the Toleration Act in 1689, which included Jews as one of several tolerated nonconforming religious groups, were they formally permitted to reside openly in the growing English Empire.[44] Nevertheless, their legal status was questioned again in discussion related to the Popery Act of 1698, which threatened English Jews with expulsion and loss of property, but this proposition received little parliamentary support. This cloud was not legally removed until the enactment of the Jews Relief Act in 1858. Even so, from the debates at Whitehall held by Cromwell in 1655, English people began to conceptualize that Jews could live among them and not necessarily as an alien other.

Accordingly, by the end of the long seventeenth century, coinciding with the accession of the House of Hanover on the British throne in 1715, acceptance of Jews had become more widespread. Indeed, the correspondence of the secretary of state for the Southern Department, James Craggs the Younger (1686–1721), reveals, from "the complaint of the Portuguese Court about Captain Prothero of *HMS Looe* who received aboard his ship a large quantity of brazilwood and gave sanctuary to a fugitive Jew who was liable to the Inquisition" that the British even came to see themselves as protectors of the Jews in the Caribbean.[45] Following the conclusion of the War of Spanish Succession (1702–13), Great Britain had begun to bring greater stability to this corner of the Americas, culminating a century later with the conclusion of the Napoleonic Wars (1799–1815).

Though Jews in Barbados and Jamaica, where the bulk of Jews resided in the British Caribbean at this time, continued to endure discrimination into the eighteenth century, they appear to have been better received in Nevis and South Carolina. Unfortunately, little documentation survives on seventeenth-century Nevis's Jewish community, largely because the Jewish presence on the island disappeared during the eighteenth century for economic reasons. Civil records indicate that Jews settled on Nevis during the 1670s and may have come from Barbados.[46] It is unclear whether Nevis's Jews came to the island because of the discriminatory laws that were alienating them on Barbados, but it could have been a "push factor" in their decisions to migrate, combined with the "pull factor" of new economic opportunity with the expanding sugarcane plantation economy on this island. Though anti-Catholic laws were passed, anti-Semitic regulations do not appear in Nevis's legal code, suggesting that the Jews were well accepted on this island.[47]

It would be in South Carolina, this furthest-most outpost of the socioeconomically defined West Indies at the onset of the American War of Independence

(1775–83), where Jews for the first time in modern history became integrated members of their adopted society: they were accepted as equals, not as aliens in the midst of the populace. This occurred in 1775 when Francis Salvador (1747–1776) was elected to South Carolina's Provincial Congress. While South Carolina's constitution, at this time, required elected officials to be Protestant, this was directed at disenfranchising Catholics.[48] Though not tested in court, the constituents who elected Salvador assumed Jews to be another "Protestant" group, though odd in their religious beliefs. Considering the accepted status Jews eventually obtained in South Carolina, which eventually spread to other corners of the Anglophone world, as well as the concessions given to Jews in the Dutch South American colonies of the Wild Coast studied by Suze Zijlstra and Tom Weterings and by Jessica Roitman, the Torrid Zone of the seventeenth century played an important proving ground where Jews demonstrated to the liberalizing governments in the Age of Enlightenment that they could be more than alien outsiders—indeed, productive citizens and members of society.

Carolina, the Torrid Zone, and the Migration of Anglo-American Political Culture

L. H. Roper

On March 24, 1663, Charles II granted a charter that delegated sweeping powers of colonization over that part "of our dominions" extending from thirty-six degrees latitude south to thirty-one degrees to George Monck, Duke of Albemarle; Edward Hyde, Earl of Clarendon; William, Lord Craven; John, Lord Berkeley; Anthony, Lord Ashley; Sir George Carteret; Sir William Berkeley; and Sir John Colleton.[1] On the face of things, the territory between Albemarle Sound and the St. John's River in modern Florida that these grantees received does not constitute a geographical part of the Caribbean Basin. Early South Carolina's relatively high reliance on enslaved labor and its correspondingly high proportion of African inhabitants are anomalous in North American terms; this seemingly distinctive socioeconomic character has enabled historians to regard the province as Caribbean in orientation. Thus, the case of seventeenth-century Carolina offers an interesting basis of analysis, especially in a comparative sense, for considering the social and political development of Anglo-America and the degree of influence played by "Caribbean" sociopolitical views beyond the immediate environs of the West Indies: how different were the island colonies from their mainland counterparts?[2]

Colonial South Carolina's demographics have enabled historians to ignore the normality of the province both within the wider context of the history of seventeenth-century Anglo-America (which properly includes the West Indies as well as North America) and that of British North America. Considering Carolina as more properly a Caribbean colony rather than an American one enables an emphasis on the purported peculiarity of the part of the United States that became the hotbed of North American slavery and of "states' rights" after independence.

The post–Civil War characterization of South Carolina's colonial history had (white) liberty-loving Carolinians chafing under the rule of absentee, grasping, yet inept proprietary overlords before casting off the imperial "yoke" in 1719, a theme followed twice: in the overthrow of British rule in the American War of Independence of 1775–83 and in the removal of the hated Reconstruction government in 1876. The dated—not to say racist—elements of this Redeemer interpretation were overthrown in the 1960s, but important—and, in their own way, misleading—elements of it have endured: a party of "Barbadian Anglicans" battled rivals who tended to dissent from the Church of England over control of the colony. These parties supposedly "switched sides" in terms of their respective relationships with the clueless (regardless of historiographical perspective) proprietors and the "fanciful ideal of hyper-feudalism"—that is, the Fundamental Constitutions of Carolina, which included provisions for serfs and manorial courts and was devised as a sociopolitical blueprint for their colony. But in the end these "Goose Creek Men" prevailed over both their local enemies and the proprietors. Their triumph insured the development of South Carolina as a "slave society" with a "black majority" population—and, indeed, it already constituted "a colony of a colony," Barbados—by the dawn of the eighteenth century.[3]

Unquestionably, Carolina, particularly the southern part of it, came into existence in large part because of the seventeenth-century expansionist initiatives of English colonies in the Caribbean; and a significant number of people, both African and European, came to this part of North America from the West Indies. Barbados was the most important of these colonies—or indeed any seventeenth-century English colony; this 166-square-mile island contained some fifty thousand inhabitants in 1680 (ten years after the founding of Charles Town). This overcrowding arose from the pursuit of what might be termed the formula for success in English America: the acquisition of a landed estate devoted to the production of a crop for export—tobacco, as was the practice prior to 1645 wherever the climate was suitable for its production, or afterwards, increasingly, sugar—by people whose labor was acquired by purchase but who were bound to their situations either for a term of years or in perpetuity.[4]

The island became something of a victim of the popularity of sugar as practically all of its suitable land came under the control of those with the wherewithal to construct works to process the cane even as servants and prisoners from the English Civil Wars (1642–51), along with increasing numbers of African slaves, continued to arrive there in substantial numbers during the 1640s. The Civil Wars and the execution of Charles I aggravated the factional political scene on the island, which in conjunction with worker discontent owing to the nature of Barbadian slavery, the overcrowding, and the lack of prospects for indentured servants created demographic and political pressure of a nature that the colony's leadership felt the need to address: as early as 1650, Barbadians such as Francis, fifth Lord Willoughby of Parham, sponsored colonizing forays to new places such as Suriname.

The new Carolina proprietors naturally linked with these objectives in their first endeavors to recruit colonists in 1664, when they reached for "Articles of Agreement" to govern the settling of Barbadian interests, such as Sir John Yeamans, on the mainland. Thus connections between the Lords and the island remained firm—if often overemphasized in particular—from the founding of Charles Town in 1670. Unquestionably, South Carolina's leaders readily transplanted the island's socioeconomic model of monocultural agriculture (rice, ultimately, in the case of the mainland colony) cultivated by enslaved or servant labor. Unquestionably, also, the leaders of Barbados provided an all-too-ready model to their mainland counterparts for "ordering" their enslaved population, having enacted a comprehensive "slave code" by 1661.[5]

The historiographical case for characterizing Carolina as a continental anomaly in terms of peculiar effects of Caribbean influences on it runs afoul of a number of realities, however. First, "West Indians" were not quite as prevalent there, either in terms of numbers or influence, as many scholars would have it. Second, a significant number of West Indians made their mark in various English-speaking parts of mainland North America, such as the Antiguan Lewis Morris in New Jersey. Third, many leading European inhabitants of Carolina who spent no or relatively little time in the Caribbean, such as Maurice Mathews, the leader of the Goose Creek Men, and Sir Nathaniel Johnson, governor of South Carolina from 1703 to 1709, appear to have seamlessly adopted the sociopolitical worldview of planters with greater experience in the West Indies, if not in America generally. Finally and most fundamentally, the "Caribbean-style" socioeconomic system and the perhaps related political convulsions that both North and South Carolina experienced prior to the end of the proprietary period (1729) were by no means distinctive, except in terms of the number of slaves brought to South Carolina on the mainland. To what degree, then, was Carolina (jointly or severally) different from other colonies, especially its North American counterparts, and to what degree can those differences be styled as "Caribbean"?[6]

One can certainly say that there was nothing extraordinary about the character of the founding of Carolina in terms of either the development or character of the seventeenth-century English Empire, but as with the issue of West Indian influence on the colony, an entrenched historiographical presumption must be rebutted. In geographical terms, the place made up one of the final pieces of the jigsaw puzzle of English claims to possession of the Atlantic seaboard of North America between Newfoundland and Florida. As such, the creation of the province would seem to constitute a further manifestation of the increasingly imperial designs and, accordingly, moves towards centralization on the part of the English state, as well as of the increasingly "absolutist" behavior of the Stuart monarchs that purportedly followed the Restoration of Charles II in 1660. Certainly, when considered in conjunction with the capture of Jamaica (1655–60), the acquisition of Tangier in Morocco (1662), and the takeover of the Dutch colony of New Netherland (1664), the founding of Carolina has suggested both a greater sense of imperial purpose and the ability to carry out that purpose from the second half of the seventeenth century.[7] According to historian Daniel Richter, these attempts at late Stuart "state building and imperial expansion" purportedly ran afoul, on the one hand, of the incompetence of the advocates of this policy and, on the other, to successful colonial adaptation to new imperial circumstances even as these imperial visions "clashed with those of the English small-planter regimes already in place in North America." Correspondingly, while the conception of Carolina may have constituted one benchmark in "the process by which a new idea of an exclusive British empire displaced the seventeenth century's 'interimperial' Atlantic community," Restoration "officials could not extend their fiscal-military state across the Atlantic until locals eschewed their cross-national, flexible origins and chose to conform to new imperial standards."[8]

Yet, these views of the character of the later seventeenth-century English state, customarily linked with a view of Anglo-American history as a modernizing phenomenon, are misleading. First, the use of a proprietorship itself, the customary form of early modern European colonization, reflected the endurance of the limited ability, in terms of both inclination and structure, of the English state to manage this sort of "public" enterprise directly. Rather than the cash-strapped central government, with its perennially overwhelming workload, retaining responsibility for recruiting, transporting, and providing for settlers, appointing officers, and pursuing relations with Indian neighbors, it devolved those duties onto "private" individuals who undertook these "public" purposes just as its predecessors had devolved the government of the border area with Scotland, for instance, onto the bishops of Durham.[9]

Then, while the English Empire increased territorially over the course of the seventeenth century, most of this expansion occurred through the sort of efforts of colonists found in the case of Barbados rather than from initiatives generated from the center. Indeed, Carolina provides further evidence of this reality in the person of the proprietor and Barbados planter, Sir John Colleton. Indeed, the impetus for colonizing the place came from three colonial regions, including the West Indies, as well as from the metropolis.[10]

There had been scattered efforts from Virginia to investigate prospects in what came to be North Carolina almost from the founding of Jamestown in 1607 that had been sparked, in part, by curiosity over the fate of the "lost," short-lived Roanoke colony (1585–89). These probes, as well as the stillborn ventures undertaken via a proprietary patent to "Carolana" that the Crown issued to Sir Robert Heath, attorney general to Charles I in 1632, generated scant results (other than lawsuits generated by the Carolana failure). After the execution of Charles I in 1649, though, this activity became more systematic and permanent: traders with the Indians, such as Abraham Wood, pursued their interests in the region of the Chowan, Meherrin, and Roanoke Rivers, while a small flurry of promotional pamphlets appeared in London extolling the qualities of the area between thirty-one and thirty-seven degrees north latitude to prospective migrants. After 1656 one Nathaniel Batts, possibly to evade creditors in Virginia, conducted his own explorations with the thanks of the colony's government and established his residence on the Pasquotank River in 1660. After the Restoration of Charles II in that same year, Sir William Berkeley, the similarly restored governor of Virginia, traveled to London to reconfigure the lines of communication and patronage between his colony and the imperial center and to secure governmental license for Virginia's southerly expansion. The presence of Sir William's brother and fellow Virginia colonizer, Sir John, Baron Berkeley of Stratton, on the newly constituted Council for Foreign Plantations, undoubtedly bolstered these prospects.[11]

Colonists from Massachusetts Bay, parts of which had become dangerously overcrowded by the mid-1630s, had, like their counterparts on Barbados, been expanding the English presence in New England and the surrounding area for three decades when a group of them followed these Virginians to the Cape Fear region. In the autumn of 1662, an exploratory voyage from Charlestown, Massachusetts, arrived to reconnoiter the region. The report of its undertakers provided the basis for the dispatch of a colonizing expedition to the "Charles River" the following February. The backers of this venture included Edward Winslow, nephew and namesake of the "Pilgrim Father" and colonial-imperialist who had died while helping lead Cromwell's Western Design against Santo Domingo in 1655, and his brother, John. The younger Edward Winslow may have served as a connection between this New England undertaking and its West Indian counterpart as he married the daughter of William Hilton, the captain (also from Massachusetts) of both of these New England voyages to Cape Fear and who conducted a sounding of the Carolina coastline in August 1663 on behalf of a group of Barbadians.[12] These latter interests had meanwhile targeted the mainland in the course of a lengthy period of colonization that also extended to Suriname (1650) and St. Lucia (1663), as well as to Jamaica (1660), after the English conquest of that island from Spain and the exploratory voyage of Hilton noted above.[13]

The accession of Charles II presented the opportunity to manure these green shoots both with a legality that could only come from the monarch in the seventeenth century and through the good offices of metropolitan patrons with an interest in colonization. At first glance, though, the membership of the Carolina proprietorship appears incongruous. The best explanation for this formation must come from the character of Restoration politics, both domestic and foreign. Accordingly, the makeup of the proprietorship sheds a healthy degree of light on the political nature of the English Empire in the third quarter of the seventeenth century.[14]

First, the list of proprietors reflected the substantial degree to which the restored monarchy carried over personnel and policy from its predecessors. This reality reflected Charles II's desire to effect a reconciliation between king and subjects following the tumults of the Civil Wars and the Interregnum. It also reflected the reality that the return of kingly government had been engineered by leading Cromwellian figures, especially Albemarle, whose Scottish-based army had led the opposition against efforts of republicans to seize power following the overthrow of the Protectorate and then secured the return of the king. Thus, Albemarle led the list of proprietors, both alphabetically and in terms of influence. Yet, to keep the importance of Carolina in perspective, his one-eighth share in this colonial venture—and it bears repeating that this included governmental responsibilities as well as land rights—ranked rather lower on the list of rewards that the newly restored monarch bestowed upon Albemarle, most notably his dukedom (one of only two nonroyal instances of this title at the time), the Garter, membership on the Privy Council, and a litany of lucrative offices, such as master of the horse. As the leading military figure in the kingdom, Albemarle served on the newly reorganized Council for Foreign Plantations.[15]

He was joined on this council by other erstwhile enemies of Charles Stuart turned servants of Charles II, including Ashley, who had been interested in overseas trade and colonization ever since the 1640s, when he had acquired a Barbados plantation. As a member of the Protectorate Council of State, he, like Albemarle, had been very sympathetic to the heterodox religious views that had gained substantial currency with the collapse of the Church of England after 1641; he retained significant ties with those deemed dissenters after the reestablishment of bishops and the Book of Common Prayer in 1662. Notwithstanding his service to Cromwell, Ashley was appointed chancellor of the exchequer at the Restoration.[16]

Clarendon, second among the proprietors in terms of influence and power, was also a member of the Council for Foreign Plantations, although his experiences of the 1640s and 1650s had been rather different from those of Albemarle and Ashley. As the chief advisor to the exiled Charles Stuart, he had shared many of the would-be Charles II's wanderings from court to court during Cromwell's ascendency (during which time he had a bitter feud with his future coproprietor, Sir John Berkeley). He became lord chancellor when Charles returned to England and, always bearing in mind the fiscal issues that had bred the constitutional difficulties that had in turn degenerated into civil war and the execution of Charles I, consistently advocated a peaceable approach to foreign and domestic religious affairs, especially in terms of England's increasingly heated relations with the Dutch Republic.[17]

In addition to Clarendon and Ashley, the ranks of Interregnum Royalists and Carolina proprietors on the Council for Foreign Plantations included the Berkeley brothers, Carteret (who was treasurer of the navy), and Colleton.[18] The collective involvement in Carolina of this politically disparate group arose from the common interest of its membership in overseas economic activity, especially the transatlantic slave trade and the state's enduring quest to acquire additional revenue streams. By 1663 it was clear to every English person with even a passing interest in overseas economic interests, including American colonization, that the control of the slave trade provided the foundation for prosperity for planters, wealth for traders, and imperial security for the Crown, as a reporter in Suriname observed. Indeed, as Sir George Downing, the virulently anti-Dutch English ambassador to The Hague under the Cromwellian and Restoration governments, noted, the States General, like the English government, were well aware "that if ye English should at this time clear ye coast of Africa of the Dutch & get ye gold trade & Negro trade to themselves that it would be of greater import than the East Indies trade."[19]

Those interested in the "Guinea trade" and who joined the Royal Company of Adventurers Trading into Africa that received a monopoly thereof included the Carolina proprietors Ashley, Craven, Sir John Berkeley, Carteret, and Colleton; but, of course, the list of those involved in English overseas trade and colonization at this time was much larger, including, most particularly, Martin Noell (an associate of Ashley's in the 1640s), Thomas Povey, Maurice Thompson, and Samuel Vassall (whose longstanding interest in the Cape Fear region of Carolina is noted below). The prospects for English involvement in this commerce—not to mention competition with the Dutch who controlled it in the mid-seventeenth century—tracked the steadily increasing resort to enslaved labor in Anglo-America or, perhaps, vice versa.[20] In 1665 the Royal Company of Adventurers held expectations of a £200,000 trade in ivory and £100,000 trade in "servants for the plantations" in the Gambia River region and claimed a contract to supply thirty-five hundred African slaves per annum to the Spanish colonies worth £86,000 annually. Not coincidentally, all these men maintained substantial interests in Barbados and most of them extended their concerns to Jamaica.[21]

These visions fueled the fierce global rivalry between English and Dutch interests during this period. Following the Dutch rejection of English overtures to unite (under English aegis) in 1650, relations between the two Protestant republics (as they then were) quickly deteriorated. The English Republic passed the first Navigation Act in response to the rebuff of its Dutch counterpart seeking to ban Dutch traders from trading with English colonies, which generated the first of the three Anglo-Dutch Wars (1652–54, 1665–67, and 1672–74). The return of the Stuarts did little to ease Anglo-Dutch relations, especially since Charles II retained the services of Downing, while English merchants with good government connections continued to covet Dutch control of trade in Africa and the East Indies. The desire to eliminate Dutch smuggling activity, compounded by Charles II's concerns about the status of his nephew, the young Prince William of Orange, and irregular Dutch concurrence with treaty obligations to dip colors to English vessels they encountered at sea also kept the temperature high at the center of the English government and in English outposts around the globe. Spain, ruler of modern Belgium (and Florida), allied itself with the Dutch Republic against the French king (and cousin of Charles II), Louis XIV—hence the agreement to marry the English king to Catherine of Braganza in support of the Portuguese in their war against the Spanish (and to acquire Tangier and Bombay as part of Catherine's dowry).[22]

The plan for colonizing Carolina, then, manifested another meeting of Restoration imperial minds, along with the acquisition (by force or otherwise) of Tangier, Bombay, Jamaica, and New Netherland/New York. By 1660 those involved in the expansion of English overseas trade and colonization recognized that the maintenance of plantations required a regular supply of bound labor, that the steadiest source of that labor was enslaved Africans, and that continuing relegation of Africans to enslavement presented further advantages to their masters—namely, no prospect of freedom and no corresponding need to provide either incentives to migrate to a colony or to honor contractual obligations as with European servants, as well as the automatic enslavement of the offspring of enslaved mothers.[23]

As often happens, however, with best-laid plans, especially of the early modern colonizing variety, the Carolina project went astray. First, the English-style pursuit of empire inevitably led to differences over tactics and, more important, interests. As soon as the proprietors received their charter, they discovered to their annoyance that the grant made to Sir Robert Heath in the 1630s had allegedly come into the hands of one of the most versatile and important "imperialists," the wealthy merchant Samuel Vassall, who was involved in the formation of the Massachusetts Bay Company and who made a substantial fortune in the "Guinea trade"; Cape Fear may have provided a nice link for his interests in "godly" colonization and advancing plantation slavery. This ubiquitous yet shadowy character, who did not trouble with legal forms unless they aligned with his ambitions, had underwritten an earlier attempt to colonize Cape Fear, using his Huguenot connections, which ran into the sand, and he had returned for a second bite at the Carolina cherry after 1660. The necessity of removing this cloud compelled Colleton to seek Albemarle's intervention, but even so, the legal wrangling took another two years and required the issuance of a second charter to the Carolina proprietors on June 30, 1665.[24]

Also, the enduring Anglo-Dutch friction erupted into another Anglo-Dutch War. This conflict, which began with English attacks on Dutch interests on the Gold Coast of West Africa and on New Netherland, quickly spread to the Caribbean, where a Franco-Dutch alliance seized the English colonies of St. Christopher's, St Lucia, and Suriname. These emergencies, along with the governmental roles of the metropolitan and colonial promoters of Carolina, put the affairs of the infant colony on hold: Yeamans, its governor-designate, was appointed deputy commander-in-chief of English forces in the West Indies shortly after the second charter passed the seals and then served as a commissioner for negotiating the restoration of the status quo on St. Christopher's with the French. The death from drowning in a hurricane of the Barbados governor and Carolina supporter, Lord Willoughby, left the government of his island in disarray and hampered the plans to recruit Barbadian settlers for the mainland plantation.[25]

Finally, Carolina's founding occurred at a time when the government of Charles II spent most of what passed for its attention to colonial affairs on Jamaica. Once the king decided, after some deliberation, to retain the island rather than return it to Spain, the members of his new Council for Foreign Trade and Plantations considered myriad petitions and proposals for advancing the colony. In

November 1660 James Ley, third Earl of Marlborough, composed a series of proposals that recommended that the "peopling" of this consolation prize from the Cromwellian Western Design to "make Jamaica the staple for the Trade of Blacks," with the Company of Royal Adventurers Trading to Africa providing "such numbers of Blacks as they shall thinke fit."[26]

The importance of Jamaica translated into the appointment of Sir Thomas Modyford as the governor of the island in February 1664 and transformed a proponent of Carolina success into an advocate of Jamaica. Modyford expected one thousand migrants every year from overcrowded Barbados to join him and encouraged the king to readily grant headrights, religious toleration, and free trade to achieve this goal, devices that the Carolina proprietors employed in the special pains they took in their own recruitment of colonists, especially from colonies like Barbados, where land had become scarce. The competition for planters, backed by royal authority, cannot have bolstered the prospects of the mainland province.[27]

Then, it seems that not all Barbadians were as keen on expanding the English presence in the Caribbean and reportedly took pains to prevent it. A writer from Suriname reported in 1663 that his colony had four thousand inhabitants and great prospects. Unfortunately, certain "Dons of Barbados," determined to "balance the power of their Negroes" and concerned about the supply and price of slaves, took steps "to disparage the country."[28] The record does not provide any similar evidence of hostility to the Carolina project on Barbados, but it is not inconceivable given the hothouse character of the colony's politics, especially with respect to the controversial career of Willoughby and the fierce disputes on the island that developed out of the Civil Wars and the subjugation of the colony by a parliamentary fleet commanded by Sir George Ayscue in 1652.[29]

In the meantime, perhaps in accordance with the 1666 exploration of the Port Royal area by the erstwhile Suriname planter Robert Sandford on behalf of the proprietors, a plan was mooted to transport the inhabitants of the English colony in South America to Carolina after its loss to the Dutch. A memorial to the Council on Foreign Trade and Plantations averred that "many of them are desirous to remove to Port Royal in Carolina," provided "their [*sic*] be provision made for their transportation & reception." Accordingly, "ye persons concerned in Carolina" asked the king for a man-of-war to collect those departing, while they would fit out two ships to convey the refugees. Nothing, though, seems to have come of this proposal and most of the Suriname planters went to Jamaica.[30] In conjunction with the interruption to shipping caused by the Second Anglo-Dutch War, which resulted in the loss of Suriname, and the contemporary distractions of a plague outbreak (1665) and the Great Fire of London (1666), as well as the overall ambiguity of the Barbadians towards the notion of resettling their island's inhabitants elsewhere, little was accomplished to advance Carolina between 1664, aside from the 1666 endeavor, and 1669. Cut off by the war from support from England, the infant Cape Fear settlement withered on the vine while its leading proponent, Vassall, who had migrated, died there leaving the trickle of settlers who had made their way south from Virginia to pick up the pieces of what came to be North Carolina. Largely free of proprietary oversight, these colonists quickly formed factions that competed fiercely for power, land, and status, all the while invoking differing sociopolitical views, especially in terms of "liberty," in the course of their internecine "rebellions."[31]

Yet, the pursuit of colonizing Carolina from a further perspective did not disappear. In 1669 Ashley and his secretary-physician, John Locke, revitalized the proprietorship. And, like Jamaica, the mainland was envisioned as a repository for English migrants from both the metropolis and other colonies, including, but not exclusively, Barbados.[32] While Ashley and Locke shared the general recognition of the centrality of the slave trade to American colonization and clearly envisioned a prominent place for African slavery in Carolina, they also moved to promote the migration of the "weighty sort" and "worthy" others from England in accordance with their own views of society building upon agreements between the proprietors and Barbados planters several years earlier. Thus, their Fundamental Constitutions guaranteed, in writing (a concept that originated in the 1650s in the course of the experimentation with new governments, with which Ashley had been involved, in the aftermath of the execution of Charles I and the abolition of the monarchy), headrights, a manorial system of government, religious toleration, and other liberties and reciprocal obligations for planters and their "inferiors." Their efforts attracted some ninety-two people for the "first fleet" that founded the first Charles Town in April 1670 after collecting other colonists at Bermuda and Barbados.[33]

Despite the experience of its drafters, the Fundamental Constitutions, the most formal and comprehensive blueprint ever devised for establishing a social and governmental framework of an American colony, proved unable to contain the ambitions of South Carolina's colonists. These fouled this clear scheme for overcoming the problem of distance that confronted seventeenth-century governments when overseeing local matters, always aggravated in imperial instances, one that included a prescription for attracting migrants across the spectrum of the society of orders to provide a "weightier sort" of planters, who obtained their status through the number of migrants they brought to the colony. The proprietary vision did attract European settlers, notably a substantial contingent of Huguenots, who provided servant labor and who became small farmers and artisans, as well as planters. Unfortunately for their fellow Carolinians and for the proprietors, these included a group, identified by contemporaries as "the Goose Creek Men" after the location of their plantations, who paid scant heed to the rule of law as they quickly identified the Indian slave trade (proscribed by the proprietors) as a ready means of advancing themselves as their counterparts in Suriname did and with similar results.[34]

On a couple of occasions, contemporaries misleadingly identified this faction as "Barbadian," which has had the effect of perpetuating the enduring view of its members as "Barbadian Anglican" even though, for instance and most particularly, its leader and arguable creator, the aforementioned Mathews, arrived in Carolina on the "first fleet" of 1669 as an agent of Ashley and even though there exists no recorded presence of a duly ordained minister of the Church of England in the colony until after 1700. Further confusion about the identities and orientations of the Goose Creek Men has arisen because of their recruitment of Johnson to their colors following his retirement to Carolina after he was compelled to leave the governorship of the Leeward Islands in the wake of the Glorious Revolution (1688–89).

The ruthless behavior of the Indian slavers, including the alleged kidnaping and public beating of their opponents, as well as the orchestration of the destruction of a Scottish colony, Stuarts Town, founded at Port Royal, may have been on the excessive side but was not atypical of political behavior in colonial Anglo-America, whether in the Caribbean or on the mainland.[35] The feverish political climate of South Carolina did, however, make a substantial contribution, along with the subtropical meteorological climate, to the colony's aforementioned peculiar demographics for North America, as contemporary observers noted: the uproarious behavior of the Goose Creek Men drove a significant number of settlers out of the colony and deterred others from migrating there. Eventually, the cycle of war and enslavement driven by the Carolinians resulted, in addition to the devastation of Native communities from the Florida Keys to the Mississippi River, in the near-destruction of their own colony in the Yamassee War of 1715–17. The nature of relations between Carolinians and Indians, of course, tracks those of other mainland colonies—especially New England, at least in terms of outcome—rather than of the West Indies, although the scope of the slave trade at Charles Town dwarfed that in any other part of North America.[36] The question that remains then is this: to what degree did Carolina constitute the northern extent of a particularly distinctive seventeenth-century Anglo-Caribbean sociopolitical orientation?

Notes

AGI   Archivo General de Indias, Seville, Spain

ANOM   Archives Nationales, Section Outre-Mer, Aix-en-Provence, France, Secrétariat d'Etat à la Marine

BL   British Library, London

BNA   Barbados National Archives, Bridgetown

CO   Colonial Office series, National Archives of Great Britain, Kew, Richmond

CSPC AWI   *Calendar of State Papers, Colonial Series, America and West Indies,* 44 vols. Edited by W. Noel Sainsbury, et al. London: H.M. Stationery Office, 1860–1963.

CSPD   *Calendar of State Papers, Domestic Series from 1509 through 1782.* Edited by M.A. Green et al. London: H.M. Stationery Office, 1858-1910.

HCA   High Court of Admiralty Papers series, National Archives of Great Britain, Kew, Richmond

JA   Jamaica Archives, Spanish Town

NAN   National Archives of the Netherlands, the Hague

SP   State Papers series, National Archives of Great Britain, Kew, Richmond

SvZ   Staten van Zeeland (States of Zeeland)

ZA   Zeeuws Archief, Middelburg, the Netherlands

Introduction

1. The index, for instance, to Bailyn, *The Barbarous Years,* a recent Pulitzer Prize nominee, includes neither mention of the Caribbean nor the West Indies in general terms or to any particular islands, save ten references to Barbados, the most important of the seventeenth-century Anglo-American colonies, in a book of over six hundred pages. Please see the bibliography for references to the literature.

2. This volume's perspective follows an approach commonly found in studies of the eighteenth- and nineteenth-century Caribbean, including, for example, Burnard and Garrigus, *The Plantation Machine,* and Ferrer, *Freedom's Mirror.* For the "genesis" of a "fragmented" Caribbean, see Knight, *The Caribbean.* I am most grateful to Laurie Wood for her considerable help in articulating the points in this paragraph.

3. See, for example, Wolinetz, "New Jersey Slavery," 2229–37.

Kalinago Colonizers

1. "La guerre que nous avons contre les holandois, contre l'empereur, et contre l'Espagnol, donnent beaucoup de chagrin au peuple des Isles, mais il craignent moins ces trois puissances que la guerre contre les Caraybes, car elle est d'une nature et d'une conduite sy difficle qu'il est presque impossible qu'on y resiste . . . qui par consequent obligent tous les habitans d'estre continuellement sous les armes . . . sy la guerre contre les Caraybes estoit bien allumée, il faudroit . . . se resoudre à l'abandonner," ANOM Fonds Ministériels [FM]

C8A 1 f. 279, de Baas Castelmore, June 8, 1674. All spellings in original. All translations are the author's own unless otherwise noted.

2.   First published in 1558, the Dominican friar's vivid account of indigenous death and enslavement at the hands of conquistadors helped create the "Black Legend" of Spanish rule in the Americas. Las Casas, *Short Account of the Destructions of the Indies.*

3.   One influential study estimates that from an initial population of almost four million people at the time of Spanish arrival in the Americas, the indigenous population of Hispaniola declined to just 125 by 1570. Cook and Borah, "Aboriginal Population of Hispaniola." In one example of how this logic has been extended to other parts of the Caribbean, James Pritchard argues, "The French met few natives in the West Indies. . . . By 1670, few Caribs remained." Pritchard, *In Search of Empire,* 3–4.

4.   For a discussion of some of the reasons why indigenous populations in the Greater Antilles were more affected by European conquest than those in the Lesser Antilles, see Wilson, "Surviving European Conquest in the Caribbean."

5.   A brief discussion of sixteenth-century Spanish slave-raiding expeditions to the Lesser Antilles can be found in Sauer, *Early Spanish Main,* 192–94.

6.   The "political and military responses of the Kalinago people to the European invasion" was first explored by Beckles, "Kalinago (Carib) Resistance to European Colonisation of the Caribbean."

7.   For a discussion of how the use of "Carib" as a subject of analysis continues to shape ethnohistorical and archaeological investigations in the island of Dominica, see Lenik, "Carib as a Colonial Category."

8.   Hulme, *Colonial Encounters,* 46 (emphasis in original).

9.   Missionary Raymond Breton's entry in his seventeenth-century Franco-Carib dictionary explains: "I finally learned from the Chiefs of the island of Dominica that the words Galibi and Carib were names that the Europeans gave them, and that their real name was Callinago, that they distinguish themselves only by the words Oubaóbanum [and] Balouébanum, that is to say, of the islands or of the mainland." In the original French: "J'ay enfin appris des Capitaines de l'isle de la Dominique, que les mots de Galibi & Caraibe estoient des noms que les Europeens leur avoient donnez, & que leur veritable nom estoit Callinago, qu'ils ne se distinguoient que par ses mots Oubaóbanum, Balouébonum, c'est-à-dire, des Isles, ou de terre ferme." Breton, *Dictionnaire caraïbe-françois,* 229.

10.   Terms quoted from historical sources have been retained.

11.   For an excellent collection of primary documents exploring European interactions with and responses to the Lesser Antilles' indigenous inhabitants, see Hulme and Whitehead, *Wild Majesty.*

12.   The well-known account of another missionary, Father Labat, has not been used here because it focuses on his experiences at the end of the seventeenth century. Labat, *Nouveau Voyage aux Iles de l'Amérique.*

13.   Although Caribbean Amerindians also challenged English settlement in the Leeward Islands, the increasing concentration of Kalinago in islands that lay in between those claimed by the French left French settlers particularly vulnerable. In his study of Barbados, Richard Dunn argues that settlement "was only feasible in sites removed as far as possible from contact with the Spanish and Indian [Kalinago] population centers"; the rapid development of the plantation complex in the English colony was facilitated in part by a lack of sustained resistance from the Kalinago. Dunn, *Sugar and Slaves,* 17–19.

14.   On seventeenth-century colonization of the Lesser Antilles, see Paquette and Engerman, *Lesser Antilles in the Age of European Expansion.* For works that focus on English colonization, see Zacek, *Settler Society in the English Leeward Islands;* and Dunn, *Sugar and Slaves.*

On early French colonizing ventures, see Boucher, *France and the American Tropics to 1700;* Chauleau, *Dans les iles du vent;* and Debien, *Les engagés pour les Antilles.*

15. On the failed Spanish attempt to colonize the Lesser Antilles, see Boromé, "Spain and Dominica, 1493–1647."

16. On the settlers' journey to the Caribbean and initial arrival in Martinique in June 1635, see Du Tertre, *Histoire générale des Antilles,* 1:75–77. On French arrival in Grenada: ibid., 1:425–28.

17. "les Sauvages ne venoient jamais voir les François les mains vides; & comme iles les voyoient dans la necessité, ils leur portoient tousjours quelques vivres." Ibid., 1:88.

18. "nos habitans s'establissent de plus en plus, ils ne se contentent pas des places que ces barbares avoient abandonnées, ils en font de nouvelles, ils abbatent du bois, & ils plantent en mesme temps des vivres & du petun." Ibid., 1:103.

19. "nos Sauvages ne sont . . . que le reste des innombrables barbares, que les Chrestiens Espagnols ont exterminé, & dont une partie des plus vieux d'entr'eux ont esté témoins occulaires de extrémes cruautez, que les Chrestiens ont exercé sur eux & sur leurs pères." *Histoire générale des Isles,* 460.

20. "Nos Francois qui ne cherchoient que l'occasion de faire des actes d'hostilité contre les Sauvages." Du Tertre, *Histoire générale des Antilles,* 1:84.

21. "pour avoir un pretexte de s'emparer de leurs vivres." Ibid., 1:82.

22. "la douceur avec laquelle ils les traitent, la charité qu'ils leurs témoignent, en fin le bon traitement, & l'affable reception que nos Religieux leur font, quand ils les viennent visiter, ce qui arrive presque tous les jours . . . pourront avec le temps adoucir leur humeur barbare." Du Tertre, *Histoire générale des Isles,* 465.

23. Breton also published a bilingual catechism in 1664 and a Carib-language grammar in 1667. See Breton, *Petit catéchisme;* and Breton, *Grammaire caraïbe.*

24. "ils vont jusques à Cayenne & Surinnames pour joindre les Gallibis leurs alliez, soit pour trocquer leur denrées & en rapporter d'autres, soit pour fair un corps d'armée, & aller attaquer les Arrouagues leur ennemis." Breton, *Dictionnaire caraïbe-françois,* 108.

25. "dix hommes, que les Sauvages tuerent." Ibid., 415.

26. "des Anglois, qui ne cherchoient qu'à leur faire la guerre, à les exterminer et à s'emparer de leur terre. Leurs foiblesses à résister à de si puissants ennemis leurs fit souhaitter du secours pour opposer à leurs mauvais desseins et se deffendre de leurs attaques." Petitjean Roget, *L'histoire de l'Isle de Grenade,* 48.

27. Ibid., 56.

28. Du Tertre confirms that attacks against French settlers in Grenada were aided by Kalinago from Dominica and St. Vincent. Du Tertre, *Histoire générale des Antilles,* 1:429.

29. "ne s'en pouvant venger sur eux pour estre trop puissans et trop esloignéz, ils vouloient descharger leur colère sur ceux qui s'estoient nouvellement establis en la Grenade pendant qu'ils estoient foibles." Ibid., 1:60–61.

30. "Les Sauvages dirent qu'on devoit donc se contenter du lieu qu'ils avoient disposé, sans se loger ailleurs," Ibid., 1:56.

31. "Les Sauvages pourtant ne se croyans pas assez forts, crurent que pour chasser entierement les Francois de l'Isle, il falloit avoir recours à leurs voisins. Pour ce sujet ils appellerent à leurs secours, ceux de la Dominique, de Saint Vincent, & de la Guadeloupe; & ayant composé un corps de quinze cens hommes, ils se presenterent sous le Fort." Du Tertre, *Histoire générale des Antilles,* 1:102. Du Tertre also describes the indigenous inhabitants of Guadeloupe making alliances with those of St. Vincent and Dominica in order to launch attacks on the new French colony. Ibid., 1:89. This display of Kalinago military strength was not an isolated incident; the anonymous settler in Grenada reported that in 1654 some 1,110

Kalinago combatants arrived in twenty-four dugout canoes to besiege the island. Petitjean Roget, *L'histoire de l'Isle de Grenade en Amérique*, 108.

32. "a été ordonné que le Sieur du Parquet ne chassera point les sauvages hors de l'isle . . . Il voulou contenter de leur en faire reprocher et les convaincre d'avoir de meilleures intentions a l'avenir et vivre en intelligence avec des personnes qui leurs veulent faire aucun tort, leur promettra toute assistance et bon traitement et les encouragent de ne rien entreprendre contre les francais meme de doner avis de ce qu'ils pourraient decouvrir d'ailleurs fois des sauvages des autres isles ou des ennemis des françois . . . A été ordonné qu'il sera envoyé aux Sieur du Parquet 1500L de poudre, savoir moitié pour mousquet et l'autre moitié pour le canon." ANOM FM F3 f. 15, January 5, 1639, extrait d'un acte d'assemblée de la Compagnie des iles relatif aux relations avec les Caraibes.

33. "apres beaucoup d'entretiens, tels qu'on les put avoir avec des gens qui s'expriments plus par signes que par paroles, & qui n'ont guéres plus de raisons que des brutes; La paix fut conclue, promesses furent reciproquement faites de part & d'autre, de ne se faire jamais aucun tort, & de se traiter d'oresnavant comme bons amys." Du Tertre, *Histoire générale des Antilles*, 1:196.

34. "Le bruit de cette paix s'estendit par toutes les Isles circonvoisines, & mesme jusques en France, ce qui attira beaucoup de monde à la Guadeloupe pour y prendre des places." Ibid., 1:197.

35. "nous apportant le rameau d'une paix générale avec trois belles tortues, un riche caret, et de lezards pour présents et marques de l'acceptation et ratification de tous autre Cariebes et Galibis des toutes les isle adjacentes. . . . on les régala comme on pust, et on leurs donna pour présens et pour gages et asseurance de paix des haches, des serpes et des cousteaux." Petitjean Roget, *L'histoire de l'Isle de Grenade*, 150 (emphasis added).

36. "ils sont tous vestus de la mesme sorte, portent les mesme couleurs, avec le mesme langage portent les mesme armes, ont les mesme intérests, vivent tous ensemble et sont de mesme intelligence. Ce qui faict q'une paix ne seauroit estre bonne si elle n'est qu'avec quelques particulier." Petitjean Roget, *L'histoire de l'Isle de Grenade en Amérique*, 149.

37. "quinze des plus nottables et recommandés entre les Caraybes des d. isles de St. Vincent, la Dominique et ceux qui ont cy devant habités l'isle Martinique." ANOM COL C8B 1 f. 4, Traité conclu entre Charles Hoüel, gouverneur de la Guadeloupe et le Caraibes, March 31, 1660.

38. "parland et entendant la langue des sauvages . . . demander aux dits Caraybes, sils avoient pouvoir de traiter pour eux et au nom de tous les autres des d. isles St. Vincent, la Dominique auroient faits reponce qu'ils se faisoient forts pour tous ayant parlé a la plus grande partie des dits sauvages qui y consentoient." Ibid.

39. "traitte d'union offensive et defensive entre les Francois et Anglois pour le maintien de la *paix avec les Caraybes contenans*. Que tous les prisonniers seront rendus de pars et d'autre. Que ny les Francois ny les Anglois n'auront point l'Isle de St. Vincent ny de la Dominique mais qu'elles resteront aux Caraybes. Et que ces Sauvages sont contents d'estre instruit par les Missionnaires Francois et s'offrent de les recevoir chez eux." ANOM COL C8B 1 f. 4, Traité conclu entre Charles Hoüel, gouverneur de la Guadeloupe et le Caraibes, March 31, 1660.

40. "Monsieur Hoüel Chevalier Seigneur et gouverneur des Isles guadeloupe ayant heurezement traittes de la paix." Ibid.

41. "la ditte isle Martinique estoit engagé dans la guerre avec les sauvages il y a plus de six ans qui a cauzé de tres grands malheurs par les meurtres incendies et enlevements de negres faits par les dits sauvages . . . les dites nations francoises et angloises habitants des isles Monsarat, Antigoa, et Nieves et les d. Caraybes des d. isles St. Vincent la Dominique et qui ont cy devant demeurez en la d. isle Martinique demeureront en paix toutes actions d'hostilitez cessantes." Ibid.

42. "A le dit Baba demandé qu'en consideration de ses peines et soins il luy soit rendus par les habitans de la Martinique ses neveux qui ont esté pris par le nommé Billaudel de la d. isle sur quoy a esté representé par les d. Pères Missionaires qu'il este non seulement juste mais necessaires de faire la d. restitution qui sera un moyen de confirmer et entretenir la paix et dacleminer la conversion des d. sauvages." Ibid.

43. "on a fait demander aux d. Caraibe s'ils ne desiraient pas apprendre a prier dieu à notre imitation et souffrir que les d. pères missionaires les aillent instruire." Ibid.

44. "l'une ou l'autre nation d'habituer les deux isles de St. Vincent et la Dominique quy seullent leur reste pour retraitte." Ibid.

45. Jean-Pierre Sainton argues that "la portée du traité de 1660 est réelle. Premier traité 'international' intra-caribéen, il ne clôt certes pas tout à fait le chapitre des guerres caraïbes, mais il instaure un équilibre durable dont bénéficieront sur le court et le moyen terme les deux parties" ("the the impact of the 1660 treaty was tangible. The first 'international' intra-Caribbean treaty, it of course did not entirely close the chapter of the Carib wars, but it established a durable equilibrium from which the two parties benefited in the short and long term"), Sainton, *Histoire et Civilisation de la Caraïbe*, 1:237.

46. ANOM DPPC G1 498 N. 54 & N. 62, Recensement générale des isles d'Amérique, 1671.

47. "deux des Caraybes de l'isle Saint-Vincent, faisants pour toutte leur nation . . . ne pourront pas aller habiter a l'isle de Grenade . . . laisser passer et repasser les Caraybes de St. Vincent sans leur porter aucun trouble ny empeschement." ANOM FM C8A 2 f. 41, Comte de Blénac, February 13, 1678.

48. "il part presantement dicy deux pirogues de sauvages quy m'ont proposé de leur faire la guerre . . . tout autant que la negrerie de St. Vincent durera, vous ne verres jamais finir le marronnage des negres." ANOM COL C8A 2 f. 87, M. de Blénac, October 1, 1678.

49. "les Caraibes, quy sont ceux aveq les negres de cette isle la, quy nous font le plus de peyne, et que l'on ne peut chasser." ANOM FM C8A 2 f. 181, Blénac, September 23, 1679.

50. "ils ont sujet de craindre que ces negres se multipliant et augmentant en nombre, ne soient plus forts et plus puissant qu'eux et ne les maltraittent dans la suitte; d'autre costé on ne peut point s'assurer que cela soit ainsy parce qu'il y a bien de ces negres alliez avec des Caraibes et qui vivent ensemble en bonne intelligence . . . ils ayment mieux voir deux mil negres establis dans leur isle, que d'y veoir desbarquer seulement 50 francois armez . . . toute leur plus grande attention est de ne point laisser prendre pié dans leur isle aux Francois en aucune manière du monde." ANOM FM C8A 12 f. 100, M. Robert, February 12, 1700.

51. Definition from the *Oxford English Dictionary* at http://www.oxforddictionaries .com/us/definition/american_english/colonize (accessed August 7, 2015).

52. "Les d. isles de St. Vincent et de la Dominique, demeureront à toujours aux dites sauvages, sans qu'elles puissent estre habitées par l'une ou l'autre des d. Nations." ANOM COL C8A 12 f. 48, "Article d'un traité fait à St. Crisophle [sic] entre les francois et les anglois, le 6 mars 1660."

Aphra Behn's *Oroonoko*, Indian Slavery, and the Anglo-Dutch Wars

1. Todd, *Secret Life of Aphra Behn*, 445n; Dickson, "Truth, Wonder, and Exemplarity in Aphra Behn's 'Oroonoko'"; Brown, "The Romance of Empire"; Hughes, Introduction, *Version of Blackness;* Rogers, "Fact and Fiction in Aphra Behn's 'Oroonoko.'"

2. Throughout this chapter, page numbers will refer to the following edition: Aphra Behn, *Oroonoko: The History of the Royal Slave,* in Hughes, *Versions of Blackness,* 117–90.

3. Visconsi, "A Degenerate Race."

4. Zijlstra, "Anglo-Dutch Suriname"; Alison Games, "Cohabitation, Suriname-Style."

5. Behn, *Oroonoko,* 169.

6. The historiography of the 1678–80 Indian War is almost entirely limited to the work of one scholar, Raymond Buve, which has not been translated into English. This accounts for the oversight in the works of English literature scholars and historians. Buve, "De Positie van de Indianen"; Buve, "Gouverneur Johannes Heinsius."

7. Brown, "The Romance of Empire," 53.

8. For a brief intellectual history of the debates over just enslavement in Europe, see Rushforth, *Bonds of Alliance*, ch. 2.

9. Behn, *Oroonoko*, 160.

10. Whitehead, *The Discoverie of the Large, Rich, and Bewtiful Empyre of Guiana*, 153, 179; Warsh, "Enslaved Pearl Divers in the Sixteenth Century Caribbean," 347.

11. Whitehead, "Carib Ethnic Soldiering in Venezuela, the Guianas, and the Antilles."

12. Behn, *Oroonoko*, 173.

13. Hughes, Introduction, *Versions of Blackness*, xix; Schmidt, Introduction, *The Discovery of Guiana by Sir Walter Raleigh*.

14. Todd, *Secret Life of Aphra Behn*, 38–44.

15. Behn, *Oroonoko*, 124.

16. Ibid., 124–25; Hughes, Introduction, *Versions of Blackness*, viii.

17. Rogers, "Fact and Fiction in Aphra Behn's 'Oroonoko,'" 7; Brown, "The Romance of Empire," 42.

18. Brown, "The Romance of Empire," 42; Hulme, *Colonial Encounters*, 241.

19. Behn, *Oroonoko*, 132, 148.

20. Ibid., 145.

21. Ibid., 149.

22. "Extracts from a further deposition by John Ellinger, 10th/20th May 1631," in Lorimer, *English and Irish Settlement on the River Amazon*, 334–36.

23. Lorimer, *English and Irish Settlement on the River Amazon*, 44.

24. "A true State of the Case between the Heires and Assignes of Sir William Courten, Knight, Deceased, and the late Earl of Carlisle, and Planters in the Island of Barbados, annexed to the Petition of William Courten Esquire, and other, exhibited in Parliament," n.d., Egerton Ms. 2395, f. 602, BL.

25. Agreement between Capt Renold Allen of the Water Dogg and Lord Carlisle, May 27, 1641, BARD RB 3/1, 852, BNA.

26. Agreement between Albert Jochemes, Cornelius Heetjes, and Christian Bodchauer, April 5, 1642, BARD RB 3/1, 143, BNA. Another article of agreement was signed between Barbados and Dutch merchants for 1,311 guilders in exchange for any "good cleaned cotton, tobacco or indigoe." December 3, 1644, BARD RB 3/1, 525, BNA.

27. Other documents use "Indian Trade" as a shorthand for the Indian slave trade—for example, Op Vrijdag den April 8, 1672 present de heeren gouverneur Pieter Versterre, Capt Nachtegael & van Muldert & d Huijbert & de heer Secretaris Baty in *Notulen, Ordonnatien (Kopieen) 10 Dec 1670–14 Dec 1680*, NAN, toegang 1.11.01.01, inv. no. 1011.

28. February 15, 1639, BARD 3/2 320–321, BNA; September 20, 1640, BARD 3/2, 320, BNA.

29. Description of a rich plantation called the Tapoywasooze, and the Towyse-yarrowes Countries, lying upon the coast of Guiana, distant from the West Indies eastwards 350 leagues, discovered by Capt. Will. Clovell, and Thos. Tyndall, [1640?], CO 1/10, f. 81 Brief relation of the present state of the business of Guiana, June 20, 1627, CO 1/4, f. 28; Inducements to be propounded to the King to take under his protection the adventurers to the river Amazon or Guiana and their plantation, 1629, CO 1/5, f. 28.

30. Koot, "An Adaptive Presence."

31. Pincus, *Protestantism and Patriotism*, 11–82.

32. Barber, "Power in the English Caribbean," 191.

33. Todd, *Secret Life of Aphra Behn*, 30–31.

34. *Declaration set forth by the Lord Lieutenant*, February 18, 1650.

35. Colonel Thomas Modyford to John Bradshaw, February 16, 1652, pp. a50-a51 of transcript of Willoughby's Settlement of Guiana, in Council Minutes of the Barbados Assembly, c. 1625 to 1667, BNA. Sarah Barber suggests that Rous and George Marten originally settled Suriname and were parliamentarians opposed to Willoughby. Barber, "Power in the English Caribbean," 196.

36. Reasons offered by the Lord Willoughbie why he ought not to bee confined in his settlement upon Serranam, [1660], Egerton Ms. 2395, f. 279, BL; Lieutenant General Byam's Journal of Guiana 1665–1667, Sloane Ms. 3662, BL.

37. [Major John Scott], "Description of Guiana," Egerton Ms. 2395, ff. 37v-42v, BL.

38. Willoughby's Settlement of Guiana, pp. a50-a51 of transcript, February 16, 1652, H1; Colonel Thomas Modyford to John Bradshaw, Council Minutes of the Barbados Assembly, c. 1625 to 1667, BNA.

39. A Proposition for erecting a West India Company for the better interest of the commonwealth in America, [1655], Egerton Ms. 2395, ff. 87–88, BL.

40. Council Minutes of the Barbados Assembly, c. 1625–1667, pp. a54-a55, June 3, 1652, BNA.

41. Koot, "An Adaptive Presence."

42. Gelfand, "A Caribbean Wind"; Zijlstra, "Anglo-Dutch Suriname," 43.

43. Menard, *Sweet Negotiations*, 16.

44. Du Tertre, *Histoire Générale des Antilles*, 2:492.

45. Schiltkamp, "On Common Ground," 78–79; Meuwese, *Brothers in Arms*, 160.

46. [Major John Scott], "Description of Guiana."

47. Deed Tobias Frere Esquire to Capt. John Frere, May 5, 1654 (entered May 24, 1654), Recopied Deeds, RB 3/2, 691–692, BNA.

48. October 12, 1659, BARD, RB 3/5, 525–527, BNA; Indenture between Thomas Noell and George Robinson and Thomas Massam, September 14, 1659, BARD RB 3/5 873–874, BNA.

49. Menard, *Sweet Negotiations*, 59. Menard argues that Maurice Thompson and the Noell family, especially Martin Noell, were the biggest investors in the Barbados "sugar boom."

50. Buve, "Gouverneur Johannes Heinsius," 14.

51. Menard, *Sweet Negotiations*, 25.

52. Letter of Francis Lord Willoughby, Governor of Barbadoes to M. De Laubier, Governor of Martinico, p. a155, September 23, 1663, item no. 565, BNA; Letter of Lord Willoughby to the King, p. a187, November 4, 1663, Council Minutes 1625 to 1667, Barbados Council Minutes 1625–1667, BNA.

53. Barber, "Power in the English Caribbean," 202.

54. Todd, *Secret Life of Aphra Behn*, 44.

55. There is little known about who George Warren was and why he was compelled to write about Suriname. Hughes, *Versions of Blackness*, 331; Warren, *Impartial Description of Suriname*, 2–3.

56. Behn, *Oroonoko*, 169–70.

57. Ibid., 173.

58. Ibid., 126.

59. "Petitie Inwoners," Inhabitants of Suriname to the Zeeland Chamber of the West Indies Company, March 11, 1671, ZA, SvZ, 2035-225. This number is even more significant

considering there were only eight hundred European colonists in Suriname in 1671. Buve, "Gouverneur Johannes Heinsius," 17.

60. De Rochefort, *Histoire Naturelle et Morale*, 531; Du Tertre, *Histoire générale des Antilles*, 1:485–86; Warren, *Impartial Description of Suriname*, 23.

61. Warren, *Impartial Description of Suriname;* de Rochefort, *Histoire Naturelle and Morale*, 438, 442, 446.

62. Du Tertre, *Histoire générale des Antilles*, 1:382–83.

63. Warren, *Impartial Description of Suriname*, 25.

64. Behn, *Oroonoko*, 126.

65. Ibid., 173.

66. Ibid., 126, 151.

67. Warren, *Impartial Description of Suriname*, 19.

68. Rogers, "Fact and Fiction in Aphra Behn's 'Oroonoko,'" 2; Dickson, "Truth, Wonder, and Exemplarity."

69. Behn, *Oroonoko*, 176.

70. Ibid., 177.

71. Ibid., 180.

72. Todd, *Secret Life of Aphra Behn*, 51.

73. Du Tertre, *Histoire Générale des Antilles*, 2:246.

74. Brown, "Romance of Empire," 52.

75. Byam's Journal of Guiana; Warren, *Impartial Description of Suriname.*

76. Todd, *Secret Life of Aphra Behn*, 113.

77. [Major John Scott], "Description of Guiana."

78. Byam's Journal of Guiana.

79. Warren, *An Impartial Description of Suriname*, 6.

80. Byam's Journal of Guiana.

81. Ibid.

82. Articles Concluded upon between Commander Abraham Crynsens, Admirall of a Squadron of shipps belonging unto the noble and mighty Lords the States of Zealand and Collonell William Byam late Lieutent Generall of Guyana, and Governour of Willoughby Land, March 6, 1667, CO 278/2.

83. Enthoven, "Suriname and Zeeland," 256.

84. Games, "Cohabitation, Suriname-Style," 212.

85. Buve, "Gouverneur Johannes Heinsius," 16.

86. February 8, 1670, SvZ 2035–105.

87. Examinatie van Majoor Nedham met zijn volck, Suriname, June 19, 1668, ZA, SvZ 2035.1–033.

88. William Willoughby to Abraham Crijnsen, August 15, 1668, Rijksarchief, Zeeland, Middleburg, SvZ 2035.1–093.

89. Instructions for Srgt Major William Neadham for this Present Voyage, Barbados, May 6, 1668, ZA Collections, Rijksarchief, Zeeland, Middelburg, SvZ 2035.1–025; Copie—Commissie van den Majoor Nedham, N1, Copy made in Suriname from the original, written in Barbados, May 1, 1668, ZA, SvZ 2035.1–027.

90. Behn, *Oroonoko*, 175.

91. BARB RB3/8, 46–47, May 30, 1670 (entered August 27, 1670), sale of slaves from Peter Wroth to John Kellicott, BNA.

92. Sir Jonathan Atkins, Governor of Barbados to the Secretary of the Council for Plantations, February 17, 1675, Minutes of the Barbados Council, 1671–1684, 439, BNA.

93. Brief of Nicholas Combe, May 1, 1675, ZA, SvZ 2035–255.

94. Richard Price has been cited by many on this point. See his essay "Caribbean Fishing and Fishermen."

95. "Petitie Inwoners," Inhabitants of Suriname to the Zeeland Chamber of the West Indies Company, March 11, 1671, ZA, SvZ, 2035–225. This number is even more significant considering there were only eight hundred European colonists in Suriname in 1671. Buve, "Gouverneur Johannes Heinsius," 17.

96. Op Vrijdag den April 8, 1672 present de heeren gouverneur Pieter Versterre, Capt Nachtegael & van Muldert & d Huijbert & de heer Secretaris Baty in *Notulen, Ordonnatien (Kopieen) 10 Dec 1670–14 Dec 1680*, NAN, toegang 1.11.01.01 inv. no. 1011.

97. Buve, "De Positie van de Indianen," 12.

98. Breslaw, *Tituba, Reluctant Witch of Salem*, 10.

99. Slavenverkoop fregat *America* te Curacaso, June 7, 1673, ZA, SvZ transcription by Philip Dikland; "Zeeuwse archivalia uit Surinamee en omliggende kwartieren 1667–1683." Available online in PDF: http://files.archieven.nl/239/f/GIDS102/2035-transcripties.pdf, 193–94.

100. Enthoven, "Islands at the Center of the Atlantic World," 67–68.

101. Minutes of the Council and Assemble of Barbados, vol. II (May 1671–1684), August 14, 1673, 151–53, BNA.

102. "Brief of Pieter Versterre to the West Indies Company," December 16, 1675, ZA, SvZ, 2035.1–271.

103. "English Commission to Pieter Versterre," ZA, SvZ 2035.2–273.

104. Buve, "Gouverneur Johannes Heinsius," 16–20.

105. Plakaat 83, "Verkoop van gevangengenomen Indiaanse Slaven" ("Sale of the Captured Indian slaves"), October 26, 1679, in Schiltkamp and Smidt, *West Indische Plakaatboek*, 101.

106. Buve, "Gouverneur Johannes Heinsius," 17.

107. Buve, "De Positie van de Indianen," 24.

108. "Hoofd en Achtergeld Schuldig," 1684, tax liability lists, NAN, Societeit van Suriname 1.05.03–213, ff. 203–42; Hoogbergen, "The History of the Suriname Maroons," 73.

Indigeneity and Authority in the Lesser Antilles

1. "The late Earle of Carlisles second Letters patents of the Caribee Islands of the seventh of Aprill 4to Caroli," Trinity College, Dublin, Ms. 736, 68–69. This is a copy made by or for Jerome Alexander, attorney to the second Earl of Carlisle, dated later 1640s–early 1650s. The first grant of July 2, 1627, is at 42–56.

2. Eden, *Decades of the new worlde*, 3.

3. SP 16/115, f. 36, p. 31. On the same day there was an Order in Council for the restoration of the above to Captains Warner and Smith, [SP 16/115 f. 28]. Letters of Marque were issued to Ralph Merrifield, the owner of the forty-ton *Gift of God* of London, with Thomas Warner captain, January 26, 1626.

4. Smith, *True Travels, Adventures, and Observations*, 51–52. "Nicnobbie" is probably an early reference to drink the English came to call "mobby," a watery mash of potatoes.

5. Jeaffreson, *Young Squire of the Seventeenth Century*, 1:3–9.

6. Thomas Warner's commission from Charles I, CO 1/3, f. 44, and fair copy at f. 45.

7. Smith, *True Travels, Adventures, and Observations*, 52–53.

8. Ibid.

9. Du Tertre, *Histoire générale des Isles*, 6.

10. Ibid., 7, translated by this author as "sinon quelques-unes des plus belles femmes pour assouvir leurs brutales passions, & en faire leurs esclaves."

11.   Ibid., 5–6. This account also gives a far more graphic and disturbing portrait of Kalinago excesses against Europeans.

12.   Egerton Ms. 2395, f. 503, BL.

13.   Du Tertre, *Histoire générale des Isles,* 8–9.

14.   That this Edward Johnson may be the same as the Puritan settler in New England and tractarian is provided by a reference to a later person of the same name. Johnson, "Merchant, at St. Christopher's in the West-Indies."

15.   Jeaffreson Box 1, M3b, Beinecke Lesser Antilles Collection, Hamilton College, Clinton, N.Y.

16.   The document at Hamilton College is endorsed on the reverse "Inrolled in the close Rolles in Chancery the fifteenth day of July in the yeare of our Lord 1658 By Humfrey Jaggard" and in a different hand. "Earle of Carlile & Jeffreson Johnson," C 10/54, f. 100, National Archives of Great Britain, Kew, Richmond: Johnson v Carlisle, James, Earl of (1653); Complaints against Governor Clement Everard, [January 25,] 1659, CO 1/13, f. 63ii, signed by John Jeaffreson. The document is torn so we do not know the descriptor after "primitive." He claimed his tenants were so oppressed by Everard that they went to Hispaniola.

17.   "Coppy extracted from the Originall of Sʳ Thomas Warners Commission for Govʳ of Sʳ Xtphers, 29 Sept 1629," Egerton Ms. 2395, ff. 15–16v, BL.

18.   Egerton Ms. 2395, f. 16, BL.

19.   D/EP/F.143, unfoliated, "Carlile Accounts," Hertfordshire Archives and Library Services, Hertford, U.K.

20.   Whitelocke Papers, vol. 2, no. 112, pp. 201–3v, Longleat House, Warminster, Wiltshire, U.K.

21.   Philip Warner had played a gallant role at sea under the command of Henry Willoughby in the taking of Cayenne and Surinam. CO 1/21, f. 90.

22.   Council of Barbados, May 6, 1673, CO 31/1, f. 234. Presiding this day was Sir Peter Colleton, with councilors John Willoughby, Daniel Searle, Samuel Farmer, Henry Walrond Snr., Henry Hawley, Thomas Warrall, John Knights, Samuel Barwick, and John Sparkes.

23.   Poyer, *History of Barbados,* 98.

24.   Letter of de la Barre to William Willoughby, an enclosure made by Willoughby to Secretary Lord Arlington, from Nevis Road, January 4, 1668, CO 1/22, f. 2i.

25.   Willoughby to de la Barre, January 3, 1668, CO 1/22, f. 2ii.

26.   William Willoughby's instructions from Antigua to Major James Walker (copy), February 2, 1668, CO 1/32, f. 32.

27.   Notes in Williamson's handwriting, attributed to 1668. Williamson says that the governor of St. Christopher's was James Russell, which must date the notes to before 1671. CO 1/23, f. 103.

28.   Notebook of Sir Joseph Williamson, CO 324/3.

29.   Extract from a Letter from the Council of Barbados to the Board of Trade, May 28, 1673, CO 1/66, f. 230.

30.   December 19, 1673, CO 29/2, f. 153.

31.   Stapleton Papers 1/1, John Rylands Library, University of Manchester.

32.   SP 44/28, ff. 131v–132v; Beckles, "Kalinago (Carib) Resistance."

33.   "To the Kings Most Excellent Majesty The humble Peticon of Dame Anne March Widdow of Sʳ George March and late Wife of Sʳ Thomas Warner deceased," CO 1/35, f. 66; Philip Warner, anchored off Barbados, to Sir Jonathan Atkins, n.d., Egerton Ms., 2395, f. 499, BL.

34.   "The Case of Coll. Philip Warner, now Prisoner in the Tower," CO 1/35, f. 64i. He was also said to have killed Edward Dering. The French Governor who took over "occupied" Antigua was Robert le Fichot des Friches.

35. Sir William Stapleton to the Committee for the Plantations, from Nevis, December 20, 1675, CO 1/35, f. 64, and enclosed depositions, ff. 64i-iv.

36. Sir Jonathan Atkins, Barbados, to the Lords of Trade and Plantations, February 17/27, 1674/5, CO 1/34, f. 13.

37. Examination of William Hamlyn, CO 1/34, ff. 13. This item, and that before, were copied into an Entry Book. Stapleton's evidence, also in the Entry Book, is not in CO 1/34.

38. CO 153/2, ff. 70–71.

39. Deposition of Walter Carwardine, December 18, 1675, copied into an Entry Book as one of the enclosures with a letter from Stapleton to the Lords of the Committee, CO 153/2, f. 72.

40. CO 153/2, f. 73.

41. CO 153/2, ff. 75–76.

42. CO 153/2, ff. 74–75.

43. Lords of Trade and Plantations to Stapleton, Whitehall, April 14, 1676, CO 153/2, f. 83.

44. CO 153/2, f. 95: "On the 27th of July 1676: is read a letter from Collonel Stapleton touching the Condition of the Leeward Islands and transmitting severall depositions and addresses about Col: Warner." Stapleton's letter was written on April 26, only twelve days after the committee had required him to prepare his account.

45. CO 153/2, ff. 101–14 (except 106–7). Dermot Duell was apparently 101 years old.

46. CO 153/2, ff. 106–7. For a reference to the way in which the Stapleton/Russells worked as a family unit, see Lafleur, *Les Caraibes des Petites Antilles,* 55–56.

47. CO 1/21, ff. 145, 288, 288v. Fellow signatories Philip Payne and Samuel Payne were presumably related to Warner by marriage to Rebecca Payne.

48. CO 153/2, f. 122.

49. Johnston, "Stapleton Sugar Plantations."

50. Whitelocke Papers, vol. 2, no. 112, f. 201, Longleat House, Warminster, U.K.

Second Is Best

1. Much of the research for this essay was done while I was a fellow at the Huntington Library in San Marino, California, as part of the Global Early Modern Caribbean Seminar. I would like to thank the Huntington Library and the University of Southern California for making my stay possible.

2. Muller, *Elisabeth van der Woude,* 106–7. There are two accounts of this attempt at colonization, both written by actual participants in the venture: De Myst, *Verloren Arbeyt ofte Klaar en kortbondigh vertoogh van de Colonie in de Lantstreke Guyana,* and Van der Woude, *Memorije van 't geen bij mijn tijt is vorgevallen soo in hollant als op ander plaetsen.* Elisabeth van der Woude's diary has been transcribed and studied by Kim Isolde Muller.

3. The river's spelling is eccentric in the sources and it is also rendered as the Oyapoc and the Wiapoco. Since 1909, it has been called the Oiapoque.

4. Ten Hoorn, *Pertinente Beschrijvinge van Guyana Gelegen aen de vaste Kust van America.*

5. De Myst, *Verloren Arbeyt,* 13.

6. Ibid., title page.

7. Muller, *Elisabeth van der Woude,* 47, 102–3.

8. De Myst, *Verloren Arbeyt,* title page.

9. Den Heijer, "'Over warem en koude landen.'"

10. Incidentally, this was also the case for Brazil, taken from the Portuguese; it was a Dutch possession (New Holland) between 1630 and 1654.

11. Schmidt, *Innocence Abroad,* 149–51.

12. Keymis, *A Relation of the second voyage to Guiana.* It was published in the Dutch

Republic two years later as *Waerachtighe ende grondighe beschryvinghe vande tweede zeevaert der Engelschen naar Guyana.*

13. Japikse, Resolution passed June 24, 1589, *Resolutiën der Staten-Generaal van 1576 tot 1609,* 355. Ten Haeff was given permission for two voyages. Jan Jacob Hartsinck, one of the first historians of the region, wrote that the Dutch had sent ships to the region in 1580, but this assertion has never been confirmed in any archival sources. Hartsinck, *Beschryving van Guyana of de Wilde Kust in Zuid-Amerika,* 206.

14. Hartsinck, *Beschryving van Guyana of de Wilde Kust in Zuid-Amerika,* 356, 809–10.

15. Ibid., 807.

16. Cabeliau's account can be found in De Jonge, *De opkomst van het Nederlandsch gezag in Oost-Indië,* 153–60, quotation at 157.

17. "Report to the States General of the earliest voyage to the coast of Guiana," in United States Commission, *Report and Accompanying Papers,* vol. 2 at 28–29.

18. Van Rees, *Geschiedenis der staathuishoudkunde in Nederland tot het einde der achttiende eeuw,* 76–78, and Appendix II, 384–408; Ligtenberg, *Willem Usselinx,* 18–19.

19. Most of these pamphlets can be found in The Hague. Many have been cataloged in Knuttel, *Catalogus van de pamfletten-verzameling berustende in de Koninklijke Bibliotheek.* In addition Thysiana, now part of the Special Collections of the Leiden University Library, is in possession of a few of these important works.

20. These descriptions are drawn from Apricius, *Een Vertoogh van de considerabele Colonie,* 5; *Beschrijvinge van Guyana,* 2; and ten Hoorn, *Pertinente Beschrijvinge van Guyana Gelegen aen de vaste Kust van America,* 7.

21. United States Commission, *Report and Accompanying Papers,* 1:27–36, quotation at 28–29.

22. De la Court, *Aanwysing der heilsame politieke Gronden en Maximen van de Republike van Holland en West-Vriesland.*

23. Keye, *Het waere onderscheyt tusschen koude en warme landen.*

24. Apricius, *Een kort en bondigh Vertoogh,* 2–3.

25. Van Meeteren, *Historie der Nederlandschen ende haerder naburen oorlogen ende geschiedenissen,* 506, 534.

26. There is a long historiography on *patroonschappen,* much of it equating them with feudalism. See Brodhead, *History of the State of New York;* O'Callaghan, *History of New Netherlands;* and Rink, *Holland on the Hudson.* Jan de Vries addresses these views in "The Dutch Atlantic Economies," 17. Other European nations employed this method of settling their overseas territories. Portugal used a system of so-called "captaincies," and the English gave large grants of land to individual settlers and/or consortiums of investors to arrange for the colonization of vast swathes of territory. Roper and Ruymbeke, *Constructing Early Modern Empires.*

27. Jan van Ryen to the Directors of the Zeeland Chamber of the West India Company, April 25 [1625], Fort Nassau, Wiapoco River, Van Rappard Manuscripts (Records of the West India Company), HM 548, ff. 2–2v, Huntington Library, San Marino, Calif.

28. Oude West-Indische Compagnie (OWIC), 1.05.01.01, inventory number 20, 24v, NAN.

29. Edmundson, "The Dutch on the Amazon and Negro in the Seventeenth Century."

30. De Forest, *Walloon Family in America,* 6, 188–89.

31. Lorimer, *English and Irish settlement on the River Amazon,* 261.

32. De Forest, *Walloon Family in America,* 189–269.

33. They are mentioned in the journal of the De Forest voyage (entry for May 23, 1625) as arriving in the area after being attacked by the Portuguese. Ibid., 259. The journal says "soldiers," which seems unlikely.

34. De Laet, *Iaerlyck Verhael van de Verrichtinghen der Geoctroyeerde West-Indische Compagnie in derthien Boecken*, 17–18.

35. Jan van Ryen to the Directors of the Zeeland Chamber of the West India Company, April 25 [1625], Fort Nassau, Wiapoco River, Van Rappard Manuscripts (Records of the West India Company), HM 548, ff. 2–2v, Huntington Library.

36. Netscher, *Geschiedenis van de koloniën Essequebo, Demerary en Berbice*, 56–57. A description of this failed voyage can be found in Jan van Ryen to the Directors of the Zeeland Chamber of the West India Company, April 25 [1625], Fort Nassau, Wiapoco River, Van Rappard Manuscripts (Records of the West India Company), HM 548, Huntington Library.

37. Muller, *Elisabeth van der Woude*, 82.

38. De Vries, *Korte historiael ende journaels aenteyckeninge van verscheyden voyagien in de vier deelen de wereldtsronde*, 187, 220–21.

39. See Oppenheim, "An Early Jewish Colony in Western Guyana, 1658–1666," and his "An Early Jewish Colony in Western Guyana: Supplemental Data"; also, Marcus, *Colonial American Jews*, 2:85–175.

40. Netscher, *Geschiedenis van de koloniën Essequebo, Demerary en Berbice, van de vestiging der Nederlanders aldaar tot op onzen tijd*, 72–75; Hartsinck, *Beschryving van Guyana*, 940–46.

41. Ternaux-Compans, *Notice historique sur la Guyana française*, 66. See also Klooster, "The Essequibo Liberties."

42. Van Alphen, *Jan Reeps en zijn onbekende kolonisatiepoging in Zuid-Amerika 1692*.

43. Van der Oest, "The forgotten colonies of Essequibo and Demerara," 325.

44. Bailyn, *Atlantic History*, 69.

45. Den Heijer, "Over warem en koude landen," 89.

46. De Myst, *Verloren Arbeyt*, 14–15.

47. Warren, *An Impartial Description of Surinam*, 4.

48. De Myst, *Verloren Arbeyt*, 15.

49. Netscher, *Geschiedenis van de koloniën Essequebo, Demerary en Berbice*, 57, 351.

50. In "'If at First You Fail . . .'" Susanah Shaw Romney makes the interesting argument that the relative lack of female colonists was one reason for the failure of Dutch settlement efforts on the Wild Coast.

51. Netscher, *Geschiedenis van de koloniën Essequebo, Demerary en Berbice*, 59.

52. In New Netherland 35.5 percent of the troops were German, compared to 32.6 percent from the Dutch Republic; Germans made up 26.3 percent of the soldiers in Brazil from 1632 to 1654, compared to 36 percent Dutch. For soldiers and family recruitment, see Klooster, *Dutch Moment in Atlantic History*, chs. 4, 6. For a good overview of these migration patterns and their cultural implications, see Kruijtzer, "European Migration in the Dutch Sphere."

53. Faber et al., "Population Changes and Economic Development in the Netherlands."

54. Oostindie and Roitman, "Repositioning the Dutch in the Atlantic," 140.

55. Muller, *Elisabeth van der Woude*, 43–45.

56. Oostindie and Van Stipriaan, "Slavery and Slave Cultures."

57. United States Commission on the Boundary between Venezuela and British Guiana, *Report and Accompanying Papers*, Appendix, 1:88–89, quotation at 88.

58. De Myst, *Verloren Arbeyt*, 12; Muller, *Elisabeth van der Woude*, 41.

59. Muller, *Elisabeth van der Woude*, 41.

60. De Myst, *Verloren Arbeyt*, 15.

61. Whitehead, "Native Peoples Confront Colonial Regimes in Northeastern South America," 412–13.

62. De Laet, *Iaerlijck Verhael*, 112. See also Goslinga, *Dutch in the Caribbean*, 413.

63. Whitehead, "Native Peoples," 412–13.

64. Scott, *Description of Guyana*, 12; Whitehead, "Native Peoples," 413.

65. De Forest, *A Walloon Family in America*, 2:246.

66. De Vries, *Korte historiael ende journaels aenteyckeninge*, 192.

67. Bailyn, *Atlantic History*, 69–70.

68. Goslinga, *Short History of the Netherlands Antilles and Suriname*, 91.

69. Whitehead, "Native Peoples," 412–13.

70. Barber, "Power in the English Caribbean," 196–97.

71. Harlow, *Colonising Expeditions to the West Indies*, 142–43n, 178–79.

72. "Certaine overtures made by ye Ld Willoughby of Parham," Sloane Ms. 159, ff. 20–21, BL.

73. "Consideraõns about the peopleing & settling the island Jamaica," n.d., but after 1660, Egerton 2395, ff. 283–86v, at 286v, BL; Lorimer, "Failure of the English Guiana Ventures, 1595–1667"; Barber, "Power in The English Caribbean," 198.

74. Games, "Cohabitation, Suriname-Style," 202.

75. Roberts and Beamish, "Venturing Out," 52. On the growth of English Suriname, see Williamson, *English Colonies in Guiana and on the Amazon*, 151, 160.

76. Barber, "Power in the English Caribbean," 197.

77. Menard, *Sweet Negotiations*, 51.

78. Warren, *Impartial Description of Suriname*. These plantations were strung out primarily along the Suriname River, although the English also settled along the Commewijne and Cottica Rivers.

79. Renatus Enys to Sec. Sir Henry Bennet, November 1, 1663, no. 577, in *CSPC, AWI* 5:166–67. This statistic was inaccurately transcribed as four thousand. Enys may have only been counting European inhabitants. Games, "Cohabitation, Suriname-Style," 202.

80. Report made by Julius Lichtenberg to the States General of the Dutch Republic, June 17, 1669, ZA, 2035.3, 164–66.

81. *Essai Historique sur la Colonie de Surinam* (Paramaribo, 1788), 35.

82. Klooster, *The Dutch Moment in Atlantic History*, 95. See also Schwartz, "Looking for a New Brazil," 20.

83. Crijnsen had initially conquered Suriname in 1667. The English briefly retook it, but it was formally ceded to the Dutch in 1667 as part of the Treaty of Breda. The colony remained under the control of the Zealanders until 1682. It was then transferred to the control of a private company, the Suriname Company, in 1683.

84. Games, "Cohabitation, Suriname Style," 223.

85. William Willoughby to Lord Arlington, May 25, 1667, CO 1/21, f. 50. See also Van der Meiden, *Betwist bestuur*, 21–23.

86. Extract of the treaty between Crijnsen and Byam, March 6, 1667, ZA, 2035.2. See also Vernooij, "Godt niet meer Engels maer geheel Zeeuws," 4, cited in Tom Weterings, "Should We Stay or Should We Go?."

87. Zijlstra, "Competing for European Settlers Jamaica, 1660–1680," 158; Games, "Cohabitation, Suriname-Style," 223.

88. *Pertinente beschrijvinge van Guiana*, 4. See also Pestana, *Protestant Empire*, 118.

89. Johan Thressrij to States of Zeeland, June 1668, ZA, 2035.2.1, 22; 2035.2.1, no. 97, Claes Reijniersen to States of Zeeland, September 18, 1668; 2035.2.1 109, Abel Thisso to States of Zeeland, January 9, 1669. See also Zijlstra, "Competing for European Settlers."

90. Weterings, "Should We Stay or Should We Go?," 139.

91. Roitman, "Creating Confusion in the Colonies," 68–69.

92. Letter of Pieter Versterre, April 10, 1676, transcribed in Karijosemito and Dikland, *Zeeuwse archivalia uit Suriname en omliggende kwartieren*, 237–39.

93. Den Heijer, *De geschiedenis van de WIC*, 145.

94. Van der Oest, "Forgotten Colonies of Essequibo and Demerara," 329.

95. Postma, *Dutch in the Atlantic Slave Trade*, 192–93.

96. For the list of men in the colony in 1675, see Baron Mulert, "De bewoners van Suriname in 1675," 404. These figures are significantly lower than the 120 English families, 1,325 Dutch men, 58 Jewish men, and garrison with 115 soldiers and 4 sailors given by Buddingh, *Geschiedenis van Suriname*, 18. Buddingh's figures seem very high.

Colonial Life in Times of War

1. The research that Suze Zijlstra conducted for this article has been generously supported by a Ph.D. grant from the Dutch Organization for Scientific Research (NWO) and a Niels Stensen Fellowship.

2. "Articles concluded upon between commander Abraham Crynsens [. . .] and Collonell William Byam," CO 278/2, f. 1.

3. See, on this phase of "cohabitation," Games, "Cohabitation, Suriname-Style."

4. Pieter Versterre to the States of Zeeland, May 1671, Overgekomen brieven uit Suriname, Staten van Zeeland (2.1), ZA, inv. no. 2035.1, no. 232; "Huisarrest voor de Engelse kolonisten," June 9, 1672, in Schiltkamp and De Smidt, *West Indische Plakaatboek*, 71; Bathshua Scott to James Bannister, September 13, 1674, CO 31/1, f. 75 I.

5. Koot, *Empire at the Periphery*; Benjamin Schmidt, "The Dutch Atlantic: From Provincialism to Globalism," in Greene and Morgan, *Atlantic History*, 163–87.

6. Notulen van Gouverneur en Politieke Raad, Aanwinsten eerste afdeling, 1905-C (1.11.01.01), inv. no. 1011, NAN; ZA, 2.1, inv. no. 2035; Intercepted mail and papers, HCA 30/223. Dutch studies have already extensively shown how much these letters reveal about the experience of the inhabitants of the Dutch Republic. See, for example, Brouwer, *Levenstekens*; Weterings, "Zeeuws Suriname."

7. Weterings, "Should We Stay or Should We Go?," 143–44.

8. Zijlstra, "Anglo-Dutch Suriname," 25–34. See also the contribution of Carolyn Arena to this volume.

9. Zeeland's grand pensionary, Pieter de Huybert, argued (to the displeasure of the province of Holland and the Dutch West India Company) that the other provinces had declined to contribute to the fleet, and hence they would receive no share in the spoils. Van der Meiden, "*Betwist bestuur*," 20–22; Den Heijer, *De geschiedenis van de WIC*, 137.

10. Extract of the treaty between Crijnsen and Byam, March 6, 1667, ZA, 2.1, inv. no. 2035.1, no. 002. See also Vernooij, "Godt niet meer Engels maer geheel Zeeuws," 4.

11. ZA, 2.1, inv. no. 2035.1, no. 009.

12. Accont of the destruction of Koyan the takeing of Surinam by William Willoughby [to Privy Council], December 16, 1667, "An exact narrative concerninge the takeinge of island off cayenne from the French and the fort and collony off Surrynam ffrom the Dutch," CO 1/21, ff. 162, 90.

13. Accont of the destruction of Koyan the takeing of Surinam by William Willoughby [to Privy Council], December 16, 1667, CO 1/21, f. 162; Letter from William Willoughby, March 9, 1667/8, CO 1/22, f. 50.

14. ZA, 2.1, 2035.1, no. 004, 007.

15. Memorie vande slaven, vee, keetels, persoonen, suijckeren ende andere goederen, door den lieutenant Generael Willoughbij uijt Suriname vervoert, May 23, 1668 [June 2, 1668], CO 1/22, f. 109.

16. "A short narrative of the state & condition of the colony of Suranam," CO 1/23, f. 31.

17. William Willoughby to James Bannister, June 28, 1668; ZA, 2.1, inv. no. 2035.1, no. 088. In various sources Bannister's rank seems to fluctuate between the extremes of sergeant and colonel, but major is most often used.

18. Court proceedings on the Bannister case, July–August 1668, ZA, 2.1, inv. no. 2035.1, no. 060–070; Abraham Crijnsen to the States of Zeeland, October 3–4, 1668, ZA, 2.1, inv. no. 2035.1, no. 076a/077.

19. Crijnsen to the States of Zeeland, August 3, 1668, ZA, 2.1, inv. no. 2035.1, no. 058/058a/058b. Crijnsen erroneously referred to Bannister as the "former governor" here.

20. Crijnsen to the States of Zeeland, October 3–4, 1668, ZA, 2.1, inv. no. 2035.1, no. 076a/077.

21. William Willoughby to Abraham Crijnsen, August 15, 1668, ZA, 2.1, inv. no. 2035.1, no. 092.

22. Crijnsen to the States of Zeeland, August 3, 1668, ZA, 2.1, inv. no. 2035.1, no. 058/058a/058b; Julius Lichtenbergh to the States of Zeeland, March 18, 1669, ZA, 2.1, inv. no. 2035.1, 124.

23. Lichtenbergh to the States of Zeeland, June 17, 1669, ZA, 2.1, inv. no. 2035.1, no. 161/162/163.

24. Ibid.; Lichtenbergh to the States of Zeeland, August 30, 1669, ZA, 2.1, inv. no. 2035.1, no. 178.

25. Lichtenbergh to the States of Zeeland, December 4, 1669, ZA, 2.1, inv. no. 2035.1, no. 196.

26. Julius Lichtenbergh to the States of Zeeland, February 24, 1671, ZA, 2.1, inv. no. 2035.1, no. 220.

27. Correspondence between Lichtenbergh and Bannister, January 22 to March 6, 1671, ZA, 2.1, inv. no. 2035.1, no. 222/223/224.

28. Lichtenbergh to the States of Zeeland, March 3, 1671, ZA, 2.1, inv. no. 2035.1, no. 226; Pieter Versterre to the States of Zeeland, March 24, 1671, ZA, 2.1, inv. no. 2035.1, no. 227.

29. Petition by the inhabitants of Surinam, March 11, 1671, ZA, 2.1, inv. no. 2035.1, no. 225. See also Schalkwijk, *Colonial State in the Caribbean,* 116.

30. Zijlstra, "Anglo-Dutch Suriname," 42–46; Games, "Cohabitation, Suriname-Style," at 217.

31. Versterre to the States of Zeeland, May 1671, ZA, 2.1, inv. no. 2035.1, no. 232. Versterre, formerly commander of the colony's garrison, would remain "temporary" governor until his death six years later.

32. Ibid.

33. Panhuysen, *Rampjaar 1672,* 98.

34. Ibid., 152.

35. Ibid., 204.

36. Weterings, "Rampjaar aan de Rivier," 53–55.

37. States of Zeeland to Dominque Potteij, April 2, 1672, ZA, 2.1, inv. no. 2035.1, no. 234.

38. Dominique Potteij to Lieutenant de Chavoones, September 11, 1672, HCA 30/223.

39. Ibid.; Dominique Potteij to Hermaenus Potteij, September 11, 1672, HCA 30/223.

40. Pieter Versterre to the States of Zeeland, May 6, 1673, ZA, 2.1, inv. no. 2035.1, no. 241.

41. Jan van Ruijven to Jacob Pietersen, August 31/September 14, 1672, HCA 30/223.

42. Jean le Grand to Pieter Sandra, September 6/15, 1672, HCA 30/223.

43. See, for example, Jan Andriese to Laurens Verpoorten, September 15, 1672, HCA 30/223; and Raquel da Silva to Ishac del Sotto, September 1, 1672, HCA 30/223. All letters written by the Jewish colonists that we use have been translated from Portuguese to Dutch by Lucia Werneck Xavier.

44. Jan van Ruijven to Adriaen Tandt, August 31/September 14, 1672, HCA 30/223. See also Jan Andriese to Laurens Verpoorten, September 15, 1672, HCA 30/223.

45. Perhaps tellingly, Captain Pieter Doncker of the *Susanna* wrote to his employer, Laurens Verpoorten, that "here [in Suriname] is nothing unusual"—a matter of perspective, probably. Doncker to Verpoorten, September 19, 1672, HCA 30/223.

46. Jean le Grand to Pieter Sandra, September 6/15, 1672, HCA 30/223; Pieter Jaspers Heerense to Johan and Pieter Boudaen Courten, September 4, 1672, HCA 30/223.

47. Jean le Grand to Samuel van Westhuijsen, September 6/15, 1672, HCA 30/223.

48. Ishak de Avilar to Jacob de Avilar, September 1, 1672, HCA 30/223.

49. Pieter Jaspers Heerense to Johan and Pieter Boudaen Courten, September 4, 1672, HCA 30/223.

50. Versterre to the States, December 29, 1672, ZA, 2.1, inv. no. 2035.1, no. 235.

51. For example, Bastiaan Thijssen Danielsen to Moijse Catteau, September 15, 1672, HCA 30/223. In times of peace nearly everyone regularly asked for supplies such as clothing to be shipped from Europe. In particular the number of shoes asked for could be enormous—in one letter, no fewer than a hundred pair were ordered. See also Weterings, "Rampjaar aan de Rivier," 37–38.

52. Zijlstra, "Anglo-Dutch Suriname," 55.

53. Jean le Grand to Pieter Sandra, September 6/15, 1672, HCA 30, inv. no. 223.

54. He had only arrived there on December 31, 1671. Jean le Grand to Moijse Catteau, January 7, 1672, HCA 30/227.

55. Pieter Versterre to the States, December 29, 1672, ZA, 2.1, inv. no. 2035.1, no. 235. By this point they had already slaughtered nearly forty cows on behalf of the garrison, which constituted an enormous value.

56. Versterre to the States, May 6, 1673, ZA, 2.1, inv. no. 2035.1, no. 241.

57. Notice of the sale of slaves arrived here [in Suriname] on the frigate *America,* June 7, 1673, ZA, 2.1, inv. no. 2035.1, no. 242.

58. S.R.D. Plessis du Bellay to Justus de Huijbert, January 2, 1674, ZA, 2.1, inv. no. 2035.1, no. 244.

59. Various entries for July 1674, in *CSP AWI* 7, *1669–1674,* 594–603; Versterre to the States, ZA, 2.1, inv. no. 2035.1, no. 249, 250, inv. no. 2035.2, no. 253.

60. Minutes of the Committee of Trade and Plantations, February 12, 1675, in *CSPC AWI* 9, *1675–1676,* 170–80.

61. Versterre to the States of Zeeland, May 8, 1675; ZA, 2.1, inv. no. 2035.2, no. 257. Apart from the hardships caused by the recent war, taxes had also gone up; as Nicolas Combe, tax officer in the colony, mentioned, this inclined more to leave the colony. Nicolas Combe to Pieter de Huybert, May 1, 1675, ZA, 2.1, inv. no. 2035.2, no. 256; Petition by the inhabitants of Suriname to the States against the high taxes, May 1675, ZA, 2.1, inv. no. 2035.2, no. 258.

62. Commission leader Edward Cranfield and one of the other members, Mark Brent, tried to make a quick profit during their stay in Suriname, but quickly fell to quarreling both among themselves and with those charged with keeping order in the colony. Luckily for them, the charges against them were dropped in the interest of diplomacy. ZA, 2.1, inv. no. 2035.2, nos. 271–78.

63. Versterre to the States of Zeeland, July 4, 1675, ZA, 2.1, inv. no. 2035.2, no. 260; Combe to the States of Zeeland, October 24, 1675, ZA, 2.1, inv. no. 2035.2, no. 269.

64. Versterre to the States of Zeeland, March 25, 1675, ZA, 2.1, inv. no. 2035.1, no. 249–50.

65. Overview of the garrison, March 25, 1675, ZA, 2.1, inv. no. 2035.1, no. 251.

66. Dominique Potteij to Hermaenus Potteij, September 11, 1672, HCA 30/223.

67. Lichtenbergh to the States of Zeeland, August 30, 1669, ZA, 2.1, inv. no. 2035.1, no. 178.

68. Pieter Versterre to the States of Zeeland, March 25, 1675, ZA, 2.1, inv. no. 2035.1, nos. 249–50; Pritchard, *In Search of Empire,* 288–90.

Notes to Pages 83–86

69. See, for instance, the letter of Abel Thisso to the States of Zeeland, January 9, 1669, ZA, 2.1, 2035.1, no. 109; Julius Lichtenbergh to the States of Zeeland, June 17, 1669, ZA, 2.1, 2035.1, nos. 161–63.

70. Lists of inhabitants, ZA, 2.1, inv. no. 2035.2, nos. 261–62; Pieter Versterre to the States of Zeeland, July 6, 1675, ZA, 2.1, inv. no. 2035.2, no. 266.

71. Hoofd-en akkergeld 1684, NAN, Sociëteit van Suriname (1.05.03), inv. no. 213.

72. Frijhoff, "Uncertain Brotherhood." On the position of other migrants in the Dutch Republic, see Kuijpers, *Migrantenstad.*

73. Letters by colonists Jean le Grand, Du Plessis du Bellay, Samuel Thierrij, and Nicolas Combe are found in HCA 30, ff. 227, 223; Combe's French correspondence to the States of Zeeland and Pieter de Huybert can also be found in ZA, 2.1, inv. no. 2035.

74. For instance, the letters of Johan d'Olijslager to Johan van de Poele, to raadsheer Hoogesteeger, to raadsheer De Ridder, and to the pensionary De Huybert, all written on December 14, 1671, HCA 30/227, f. 1.

75. "François Chaillou aengestelt tot predicant in Suriname," ZA, 2.1, inv. no. 667, f. 236v.

76. Samuel de Witt to his cousin [Abraham de Hartogh, 16 December 1671], Willem Blaeu to his brother, January 10, 1671, HCA 30, inv. nos. 227/2 and 227/1, respectively; Pieter Versterre to the States of Zeeland, May 6, 1673, ZA, 2.1, ff. 2035.1, no. 241.

77. List of departing people in 1675, CO 278/3, ff. 119–31.

78. Pieter Versterre to unknown recipient, 4–7-1675, ZA, 2.1, inv. no. 2035.2, no. 260.

79. For estimates on the number of immigrants, see Zijlstra, "Om te sien of ick een wijf kan krijge," 69; On the taxes and the day of prayer: petition of the colonists of Suriname, May 1675, ZA, 2.1, 2035.2, no. 258; Ordinance of August 5, 1676, NAN, 1.11.01.01, inv. no. 1101, f. 49v. This entire inventory number is a set of modern transcriptions of the seventeenth-century originals. The folio numbers are not always copied; we refer to the folio numbers whenever possible.

80. Ordinance of November 29, 1677, and minutes of the council of war on December 7, 1677, NAN, 1.11.01.01, inv. no. 1101, f. 67v-68, unnumbered folio.

81. Resolutions of December 11, 1677, NAN, 1.11.01.01, inv. no. 1101, f. 67v-68, unnumbered folios.

82. Ibid.

83. "Publicatie vanden vrede," September 30, 1678, ZA, 2.1, inv. no. 681, f. 28v.

84. Ordinance of November 19, 1678, NAN, 1.11.01.01, inv. no. 1101, f. 96v.

85. "ten tijde van alarme," Petition of colonists, 4–4-1678, NAN, 1.11.01.01, inv. no. 1011, request no. 8, f. 87v.

86. Zeeland's response to the planters' requests, August 9, 1678, ZA, 2.1, inv. no. 680, ff. 235v-239r.

87. Den Heijer, *De geschiedenis van de WIC,* 140, 187; Klooster and Oostindie, *Curaçao in the Age of Revolutions;* Kars, "Dodging Rebellion"; Dragtenstein, *'De ondraaglijke stoutheid der wegloopers.'*

Reassessing Jamayca Española

1. The exceptions to these general rules include Padrón, *Spanish Jamaica;* Wright, *Spanish Documents Concerning English Voyages to the Caribbean;* and Wright, *Documents Concerning English Voyages to the Spanish Main.*

2. Padrón, *Spanish Jamaica,* 44.

3. AGI legajos de Santo Domingo 178A and B, as well as AGI, *Santo Domingo,* 1: "Isla Española. Consultas y Decretos, 1568–1569," part 1, 1568–1612; documents #11 (July 23, 1594),

#12 (October 12, 1594), #200 (March 31, 1629); and AGI, Patronato, 265, R44: "Autos contra corsarios inglese: costa de jamaica," 1–5.

4. Korr, *Cromwell and the New Model Foreign Policy*, 1.

5. Venning, *Cromwellian Foreign Policy*. Hence, why did Cromwell have different policies in Ireland than in the West Indies, and why scholars should study the two as separate and distinct policies? A good part of Cromwell's success certainly stemmed from his aggressive naval policies. I do not include Cromwell's Irish designs under "foreign policy." Scholars agree that Cromwell took his anti-Catholic tendencies to an extreme in his domination of the Irish countryside.

6. Certainly market and merchant demands affected the Protectorate's decisions, just as those concerns had influenced previous piracy and privateering ventures. However, there was also an understanding that the Commonwealth needed to assert itself on an international stage and gain diplomatic recognition by acquiring its own colony. A fleet of "sixty ships . . . [with] Four-thousand soldiers" was "augmented at Barbados, with a still more unruly set, to Nine-thousand," Letters CCIV-CCVI regarding Jamaica. See Lomas, *Letters and Speeches of Oliver Cromwell*, 2:465.

7. Scholars estimate that as many as three hundred thousand Englishmen migrated to the Caribbean during the seventeenth century. Snyder, "Pirates, Exiles, and Empire." Discussions there further draw from works such as Armitage and Braddick, *British Atlantic World*, 37–42; and Games, *Migration and the Origins of the British Atlantic World*. See also Burnard, "European Migration to Jamaica." J. H. Elliott estimates the numbers at two hundred thousand, "Afterword," in Armitage and Braddick, *British Atlantic World*, 233–49.

8. James I, *Proclamation concerning Warlike ships at Sea*, Greenwich, June 23, 1603, Larkin and Hughes, *Stuart Royal Proclamations*, 1:30-31; "To Mariners, Cancelling Letters of Reprisal which they had from Elizabeth," SP 14/1, f. 111.

9. Larkin and Hughes, *Stuart Royal Proclamations*, 1:31.

10. "Proclamation for the search and apprehension of certain Pirates," November 12, 1604, HCA 1/5, ff. 4–11. Other executions carried out from this search are found in HCA 1/5, ff. 71–73.

11. SP 94/10, f. 147.

12. See, for example, *Proclamation for the due and speedy execution of the Statute against Rogues, Vagabonds, Idle, and dissolute persons*, Woodstock, September 17, 1603, in Larkin and Hughes, *Stuart Royal Proclamations*, 1:52–53.

13. *Proclamation for Revocation of Mariners from Forreine Services*, March 1, 1605, in Larkin and Hughes, *Stuart Royal Proclamations*, 1:108–11.

14. *Proclamation for better furnishing the Navy and Shipping of the Realme*, August 6, 1622, in Larkin and Hughes, *Stuart Royal Proclamations*, 1:230.

15. The neighboring island of Tortuga, among others, was a haven as well.

16. Decree of January 14, 1514, quoted in Padrón, *Spanish Jamaica*, 38.

17. Padrón, *Spanish Jamaica*, 43.

18. Ibid., 31.

19. AGI, Patronato, 265, R14, 1570.

20. AGI, Patronato, 265, R15, July 20, 1571.

21. AGI, Santo Domingo, 177, February 22, 1586.

22. Padrón, *Spanish Jamaica*, 71–73.

23. AGI, Santo Domingo, 177, February 22, 1586.

24. Archivo Historico Nacional Madrid, Board, 265, R15, Chapters of Don Gerau, July 1571.

25. AGI, sección Gobierno, Indiferente General, 743, no. 144, Juan de Ibarra, Consejo de India a Felipe II, October 27, 1595.

Notes to Pages 92–96

26. Stradling, *Armada of Flanders,* 276.

27. Archivo General de Simancas, Guerra Antigua legajo 405, no 142, De Soto to Philip II, September 23, 1594, Lisbon.

28. Goodman, *Spanish Naval Power,* 9.

29. Elliott and de la Peña, *Memoriales y cartas del Conde Duque de Olivares,* 2:1441–43.

30. *Viage y sucesso y sucesso de los carauelones, galeoncetes de la guarda de Cartagena de las Indias, y su costa.*

31. Powell and Timings, *Documents Relating to the Civil War,* 69–72.

32. Council of State Day's Proceedings, March 29, 1650, and Admiralty Commissioners to the Navy Commissioners, April 12, 1650, *CSPD, Interregnum, 1649–1650,* 59, 82.

33. Council of State, Day's Proceedings, October 4, 1651, *CSPD, Interregnum, 1651–1652,* 429–30.

34. For more on the New Model Navy and Cromwellian naval policy, supply, and support, see Snyder, "Pirates, Exiles, and Empire," ch. 4.

35. Padrón, *Spanish Jamaica,* 130.

36. AGI, Santo Domingo, 177, 1604.

37. AGI, Santo Domingo, 178B.

38. AGI, Indiferente General, Letter to Lerma, July 20, 1608, 473, I, 173.

39. AGI, Santo Domingo, Royal Cédula to Governor Don Francisco Terril, May 3, 1627, 870, 84.

40. See sources cited in Hoffman, *Spanish Crown and the Defense of the Caribbean,* 75.

41. For one instance of trade protection, see account in AGI, Patronato 267, no. 1, R. 34.

42. Henry Kamen even claims that the crown "had no vessels at all" for much of the century. See *Spain's Road to Empire,* 170.

43. Ibid., 305. Naples and Sicily were dependencies of the Crown of Aragon, though not all of the ships from these dependencies belonged to the provincial government and therefore to the Spanish Crown. Many of the ships remained in the hands of private merchants and the Crown could not necessarily lay claim to them. These numbers are in contrast to those cited by other scholars who claim that by 1547 Spain, under Charles I, had 150 galleys, and over 200 galleys to fight at the famed Battle of Lepanto (1571) under Philip II. Kamen, *Spain's Road to Empire,* 305. See also Goodman, *Spanish Naval Power,* 2.

44. Archivo General de Simancas, Sección Varios Galeras, legajo 8, Asiento, *que los señores . . . del consejo real de las indias tomaron con adriano de legaso* (Madrid, 1627).

45. Goodman, *Spanish Naval Power,* 260.

46. Spanish sailors constantly deserted upon arrival in the New World, seeing employment on a ship as the best, most profitable way to reach the New World. See Pérez-Mallaína, *Spain's Men of the Sea,* 25.

47. Kamen, *Spain's Road to Empire,* 170.

48. Goodman, *Tobacco in History,* 80.

49. Phillips, *Six Galleons for the King of Spain,* 26.

50. De Escalante de Mendoza, *Itinerario de navegación de los mares y tierras occidentales.* Ralph Davis wrote of English seamen that men became sailors "to see the world, to get a good rate of pay, to get a job of some sort at any price, to do what father did; these were the motives of those who went to sea; perhaps some went willy-nilly, drunk or unconscious, as the crimp made up the required crew as best he could." Davis, *Rise of English Shipping Industry,* 158.

51. Pérez-Mallaína, *Spain's Men of the Sea,* 33.

52. Padrón, *Spanish Jamaica,* 131. There were two Juan Bautista Antonellis, a father (1550–1616) and son (1585–1649), who worked as engineers for the Spanish government throughout the Caribbean and Central America.

Notes to Pages 96–100

53. Padrón, *Spanish Jamaica*, 132.
54. AGI, Real Cedula, Santo Domingo, 1126, 1631.
55. AGI, Santo Domingo, 178B, September 19, 1634.
56. AGI, Santo Domingo, 178B, September 25, 1634.
57. Padrón, *Spanish Jamaica*, 135.
58. AGI, Santo Domingo, 178B, written from Santo Domingo, December 8, 1638.
59. Padrón, *Spanish Jamaica*, 85.
60. Ibid., 84–85.
61. AGI, Santo Domingo, 178B.
62. AGI, Santo Domingo, 178B, 1638.
63. AGI, Santo Domingo, 178B, April 15, 1646.
64. AGI, Santo Domingo, 178A.
65. Jason McElligott claims that Roundhead scholars have been much more willing to take up the mantle of an Atlantic history of the Civil War than Royalist scholars, who have remained "doggedly Anglo-centric." McElligott, "Atlantic Royalism?," in McElligott and Smith, *Royalists and Royalism during the Interregnum*, 214.
66. McElligott, Smith, and Pestana are some of the first scholars to extensively discuss the significance of the Civil War as it pertains the Caribbean. See McElligott and Smith, *Royalists and Royalism during the Interregnum*, and Pestana, *English Atlantic in an Age of Revolution*.
67. "The Draft of an Act concerning the settling of the plantation of Virginia under the government of the Commonwealth, to be presented to the Council of State, for presentation to Parliament," SP 25/123, f. 173.
68. Davis, *Cavaliers and Roundheads of Barbados*, 6.
69. See also Geoffrey Smith, "Royalists in Exile."
70. Davis, *Cavaliers and Roundheads of Barbados*, 55, 80–86.
71. McElligott, "Atlantic Royalism?," 215.
72. SP 25/146/123; 138; CO 1/11, f. 14.
73. McElligott, "Atlantic Royalism?," 214.
74. R. A. Stradling claims that this was made "with indecent haste." Stradling, *Philip IV and the Government of Spain*, 297.
75. Giacomo Quirini, Venetian Ambassador in Spain, to the Doge and Senate, March 4, 1654, in Hinds, *Calendar of State Papers Venetian*, 29:187.
76. Quoted in Venning, *Cromwellian Foreign Policy*, 47.
77. Venning, *Cromwellian Foreign Policy*, 49. As occurred so often in the history of Jamaica, the Spanish crown largely ignored reports from the island about a possible English invasion in 1654. The Spanish ambassador in London, Don Alonso de Cárdena, warned Philip IV of English preparation for an expedition to the Indies, "specifically against Santo Domingo." Quoted in Padrón, *Spanish Jamaica*, 182–83.
78. See Powell, *Navy in the English Civil War*.
79. Lomas, *Letters and Speeches of Oliver Cromwell*, 2:465.
80. Ibid., 2:467.
81. Eagle, "Restoring Spanish Hispaniola," 385; Lane, *Blood and Silver*, 97–102.

Making Jamaica English

1. I am grateful to Linda Sturtz for commenting on earlier drafts of this essay.
2. On these categories see Knight, *The Caribbean*, 66–87, and Shoemaker, "A Typology of Colonialism."
3. Greene, "Reformulating Englishness."
4. On the Western Design, see Pestana, "English Character and the Fiasco of the Western Design"; Taylor, *The Western Design*; and Watts, *Une Histoire des Colonies Anglaises aux*

Antilles, 87–249. Considering the militarized society that resulted, see Webb, *The Governors-General,* 160–206.

5. On this choice, see Taylor, *Western Design,* ch. 12.

6. Satchell, *Hope Transformed,* 43.

7. On wealth generating, see Zahedieh, "Trade, Plunder and Economic Development," and Robertson, "Jamaican Architectures before Georgian."

8. Griffin, "Specter of Spain in John Smith's Colonial Writing," 122. On the transitions in Spanish policy between 1660 and 1670, see Padrón, *Spanish Jamaica,* 223–33, and Thornton, *West-India Policy under the Restoration,* 67–123.

9. For the English army's wandering in Hispaniola, see Taylor, *Western Design,* 8–30.

10. Padrón, *Spanish Jamaica,* 197–205, 207–10.

11. Wright, "Spanish Resistance to the English Occupation of Jamaica."

12. See Amanda Snyder's contribution to this volume. For the island's transfer to the Columbus family in 1536, see Padrón, *Spanish Jamaica,* 62–66, and Pawson and Buisseret, *Port Royal,* 8–15.

13. Robertson, *Gone is the Ancient Glory,* 38–39, 43–52.

14. For an overview of the campaign in Jamaica, see Taylor, *Western Design,* 98–110, 146–83, 184–93. On de Bolas' decision and its consequences, see Robertson, "'The Land of the Spanish Negroes.'" For an alternate view, Taylor and Buisseret, "Juan de Bolas and his Pelinco."

15. Report on Jamaica, June 20, 1657, Ms. 381, National Library of Jamaica, Kingston, and another copy, To his Highness the Lord Protector, n.d., Sloane Ms. 3662, ff. 122–23, BL.

16. Lord Broghill to John Thurloe, September 18, 1655, Birch, *Papers of John Thurloe,* 4:41.

17. Manning, "Reformation and Wickedness," 152n; Henry Cromwell to John Thurloe, November 14, 1655, Birch, *Papers of John Thurloe,* 4:198.

18. This proposal was not followed through. See de Jong, "The Irish in Jamaica during the Seventeenth Century," 15–20. On "shovelling out," see Rogers, "A Changing Presence," 18. For "the Dirge," see Seán ó Connaill's "Tuireamh na h-Éireann," quoted in Ó Ciardha, "Tories and Moss-troopers in Scotland and Ireland in the Interregnum," 145.

19. An articulate protest against such enforced service is described in Beckles, "English Parliamentary Debate on 'White Slavery' in Barbados."

20. From Nevis, Luke Stokes to Robert Sedgwick, March 12, 1656, Birch, *Papers of John Thurloe,* 4:603. For the casualty report, see Vice-Admiral William Goodson to Thurloe, January 9, 1657, Birch, *Papers of John Thurloe,* 5:771; for the posting of troops at Port Morant, see William Brayne to Thurloe, January 9, 1657, Birch, *Papers of John Thurloe,* 5:770.

21. Pawson and Buisseret, *Port Royal,* 16–22.

22. For the grants, see Penn to Council, 12 September, 1655, Birch, *Papers of John Thurloe,* 4:30; for their lapsing, see A Council of War held at St Jago de la Vega, June 7, 1655, Birch, *Papers of John Thurloe,* 3:523.

23. Francis Barrington to John Hawkins, March 15, 1656, Egerton Ms. 2648, f. 263, BL.

24. Francis Barrington to John Hawkins, October 8, 1656, Egerton Ms. 2648, f. 280, BL.

25. Francis Barrington to Sir John Barrington, July 1, 1657, Egerton Ms. 2648, f. 302, BL.

26. Whitson, *Constitutional Development of Jamaica,* 85–89, 93–97, 103–9.

27. Pestana, *English Atlantic,* 216.

28. Robertson, "Battle of Rio Nuevo."

29. Beeston, "A Journal Kept by Col. William Beeston from his first coming to Jamaica," [April 27, 1660], 272.

30. On these developments, see Thornton, *West-India Policy*, 39–60. For the brandy duty, see "The Distribution of the Royal Donative which King Charles II sent to the Officers and Soldiers in Jamaica," October 17, 1662, in *Interesting Tracts, Relating to the History of Jamaica*, 269–70, and the royal proclamation of December 14, 1660, in the same volume, 135–36.

31. For Barbados's ill-treated Quakers, see Dunn, *Sugar and Slaves*, 103–6; and Gragg, *The Quaker Community on Barbados*, 104–10, 113–15. On those who relocated to Jamaica, see Manning, "Reformation and Wickedness," 140–41.

32. For the development of this agricultural system, see Higman, "The Sugar Revolution." For its practices, see Zahedieh, *Capital and the Colonies*, 210–18; Menard, *Sweet Negotiations;* Watts, *The West Indies*, 176–231; Dunn, *Sugar and Slaves*, 59–67, 168–71, 188–223; and Batie, "Why Sugar?" On slavery, see Gaspar, "'Rigid and Inclement.'" On sugar's initial repercussions on the white members of island societies, see Barber, *Disputatious Caribbean*, 59–62, 78–81.

33. Robertson, "Re-inventing the English conquest of Jamaica in the late seventeenth century."

34. Rashford, "Arawak, Spanish and African Contributions"; Atkinson, "Exploitation and Transformation," 106–10.

35. On the oranges, lemons, limes, and pomegranates, see Hickeringill, *Jamaica Viewed*, 10. On adding figs and bananas, see Buisseret, *Jamaica in 1687*, 187–89, 208–10. For the transfer of coconuts from the Indian Ocean, see Harries, "The Cape Verde Region."

36. For the guava walk, see Survey for William Morris, December 21, 1664, Platt Book, St. Catherine, 2, f. 103, 1B/11/2/6, JA. For the plum walk, see Survey for Edward Nicholls, August 6, 1666, Platt Book, St. Catherine, 2, f. 130, JA. Discussing tamarind trees as an introduced species that offer a marker for earlier foreigners' passage, Connah, "Of the hut I builded," 10; for a roadside tamarind, see Survey for James Wellin, December 8, 1710, Platt Book, St. Catherine, 1, f. 115, 1B/11/2/5, JA. For earlier references to tamarinds, see Ms. Eng. 179, Dr. Smallwood's Memoranda, n.d. [c. 1670], f. 3, Boston Public Library; and Buisseret, *Jamaica in 1687*, 185.

37. Rampini, *Letters from Jamaica*, 46; Harvey and Brewin, *Jamaica in 1866*, 62.

38. Barham, *Hortus Americanus*, 5.

39. Colon de Portugal y Castro, *The Columbus Petition Document for the island of Jamaica 1672*, H2v. On the Sixteen Mile Walk, see Survey for [Thomas] Ballard, June, 28, 1665, Platt Book, St. Catherine, 3, f. 38, 1B/11/2/7, JA. On cocoa captured by the frigate *Pearl*, February 3, 1659, see Add. Ms. 12423, f. 69r, BL. I consulted a modern transcript of this text at the West Indies Collection, Main Library, University of the West Indies, Mona; used to pay various military units' wages, February 10, 1659 and May 25, 1659, Ms. 12423, f. 71r. On paying council members' attendance expenses, see September 2, 1659, Ms. 12423, f. 78r. On certifying that 6,983 pounds of cocoa nuts were grown in Jamaica, July 30, 1660, Ms. 12423, f. 92v.

40. Hickeringill, *Jamaica Viewed*, 26.

41. Stubbs, *Indian Nectar.*

42. On English practices, see Cowan, *Social Life of Coffee;* On Port Royal, see Buisseret, *Jamaica in 1687*, 239.

43. Higman and Hudson, *Jamaican Place Names*, 155–95. On "Hutt Hill," see Survey for Lieutenant Henry Vazey, February 4, 1664, St. Catherine Platts, 2, 1B/11/2/6, f. 75, JA. For cocoa walks known as "the Labyrinth," see Survey for Captain Edward Walred and Captain Richard Beckford, June 10, 1663, St. Catherine Platts, 2, f. 106, JA.

44. Articles of Agreement between Sir Thomas Modyford and Francis Palmer, April 1, 1675, Deeds o.s. 1, ff. 175–75v, Island Records Office, Spanish Town, Jamaica. Modyford was acting as executor for his son, Sir James Modyford.

45. For the site, see Taylor, *Western Design,* 54. Early land grants there include one to Joseph Peters et al., March 26, 1660, Add. Ms. 12423, f. 84v, BL, and a further post-Restoration sequence that includes the following: survey for Edward Keen, et al. partners, January 12, 1663, St. Catherine Platts, 1, f. 20, 1B/11/2/5, JA; survey for William Herbert, 1666, St. Catherine Platts, f. 47; survey for John Vine, May 18, 1666, St. Catherine Platts, 2, f. 74, 1B/11/2/6, JA; two surveys for Francis Barnes, May 18, 1666, St. Catherine Platts, 3, ff. 34, 67, 1B/11/2/7, JA; survey for John Wint, June 7, 1666, St. Catherine Platts, 2, f. 79, 1B/11/2/6, JA; survey for George Dunkin and Christopher Bulmer, November 7, 1666, St. Catherine Platts, 3, f. 109, 1B/11/2/7, JA; survey for John Wallers, August 31, 1671, St. Catherine Platts, 2, f. 80, 1B/11/2/6, JA; grant to Lieutenant John Wint (a survey for his orphaned daughters), June 3, 1673, St. Catherine Platts, 2, f. 80; survey for Henry Phenwick, June 21, 1673, St. Catherine Platts, 1, f. 145, 1B/11/2/5, JA; survey for Henry Fenwicks, December 5, 1676, St. Catherine Platts, 3, f. 132, 1B/11/2/7, JA; and patent for Captain Peter Quadman, a re-grant of Francis Barnes's escheated patent, September 8, 1674, St. Catherine Platts, 1, f. 23 1B/11/1/5, JA.

46. Barham, *Hortus Americanus,* 56.

47. William Whaley to William Helyar, January 20, 1672, quoted in Bennett, "William Whaley," 114.

48. For example, a thousand acres in St. David's Parish, with "between thirty & forty Acres of Canes in the ground and six acres of provisions," lease between Thomas Smith and Luke Phillips, and Hender Molesworth et al., executors of Richard Richardson, October 30, 1672, Deeds o.s. 5, ff. 105v–108, Island Records Office, Spanish Town, Jamaica. At Cary Helyar's Bybrook plantation the same year, twenty-four acres were in sugar cane, twenty in pasture, and sixteen in provision crops. Bennett, "William Whaley," 114.

49. Limes, Buisseret, *Jamaica in 1687,* 189. For "doodledoes," see Barham, *Hortus Americanus,* 16.

50. Higman, *Jamaica Surveyed.*

51. Survey for Richard Holmes, February 1, 1663, St. Catherine Platts, 1, f. 31, 1B/11/2/5, JA; Buisseret, "A Frenchman looks at Jamaica in 1706," 8. On English efforts to comprehend this landscape, see Robertson, "Late Seventeenth-Century Spanish Town."

52. Buisseret, "Fresh Light on Spanish Jamaica."

53. Lease from Thomas Lynch to Thomas Bourne and John Newman, April 10, 1664, Deeds, o.s. 1, ff. 5–6v, Island Records Office, Spanish Town, Jamaica.

54. This occurred in multiple parishes. See, for example, in St. Catherine's, patent to Robert Edy, Patents 4, 1670–1673, ff. 75v-76, March 13, 1672, 1B/11/1/4, JA, and a late Victorian map, "Angels: Plan of area known as Angells and Red Hills; giving names of original Owners," St.C 256, National Library of Jamaica, Kingston; in St. Elizabeth's, patent to Christopher Pindar, July 20, 1674, Patents 5, 1673–1674, ff. 129v-30, 1B/11/1/5, JA; in St. Andrew's, patent to Harman Atkins, July 3, 1678, Patents 7, 1677–79, ff. 77v-78, 1B/11/1/7, JA; and in Clarendon, patent to John Bodle and Dorothy Cary, July 6, 1688, Patents 11, 1686–1689, ff. 185-85v, 1B/11/1/11, JA.

55. Claypole, "Land Settlement and Agricultural Development," 80–82.

56. "An Act for keeping open old Paths to Publick Watering Places," in *Laws of Jamaica, 1683,* 123–24.

57. Earliest Chancery Records, 1676–1678 and 1684, Deposition of Samuel Trussell of Passage Fort, Butcher, 1A/3/1, JA. For Port Royal as a major market for Jamaican produce, see Zahedieh, "'The wickedest city in the world.'"

58. Council Minutes, 1661–1678, f. 2, June 18, 1661, 1B/5/3/1, JA; also, the proclamation, Council Minutes, 1661–1678, ff. 17–19, June 26, 1661, JA. These values were reaffirmed fifteen months later by the first royal governor, Lord Windsor. See Council Minutes, 1661–1678, ff. 61–63, October 10, 1662, JA.

Notes to Pages 112–113

59. Council Minutes, 1661–1678, f. 25, July 30, 1661, 1B/5/3/1, JA.

60. Council Minutes, 1661–1678, ff. 88–99, November 6, 1663, Deputy Governor and Council, 1B/5/3/1, JA. For tobacco's decline across all the English islands except Antigua, see Zahedieh, *The Capital and the Colonies*, 197–201. For the French case, see Lafleur, "Le tabac en Guadeloupe."

61. For cotton growing, see Buisseret, *Jamaica in 1687*, 216. For the rebellion at Madam Grey's, see ibid.

62. Buisseret, *Jamaica in 1687*, 258–60; Barham, *Hortus Americanus*, 11. For indigo plants in Yallas, see Buisseret, *Historic Jamaica from the Air*, 13.

63. Add. Ms. 12432, f. 75r., September 19, 1659, BL. In "Early English Jamaica without Pirates," Carla Pestana makes a persuasive case that in his much-cited invitation to Hispaniola's buccaneers, Governor D'Oyley was seeking such hunters rather than naval auxiliaries.

64. Patent to Thomas More, December 13, 1686, Patents 11, ff. 24v-25, 1B/11/1/11, JA.

65. Survey for Sir James Modyford, August 8, 1671, St. Mary Platt Book, f. 73, 1B/11/2/26, JA.

66. Grant to David Spence, September 29, 1676, Patents 5, ff. 502–3, 1B/11/1/5, JA; grant to Hirome Westbury, September 29, 1676, Patents 7, ff. 104v-105, 1B/11/1/7, JA; grant to William Watts, November 12, 1674, Patents 5, ff. 164v-65, 1B/11/1/5, JA.

67. Survey for Sir Thomas Modyford, January 10, 1671, St. Mary Platts, f. 67, 1B/11/2/26, JA.

68. "An Act For preventing Damages in Plantations, Preserving of Cattle, and Regulating Hunting" in *Laws of Jamaica* (1683), 71–74. This repassage of the law removed the veterans' exception that had been included in earlier versions.

69. Buisseret, *Jamaica in 1687*, 295, discussed in Crow Via, "A Comparison of the Colonial Laws of Jamaica under Governor Thomas Lynch," 243–44. The source and status of the laws Taylor transcribed remains uncertain. See Crow Via, "New Light from the Taylor Manuscript." That these issues were even considered to merit legislation in 1680s Jamaica is striking.

70. "An Act For Clearing of *Rio Cobre* above and below *Caymana's*," in *Laws of Jamaica* (1683), 105–14.

71. Buisseret, *Jamaica in 1687*, 178.

72. Peter Heywood to Charles Long, October 27, 1708–January 31, 1709, West Indies Collection, Main Library, University of the West Indies, Mona.

73. Henry Barham, "Account of Jamaica," Sloane Ms. 3918, ff. 143, 230, BL.

74. Robertson, "Land of the Spanish Negroes"; Buisseret and Taylor, "Juan de Bolas and His Pelinco."

75. "A Gate formerly belonging to the Spanish Negroes," survey for Captain John Ellis, January 8, 1687, St. Catherine Platts, 2, f. 122, 1B/11/2/7, JA.

76. Sloane, *Voyage to the Islands*, 1:xix.

77. Ibid., 1:B2. On these garden plots, see Brierley, "Kitchen Gardens in the Caribbean," and Parry, "Plantation and Provision Ground." While valuing his research, Jamaican settlers would critique Sloane's *Voyage* for some mistakes resulting from unfamiliarity during a fairly short visit and also complained about his use of Latin names rather than familiar English ones. Their criticisms were provoked because they used his book. Robertson, "Knowledgeable Readers."

78. Barham, *Hortus Americanus*, 38, 86, 99, 113, 122, 163.

79. Council Minutes, 3, ff. 313–14, September 24, 1686, May 1682–June 1687, 1B/5/3/3A, JA. See also Campbell, *Maroons of Jamaica;* and Patterson, "Slavery and Slave Revolts."

80. Order, May 2, 1670, Council Minutes, ff. 171–74 at 171, 1B/5/3/1, JA.

81. Buisseret, "The French Come to Wood and Water in 1679."

82. Essays on the 1692 earthquake are legion. See, for example, Manning, "Reformation and the Wickedness of Port Royal"; Mulcahy, "The Port Royal Earthquake and the World of Wonders in Seventeenth-Century Jamaica"; and Pawson and Buisseret, *Port Royal*, 165–72.

83. Buisseret, "The French Invasion of Jamaica"; Beeston, "A narrative by Sir William Beeston of the Descent on Jamaica by the French." On possible Spanish cooperation for English attacks on the French at St. Domingue, see William Blathwayte to William Beeston, January 5, 1692/3, Ms. 45.2, Blathwayte Ms. XXI folder 2, Colonial Williamsburg Foundation, John D. Rockefeller Jr. Library, Special Collections (CWF). On an English assault from Jamaica, see Peter Beckford to William Blathwayte, September 20, 1694, Ms. 45.2, Blathwayte Ms. XXII, folder 5, CWF.

84. Minter, *Episcopacy without Episcopate.*

85. On the poor exchange on English imports to Jamaica, see Barber, *Disputatious Caribbean*, 62–68. On the colonists' "worldly vanity," see Manning "Reformation and Wickedness," 135. See also Burnard, "'The Countrie Continues Sicklie'"; McNeill, *Mosquito Empires*, 142–49; and Burnard, "Not a Place for Whites?"

86. On Bannister and the English planters who had remained in Surinam after the Dutch conquest in 1667, see the essay by Suze Zijlstra and Tom Weterings in this volume. On Bannister's commission as general, see November 9, 1670, 1B/11/1/4, Patents 4, f. 76, JA. On families already established and "Surinam Quarters," see Dunn, *Sugar and Slaves*, 38, 157, 176. Bannister's land grants included 416 acres in St. Catherine, October 31, 1672, 1B/11/1/4, ff. 110–110v, JA; 11¼ acres in St. Catherine, October 13, 1672, 1B/11/1/4, f. 110v, JA; 2,540 acres in St. Elizabeth at "Bannister Bay," January 14, 1673, 1B/11/1/4, ff. 126r-27, JA; and a house at Old Harbour (grant entered), May 11 1674, 1B/11/1/5, f. 53, JA. Mrs. Dorothy Bannister's grants included five hundred acres at Orange Bay, St. Elizabeth, February 22, 1675, 1B/11/1/6, ff. 45–46, JA; one thousand acres at Orange Bay, February 22, 1675, 1B/11/1/6, ff. 46–47, JA; another one thousand acres there, October 2 1674, 1B/11/1/6, f. 46, JA; and eleven hundred acres at Paros in Clarendon Parish, 22 February 1675, 1B/11/1/6, ff. 47–48, JA. On James Bannister Jr. See William Beeston to William Blathwayt, August 26, 1694, Ms. 45.2, Blathwayte Ms. XXI, folder 3, Colonial Williamsburg Foundation, John D. Rockefeller Jr. Library, Special Collections, Williamsburg, Va.

87. Robertson, "'Stories' and 'Histories.'"

The Danish West Indies, 1660s–1750s

1. General histories in English of the Danish West Indies can be found in Westergaard, *Danish West Indies under Company Rule;* Dookhan, *History of the Virgin Islands;* Gøbel, *Guide to Sources for the History of the Danish West Indies;* and Highfield and Tyson, *Slavery in the Danish West Indies.* In addition, there exists a comprehensive literature in Danish; the standard works are Brøndsted, *Vore gamle Tropekolonier,* vols. 1 and 2; Olsen, *Vest indierl.*

2. In this text "Denmark" includes all the Danish king's realms—that is, Denmark, Norway, and Schleswig-Holstein, as well as colonies in Asia, Africa, the Caribbean, and the North Atlantic.

3. Sieveking, "Die Glückstädter Guineafahrt im 17. Jahrhundert"; Kellenbenz, "La place de l'Elbe inférieure dans le commerce triangulaire au milieu du XVIIIe siècle."

4. Gøbel, *Vestindisk-guineisk Kompagni 1671–1754.*

5. Bookkeeper's return book, 1673–1677, West India and Guinea Company box 386, Danish National Archives, Copenhagen (all translations by the author).

6. Knight, *1688 Census of the Danish West Indies.*

7. Highfield, *Sainte Croix, 1650–1733.*

8. Abrahams, "Nogle Bidrag til den dansk-vestindiske Handels Historie i de første Aar."

9. Gøbel, "Danish Shipping along the Triangular Route, 1671–1802."

10. Gøbel, "Danish Trade to the West Indies and Guinea."

11. Olsen, "Sørøvere i Vestindien."

12. Justesen, *Danish Sources for the History of Ghana.*

13. Schmitt, "Brandenburg Overseas Trading Companies"; Westergaard, *Danish West Indies under Company Rule,* 71–94.

14. Report from the Board of Police and Trade to King Frederick IV, 1716, in Westergaard, *Danish West Indies under Company Rule,* 306–14.

15. Sebro, "1733 Slave Revolt"; Highfield and Caron, *French Intervention in the St. John Slave Revolt;* Pannet, *Report on the Execrable Conspiracy.*

16. Highfield, *Sainte Croix, 1650–1733;* Caron, *Sainte Croix and Saint Thomas.*

17. Hayes, *Christiansted at 275.*

18. A contemporary description can be found in Highfield, *J. L. Carstens' St. Thomas.*

19. Gøbel, "Danish Shipping along the Triangular Route"; Gøbel, *Danish Slave Trade and Its Abolition.*

20. Computed by means of Eltis, *Trans-Atlantic Slave Trade Database* (accessed January 20, 2015).

21. Gøbel, "Danish Shipping along the Triangular Route."

22. Hernæs, *Slaves, Danes, and African Coast Society,* 251–55. I have calculated mortality as loss of life in transit, no matter how long the Middle Passage took.

23. The charters of 1671 and 1697 can be found in Westergaard, *Danish West Indies under Company Rule,* 294–302. The charter of 1734 (and all bylaws) can be found in Feldbæk, *Danske handelskompagnier 1616–1843,* 364–438.

24. A list of governors can be found in Westergaard, *Danish West Indies under Company Rule,* 285–87.

25. Bro-Jørgensen, *Dansk Vestindien indtil 1755,* 81–82, 130, 199–215.

26. Hall, *Slave Society in the Danish West Indies,* 56–62; Olsen, "Slavery and the Law in the Danish West Indies."

27. West India and Guinea Company box 515, September 5, 1733, Danish National Archives, Copenhagen. An English translation can be found online at *Eurescl: Slave Trade, Slavery Abolitions, and Their Legacies in European Histories and Identities,* http://www.eurescl .eu/images/files_wp3/danishregulations/17330905.pdf (accessed January 27, 2015).

28. Hall, *Slave Society in the Danish West Indies,* 139–56.

29. *Eurescl: Slave Trade, Slavery Abolitions, and Their Legacies in European Histories and Identities,* http://www.eurescl.eu/images/files_wp3/danishregulations/17330905.pdf (accessed January 27, 2015).

30. Sebro, "The 1733 Slave Revolt on the Island of St. John"; Sebro, "Freedom, Autonomy, and Independence."

31. Highfield, "Domingo 'Mingo' Gesoe."

32. Gøbel, *Det danske slavehandelsforbud 1792.*

33. Smith, *Inquiry into the Nature and Causes of the Wealth of Nations,* 2:570, 575. Smith does not mention St. John.

34. Andersen, "Denmark-Norway, Africa, and the Caribbean."

35. The full West India and Guinea Company record group, together with other records concerning the Danish West Indies, are available online at https://www.virgin-islands-history.org.

Creating a Caribbean Colony in the Long Seventeenth Century

1. Demorizi, *Relaciones históricas de Santo Domingo,* 2:109–445; Moreau, "De la flibuste nord-européenne à la flibuste antillaise," 121. For Choiseul-Beaupré's charge from the Minister of Marine, see Choiseul-Beaupré to Pontchartrain, June 1710, ANOM, f.c., C9^A, reg. 9, ff. 58–59.

2. Ordonnance qui fixe la ville de Léogane au quartier de la pointe, Léogane, May 25, 1710, ANOM, f.c., C9^A, reg. 9, ff. 31–32; Projet du Petit-Goave, June 1, 1710, ANOM, f.c., C9^A, reg. 9, ff. 34–50.

3. Moreau de Saint-Mery, *Loix et constitutions des colonies françoises de l'Amérique sous le Vent*, 6:71–72.

4. *Règlement concernant l'entretien des routes*, Léogane, October 24, 1709, ANOM, f.c., C9^A, reg. 8, ff. 413–19; Ordonnance qui fixe le bourg du Cap dans le lieu ou il se trouve, Léogane, March 12, 1710, ANOM, f.c., C9^A, reg. 9, ff. 24–25; Ordonnance qui fixe la ville de Léogane au quartier de la pointe, Léogane, May 25, 1710, ANOM, f.c., C9^A, reg. 9, ff. 31–32. Prior to the War of Austrian Succession (1740–48), all major ports and villages of the colony were connected via a network of dirt roads.

5. Pagden, "Plus Ultra."

6. Choiseul-Beaupré to Minister, August 29, 1708, ANOM, f.c., C9^A, reg. 8, ff. 181–82.

7. "Notre intentions [. . .] est d'établir dans ce quartier de Petit-Goave, où est le gros des troupes un hopital pour leur soulagement, et pour celuy des flibustiers qui sy sont habitués de tous temps pour y faire leurs armements, et leur retraitte," Ordonnance de Mr de Choiseul pour l'establissement d'un hôpital au Petit-Goave, June 8, 1710, ANOM, f.c., C9^A, reg. 9, ff. 51–53.

8. *Mémoire de Mr. de Paty,* June 30, 1711, ANOM, f.c., C9^A, reg. 9, ff. 117–19.

9. Ordonnance de Mr de Choiseul pour l'establissement d'un hopital au Petit-Goave, June 8, 1710, ANOM, f.c., C9^A, reg. 9, ff. 51–53.

10. Lane, *Pillaging the Empire,* 164–80. For further information on this subject, see James Robertson's essay in this volume.

11. Ordonnance d'amnistie en faveur des forbans de Saint-Domingue, April 12, 1702, ANOM, f.c., série B, reg. 24, f. 396.

12. Extract of a letter from Choiseul-Beaupré to Pontchartrain, Petit-Goave, January 1, 1710, ANOM, f.c., C9^A, reg. 9, f. 22; Choiseul-Beaupré to Pontchartrain, June 1710, ANOM, f.c., C9^A, reg. 9, ff. 58–59; Ordonnance du Roi, portant Amnistie en faveur des Flibustiers et Déserteurs, June 1, 1707, cited in Moreau de Saint-Mery, *Loix et constitutions des colonies françoises de l'Amérique sous le Vent,* 6:98–99.

13. De Paty and Mithon to Minister, July 3, 1711, ANOM, f.c., C9^A, reg. 9, ff. 220–41.

14. Choiseul-Beaupré to Minister, July 14, 1707, ANOM, f.c., C9^A, reg. 8, ff. 119–21; Pritchard, *In Search of Empire,* 398.

15. Blénac and Mithon to Minister, August 10, 1713, ANOM, f.c., C9^A, reg. 10, ff. 8–31; Ordonnance concernant les récompenses à donner aux Garçons Flibustiers et Boucaniers en cas d'estropiement dans la défense de la colonie, June 30, 1714, cited in de Saint-Mery, *Loix et constitutions des colonies françoises de l'Amérique sous le Vent,* 6:423; Blénac and Mithon to Minister, August 1st, 1714, ANOM, f.c., C9^A, reg. 10, ff. 291–317.

16. Blénac and Mithon to Minister, August 10, 1713, ANOM, f.c., C9^A, reg. 10, ff. 8–31; Pollet, "Saint-Domingue et l'autonomie," 39.

17. Blénac and Mithon to Minister, Léogane, March 1, 1715, ANOM, f.c., C9^A, reg. 10, ff. 34–46.

18. Frostin, *Histoire de l'autonomisme colon de la partie française de Saint-Domingue aux XVIIème et XVIIIème siècles,* 182–93.

19. Lane, *Pillaging the Empire,* 171.

20. Captain Cherpin to Du Casse, Martinique, July 1, 1691, ANOM, f.c., série C9^A, reg. 2, ff. 355–58.

21. Johnson, *A general history of the pyrates,* 233–34.

22. De Paty to Minister, Petit-Goave, June 30, 1711, ANOM, f.c., C9^A, reg. 9, ff. 213–20.

23. Furetière, *Dictionnaire universel,* vol. 2.

24. Résumé de l'enquête faite par Pierre Juers et René Bédu, commissaires, ANOM, f.c., C9ᴬ, reg. 1, ff. 259–83.

25. De Lussan, *Journal du voyage fait à la mer de Sud;* Johnson, *A general history of the pyrates,* 232–34.

26. Linebaugh and Rediker, *Many-Headed Hydra,* 162–63.

27. Jacques Helin to Galiffet, 1699, ANOM, f.c., C9ᴬ, reg. 4, f. 343.

28. Extrait des minutes du greffe du Siége Royal du Cap François, Coste St. Domingue, January 18, 1708, ANOM, f.c., C9ᴬ, reg. 8, ff. 208–11; Coppie d'un recue fait par le s.r La Grave à Mr. Grave á M. de Charritte, Le Cap, November 14, 1707, ANOM, f.c., C9ᴬ, reg. 8, f. 199.

29. Choiseul-Beaupré to Pontchartrain, June 1710, ANOM, f.c., C9ᴬ, reg. 9, ff. 54–63.

30. De Paty to Minister, Petit-Goave, Juin 30, 1711, ANOM, f.c., C9ᴬ, reg. 9, ff. 213–18).

31. Exquemelin, *Histoire des Avanturiers qui se sont signalez dans les Indes,* 1:153–55; Jean Charpin to Du Casse, Martinique, July 1, 1691, ANOM, f.c., série C9ᴬ, reg. 2, ff. 355–58.

32. Goubert, *L'ancien régime,* 58–61.

33. Choiseul-Beaupré and Mithon to Minister, Léogane, September 9, 1709, ANOM, f.c., C9ᴬ, reg. 8, ff. 402–3.

34. Arquian and Mithon to Minister, Saint-Louis, January 1, 1713, ANOM, f.c., C9ᴬ, reg. 10, ff. 135–36.

35. Boucher, "The 'Frontier Era' of the French Caribbean," 209.

36. Gruzinski, *La colonisation de l'imaginaire;* Gruzinski, "Les mondes mêlés de la Monarchie Catholique et autres connected histories"; Gruzinski, *Les Quatre parties du monde;* Boucher, *Cannibal Encounters;* Lestringant, *Le Huguenot et le sauvage;* Pagden, *European Encounters with the New World;* Pagden, "Plus Ultra"; Pagden, *Peoples and Empires.* For more information regarding free blacks, slaves, and maroon cultures in Saint-Domingue, see Garrigus, "Blue and Brown," and Garrigus, *Before Haiti.*

37. Greene, *Peripheries and Center,* 47.

38. Vauban's project was elaborated during a heavy reduction of the financial support to the Marine Royale (1694). These years prior to the crisis of the *Flotte* marked a definitive mutation toward privateering, Symcox, *Crisis of the French Sea Power;* Bromley, "Les prêt de vaisseaux de la marine française aux corsaires," 85; Virol, *Vauban,* 116–17. At the time, French sailors and officers were divided into classes, grouped according to the qualifications of the sailors: "captains and masters," "officers," "sailors," and "without class." Villiers, "Du système des classes à l'inscription maritime, le recrutement des marins français de Louis XIV à 1952"; Villiers, *Marine royale, corsaires et trafic dans l'Atlantique de Louis XIV à Louis XVI,* 24–26.

39. Pollet, "Saint-Domingue et l'autonomie," 57.

40. Similarly, the coeval French term for plantation was *habitation.*

The Martinican Model

1. Du Tertre, *Histoire générale des Antilles habitées par les François,* frontispiece.

2. As noted for the Anglophone Caribbean by L. H. Roper and for the Danish Caribbean by Erik Gøbel.

3. For pirates, see Giovanni Venegoni's contribution to this volume; for conflict with the Dutch, see those of Jessica Vance Roitman and of Suze Zijlstra and Tom Weterings. For the transition to plantation agriculture, compare this example with Amanda Snyder and James Robertson's accounts of Jamaica above.

4. For Saint-Domingue's development, see Venegoni's contribution in this volume. Another literature has charted the other, less violent, but no less contested road taken by Martinique and Guadeloupe. See Chauleau, *Dans les îles du vent la Martinique;* Abénon, *La Guadeloupe de 1671 à 1759;* and Pérotin-Dumon, *Être patriote sous les tropiques.*

5.   Garrigus, *Before Haiti;* Ghachem, *Old Regime and the Haitian Revolution.* For the revolutionary era, see, for example, Dubois, *Colony of Citizens;* and Geggus and Fiering, *World of the Haitian Revolution.*

6.   Contributions to this volume that similarly emphasize circum-Caribbean developments include Murphy, Barber, Snyder, Gøbel, and Roper. The literature on peripheries versus centers in the early modern Atlantic is vast. For an overview of some of the key issues at stake, see Daniels and Kennedy, *Negotiated Empires.*

7.   Dunn, *Tale of Two Plantations.* Earlier comparative studies of empire have tended to focus similarly on discrete sites of colonial involvement. See, for example, McNeill, *Atlantic Empires of France and Spain.*

8.   Andrews's work is, in fact, an empirically grounded rebuttal to many of the arguments presented in Foucault, *Discipline and Punish.* Aside from these examples, several of the most influential explorations of early modern French legal and political culture rely upon cases centered in Paris—for example, Maza, *Private Lives and Public Affairs,* and Hanley, "'Jurisprudence of the *Arrets.*'"

9.   Andrews, *Law, Magistracy, and Crime in Old Regime Paris.*

10.   Liu, "Legal Profession as a Social Process," 671.

11.   For example, Shannon Lee Dawdy's work on Louisiana's *conseil* and her identification of their "rogue colonialism" arguably reveals the contours of both "boundary work over professional jurisdictions" and the "exchange between professions and the state," themes that are also relevant to Malick Ghachem's work on creole legal experts in Saint-Domingue. Dawdy, *Building the Devil's Empire;* Ghachem, "Montesquieu in the Caribbean."

12.   For the former, see Dessens, *From Saint-Domingue to New Orleans;* and Dawdy, *Building the Devil's Empire.* For the latter, see Hodson, *Acadian Diaspora;* and Spieler, *Empire and Underworld.*

13.   Bouton, *Relation de l'establissement des François depuis l'an 1635 en l'isle de la Martinique.*

14.   Two examples are Petit de Viévigne, *Code de La Martinique;* and Dessalles, *Les Annales du Conseil Souverain de la Martinique.*

15.   Specifically, Chanvalon complained that Martinique was governed by the Paris Coûtume rather than by Normandy's customary law, but he recognized this as an outcome of royal rule. Thibault de Chanvalon, *Voyage à la Martinique,* 3.

16.   ANOM COL E 210, David Gradis, et al.

17.   Hayot, *Les Officiers du Conseil Souverain de la Martinique,* 240.

18.   ANOM FM F/3/247, *Code de la Martinique—Receuil des documents principalement législatifs 1629–1784,* 430–31.

19.   ANOM COL E 135, Guillaume Dorange.

20.   ANOM COL E 241, de La Calle. De La Calle is best known for his first-hand account of the 1674 Dutch attack on Martinique, *Relation du S. de la Calle: sur ce qui s'est passé a l'attaque du Fort Royal de la Martinique par la flote de Ruiter.*

21.   ANOM COL E 83, Michel de Clermont.

22.   ANOM COL E 211, Grandval de La Vigne, letters dated March 9, 1774, and August 16, 1775.

23.   The origins of Saint-Christophe's *conseil* remain murky, despite this reference. ANOM COL E 95, de Courpon, and ANOM COL A 24 f. 29, August 3, 1682, "Extrait de la lettre du marquis de Seignelay à Blénac, où il est reproché à Courpon, conseiller du conseil de Saint-Christophe, d'avoir prescrit des ordonnances de son propre chef, et où il est spécifié que toute l'autorité pour l'exécution des arrêts du roi émane des conseils seulement" (no. 26).

24.   ANOM COL E 95, Courpon.

25.   ANOM COL E 95, Courpon de La Vernade, capitaine de milices à la Martinique, et Courpon de La Vernade, enseigne d'Infanterie à Saint-Domingue.

26. For more on militia members in court, as criminal case participants and members of the wider legal culture, see Wood, "Archipelago of Justice."

27. This latter evidence appears in a letter from Courpon de La Vernade *père* at Martinique, April 10, 1751. ANOM COL E 95, Courpon de La Vernade, capitaine de milices à la Martinique, et Courpon de La Vernade, enseigne d'Infanterie à Saint-Domingue.

28. James Pritchard reports that the best population statistics indicate that Saint-Domingue had 13,642 people in 1700 and 43,523 people by 1715. For the same years, Martinique (including Grenada) had 22,573 and 39,758 residents respectively. Pritchard, *In Search of Empire,* 424.

29. Thibault de Chanvalon, *Voyage à la Martinique,* 4. Chanvalon quotes Locke on Pennsylvania as a good example of writing about colonial law.

30. Petit de Viévigne, *Code de la Martinique,* cover page. The quotation is, "In Societate Civili, aut Lex, aut vis Valet" ("In civil society, either law or force prevails"). I thank Tara Leithart for the translation.

31. See especially Malick Ghachem's section on Moreau de Saint-Méry, who was perhaps the most successful at playing this game, becoming a client of the minister of the marine, the Marquis de Castries. However, like Faure de Lussac, Moreau de Saint-Méry ended up in Saint-Domingue as a result of financial problems. Ghachem, "Montesquieu in the Caribbean," 202–6.

32. For his compilation of French laws and later membership in the Constituent Assembly during the French Revolution, see Moreau de Saint-Méry, *Loix et constitutions des colonies françoises de l'Amérique sous le vent.*

33. In 1713. John Garrigus, "'Le Patriotisme americain,'" 20.

34. Both Ghachem and Garrigus state that Saint-Domingue had only two Superior Councils (Cap-Français and Port-au-Prince), as does one of the letters in Faure de Lussac's personnel file. However, my survey of personnel records lists at least five different named councils (Léogane, Petit-Goave, and Saint-Domingue in addition to the above), which probably indicate changes in jurisdiction over time. I have yet to find an easily accessible guide to Saint-Domingue councils. Ghachem, "Montesquieu in the Caribbean," 203. Garrigus states that Petit worked for Léogane's Superior Council in the 1750s, as do my sources, implying that the council moved to Port-au-Prince sometime in the middle of the eighteenth century. Garrigus, *Before Haiti,* 42; Garrigus, "Le Patriotisme americain"; ANOM COL E 177, letter dated August 9, 1776.

35. Petit, *Droit public,* 35. The full quotation is "Le choix des matières et les observations sur les raisons de décider, et sur l'usage don't peuvent actuellement être ces décisions, prouvent autant d'intelligence en cet officier, que de zele pour le bien de la colonie" ("The selection of subjects and the observations on the motives for deciding [them], and on the usage of which can actually be these decisions, prove as much the intelligence of this officer, as [his] zeal for the good of the colony").

36. Petit de Viévigne, *Code de la Martinique.* Another example is Pierre Dessalles, who collected and published the records of Martinique's *conseil supérieur.* He revised and finished the project started by Assier, Dessalles, *Les Annales du Conseil Souverain de la Martinique,* 1:1, ix.

37. Petit de Viévigne, *Code de la Martinique,* i.

38. Hayot, *Les Officiers du Conseil,* 69. The brevet was written on April 20, 1774, according to Faure de Lussac's personnel file (ANOM COL E 177). The only other member of Martinique's Superior Council who moved to a different island was a Le Blond, nominated in 1686, who moved to Guadeloupe in 1688 and became a member of its council that year. By the 1770s his descendant Charles Gabriel Le Blond was running Guadeloupe's council as its doyen. ANOM COL E 266.

39. Hayot does not list Faure de Lussac's children, so I have been unable to track down this connection except through his personnel file. As far as I know, there is no study of Saint-Domingue's Superior Councils to complement Hayot's study of Martinique, so I have yet to cross-reference or fully describe the families of those council members.

40. ANOM COL E 177, letter dated May 24, 1776, from a M. de Sartine.

41. ANOM COL E 177. I am still a bit uncertain about the financial recompense for council members. Chanvalon ascribes moral superiority to council members for not getting paid, but I have been unable to corroborate his statement, Thibault de Chanvalon, *Voyage à la Martinique*, 4.

42. Hayot, *Les Officiers du Conseil*, 71.

43. For more on this phenomenon, see Wood "Archipelago of Justice. A more complete interrogation of Superior Council records will reveal which council members (whether planters, traders, or military officials) were more likely to rely upon Martinican commentary and why. Further investigation will also uncover new insights into the classic conflict between colonial administrators (such as Marine officials) and local elites (such as the Martinican commentators). For a summary of this tension for the eighteenth century, see Ghachem, *Old Regime and the Haitian Revolution*, 183–210, and throughout.

44. ANOM COL E 226, Martin Hussey.

45. ANOM COL E 98, Walter Hussey (with three other Guadeloupean resident aliens: André Cram, Isaac Lion, and David Fletcher). This request was approved in 1774.

46. For English Atlantic comparisons of legal knowledge acquired by colonial elites in European law schools and courtrooms, see Flavell, "'School for Modesty and Humility,'" and Hadden and Minter, "Legal Tourist Visits Eighteenth-Century Britain."

47. ANOM COL E 16, Nicolas François Barbé de Marbois.

48. ANOM COL E, 271, François Millon.

49. For lawyers in Europe at the same time, see especially Kagan, *Lawsuits and Litigants in Castile;* Brooks, *Pettyfoggers and Vipers of the Commonwealth;* and Bell, *Lawyers and Citizens.*

50. Québec's legal culture, including connections between Québecois and Caribbean themistocrats, deserves separate attention. For a civil law practice in one seventeenth-century court, see Dickinson, *Justice et justiciables.* Around 1628 Du Tertre himself noted that Canadian trading company problems prompted migration to the Antilles, aided by the prospect of fertile land. Du Tertre, *Histoire générale des Antilles habitées par les François,* 3:44. For the Canadian dimensions of Atlantic trade and migration, though oriented more towards the eighteenth century, see Miquelon, *Dugard of Rouen;* Bosher, *Canada Merchants;* Hodson, *Acadian Diaspora;* and Rushforth, *Bonds of Alliance.*

51. *L'État de la France,* at 284–85. For more on the *conseils,* see Wood, "Archipelago of Justice."

52. Hayot, *Les officiers du Conseil souverain de la Martinique;* Moreau de Saint-Méry, *Loix et constitutions des colonies française de l'Amérique;* ANOM, Série A—Actes du Pouvoir Souverain (1628–1779); ANOM, Série E—Personnel Colonial Ancien (17th–18th centuries). For a similar approach in the study of other colonies, see Scott and Hébrard, *Freedom Papers;* Games, *Migration and the Origins of the English Atlantic World;* Hatfield, *Atlantic Virginia;* Kupperman, *Providence Island;* Kupperman, *Jamestown Project;* Meadows, "Engineering Exile"; Ferreira, "Atlantic Microhistories"; Pearsall, *Atlantic Families;* and Romney, *New Netherland Connections.* For an overview of recent approaches to Atlantic family history, consult Hardwick, Pearsall, and Wulf, "Introduction: Centering Families."

53. For thoughtful discussion of the interpretive dangers and opportunities associated with network analysis, see Lemercier, "Formal network methods in history," n.p.; Erickson, "Historical Research and the Problem of Categories: Reflections on 10,000 Digital. Note

Cards," n.p.; and Lynch, "Social Networks and Archival Context Project," n.p. I thank Will Hanley for bringing this literature to my attention.

Experimenting with Acceptance, Caribbean-Style

1.	See Stiefel, *Jewish Sanctuary in the Atlantic World*, 95–119, for in-depth discussion of this historic context.

2.	Jacobs, *Origins of a Creole*, 33.

3.	Stiefel, *Jewish Sanctuary in the Atlantic World*, 62–65.

4.	"Memorandum respecting Lopez's treason against Her Majesty, March 9 [?], 1594," in *CSPD*, Elizabeth I, 1591–1594, 455–56.

5.	"Lopez, Rodrigo," in Richards, *Who's Who in British History*, 810–11.

6.	"The Declaration deliver'd (in March 1593–94) by Judazer Fatim, a Jew," in *A Catalogue of the Harleian Collection of Manuscripts*, vol. 1, no. 871.

7.	Kohen, *History of the Turkish Jews and Sephardim*, 101.

8.	See the detailed biography in García-Arenal and Wiegers, *Man of Three Worlds*.

9.	Acts of the Privy Council, 33:665–66.

10.	Hyamson, *History of the Jews in England*, 135–36; Feldberg, "Joachim Gaunse: The Jew with Sir Walter Raleigh," in Feldberg, *Blessings of Freedom*, 2–3.

11.	Stick, *Roanoke Island*, 27–33. See also Wallace, "List of Participants" (accessed August 7, 2015).

12.	Stiefel, *Jewish Sanctuary in the Atlantic World*, 51–94.

13.	"Report by the Admiralty Judges to Council, April 12, 1654," in *CSPD* [Commonwealth], 1649–1660, 1654, 91.

14.	Endelman, *Jews of Georgian England*.

15.	Arbell, *Jewish Nation of the Caribbean*, 268–71.

16.	Andrews, *Trade, Plunder, and Settlement*, 301–2.

17.	Davis, "Notes on the History of the Jews in Barbados," 146.

18.	Pestana, *English Atlantic in an Age of Revolution*, 37.

19.	Ben Israel and Wolf, *Menasseh ben Israel's Mission to Oliver Cromwell*, xxxvi–xxxvii.

20.	Delevante and Alberga, *Island of One People*, 6–14; Marcus, *Colonial American Jew*, 96.

21.	Bodian, "Hebrews of the Portuguese Nation."

22.	Barnett, et. al., *Bevis Marks Records*, 1–3.

23.	"Requests to the Protector by Manasseh Ben Israel, on behalf of the Hebrew nation, [November 13, 1655]," in *CSPD* [Commonwealth], 1649–1660, 1655–56, 15.

24.	"Petition of Ant. Rodrigues Robles to the Protector, April 25, 1656," in *CSPD*, [Commonwealth], 1649–1660, 1655–56, 294–95.

25.	Samuel, "Antonio Rodrigues Robles."

26.	Arbell, *Jewish Nation of the Caribbean*, 195.

27.	"Remonstrance, addressed to the King, concerning the English Jews, showing the mischiefs accomplished by them since their coming in at the time of William the Conqueror, [November 30, 1660]," in *CSPD*, Charles II, 1660–61, 366.

28.	Holzberg, *Minorities and Power in a Black Society*, 16.

29.	American Jewish Archives, Cincinnati, Ohio, Small Collections, document SC-3232, dated 1661, my translation.

30.	Wilensky, "Royalist Position Concerning the Readmission of Jews to England."

31.	Arbell, *Jewish Nation of the Caribbean*, 85–86.

32.	Thorpe, *Federal and State Constitutions*, 2772–86.

33.	Petition of Jean d'Illan, Jew of Amsterdam, to the King, for a pass for a Holland ship to transport himself and fifty families of Jews from Amsterdam to Palestine, February 5, 1666, in *CSPD*, Charles II, 1665–66, 232.

34. Rupert, *Creolization and Contraband*, 53.

35. Petition of Jean d'Illan, Jew of Amsterdam, Gale Document Number: MC4327702087.

36. Stavans, *The Scroll and the Cross*, 136.

37. "Ya, en seis ciudades anglas, se publica luz de seis juntas de Israël sagradas: tres en Nieves, London, Iamaica; Quarta y quinta en does partes de Barbadas; Sexta en Madras Patân se vérifica." Daniel Levi de Barrios, *Historia real de Gran Bretaña* (Amsterdam, 1688), quoted in De Bethencourt, "Notes on the Spanish and Portuguese Jews in the United States," 38, my translation.

38. Pencak, *Historical Dictionary of Colonial America*, 24–25.

39. See Jessica Roitman's essay in this volume and Arbell, *Jewish Nation of the Caribbean*, 67–81, 82, 125, 172, 261–67.

40. "Proceedings upon the petition of Isaac Fernandez Dias, Isaac Motes Baruch, Isaac Nunes, and other Jews, late of Jamaica, merchants, August 30, 1692," in *CSPD*, William and Mary, 1691–1692, 425.

41. Delevante and Alberga, *Island of One People*, 23–31.

42. Stiefel, *Jewish Sanctuary in the Atlantic World*, 165.

43. Arbell, *Jewish Nation of the Caribbean*, 207.

44. Marcus, *Colonial American Jew, 1492–1776*, 500; Wilensky, "Royalist Position Concerning the Readmission of Jews to England."

45. Extract of Mr Secretary Cragg's letter, November 15, 1720, SP 42/17, f. 65.

46. Terrell, *Jewish Community of Early Colonial Nevis*, 44–48.

47. *Acts of Assembly, passed in the Island of Nevis*, London, 1740.

48. Godfrey and Godfrey, *Search Out the Land*, 119; Miller, *Discovering a Lost Heritage*, 186.

Carolina, the Torrid Zone, and the
Migration of Anglo-American Political Culture

1. A version of this essay was read at the 2013 meeting of the Southern Historical Association in St. Louis. I would like to thank Daniel C. Littlefield for his helpful commentary at that session. My thanks also to the contributors to the present volume for their critiques.

2. Charter of Carolina, March 24, 1663 ("the fifteenth year of our reign," which "began" with the execution of Charles I on January 30, 1649), http://avalon.law.yale.edu/17th_century /nc01.asp#1 (accessed August 1, 2013).

3. Quotation from Richter, *Before the Revolution*, 242. The standard view of the predominance of West Indian connections and influence on South Carolina's early history has been most recently restated in Roberts and Beamish, "Venturing Out." The classic "colony of a colony" formulation appears in Wood, *Black Majority*, 13–34. For the Redeemer view of South Carolina history, see McCrady, *History of South Carolina under the Proprietary Government*.

4. This "formula" was devised by the leadership of the Virginia Company and Virginia planters in the 1610s, Roper, *English Empire in America*, 93–120. For the Barbados situation, see Dunn, "The Barbados Census of 1680."

5. Roper, "The 1701 'Act for the Better Ordering of Slaves.'" For the expansion of Barbados, including its effects on Suriname, see Barber, "Power in the English Caribbean"; Weterings, "Should We Stay or Should We Go?"; and Zijlstra, "Competing for European Settlers."

6. For cautions with respect to the West Indian influence on South Carolina, see Bull, "Barbados Settlers in Early Carolina." Mathews arrived in Carolina on the "first fleet" that founded the Ashley River colony in 1670 as the agent of Anthony Ashley Cooper. He spent several months at Barbados while the fleet recovered from storm damage, but no evidence

exists that he had "strong ties to the island" otherwise. Roper, *Conceiving Carolina*, 6–7, 45; compare Roberts and Beamish, "Venturing Out," 63. While he did serve as governor of the Leeward Islands from 1686 to 1689 and so, technically, was "from the Caribbean," Sir Nathaniel Johnson originated from Newcastle, where he had been a prominent Baltic merchant and member of parliament. Roper, *Conceiving Carolina*, 57–61; compare Roberts and Beamish, "Venturing Out," 71n.

7. There can be no question that the Restoration government either sought—or was encouraged—to take stock of plantation affairs (as happened with all other affairs with which it had to deal). See, for example, "A State of your Majesties Interest in the West Indies," [1662], Egerton Ms. 2543, f. 123; and Nathaniel Butler, "That the Sommer Islands are of necessity to be taken into his Majesties peculiar care government and command," Egerton Ms. 2543, f. 125, both BL.

8. Richter, *Before the Revolution*, 241–56, quotations at 241–42; Koot, *Empire at the Periphery*, 5; Games, *Web of Empire*.

9. Roper and Van Ruymbeke, Introduction, *Constructing Early Modern Empires*, 1–19.

10. As in the case of Thomas Breedon, Samuel Maverick, and John Winthrop Jr., who lobbied the government successfully to support an attack on New Netherland. Roper, "Fall of New Netherland."

11. "Depositions of inhabitants of Nansemond County, Virginia concerning the North Carolina/Virginia boundary," March 25, 1708, in Saunders, *Colonial Records of North Carolina*, 1:676–77; Lefler, "A Description of 'Carolana' by a 'Well-Willer'"; Powell, "Carolana and the Incomparable Roanoke"; McPherson, "Nathaniel Batts, Landholder"; Bland, *Discovery of New Brittaine;* Billings, *Sir William Berkeley,* 74–78; Butler, "The Early Settlement of Carolina"; Billings, "Sir William Berkeley and the Carolina Proprietary." Sir John Berkeley was one of the grantees of a 1649 patent issued by Charles II during the king's exile to the Rappahannock Country. CO 1/17, f. 177.

12. English Members of the Cape Fear Company to the Lords Proprietors, August 6, 1663, in Saunders, *Colonial Records of North Carolina,* 1:36–39; Hall, "New Englanders at Sea."

13. Lord Willoughby of Parham to Council on Foreign Trade and Plantations, September 23, 1663, CO 1/17, f. 203.

14. In *Before the Revolution,* Daniel Richter claims that the proprietors received their grant as a reward "for their service to the Stuart family" (236). This may have been the case for the Berkeleys, Carteret, Clarendon, and Craven, although they, especially Clarendon, received a healthy share of the greater rewards—and responsibilities—on offer at the Restoration. The inclusion of Albemarle, Ashley, and Colleton, though, renders this view unsatisfactory.

15. The nature and timing of the behavior of the behavior of key players, especially Albemarle and his fellow proprietor, Ashley, in the advent of the Restoration necessarily remains murky. De Krey, *London and the Restoration,* 19–66. For the membership of the first Restoration Council for Foreign Plantations, see Order appointing a Committee for Plantation affairs, July 4, 1660, in O'Callaghan and Ferlow, *Documents Related to the Colonial History,* 3:30.

16. It has not been established whether his island interests qualify him as a "Barbadian" in the minds of those who adhere to the view that West Indian planters exercised a dominant influence on Carolina. Ashley sold this plantation in 1654, but by the time the Carolina proprietorship was formed, he had extended his personal overseas interests from Hudson's Bay to the Gold Coast. Thomas Leng, "Shaftesbury's Aristocratic Empire," 104. For his involvement in religious politics, see Spurr, "Shaftesbury and the Politics of Religion."

17. Curiously, no modern treatment of Clarendon's life exists either. For his entry in the *Oxford Dictionary of National Biography,* see Paul Seaward, "Hyde, Edward, first earl

of Clarendon (1609–1674)," first published 2004, online ed., October 2008, http://dx.doi
.org/10.1093/ref:odnb/14328 (accessed August 15, 2013).

18. For the membership of the Council for Foreign Plantations, see His Majesty's Commission for a Council for Foreign Plantations, December 1, 1660, in O'Callaghan and Ferlow, *Documents Related to the Colonial History,* 3:2–34.

19. Sir George Downing to Sir Henry Bennett, August 4, 1664, SP 84/171, ff. 106–10 at 108r. As observed in, for example, a "letter from Surinam," November 8, 1663, CO 1/17, ff. 226–27, at 226–27v.

20. Gragg, "'To Procure Negroes'"; McCusker and Menard, "Sugar Industry in the Seventeenth Century."

21. "A Brief Narrative of the Trade and Present Condition of the Company of Royal Adventurers of England trading into Africa," 1665, CO 1/19, ff. 7–8. Sir Peter Colleton, successor to the proprietary interest of his father, served as agent on Barbados for the Royal Adventurers along with his friend and fellow Carolina advocate, Sir Thomas Modyford. Zook, "Company of Royal Adventurers," 74–75. For Noell, see, for example, East India Company in London to the Agent and factors at Fort Cormontine, July 16, 1658, and November 8, 1659, in Makepeace, *Trade on the Guinea Coast, 1657–1666,* 15–17, 42–46; and The Humble Petition of Martin Noel and William Watts merchants in the behalf of themselves and others interested with them, [1656?], Egerton Ms. 2395, ff. 107–13, BL. For Povey, see Register of Letters Relating to the West Indies, 1655–1661, Add. Ms. 11411, BL; and AO 1/1309, f. 1218 and E 351, f. 357, National Archives of Great Britain, Kew, Richmond. For Thompson and Vassall, see Lancelot Stavely at Fort Cormontine to Maurice Thompson, Samuel Vassall, and John Wood of the Guinea Company in London, May 1, 1658, in Makepeace, *Trade on the Guinea Coast,* 9–10; and Captain John Blake to the Guinea Company, February 15, 1652, in Donnan, *Documents Illustrative of the Slave Trade to America,* 1:134–36.

22. Sir George Downing to The Lord Chancellor Clarendon, June 21/July 1, 1661, Downing to Clarendon, July 15, 1661, Clarendon to Downing, August 16, 1661, Downing to Clarendon, September 18, 1663, in Lister, *Life and Administration of Edward, Earl of Clarendon,* 3:144–148, 152–55, 166–69, 249–53; Charles II to Dutch Ambassadors, June 26, 1661, in Routledge, *Calendar of the Clarendon State Papers Preserved in the Bodleian Library,* 5:110; Desires of the East India Company to the Lords Commissioners appointed to treat with the Dutch, [February 1661] in Sainsbury, *Calendar of the Court Minutes of the East India Company,* 86–88; Stein, "Tangier in the Restoration Empire"; Petition of the Company of Royal Adventurers in England Trading into Africa, August 26, 1663, SP 44/13, f. 355.

23. Without engaging in the seemingly endless scholarly debates over "transitions from servitude to slavery," it should be noted that the 1660s saw the first Anglo-American codifications of "slave codes" beginning in Barbados in 1661 and the shift in the designation of children from the status of their fathers to that of their mothers. See, for example, An Act Concerning Negroes & other Slaves, September 1664, *Proceedings and Acts of the General Assembly* [of Maryland] *January 1637/8-September 1664,* Archives of Maryland Online, 1:533–34, http://aomol.msa.maryland.gov/html/index.html (accessed January 2, 2015).

24. "State of the case of the Duke of Norfolk's pretensions to Carolina," CO 1/17, f. 106; Kopperman, "Profile of Failure." Vassall, who knew well the wealth generated by the transatlantic slave trade, headed a predecessor of the Royal Company Adventurers Trading into Africa. Captain John Blake to the Guinea Company, February 15, 1652, in Donnan, *Documents Illustrative of the Slave Trade to America,* 1:134–36. The wide-ranging activities of the Vassall family extended to the West African coast. Thus, the *Mayflower, Peter,* and *Benjamin,* jointly owned by Samuel Vassall, his brother-in-law Peter Andrews, and others made a 1647–48 voyage to the Guinea coast; *Mayflower* and *Peter* were captured by Spaniards after embarking a total of four hundred slaves at Santo Domingo, but *Benjamin* escaped

after embarking 174 slaves, out of an original consignment of 251 individuals, voyages 21879, 26255, and 26256, Voyages Database. 2009, Eltis, *Voyages* (accessed March 20, 2013). The Vassalls were also involved in the failed Providence Island venture, "A Coppie of Providence Charter," March 14, 1644, CO 1/11, ff. 4–6; in New England, where they were among the founders of Massachusetts Bay, Wall, *Massachusetts Bay*, 102–5, 157–224. Their interests also included the West Indies as well as Carolina. Harris, *John Vassal and His Descendants*, 6–10; Smith, *Slavery, Family, and Gentry Capitalism*, 22–25; e.g., Commission to appoint John Vassall as Surveyor General of Clarendon County, November 24, 1664, and Henry Vassall to the Lords Proprietors of Carolina, August 15, 1666, both in Saunders, *Colonial Records of North Carolina*, 1:73, 144–45.

25. His commissions may be found, respectively, at CO 1/19, f. 227, and September 16, 1670, CO 1/24, f. 149. For Willoughby and the plans for Carolina, see Albemarle to Lord Willoughby, August 31, 1663, CO 5/286, ff. 6–7.

26. "Proposals concerning Jamaica by my lord Marlborough," [November 1660?], CO 123–24, at 123r; Thomas Povey's letters on the West Indies, 1655–1661, Add. Ms. 11411, BL; CO 138/1.

27. Modyford's commission is dated February 15, 1664 (CO 1/18, ff. 35–40), and he arrived in his new post in June. Joseph Martin to Secretary Bennett from Port Royal, June 26, 1664, CO 1/18, f. 171. For his partnership with Colleton, see, for example, Sir Thomas Modyford and Sir Peter Colleton to Governor, Deputy-Governor, Court of Assistants [of Royal Company of England Trading into Africa], March 20, 1664, and March 31, 1664, CO 1/18, ff. 84–86. For his involvement in Carolina, see "Proposal by Thomas Modyford and Peter Colleton concerning the settlement of Carolina by inhabitants of Barbados," August 12, 1663, and George Monck, Duke of Albemarle, to Thomas Modyford and Peter Colleton, August 30, 1663, both in Saunders, *The Colonial Records of North Carolina*, 1:39–42, 46–47. For proprietary plans, see Sir Robert Harley to Sir Edward Harley, November 3, 1662, Royal Commission on Historical Manuscripts, *Manuscripts of His Grace the Duke of Portland, Preserved at Welbeck Abbey, Fourteenth Report, Appendix, Part II* (London, 1894), vol. 3, 268; "Concessions and Agreements of the Lords Proprietors of the Province of Carolina, 1665," http://avalon.law.yale.edu/17th_century/nc03.asp#1 (accessed July 3, 2013). For Modyford's promotion of Jamaica, see Sir Thomas Modyford to Secretary of State Henry Bennett, May 10, 1664, CO 1/18, ff. 133–36.

28. CO 1/17, f. 226.

29. Barber, "Power in the English Caribbean."

30. Memorial touching the removal of the planters from Suriname to Carolina, received March 24, 1669, CO 1/24, f. 66; James Bannister to Arlington, January 26, 1672, CO 1/28, f. 7; Bathshua Scott to Bannister, September 13, 1674, CO 1/31, f. 223. The planters continued to resist the Dutch, and the relicts, including Bannister, did not depart Suriname until 1675. Conceivably (although I have found no proof), Sandford's prickly relations with other Suriname planters may have contributed to the abandonment of the Carolina plan.

31. Sandford, "Relation of a Voyage on the Coast." For Sandford's disagreements with other Suriname colonists, see Sandford, *Suriname Justice;* John Vassall to Sir John Colleton, October 6, 1667, in Cheves, *Shaftesbury Papers,* 89–90. The latest examination of North Carolina's early history is an unsatisfactory one in that it privileges the vision of reality espoused by "Levellers." McIlvenna, *Very Mutinous People.*

32. "An Essaie or overture for the regulating the Affaires of His Highness in the West Indias," [1655], Add. Ms. 11411, ff. 22–24; "Certaine queries concerning his Highness interest in the West Indias," [circa 1656–1658], Egerton Ms. 2395, ff. 86–87. The latter document is accompanied by various proposals for a West India Company and reasons for settling Jamaica and attacking the Spaniards. Egerton Ms. 2395, ff. 88–112. All sources in BL.

33. Leng, "Shaftesbury's Atlantic Empire." The passenger figure is inexact, but so is Cheves's attempt at correction; Sir John Yeamans, for instance, did not go to the colony until 1672. Cheves, *Shaftesbury Papers*, 135. For Ashley's relations with the English governments of the 1650s, see Marshall, "'Mechanic Tyrannie.'"

34. For those results, see the contributions by Carolyn Arena and Jessica Roitman to this volume.

35. See, for example, Bonomi, *A Factious People;* McConville, *Those Daring Disturbers;* and Nash, *Quakers and Politics.*

36. For a detailed account of South Carolina's history under the proprietors, see Roper, *Conceiving Carolina.*

Bibliography

Abénon, Lucien-René. *La Guadeloupe de 1671 à 1759: étude politique, économique et sociale.* 2 vols. Paris: L'Harmattan, 1987.

Abrahams, Nicolai. "Nogle Bidrag til den dansk-vestindiske Handels Historie i de første Aar (1671–c.1680)." *Historisk Tidsskrift*, ser. 7, no. 4 (1902): 283–316.

Acerra, Martine, José Merino, and Jean Meyer, eds. *Les marines de guerre européennes: XVIIe–XVIIIe siècles: actes du colloque organisé au Musée de la Marine et à l'Université de Paris-Sorbonne.* Paris: Presses de l'Université Paris-Sorbonne, 1998.

Acts of Assembly, passed in the Island of Nevis, from 1664 to 1739, inclusive. London, 1740.

Adams, Simon. "Early Stuart Politics: Revisionism and After." In *Theatre and Government under the Early Stuarts,* edited by J. R. Mulryne and Margaret Shewring, 29–56. Cambridge, U.K.: Cambridge University Press, 1993.

Andersen, Dan H. "Denmark-Norway, Africa, and the Caribbean, 1660–1917: Modernisation Financed by Slaves and Sugar?" In *A Deus ex Machina Revisited: Atlantic Colonial Trade and European Economic Development,* edited by P. C. Emmer, O. Pétré-Grenouilleau, and J. V. Roitman, 291–315. Leiden, the Netherlands: Brill 2006.

Andrews, Kenneth R. *Trade, Plunder, and Settlement: Maritime Enterprise and the Genesis of the British Empire, 1480–1630.* Cambridge, U.K.: Cambridge University Press, 1984.

Andrews, Richard Mowery. *Law, Magistracy, and Crime in Old Regime Paris, 1735–1789.* Cambridge, U.K.: Cambridge University Press, 1994.

Apricius, Johannes. *Een kort en bondigh Vertoogh van de considerabele Colonie, die de . . . Staten van Hollandt . . . hebben goedt-gevonden ende geresolveert . . . uyt te setten op de vaste Kuste van America, vervattende het fundament tot beter establissement, bevolckinghe en beschreminge van dien; de favorabele condition.* The Hague, 1676. Bibliotheca Thysiana, UBL.

Arbell, Mordechai. *The Jewish Nation of the Caribbean: The Spanish-Portuguese Jewish Settlements in the Caribbean and Guianas.* Jerusalem: Gefen Publishing House, 2002.

Archives of Maryland Online, Maryland State Archives, 864 vols. http://aomol.msa.maryland .gov/000001/000001/html/am1–533.html.

Armitage, David, and Michael Braddick, eds. *The British Atlantic World, 1500–1800.* New York: Palgrave Macmillan, 2002.

Atkinson, Lesley-Gail. "The Exploitation and Transformation of Jamaica's Natural Vegetation." In *The Earliest Inhabitants: The Dynamics of the Jamaican Taíno,* edited by Atkinson, 97–112. Kingston, Jamaica: University of the West Indies Press, 2006.

Bailyn, Bernard, *Atlantic History: Concept and Contours.* Cambridge, Mass.: Harvard University Press, 2005.

———. *The Barbarous Years: The Peopling of British North America: The Conflict of Civilizations, 1600–1675.* New York: Knopf, 2012.

Barber, Sarah. *The Disputatious Caribbean: The West Indies in the Seventeenth Century.* New York: Palgrave Macmillan, 2014.

———. "Power in the English Caribbean: The Proprietorship of Lord Willoughby of Parham." In *Constructing Early Modern Empires: Proprietary Ventures in the Atlantic World,*

1500–1750, edited by L. H. Roper and Van Ruymbeke, 189–212. Leiden, the Netherlands: Brill, 2007.

Barham, Henry. *Hortus Americanus: Containing an Account of the Trees, Shrubs and other Vegetable Productions of South-America and the West-India Islands and Particularly of the Island of Jamaica.* Kingston, Jamaica: Alexander Aikman, 1794.

Barnett, Lionel D., ed. *Bevis Marks Records: Being Contributions to the History of the Spanish and Portuguese Congregation of London.* Oxford, U.K.: Oxford University Press, 1940.

Baron Mulert, F. E. "De bewoners van Suriname in 1675." *De Navorscher* 66 (1917): 401–6.

Barr, Juliana. *Peace Came in the Form of a Woman: Indians and Spaniards in the Texas Borderlands.* Chapel Hill: University of North Carolina Press, 2007.

Batie, Robert Carlyle. "Why Sugar? Economic Cycles and the Changing of Staples in the English and French Antilles, 1624–1654." *Journal of Caribbean History* 8 (November 1976): 1–41.

Beckles, Hilary McD. *Britain's Black Debt: Reparations for Slavery and Native Genocide.* Kingston, Jamaica: University of West Indies Press. 2013.

———. "English Parliamentary Debate on 'White Slavery' in Barbados, 1659." *Journal of the Barbados Museum and Historical Society* 36, no. 4 (1982): 344–52.

———. "Kalinago (Carib) Resistance to European Colonisation of the Caribbean." *Caribbean Quarterly* 54, no. 4 (2008): 77–94.

Beeston, William. "A Journal Kept by Col. William Beeston from his first coming to Jamaica." In *Interesting Tracts relating to Jamaica*, 271–300. St. Jago de la Vega [Jamaica]: Lewis, Luna and Jones, 1800.

———. "A narrative by Sir William Beeston of the Descent on Jamaica by the French." In *Interesting Tracts Relating to the History of Jamaica*, 249–59. St. Jago de la Vega [Jamaica]: Lewis, Luna and Jones, 1800.

Behn, Aphra. *Oroonoko* [London: 1688]. Citations to the text found at http://ebooks.adelaide .edu.au/b/behn/aphra/b420/.

Belcher, Gerald L. "Spain and the Anglo-Portuguese Alliance of 1661: A Reassessment of Charles II's Foreign Policy." *Journal of British Studies* 15, no. 1 (1975): 67–88.

Bell, David Avrom. *Lawyers and Citizens: The Making of a Political Elite in Old Regime France.* New York: Oxford University Press, 1994.

Ben Israel, Manasseh, and Lucien Wolf. *Menasseh ben Israel's Mission to Oliver Cromwell: Being a reprint of the pamphlets published by Menasseh ben Israel to promote the re-admission of the Jews to England, 1649–1656.* London: Jewish Historical Society of England and Macmillan, 1901.

Bennett, J. Harry. "William Whaley, Planter of Seventeenth-Century Jamaica." *Agricultural History* 40, no. 2 (1966): 113–23.

Beschrijvinge van Guyana; Des selfs Cituatie, Gesontheyt, Vruchtbaerheyt endeongemeene Profijten en Voordeelen boven andere landen. Discourerender wijse voorgestelt, tusschen Een Boer . . . Een Burger . . . Een Schipper . . . en een Haeghsche Bode. Hoorn: Stoffel Jansz. Kortingh, 1676. Bibliotheca Thysiana, University of Leiden Library.

Billings, Warren M. "Sir William Berkeley and the Carolina Proprietary." *North Carolina Historical Review* 72 (July 1995): 329–42.

———. *Sir William Berkeley and the Forging of Colonial Virginia.* Baton Rouge: Louisiana State University Press, 2004.

Bilson, Thomas. *The True Difference Betweene Christian Subjection and Unchristian Rebellion.* Oxford, England, 1585.

Birch, Thomas, ed. *A Collection of the State Papers of John Thurloe, Esq.* 7 vols. London, 1742. Accessible at *British History Online:* http://www.british-history.ac.uk/search/series /thurloe-papers.

Bland, Edward. *The Discovery of New Brittaine.* London, 1651.

Block, Kristen. *Ordinary Lives in the Early Caribbean: Religion, Colonial Competition, and the Politics of Profit.* Athens: University of Georgia Press, 2012.

Blussé, Leonard, and Femme Gaastra, eds. *Companies and Trade.* Leiden, the Netherlands: Brill, 1981.

Bodian, Miriam. "Hebrews of the Portuguese Nation: The Ambiguous Boundaries of Self-Definition." *Jewish Social Studies* 15, no. 1 (2008): 166–80.

Bonney, Richard. "The European Reaction to the Trial and Execution of Charles I." In *The Regicides and the Execution of Charles I,* edited by Jason Peacey, 247–79. New York: Palgrave, 2001.

Bonomi, Patricia U. *A Factious People: Politics and Society in Colonial New York.* New York: Columbia University Press, 1971.

Boromé, Joseph. "Spain and Dominica, 1493–1647." *Caribbean Quarterly* 12, no. 4 (1966): 30–46.

Bosher, J. F. *The Canada Merchants, 1713–1763.* Oxford, U.K.: Clarendon Press, 1987.

Boucher, Philip P. *Cannibal Encounters: Europeans and Island Caribs, 1492–1763.* Baltimore: Johns Hopkins University Press, 1992.

———. *France and the American Tropics to 1700: Tropics of Discontent?* Baltimore: Johns Hopkins University Press, 2008.

———. "French Proprietary Colonies in the Greater Caribbean, 1620s–1670s." In *Constructing Early Modern Empires: Proprietary Ventures in the Atlantic World, 1500–1750,* edited by L. H. Roper and Bertrand Van Ruymbeke, 163–88. Leiden, the Netherlands: Brill, 2007.

———. "The 'Frontier Era' of the French Caribbean, 1620s–1690s." In *Negotiated Empires: Centers and Peripheries in the Americas, 1500–1820,* edited by Christine Daniels and Michael V. Kennedy, 207–34. London: Routledge, 2002.

Bouton, Jacques. *Relation de l'establissement des François depvis l'an 1635 en l'isle de la Martinique.* Paris, 1640. Available online at *Banque Numérique des Patrimoines Martiniquais:* http://www.patrimoines-martinique.org/.

Boxer, C. R. *The Anglo-Dutch Wars of the 17th Century.* London: National Maritime Museum and Her Majesty's Stationary Office, 1974.

Breslaw, Elaine. *Tituba, Reluctant Witch of Salem: Devilish Indians and Puritan Fantasies.* New York: New York University Press, 1996.

Breton, Raymond. *Dictionnaire caraïbe-françois: meslé de quantité de remarques historiques pour l'esclaircissement de la langue.* Auxerre, France, 1665.

———. *Grammaire caraïbe.* Auxerre, France, 1667.

———. *Petit catéchisme, ou Sommaire des trois premières parties de la doctrine chrestienne, traduit du françois en la langue des Caraïbes insulaires.* Auxerre, France, 1664.

Brierley, John S. "Kitchen Gardens in the Caribbean, Past And Present: Their Role In Small-Farm Development." *Caribbean Geography* 3, no. 1 (1991): 15–28.

Bro-Jørgensen, J. O. *Dansk Vestindien indtil 1755: Kolonisation og kompagnistyre.* Vol. 1 of *Vore gamle Tropekolonier.* Copenhagen: Fremad, 1966.

Bromley, John Selwyn. "Les prêt de vaisseaux de la marine française aux corsaires (1688–1715)." In *Les marines de guerre européennes: XVIIe-XVIIIe siècles: actes du colloque organisé au Musée de la Marine et à l'Université de Paris-Sorbonne,* edited by Martine Acerra, José Merino, and Jean Meyer, 81–107. Paris: Presses de l'Université Paris-Sorbonne, 1998.

Brøndsted, Johannes, ed. *Vore gamle Tropekolonier.* 4 vols. Copenhagen: Fremad, 1966.

Brooks, C. W. *Pettyfoggers and Vipers of the Commonwealth: The "Lower Branch" of the Legal Profession in Early Modern England.* Cambridge, U.K.: Cambridge University Press, 1986.

Brouwer, Judith. *Levenstekens. Gekaapte brieven uit het Rampjaar 1672.* Hilversum: Verloren, 2014.

Brown, Laura. "The Romance of Empire: Oroonoko and the Trade in Slaves." In *The New Eighteenth Century: Theory, Politics, English Literature*, edited by Laura Brown and Felicity Nussbaum, 41–61. New York: Methuen, 1987.

Buddingh, H. *Geschiedenis van Suriname*. Utrecht, the Netherlands, 1999.

Buisseret, David. "The French Come to Wood and Water in 1679." *Jamaica Journal* 8, nos. 2 and 3 (Summer 1974): 38–39.

———. "The French Invasion of Jamaica—1694." *Jamaica Journal* 16, no. 3 (1983): 31–33.

———, ed. "A Frenchman Looks at Jamaica in 1706." *Jamaica Journal* 2, no. 2 (1968): 6–9.

———. "Fresh Light on Spanish Jamaica." *Jamaica Journal* 16, no. 1 (1983): 72–73.

———. *Historic Jamaica from the Air*. Kingston, Jamaica: Ian Randle, 1996.

———, ed. *Jamaica in 1687: The Taylor Manuscript at the National Library of Jamaica*. Kingston, Jamaica: University of the West Indies Press, 2008.

Buisseret, David, and S. A. G. Taylor. "Juan de Bolas and His Pelinco." *Caribbean Quarterly* 24 (1978): 1–7.

Bull, Kinloch. "Barbados Settlers in Early Carolina: Historiographical Notes." *South Carolina Historical Magazine* 96 (October 1995): 329–39.

Burnard, Trevor. "'The Countrie Continues Sicklie': White Mortality in Jamaica, 1655–1780." *Social History of Medicine* 12, no. 1 (1999): 45–72.

———. "European Migration to Jamaica, 1655 to 1780." *William and Mary Quarterly*, 3rd ser., 53, no. 4 (1996): 769–96.

———. "Not a Place for Whites? Demographic Failure and Settlement in Comparative Context: Jamaica, 1655–1780." In *Jamaica in Slavery and Freedom: History, Heritage and Culture*, edited by Kathleen E. A. Monteith and Glen Richards, 73–88. Kingston, Jamaica: University of the West Indies Press, 2002.

———. *Planters, Merchants, and Slaves: Plantation Societies in British America, 1650–1820*. Chicago: University of Chicago Press, 2015.

Burnard, Trevor, and John Garrigus. *The Plantation Machine: Atlantic Capitalism in French Saint-Domingue and British Jamaica*. Philadelphia: University of Pennsylvania Press, 2016.

Butler, Lindley S. "The Early Settlement of Carolina: Virginia's Southern Frontier." *Virginia Magazine of History and Biography* 79 (January 1971): 20–26.

Buve, Raymond. "De Positie van de Indianen in de Surinaamse Plantagekolonie gedurende de 17e en de 18e Eeuw: een poging tot sociaal-historische studie." M.A. thesis, University of Leiden, the Netherlands, 1960.

———. "Gouverneur Johannes Heinsius de rol van aerssen's voorganger in de surinaamse indianenoorlog, 1678–1680." *New West Indian Guide/Nieuwe West-Indische Gids* 45, no. 1 (1966): 14–26.

[Campbell, John]. *Candid and Impartial Considerations On the Nature of the Sugar Trade; The Comparative Importance Of The British and French islands In The West-Indies: With The value and Consequence of St. Lucia and Granada, truly stated*. London, 1763.

Campbell, Mavis C. *The Maroons of Jamaica, 1655–1796: A History of Resistance, Collaboration and Betrayal*. Trenton: Africa World Press, 1990.

Carlton, Charles. *Going to the Wars: The Experience of the British Civil Wars, 1638–1651*. London: Routledge, 1992.

Caron, Aimery P. *Sainte Croix and Saint Thomas through French Documents (1629–1737)*. St. Thomas, Virgin Islands: Bureau of Libraries, Museums and Archaeological Services, 2013.

A Catalogue of the Harleian Collection of Manuscripts, Purchased by the Authority of Parliament. 2 vols. London, 1759.

Chauleau, Liliane. *Dans les îles du vent: La Martinique XVIIe-XIXe siècle*. Paris: Éditions Harmattan, 1993.

Cheves, Langdon III, ed. *The Shaftesbury Papers*. Charleston, S.C.: South Carolina Historical Society, 2000 [1897].

Claypole, William A. "Land Settlement and Agricultural Development in the Liguanea Plain 1655 to 1700." M.A. thesis, University of the West Indies, 1970.

Coke, Thomas. *A History of the West Indies*. 3 vols. Liverpool, U.K.: 1808.

Colon de Portugal y Castro, Don Pedro. *The Columbus Petition Document for the island of Jamaica 1672*. Translated by Jeremy Lawrence. Kingston, Jamaica: Mill Press, 1992.

Cook, Sherburne F., and Woodrow Borah. "The Aboriginal Population of Hispaniola." In *Essays in Population History*. Vol. 1: *Mexico and the Caribbean*, edited by Sherburne F. Cook and Woodrow Borah, 376–410. Berkeley: University of California Press, 1971.

Connah, Graham. *"Of the hut I builded": The Archaeology of Australia's History*. Cambridge, U.K.: Cambridge University Press, 1988.

Cope, Robert Douglas. "The Underground Economy in Eighteenth-Century Mexico City." Paper presented at the David Rockefeller Center, Harvard University, 2006.

Cowan, Brian. *The Social Life of Coffee: The Emergence of the British Coffee House*. New Haven: Yale University Press, 2005.

Crow Via, Viki. "A Comparison of the Colonial Laws of Jamaica under Governor Thomas Lynch 1681–1684 with Those Enumerated in the John Taylor Manuscript of 1688." *Journal of Caribbean History* 39, no. 2 (2005): 236–48.

———. "New Light from the Taylor Manuscript on Early Jamaican Law." *Bulletin of the Jamaican Historical Society* 11, no. 15 (2005): 427–29.

Cumming, William Patterson. "Cartography and Exploration." *North Carolina Historical Review* 22 (1945): 34–42.

Daniels, Christine, and Michael V. Kennedy, eds. *Negotiated Empires: Centers and Peripheries in the Americas, 1500–1820*. New York: Routledge, 2002.

Dasent, John Roche, et al., eds. *Acts of the Privy Council of England, 1542–1631*, 44 vols., British History Online: http://www.british-history.ac.uk/acts-privy-council.

Davis, N. Darnell. *The Cavaliers and Roundheads of Barbados, 1650–1652*. 1883. Reprint, London: Forgotten Books, 2013.

———. "Notes on the History of the Jews in Barbados." *Publications of the American Jewish Historical Society* 18 (1909): 129–48.

Davis, Ralph. *The Rise of the English Shipping Industry in the Seventeenth and Eighteenth Centuries*. New York: St. Martin's Press, 1962.

Dawdy, Shannon Lee. *Building the Devil's Empire: French Colonial New Orleans*. Chicago: University of Chicago Press, 2008.

Debien, Gabriel. *Les engagés pour les Antilles (1634–1715)*. Paris: Société de l'histoire des colonies françaises, 1952.

de Bethencourt, Cardoza. "Notes on the Spanish and Portuguese Jews in the United States, Guiana, and the Dutch and British West Indies during the Seventeenth and Eighteenth Centuries." *American Jewish Historical Society Journal* 29, nos. 1–4 (1925): 7–38.

A Declaration set forth by the Lord Lieutenant the Gentlemen of the Councell and assembly occasioned from the view of a printed paper Entitled an Act prohibited trade with the Barbados, Virginia, Bermudes and Antegoe. London, 1650.

de Escalante de Mendoza, Juan. *Itinerario de navegación de los mares y tierras occidentales*. 1575. Reprint, Madrid: Museo Naval, 1985.

de Forest, Mrs. Robert W. *A Walloon Family in America: Lockwood de Forest and His Forbears, 1500–1848; Together with a Voyage to Guyana Being the Journal of Jesse de Forest and His Colonists 1623–1625*. Vol. 2. Boston: Houghton Mifflin, 1914.

de Jong, Karst. "The Irish in Jamaica during the Seventeenth Century, 1655–1693." M.A. thesis, Queen's University, Belfast, 2010.

de Jonge, J. K. J., ed. *De opkomst van het Nederlandsch gezag in Oost-Indië (1595–1610).* Vol. 1. The Hague: Martinus Nijhoff and Frederik Muller, 1862.

De Krey, Gary S. *London and the Restoration, 1659–1683.* Cambridge, U.K.: Cambridge University Press, 2005.

de la Calle, Sieur. *Relation du S. de la Calle: sur ce qui s'est passé a l'attaque du Fort Royal de la Martinique par la flote de Ruiter.* Newberry Library, Chicago, Edward E. Ayer Manuscript Collection, MS 480 [1674?].

de la Chesnaye des Bois, François-Alexandre Aubert. *Dictionnaire de la noblesse, contenant les généalogies, l'histoire & la chronologie des familles nobles de France, l'explication de leurs armes, & l'état des grandes terres du royaume.* 15 vols. Paris, 1772.

de la Court, Pieter. *Aanwysing der heilsame politieke Gronden en Maximen van de Republike van Holland en West-Vriesland.* Leiden/Rotterdam, 1669.

de Laet, Johannes *Iaerlijck Verhael van de Verrichtinghen der Geoctroyeerde West-Indische Compagnie in derthien Boecken.* Vol. 2. The Hague: Martinus Nijhoff, 1932.

Delevante, Marilyn, and Anthony Alberga. *The Island of One People: An Account of the History of the Jews of Jamaica.* Kingston, Jamaica: Ian Randle, 2005.

de Lussan, Raveneau. *Journal du voyage fait à la mer de Sud, avec les flibustiers de l'Amérique en 1684. & années suivantes.* Paris, 1690.

Demorizi, Emilio Rodriguez, ed. *Relaciones históricas de Santo Domingo.* 4 vols. Ciudad Trujillo: Editora Montalvo, 1942.

de Myst, Gerardus. *Verloren Arbeyt ofte Klaar en kortbondigh vertoogh van de Colonie in de Lantstreke Guyana, aan de vast kust van America Op de Revier Wiapoca.* Amsterdam, 1678. Bibliotheca Thysiana, University of Leiden Library, 10164.

de Rochefort, Charles. *Histoire Naturelle et Morale Des Iles Antilles de L'Amerique. Enrichie D'un Grand Nombre de Belles Figures En Taille Douce, Des Places & Des Raretez Les plus Considerables, Qui Y Sont Décrites. Avec Un Vocabulaire Caraibe. Reveuë & Augmentée de Plusieurs Descriptions, & de Quelques Èclaircissemens, Qu'on Desiroit En La Precedente.* 2nd ed. Rotterdam, 1665.

Dessalles, Pierre-François-Régis. *Les Annales du Conseil Souverain de la Martinique.* 2 vols. 1786. Reprint, Paris: L'Harmattan, 1995.

Dessens, Nathalie. *From Saint-Domingue to New Orleans: Migration and Influences.* Gainesville: University Press of Florida, 2007.

de Vassière, Pierre. *Saint-Domingue: La société et la vie créoles sous l'Ancien Régime (1629–1789).* Paris: Perrin, 1909.

de Vries, D. P. *Korte historiael ende journaels aenteyckeninge van verscheyden voyagien in de vier deelen de wereldtsronde, als Europa, Africa, Asia, ende America gedaen.* The Hague, 1911.

Den Heijer, Henk. *De geschiedenis van de WIC.* Zutphen: Walburg Pers, 2002.

———. "'Over warem en koude landen': Mislukte Nederlandse volksplantingen op de Wilde Kust in de zeventiende eeuw." *De zeventiende eeuw* 21 (2005): 79–91.

Dickson, Vernon Guy. "Truth, Wonder, and Exemplarity in Aphra Behn's 'Oroonoko.'" *Studies in English Literature, 1500–1900* 47, no. 3 (2007): 573–94.

Dickinson, John Alexander. *Justice et justiciables. La procédure civile à la Prévôté de Québec, 1667-1759.* Québec: Les Presses de l'Université Laval, 1982.

Donnan, Elizabeth, ed. *Documents Illustrative of the Slave Trade to America.* 4 vols. 1930. Reprint, New York: Octagon Books, 1965.

Dookhan, Isaac. *A History of the Virgin Islands of the United States.* St. Thomas, Virgin Islands: Caribbean Universities Press, 1974.

Dragtenstein, Frank. *'De ondraaglijke stoutheid der wegloopers.' Marronage en koloniaal beleid in Suriname, 1667–1768.* Utrecht, the Netherlands: CLACS 2002.

Dubois, Laurent. *A Colony of Citizens: Revolution and Slave Emancipation in the French Caribbean, 1787–1804.* Chapel Hill: University of North Carolina Press, 2004.

Dunn, Richard S. "The Barbados Census of 1680: Profile of the Richest Colony in English America." *William and Mary Quarterly,* 3rd ser., 26, no. 1 (1969): 3–30.

———. *Sugar and Slaves: The Rise of the Planter Class in the English West Indies, 1624–1713.* Chapel Hill: University of North Carolina Press, 1972.

———. *A Tale of Two Plantations: Slave Life and Labor in Jamaica and Virginia.* Cambridge, Mass.: Harvard University Press, 2014.

Du Tertre, Jean-Baptiste. *Histoire générale des Isles de St. Christophe, de la Guadeloupe, de la Martinique, et autres dans L'Amerique.* Paris, 1654.

———. *Histoire générale des Antilles Habitées par les François.* 4 vols. Paris, 1667–1671.

Eagle, Marc. "Restoring Spanish Hispaniola, the First of the Indies: Local Advocacy and Transatlantic *Arbitrismo* in the Late Seventeenth Century." *Colonial Latin American Review* 23, no. 3 (2014): 385–412.

Edelson, S. Max. *Plantation Enterprise in Colonial South Carolina.* Cambridge, Mass.: Harvard University Press, 2006.

Eden, Richard. *The Decades of the new worlde or West India.* London, 1555.

Edmundson, George. "The Dutch on the Amazon and Negro in the Seventeenth Century, Part I: Dutch Trade on the Amazon." *English Historical Review* 18, no. 72 (1903): 642–63.

Elliott, J. H., and J. F. de la Peña, eds. *Memoriales y cartas del Conde Duque de Olivares.* 2 vols. Madrid: Alfaguara, 1978–1981.

Eltis, David B., et al., eds. *Voyages: The Trans-Atlantic Slave Trade Database,* http://www.slavevoyages.org.

Emmer, P. C., O. Pétré-Grenouilleau, and J. V. Roitman, eds. *A Deus ex Machina Revisited. Atlantic Colonial Trade and European Economic Development.* Leiden, the Netherlands: Brill 2006.

Endelman, Todd M. *The Jews of Georgian England, 1714–1830: Tradition and Change in a Liberal Society.* Philadelphia: The Jewish Publication Society of America, 1979.

Enthoven, Victor. "The Islands at the Center of the Atlantic World: The Early Presence of the Dutch in the West Indies." *De Halve Maen* 78, no. 4 (2005): 63–68.

———. "Suriname and Zeeland: Fifteen Years of Misery on the Wild Coast, 1667–1682." In *International Conference on Shipping, Factories and Colonization,* edited by J. Everaert and J. Parmentier, 249–60. Brussels: Académie Royale des Sciences d'Outre Mer, 1996.

Erickson, Ansley T. "Historical Research and the Problem of Categories: Reflections on 10,000 Digital Note Cards." In *Writing History in the Digital Age,* edited by Kristen Nawrotzki and Jack Dougherty. Ann Arbor: University of Michigan Press, 2013. Available online at *Digital Culture Books:* http://hdl.handle.net/2027/spo.12230987.0001.001.

Exquemelin, Alexandre-Olivier. *Histoire des Avanturiers qui se sont signalez dans les Indes, contenant ce qu'ils ont fait de plus remarquable depuis vingt années.* 2 vols. Paris, 1686.

———. *Essai Historique sur la colonie de Surinam.* Paramaribo: s.n., 1788.

Faber, J. A., H.K. Roessingh, B.H. Slicher von Bath, A.M. van der Woude, and H.J. van Xanten. "Population Changes and Economic Development in the Netherlands: A Historical Survey." *A.A.G. Bijdragen* 12 (1965): 47–113.

Feldbæk, Ole. *Danske handelskompagnier 1616–1843. Oktrojer og interne ledelsesregler.* Copenhagen: Selskabet for Udgivelse af Kilder til Dansk Historie, 1986.

Feldberg, Michael, ed. *Blessings of Freedom: Chapters in American Jewish History.* Hoboken: KTAV Publishing and the American Jewish Historical Society, 2002.

Ferreira, Roquinaldo. "Atlantic Microhistories: Mobility, Personal Ties, and Slaving in the Black Atlantic World (Angola and Brazil)." In *Cultures of the Lusophone Black Atlantic,* edited by Nancy Priscilla Naro, Roger Sansi-Roca, and Dave Treece, 99–128. New York: Palgrave Macmillan, 2007.

Ferrer, Ada. *Freedom's Mirror: Cuba and Haiti in the Age of Revolution*. New York: Cambridge University Press, 2014.

Finch, Heneage. *Reports of Cases decreed in the High Court of Chancery (1678–1679)*. London, 1725.

Flavell, Julie M. "The 'School for Modesty and Humility': Colonial American Youth in London and Their Parents, 1755–1775." *Historical Journal* 42, no. 2 (1999): 377–403.

Foucault, Michel. *Discipline and Punish: The Birth of the Prison*. Trans. Alan Sheridan. New York: Pantheon Books, 1977.

Frijhoff, Willem. "Uncertain Brotherhood: The Huguenots in the Dutch Republic." In *Memory and Identity: The Huguenots in France and the Atlantic Diaspora*, edited by Bertrand Van Ruymbeke and Randy J. Sparks, 128–71. Columbia: University of South Carolina Press, 2003.

Frostin, Charles. "Histoire de l'autonomisme colon de la partie française de Saint-Domingue aux XVIIème et XVIIIème siècles: Contribution à l'étude du sentiment américain d'indépendance." 2 vols. Ph.D. diss., University of Paris, 1972.

Furetière, Antoine. *Dictionnaire universel, contenant généralement tous les mots françois tant vieux que modernes, et les termes de toutes les sciences et des arts*. 3 vols. The Hague, 1690.

Games, Alison. "Cohabitation, Suriname-Style: English Inhabitants in Dutch Suriname after 1667." *William and Mary Quarterly*, 3rd ser., 72, no. 2 (2015): 195–242.

———. *Migration and the Origins of the English Atlantic World*. Cambridge, Mass.: Harvard University Press, 1999.

———. *The Web of Empire: English Cosmopolitans in an Age of Expansion, 1560–1660*. New York: Oxford University Press, 2008.

García-Arenal, Mercedes, and Gerard A. Wiegers. *A Man of Three Worlds: Samuel Pallache, a Moroccan Jew in Catholic and Protestant Europe*. Baltimore: Johns Hopkins University Press, 2003.

Garrigus, John D. *Before Haiti: Race and Citizenship in French Saint-Domingue*. New York: Palgrave Macmillan, 2006.

———. "Blue and Brown: Contraband Indigo and the Rise of a Free Colored Planter Class in French Saint-Domingue." *The Americas* 50, no. 2 (1993): 233–63.

———. "'Le Patriotisme americain': Emilien Petit and the Dilemma of French-Caribbean Identity Before and After the Seven Years' War." *Proceedings of the Annual Meeting of the Western Society for French History* 30 (2002): 18–29.

Gaspar, David Barry. "'Rigid and Inclement': Origins of the Jamaican Slave Laws of the Seventeenth Century." In Christopher L. Tomlins and Bruce H. Mann, eds., *The Many Legalities of Early Modern America*, 78–96. Chapel Hill: University of North Carolina Press, 2001.

Geggus, David Patrick, and Norman Fiering, eds. *The World of the Haitian Revolution*. Bloomington: Indiana University Press, 2009.

Gehring, Charles T., ed. and trans. *Correspondence, 1654–1658: Volume XII of the Dutch Colonial Manuscripts (New Netherland Documents)*. Syracuse: Syracuse University Press, 2003.

Gelfand, Noah L. "A Caribbean Wind: an Overview of the Jewish Dispersal from Dutch Brazil." *De Halve Maen* 78 no. 4 (2005): 49–56.

Ghachem, Malick W. "Montesquieu in the Caribbean: The Colonial Enlightenment between Code Noir and Code Civil." *Historical Reflections/Réflexions Historiques* 25, no. 2 (1999): 183–210.

———. *The Old Regime and the Haitian Revolution*. New York: Cambridge University Press, 2012.

Gøbel, Erik. "Danish Shipping along the Triangular Route, 1671–1802: Voyages and Conditions on Board." *Scandinavian Journal of History* 36 (2011): 135–55.

———. *The Danish Slave Trade and Its Abolition.* Leiden, the Netherlands: Brill, 2016.

———. "Danish Trade to the West Indies and Guinea, 1671–1754." *Scandinavian Economic History Review* 31 (1983): 21–49.

———. *Det danske slavehandelsforbud 1792. Studier og kilder til forhistorien, forordningen og følgerne.* Odense: University Press of Southern Denmark, 2008.

———. *A Guide to Sources for the History of the Danish West Indies (U. S. Virgin Islands), 1671–1917.* Odense: University Press of Southern Denmark, 2002.

———. *Vestindisk-guineisk Kompagni 1671–1754: Studier og kilder til kompagniet og kolonierne.* Odense: University Press of Southern Denmark, 2015.

Godfrey, Sheldon J., and Judy Godfrey. *Search Out the Land: The Jews and the Growth of Equality in British Colonial America, 1740–1867.* Montréal: McGill-Queen's University Press, 1995.

Goodman, David C. *Spanish Naval Power, 1589–1665: Reconstruction and Defeat.* Cambridge, U.K.: Cambridge University Press, 1997.

Goodman, Jordan. *Tobacco in History: The Cultures of Dependence.* London: Routledge, 1993.

Goslinga, Cornelis. *The Dutch in the Caribbean and on the Wild Coast, 1580–1680.* Assen, the Netherlands: Van Gorcum, 1971.

———. *A Short History of the Netherlands Antilles and Suriname.* The Hague: Martinus Nijhoff, 1979.

Goubert, Pierre. *L'ancien régime: La società, i poteri.* 4th ed. Milan: Jaca Books, 1999.

Gragg, Larry. "'To Procure Negroes': The English Slave Trade to Barbados, 1627–1660." *Slavery and Abolition* 16 (April 1995): 65–84.

Green, R. *The History, Topography and Antiquities of Framlingham and Saxsted.* London: Whittaker, Treacher, 1834.

———. *The Quaker Community on Barbados: Challenging the Culture of the Planter Class.* Columbia: University of Missouri Press, 2009.

Greene, Jack P. *Peripheries and Center: Constitutional Development in the Extended Polities of the British Empire and the United States, 1607–1788.* New York: W. W. Norton, 1990.

———. "Reformulating Englishness: Cultural Adaptation and Provinciality in the Construction of Corporate Identity in Colonial British America." In *Creating the British Atlantic: Essays on Transplantation, Adaptation, and Continuity,* edited by Greene, 19–32. Charlottesville: University of Virginia Press, 2013.

Greene, Jack P., and Philip D. Morgan, eds. *Atlantic History: A Critical Appraisal.* New York: Oxford University Press, 2009.

Griffin, Eric. "The Specter of Spain in John Smith's Colonial Writing." In *Envisioning an English Empire: Jamestown and the Making of the North Atlantic World,* edited by Robert Applebaum and John Wood Sweet, 111–34. Philadelphia: University of Pennsylvania Press, 2005.

Gruzinski, Serge. *La colonisation de l'imaginaire: sociétés indigènes et occidentalisation dans le Mexique espagnol XVIe–XVIIIe siècle.* Paris: Gallimard, 1988.

———. "Les mondes mêlés de la Monarchie Catholique et autres 'connected histories.'" *Annales: Histoire, Sciences Sociales* 56, no. 1 (2001): 85–117.

———. *Les Quatre parties du monde: Histoire d'une mondialisation.* Paris: La Martinière, 2004.

Hadden, Sally, and Patricia Hagler Minter. "A Legal Tourist Visits Eighteenth-Century Britain: Henry Marchant's Observations on British Courts, 1771 to 1772." *Law and History Review* 29, no. 1 (2011): 133–79.

Bibliography

Hall, Louise. "New Englanders at Sea: Cape Fear before the Royal Charter of 24 March 1662/3." *New England Historical and Genealogical Register* 124 (April 1970): 88–108.

Hall, Neville. *Slave Society in the Danish West Indies.* Mona, Jamaica: University of the West Indies Press, 1992.

Handler, Jerome. "The Amerindian Slave Population of Barbados in the 17th and Early 18th Centuries." *Caribbean Studies* 8 (1969): 38–64.

Handler, Jerome, and F. W. Lange. "Amerindians and Their Contributions to Barbadian Life in the Seventeenth Century." *Journal of the Barbados Museum and Historical Society* 35 (1977): 189–210.

———. *Plantation Slavery in Barbados: An Archaeological and Historical Investigation.* Cambridge, Mass.: Harvard University Press, 1978.

Hanley, Sarah. "'The Jurisprudence of the *Arrets*': Marital Union, Civil Society, and State Formation in France, 1550–1650." *Law and History Review* 21, no. 1 (2003): 1–40.

Hardwick, Julie, Sarah M. S. Pearsall, and Karin Wulf. "Introduction: Centering Families in Atlantic Histories." *William and Mary Quarterly*, 3rd ser., 70, no. 2 (2013): 205–24.

Harlow, Vincent T., ed. *Colonising Expeditions to the West Indies, 1623–1667.* London: Hakluyt Society, 1923.

Harries, H. C. "The Cape Verde Region (1499–1549): The Key to Coconut Cultivation in the Western Hemisphere?" *Turrialba* 27 (1977): 227–31.

Harris, Edward Doubleday. *John Vassal and His Descendants.* Albany, N.Y.: Munsell, 1862.

Hartsinck, J. *Beschryving van Guyana of de Wilde Kust in Zuid-Amerika.* Vol. 1. Amsterdam, 1770.

Hatfield, April Lee. *Atlantic Virginia: Intercolonial Relations in the Seventeenth Century.* Philadelphia: University of Pennsylvania Press, 2004.

Harvey, Thomas, and William Brewin. *Jamaica in 1866: A Narrative of a Tour Through the Island, with Remarks on its Social, Educational and Industrial Condition.* London: A. W. Bennet, 1867.

Hayes, David, ed. *Christiansted at 275: Celebrating the 275th Anniversary of the Founding of Christiansted, St. Croix.* St. Croix: Society of Virgin Islands Historians, 2013.

Hayot, Émile. *Les Officiers du Conseil Souverain de la Martinique et leurs Successeurs les Conseillers de la Cour d'Appel: Notices Biographiques et Généalogiques.* Fort-de-France, Martinique: Annales des Antilles, 1965.

Hernæs, Per. *Slaves, Danes, and African Coast Society: The Danish Slave Trade from West Africa and Afro-Danish Relations on the 18th Century Gold Coast.* Trondheim, Norway: University of Trondheim Press, 1995.

Hibbert, Christopher. *Charles I: A Life of Religion, War and Treason.* New York: Palgrave Macmillan, 2007.

Hickeringill, Edward. *Jamaica Viewed: With All the Ports, Harbours, and their several Soundings, Towns and Settlements thereunto belonging.* London, 1661.

Highfield, Arnold R. "Domingo 'Mingo' Gesoe: An Improbable Life." In *Negotiating Enslavement: Perspectives on Slavery in the Danish West Indies,* edited by Arnold R. Highfield and George F. Tyson, 77–87. St. Croix, Virgin Islands: Antilles Press, 2009.

———, ed. *J. L. Carstens' St. Thomas in Early Danish Times: A General Description of all the Danish, American West Indian Islands.* St. Croix: Virgin Islands Humanities Council, 1997.

———, ed. *Negotiating Enslavement: Perspectives on Slavery in the Danish West Indies.* St. Croix, Virgin Islands: Antilles Press, 2009.

———. *Sainte Croix, 1650–1733: A Plantation Society in the French Antilles.* St. Croix, Virgin Islands: Antilles Press, 2013.

Highfield, Arnold R., and Aimery P. Caron. *The French Intervention in the St. John Slave Revolt of 1733–34.* St. Thomas, Virgin Islands: Bureau of Libraries, Museums, and Archeological Services, 1981.

Highfield, Arnold R., and George F. Tyson. *Slavery in the Danish West Indies: A Bibliography.* St. Croix: Virgin Islands Humanities Council, 1994.

Higman, B. W. *Jamaica Surveyed: Plantation Maps and Plans of the Eighteenth and Nineteenth Centuries.* Kingston: Institute of Jamaica, 1988.

———. "The Sugar Revolution." *Economic History Review* 53, no. 2 (2000): 213–36.

Higman, B. W., and B. J. Hudson. *Jamaican Place Names.* Kingston, Jamaica: University of the West Indies, 2009.

Hill, Christopher. *Intellectual Origins of the English Revolution.* Oxford, U.K.: Clarendon Press, 1965.

———. *The World Turned Upside Down: Radical Ideas During the English Revolution.* New York: Viking Press, 1972.

Hinds, Allen B., et al., eds. *Calendar of State Papers Relating to English Affairs in the Archives of Venice,* 38 vols. London: H.M. Stationery Office, 1864–1947.

Hodson, Christopher. *The Acadian Diaspora: An Eighteenth-Century History.* New York: Oxford University Press, 2012.

Hoffman, Paul E. *The Spanish Crown and the Defense of the Caribbean, 1535–1585: Precedent, Patrimonialism, and Royal Parsimony.* Baton Rouge: Louisiana State University Press, 1980.

Holinshed, Raphael. *The First and second volumes of Chronicles.* N.p., 1587.

Holzberg, Carol S. *Minorities and Power in a Black Society: The Jewish Community of Jamaica.* Lanham, Md.: North-South Publishing, 1987.

Hoogbergen, Wim S. M. "The History of the Suriname Maroons." In *Resistance and Rebellion in Suriname: Old and New,* edited by Gary Brana-Shute, 65–102. Williamsburg, Va.: Department of Anthropology, College of William and Mary, 1990.

Hughes, Derek, ed. *Versions of Blackness: Key Texts on Slavery from the Seventeenth Century.* Cambridge, U.K.: Cambridge University Press, 2007.

Hulme, Peter. *Colonial Encounters: Europe and the Native Caribbean, 1492–1797.* London: Methuen, 1986.

Hulme, Peter, and Neil L. Whitehead, eds. *Wild Majesty: Encounters with Caribs from Columbus to the Present Day.* New York: Oxford University Press, 1992.

Hulsman, L. A. H. C. "Nederlands Amazonia: Handel met indianen tussen 1580 en 1680." Ph.D. diss., University of Amsterdam, 2009.

Hyamson, Albert Montefiore. *A History of the Jews in England.* London: Chatto and Windus, 1908.

Interesting Tracts, Relating to the Island of Jamaica, consisting of curious State-Papers, Councils of War, Letters, Petitions, Narratives, &c. &c., which throw great light on the history of that island, from its conquest, down to the year 1702. St. Jago de la Vega [Jamaica]: Lewis, Luna and Jones, 1800.

Jacobs, Bart. *Origins of a Creole: The History of Papiamentu and Its African Ties.* Boston: De Gruyter Mouton, 2012.

Japikse, N., ed. *Resolutiën der Staten-Generaal van 1576 tot 1609.* Vol. 10, *1598–1599.* The Hague, 1930.

Jeaffreson, John Cordy. *A Young Squire of the Seventeenth Century.* 2 vols. London: Hurst and Blackett, 1878.

Johnson, Charles. *A general history of the pyrates: from their first rise and settlement in the Island of Providence, to the present time: with the remarkable actions and adventures of the two female pyrates Mary Read and Anne Bonny, contain'd in the following chapters . . . to*

Bibliography

which is added a short abstract of the statute and civil law in relation to pyracy. 2nd ed. London, 1724.

Jekabson-Lemanis, Karin. "Balts in the Caribbean: The Duchy of Courland's Attempts to Colonize Tobago Island, 1638 to 1654." *Caribbean Quarterly* 46, no. 2 (2000): 25–44.

Johnson, Edward. "Merchant, at St. Christophers in the West-Indies." *A Primitive Discourse upon Prayer.* London, 1740.

Johnston, J. R. V. "The Stapleton Sugar Plantations in the Leeward Islands." *Bulletin of the John Rylands Library* 48, no. 1 (1965): 175–206.

Justesen, Ole. *Danish Sources for the History of Ghana, 1657–1754.* 2 vols. Copenhagen: Royal Danish Academy of Sciences, 2005.

Kagan, Richard L. *Lawsuits and Litigants in Castile, 1500–1700.* Chapel Hill: University of North Carolina Press, 1981.

Kamen, Henry. *Spain's Road to Empire: The Making of a World Power, 1492–1763.* London: Penguin, 2002.

Karijosemito, R., and P. Dikland, eds. *Zeeuwse archivalia uit Suriname en omliggende kwartien, 1667–1683.* Paramaribo: s.n., 2003.

Kars, Marjoleine. "Dodging Rebellion: Politics and Gender in the Berbice Slave Uprising of 1763." *American Historical Review* 121, no. 1 (2016): 39–69.

Kellenbenz, Hermann. "La place de l'Elbe inférieure dans le commerce triangulaire au milieu du XVIIIe siècle." *Revue francaise d'histoire d'outre-mer* 62, no. 226 (January 1975): 186–95.

Kenyon, John, and Jane Ohlmeyer, eds. *The Civil Wars: A Military History of England, Scotland, and Ireland 1638–1660.* Oxford, U.K.: Oxford University Press, 1998.

Keye, O. *Het waere onderscheyt tusschen koude en warme landen.* The Hague, 1659.

Keymis, Lawrence. *A Relation of the second voyage to Guyana: performed and written in the yeare 1596.* London, 1596.

Klooster, Wim. *The Dutch Moment: War, Trade, and Settlement in the Seventeenth-Century Atlantic World.* Ithaca: Cornell University Press, 2016.

———. "The Essequibo Liberties: The Link between Jewish Brazil and Jewish Suriname." *Studia Rosenthaliana* 42–43 (2010–11): 77–82.

———. "Networks of Colonial Entrepreneurs: The Founders of the Jewish Settlements in Dutch America, 1650s and 1660." In *Atlantic Diasporas: Jews, Conversos, and Crypto-Jews in the Age of Mercantilism, 1500–1800,* edited by Richard Kagan and Philip D. Morgan, 33–49. Baltimore: Johns Hopkins University Press, 2008.

Klooster, Wim, and Gert Oostindie, eds. *Curaçao in the Age of Revolutions, 1795–1800.* Leiden, the Netherlands: KITLV Press, 2011.

Knight, David W. *The 1688 Census of the Danish West Indies: Portrait of a Colony in Crisis.* St. Thomas, Virgin Islands: Little Nordside Press, 1998.

Knight, Franklin W. *The Caribbean: The Genesis of a Fragmented Nationalism,* 2nd ed. New York: Oxford University Press, 1990.

Knuttel, W. P. C. *Catalogus van de pamfletten-verzameling berustende in de Koninklijke Bibliotheek.* Utrecht, 1978.

Kohen, Elli. *History of the Turkish Jews and Sephardim: Memories of a Past Golden Age.* Lanham, Md.: University Press of America, 2007.

Koot, Christian J. "An Adaptive Presence: The Dutch Role in the English Caribbean before and after the fall of Dutch Brazil." *De Halve Maen* 78, no. 4 (2005): 69–76.

———. *Empire at the Periphery: British Colonists, Anglo-Dutch Trade, and the Development of the British Atlantic, 1621–1713.* New York: New York University Press, 2011.

Kopperman, Paul E. "Profile of Failure: The Carolana Project, 1629–1640." *North Carolina Historical Review* 59 (1982): 1–23.

Korr, Charles. *Cromwell and the New Model Foreign Policy: England's Policy towards France, 1649–1658.* Berkeley: University of California Press, 1975.

Kruijtzer, Gijs. "European Migration in the Dutch Sphere." In *Dutch Colonialism, Migration and Cultural Heritage,* edited by Gert Oostindie, 97–154. Leiden, the Netherlands: Brill, 2008.

Kuijpers, Erika. *Migrantenstad. Immigratie en sociale verhoudingen in zeventiende-eeuws Amsterdam.* Hilversum, the Netherlands: Verloren, 2005.

Kupperman, Karen Ordahl. *The Jamestown Project.* Cambridge, Mass.: Harvard University Press, 2007.

———. *Providence Island, 1630–1641: The Other Puritan Colony.* Cambridge, U.K.: Cambridge University Press, 1993.

Labat, Jean-Baptiste. *Nouveau Voyage aux Iles de l'Amérique.* Paris, 1722.

Lafleur, Gérard. *Les Caraïbes des Petites Antilles.* Paris: Éditions Karthala, 1992.

———. "Le tabac en Guadeloupe: de la culture principale à la culture secondaire." In *Construire l'historie antillaise: Mélanges offerts à Jacques Adélaïde-Merlande,* edited by Lucien Abenon, Danielle Bégot, and Jean-Pierre Sainton, 252–71. Paris: Comité des travaux historiques et scientifiques, 2002.

Lane, Kris E. *Pillaging the Empire: Global Piracy on the High Seas, 1500–1750.* London: Routledge, 2015.

Larkin, James, and Paul Hughes, eds. *Stuart Royal Proclamations.* Vol. 1, *Royal Proclamations of King James I, 1603–1625.* Oxford, U.K.: Clarendon Press, 1973.

Las Casas, Bartolomé de. *A Short Account of the Destructions of the Indies.* Ed. Anthony Pagden. 1552. Reprint, London: Penguin, 2004.

Lauring, Kaare. *Slaverne dansede og holdt sig lystige. En fortælling om den danske slavehandel.* Copenhagen: Gyldendal, 2014.

The Laws of Jamaica Passed by the Assembly, And Confirmed by His Majesty in Council, Feb. 23 1683. London, 1683.

The Laws of Jamaica, Passed by the Assembly, And Confirmed by His Majesty in Council, April 17, 1684. London, 1684.

Lefler, Hugh Talmage, ed. "A Description of 'Carolana' by a 'Well-Willer,' 1649." *North Carolina Historical Review* 32 (1955): 102–5.

Lemercier, Claire. "Formal Network Methods in History: Why And How?" In *Social Networks, Political Institutions, and Rural Societies,* edited by Georg Fertig. Turnhout, Belgium: Brepols, 2011, https://hal.archives-ouvertes.fr/halshs-00521527/document.

Leng, Thomas. "Shaftesbury's Aristocratic Empire." In *Anthony Ashley Cooper, First Earl of Shaftesbury, 1621–1683,* edited by John Spurr, 101–26. Farnham, U.K.: Ashgate, 2011.

Lenik, Stephan. "Carib as a Colonial Category: Comparing Ethnohistoric and Archaeological Evidence from Dominica, West Indies." *Ethnohistory* 59, no. 1 (2012): 79–107.

Lestringant, Franck. *Le Huguenot et le sauvage: L'Amérique et la controverse coloniale, en France, au temps des guerres de Religion (1555–1589).* Paris: Diffusion Klincksieck, 1990.

L'État de la France: Tome Cinquième, De l'établissement des Parlemens, Cours Supérieurs & autres Jurisdictions du Royaume. Des Généralités, Intendances & Recettes Générales. Paris, 1749.

Ligtenberg, C. *Willem Usselinx.* Utrecht, the Netherlands: A. Oosthoek, 1915.

Linebaugh, Peter, and Marcus Rediker. *The Many-Headed Hydra: Sailors, Slaves, Commoners, and the Hidden History of the Revolutionary Atlantic.* Boston: Beacon Press, 2000.

Lipman, Andrew. *The Saltwater Frontier: Indians and the Contest for the American Coast.* New Haven: Yale University Press, 2015.

Lister, T. H., ed. *Life and Administration of Edward, Earl of Clarendon with Original Correspondence and Authentic Papers Never Before Published.* 3 vols. London: Longman, Orme, Brown, Green and Longmans, 1837.

Liu, Sida. "The Legal Profession as a Social Process: A Theory on Lawyers and Globalization." *Law & Social Inquiry* 38, no. 3 (2013): 670–93.

Lomas, S. C., ed. *The Letters and Speeches of Oliver Cromwell with Elucidations by Thomas Carlyle.* 3 vols. London: Methuen, 1904.

Lorimer, Joyce. *English and Irish Settlement on the River Amazon, 1550–1646.* London: Hakluyt Society, 1989.

———. "The Failure of the English Guiana Ventures, 1595–1667, and James I's Foreign Policy." *Journal of Imperial and Commonwealth History* 21, no. 1 (1993): 1–30.

———. ed. *Sir Walter Ralegh's* Discoverie of Guiana. London: Ashgate, 2007.

Lynch, Tom J. "Social Networks and Archival Context Project: A Case Study of Emerging Cyberinfrastructure." *Digital Humanities Quarterly* 8, no. 3 (2014): http://www.digital humanities.org/dhq/vol/8/3/000184/000184.html.

Makepeace, Margaret, ed. *Trade on the Guinea Coast, 1657–1666: The Correspondence of the English East India Company.* Madison, Wis.: African Studies Program, University of Wisconsin, 1991.

Manning, David. "Reformation and the Wickedness of Port Royal, Jamaica, 1655–c.1692." In *Puritans and Catholics in the Trans-Atlantic World 1600–1800,* edited by Crawford Gribben and Scott Spurlock, 131–63. Basingstoke, U.K.: Palgrave Macmillan, 2016.

Marcus, Jacob Rader. *The Colonial American Jew, 1492–1776.* 3 vols. Detroit: Wayne State University Press, 1970.

Marino, John A., ed. *Early Modern History and the Social Sciences: Testing the Limits of Braudel's Mediterranean.* Kirksville, Mo.: Truman State University Press, 2002.

Marshall, Alan. "'Mechanic Tyrannie': Anthony Ashley Cooper and the English Republic." In *Anthony Ashley Cooper, First Earl of Shaftesbury, 1621–1683,* edited by John Spurr, 27–50. Farnham, U.K.: Ashgate, 2011.

Maza, Sarah C. *Private Lives and Public Affairs: The Causes Célèbres of Prerevolutionary France.* Berkeley: University of California Press, 1993.

McConville, Brendan. *Those Daring Disturbers of the Public Peace: The Struggle for Property and Power in Early New Jersey.* Ithaca: Cornell University Press, 1999.

McCrady, Edward M. *The History of South Carolina under the Proprietary Government, 1670–1719.* New York: Macmillan, 1897.

McCusker, John J., and Russell R. Menard. "The Sugar Industry in the Seventeenth Century: A New Perspective on the Barbadian 'Sugar Revolution.'" In *Tropical Babylons: Sugar and the Making of the Atlantic World,* edited by Stuart B. Schwartz, 289–330. Chapel Hill: University of North Carolina Press, 2004.

McElligott, Jason. "Atlantic Royalism? Polemic, Censorship and the Declaration and the Protestation of the Governour and Inhabitants of Virginia." In *Royalists and Royalism during the Interregnum,* edited by McElligott and David L. Smith, 214–34. Manchester, U.K.: Manchester University Press, 2010.

McIlvenna, Noeleen. *A Very Mutinous People: The Struggle for North Carolina, 1660–1713.* Chapel Hill: University of North Carolina Press, 2009.

McNeill, John Robert. *Atlantic Empires of France and Spain: Louisbourg and Havana, 1700–1763.* Chapel Hill: University of North Carolina Press, 1985.

McNeill, J. R. *Mosquito Empires: Ecology and War in the Greater Caribbean, 1620–1914.* Cambridge, U.K.: Cambridge University Press, 2010.

McPherson, Elizabeth Gregory. "Nathaniel Batts, Landholder on Pasquotank River, 1660." *North Carolina Historical Review* 43 (1960): 66–81.

Meadows, R. Darrell. "Engineering Exile: Social Networks and the French Atlantic Community, 1789–1809." *French Historical Studies* 23, no. 1 (2000): 67–102.

Menard, Russell. *Sweet Negotiations: Sugar, Slavery, and Plantation Agriculture in Early Barbados.* Charlottesville: University of Virginia Press, 2006.

Merrell, James. *The Indians' New World: Catawbas and Their Neighbors from European Contact through the Era of Removal.* Chapel Hill: University of North Carolina, 1989.

Meuwese, Mark. *Brothers in Arms, Partners in Trade: Dutch-Indigenous Alliances in the Atlantic World, 1595–1674.* Leiden, the Netherlands: Brill, 2012.

Miller, Adam S. *Discovering a Lost Heritage: The Catholic Origins of America.* Monrovia: Marian Publications, 2006.

Minter, R. A. *Episcopacy without Episcopate: The Church of England in Jamaica before 1824.* Upton-upon-Severn, U.K.: Self-Publishing Association, 1990.

Mintz, Sidney W. *Sweetness and Power: The Place of Sugar in Modern History.* New York: Viking Penguin, 1985.

Miquelon, Dale. *Dugard of Rouen: French Trade to Canada and the West Indies, 1729–1770.* Montréal: McGill-Queen's University Press, 1978.

Montbrun, Christian. *Les Petites Antilles avant Christophe Colomb. Vie quotidienne des Indiens de la Guadeloupe.* Paris: Karthala, 1984.

Moreau, Jean-Pierre. "De la flibuste nord-européenne à la flibuste antillaise. L'exemple français 1504–1625." In *Dans le sillage de Colomb. L'Europe du Ponant et la découverte du Nouveau Monde (1450–1650), Actes du Colloque International, Université Rennes 2, 5, 6 et 7 mai 1992,* edited by Jean-Pierre Sanchez, 119–24. Rennes, France: Presses Universitaires de Rennes, 1995.

Moreau de Saint-Méry, M. L. E. [Médéric Louis Elie]. *Loix et constitutions des colonies françoises de l'Amérique sous le vent.* 6 vols. Paris, 1784.

Mulcahy, Matthew. *Hubs of Empire: The Southeastern Lowcountry and British Caribbean.* Baltimore: Johns Hopkins University Press, 2014.

———. "The Port Royal Earthquake and the World of Wonders in Seventeenth-Century Jamaica." *Early American Studies* 8, no. 2 (2008): 391–421.

Muller, Kim Isolde. *Elisabeth van der Woude: Memorije van 't geen bij mijn tijt is voorgevallen. Met het opzienbarende verslag van haar reis naar de Wilde Kust, 1676–1677.* Amsterdam: Terra Incognita, 2001.

Nash, Gary B. *Quakers and Politics: Pennsylvania, 1691–1726.* Princeton: Princeton University Press, 1968.

Naum, Magdalena, and Jonas M. Nordin, eds. *Scandinavian Colonialism and the Rise of Modernity. Small Time Agents in a Global Arena.* New York: Springer, 2013.

Netscher, P. M. *Geschiedenis van de koloniën Essequebo, Demerary en Berbice, van de vestiging der Nederlanders aldaar tot op onzen tijd.* The Hague: M. Nijhoff, 1888.

Newman, Simon. *A New World of Labor: The Development of Plantation Slavery in the British Atlantic.* Philadelphia: University of Pennsylvania Press, 2013.

Nicholson, D. V. "The Legend of Ding-a-Dong Nook." *History and Archaeological Society Museum of Antigua and Barbuda Newsletter,* no. 112 (January, February, March 2011): 9–11.

O'Callaghan, E. B., and Berthold Ferlow, eds. *Documents Related to the Colonial History of the State of New York.* 15 vols. Albany, N.Y. 1856–1887.

Ó Ciardha, Éamonn. "Tories and Moss-troopers in Scotland and Ireland in the Interregnum: A Political Dimension." In *Celtic Dimensions of the British Civil Wars,* edited by John R. Young, 143–63. Edinburgh: John Donald, 1997.

Oliver, Vere Langford. *The History of the Island of Antigua.* 3 vols. London: Mitchell and Hughes, 1899.

Olsen, Poul. "Slavery and the Law in the Danish West Indies." In *Negotiating Enslavement. Perspectives on Slavery in the Danish West Indies,* edited by Arnold R. Highfield and George F. Tyson, 1–14. St. Croix, Virgin Islands: Antilles Press, 2009.

———. "Sørøvere i Vestindien." *Siden Saxo* 20, no. 1 (2003): 5–9.

Olsen, Poul, ed. *Vest indien*. Copenhagen: Gads Forlag, 2017.

Oostindie, Gert, and Jessica Vance Roitman. "Repositioning the Dutch in the Atlantic, 1680–1800." *Itinerario* 36, no. 2 (2012): 129–60.

Oostindie, Gert, and Alex van Stipriaan. "Slavery and Slave Cultures in a Hydraulic Society: Suriname." In *Slavery and Slave Cultures in the Americas,* edited by Stephan Palmié, 78–99. Knoxville: University of Tennessee Press, 1996.

Oppenheim, Samuel. "An Early Jewish Colony in Western Guyana, 1658–1666: And Its Relation to the Jews in Surinam, Cayenne and Tobago." *Publications of the American Jewish Historical Society* 16 (1907): 75–186.

———. "An Early Jewish Colony in Western Guyana: Supplemental Data." *Publications of the American Jewish Historical Society* 17 (1909): 53–70.

Padrón, Francisco Morales. *Spanish Jamaica*. Translated by Patrick Bryan. 1953. Reprint, Kingston, Jamaica: Ian Randle, 2003.

Pagden, Anthony. *European Encounters with the New World: From Renaissance to Romanticism*. New Haven: Yale University Press, 1993.

———. *Lords of All the World: Ideologies of Empire in Spain, Britain and France, c. 1500–c. 1800*. New Haven: Yale University Press, 1995.

———. *Peoples and Empires: A Short History of European Migration, Exploration, and Conquest*. New York: Random House, 2007.

———. "Plus Ultra: America and the Changing European Notions of Time and Space." In *Early Modern History and the Social Sciences: Testing the Limits of Braudel's Mediterranean,* edited by John A. Marino, 255–73. Kirksville, Mo.: Truman State University Press, 2002.

Panhuysen, Luc. *Rampjaar 1672: Hoe de Republiek aan de ondergang ontsnapte*. Amsterdam: Atlas-Contact, 2009.

Pannet, Pierre J. *Report on the Execrable Conspiracy Carried out by the Amina Negroes on the Danish Island of St. Jan in America, 1733*. Edited by Aimery P. Caron and Arnold R. Highfield. St. Croix, Virgin Islands: Antilles Press, 1984.

Paquette, Robert L., and Stanley L. Engerman, eds. *The Lesser Antilles in the Age of European Expansion*. Gainesville: University Press of Florida, 2001.

Parker, Geoffrey. *Philip II*. Boston: Little, Brown, 1978.

Parmenter, Jon. *Edge of the Woods: Iroquoia, 1534–1701*. East Lansing: Michigan State University Press, 2010.

Parry, J. H. "Plantation and Provision Ground: An Historical Sketch of the Introduction of Food Crops into Jamaica." *Revista de Historia de América*, no. 39 (June 1955): 1–20.

Patterson, Orlando. "Slavery and Slave Revolts: A Socio-Historical Analysis of the First Maroon War, 1655–1740." *Social and Economic Studies* 19, no. 3 (1970): 289–325.

Pawson, Michael, and David Buisseret. *Port Royal, Jamaica*. Rev. ed. Kingston, Jamaica: University of the West Indies Press, 2000.

Pearsall, Sarah M. S. *Atlantic Families: Lives and Letters in the Later Eighteenth Century*. Oxford, U.K.: Oxford University Press, 2008.

Pencak, William. *Historical Dictionary of Colonial America*. Lanham, Md.: Scarecrow Press, 2011.

Pérez-Mallaína, Pablo. *Spain's Men of the Sea: Daily Life on the Indies Fleets in the Sixteenth Century*. Translated by Carla Rahn Phillips. Baltimore: Johns Hopkins University Press, 1998.

Pérotin-Dumon, Anne. *Être patriote sous les tropiques: la Guadeloupe, la colonisation et la Révolution (1789–1794)*. Basse-Terre: Société d'histoire de la Guadeloupe, 1985.

Pertinente beschrijvinge van Guiana. Geleen aen de vaste Kust van America. Amsterdam, 1676.

Pestana, Carla Gardina. "Early English Jamaica without Pirates." *William and Mary Quarterly*, 3rd ser., 71, no. 3 (2014): 321–60.

———. *The English Atlantic in an Age of Revolution, 1640–1661.* Cambridge, Mass.: Harvard University Press, 2004.

———. "English Character and the Fiasco of the Western Design." *Early American Studies* 3, no. 1 (2005): 1–31.

———. *Protestant Empire: Religion and the Making of the British Atlantic World.* Philadelphia: University of Pennsylvania Press, 2009.

Petit, Emilien. *Droit public; ou, Gouvernement des colonies françoises d'après les loix faites pour ces pays.* Paris, 1771.

Petit de Viévigne, Jacques, ed. *Code de La Martinique.* Saint-Pierre, Martinique: P. Richard, 1767. Available online at *Gallica:* http://gallica.bnf.fr/ark:/12148/bpt6k113036j.

Petitjean Roget, Jacques, ed. *L'histoire de l'Isle de Grenade en Amérique, 1649–1659. Manuscrit anonyme de 1659.* Montréal: Les Presses Universitaires de Montréal, 1975.

Phillips, Carla Rahn. *Six Galleons for the King of Spain: Imperial Defense in the Early Seventeenth Century.* Baltimore: Johns Hopkins University Press, 1986.

Pincus, Steven C. A. *Protestantism and Patriotism: Ideologies and the Making of English Foreign Policy, 1650–1668.* Cambridge, U.K.: Cambridge University Press, 1996.

Pollet, Georges. "Saint-Domingue et l'autonomie (1629–1730)." Ph.D. diss., University of Paris, 1934.

Postma, Johannes. *The Dutch in the Atlantic Slave Trade, 1600–1815.* Cambridge, U.K.: Cambridge University Press, 1990.

Powell, J. R. *The Navy in the English Civil War.* Hamden, Conn.: Archon, 1962.

Powell, J. R., and Edward Timings, eds. *Documents Relating to the Civil War, 1642–1648.* London: Navy Records Society, 1963.

Powell, William S. "Carolana and the Incomparable Roanoke: Explorations and Attempted Settlements, 1620–1663." *North Carolina Historical Review* 51 (1974): 1–21.

Poyer, John. *The History of Barbados.* London: J. Mawman, 1808.

Price, Richard. "Caribbean Fishing and Fishermen: A Historical Sketch." *American Anthropologist* 68, no. 6 (1966): 1363–83.

Pritchard, James S. *In Search of Empire: The French in the Americas, 1670–1730.* Cambridge, U.K.: Cambridge University Press, 2004.

Ralegh, Sir Walter. *The Discovery of the Large, Rich, and Beautiful Empire of Guiana.* London, 1595.

Rampini, Charles Joseph Galliari. *Letters from Jamaica: The Land of Streams and Woods.* Edinburgh: Edmonston and Douglas, 1873.

Rashford, John. "Arawak, Spanish and African Contributions to Jamaica's Settlement Vegetation." *Jamaica Journal* 24, no. 3 (1993): 17–23.

Reyce, Robert. *Suffolk in the Seventeenth Century: The Breviary of Suffolk by Robert Reyce, 1618.* London, John Murray: 1902.

Richter, Daniel K. *Before the Revolution: America's Ancient Pasts.* Cambridge, Mass.: Harvard University Press, 2011.

Roberts, Justin. *Slavery and the Enlightenment in the British Atlantic, 1750–1807.* New York: Cambridge University Press, 2013.

———. "Surrendering Surinam: The Barbadian Diaspora and the Expansion of the English Sugar Frontier, 1650–75." *William and Mary Quarterly*, 3rd ser., 73, no. 2 (2016): 225–56.

Roberts, Justin, and Ian Beamish. "Venturing Out: The Barbadian Diaspora and the Carolina Colony, 1650–1685." In *Creating and Contesting Carolina: Proprietary Era Histories,* edited by Michelle LeMaster and Bradford J. Wood, 49–72. Columbia: University of South Carolina Press, 2013.

Robertson, James. "The Battle of Rio Nuevo." In *Rio Nuevo*, edited by Jonathan Greenland, 10–24. Kingston: Jamaica National Heritage Trust, 2009.

———. *Gone is the Ancient Glory: Spanish Town, Jamaica, 1534–2000.* Kingston, Jamaica: Ian Randle, 2005.

———. "Jamaican Architectures before Georgian." *Winterthur Portfolio* 36, no. 2/3 (2001): 73–95.

———. "Knowledgeable Readers: Jamaican Critiques of Hans Sloane's Botany." In *From Books to Bezoars: Sir Hans Sloane,* edited by Alison Walker, Arthur MacGregor, and Michael Hunter, 80–89. London: British Library, 2012.

———. "'The Land of the Spanish Negroes': Local Alliances and African Jamaican Landholders in Late Seventeenth-Century Jamaica." *Jamaican Historical Review* 27 (2016): 1–22.

———. "Late Seventeenth-Century Spanish Town, Jamaica: Building an English City on Spanish Foundations." *Early American Studies* 6, no. 2 (2008): 346–90.

———. "Re-inventing the English Conquest of Jamaica in the Late Seventeenth Century." *English Historical Review* 117, no. 473 (2002): 813–39.

———. "'Stories' and 'Histories' in Late-Seventeenth-Century Jamaica." In *Jamaica in Slavery and Freedom: History, Heritage and Culture,* edited by Kathleen E. A. Monteith and Glen Richards, 25–51. Kingston, Jamaica: University of the West Indies Press, 2002.

Rogers, Katharine M. "Fact and Fiction in Aphra Behn's 'Oroonoko.'" *Studies in the Novel* 20, no. 1 (1988): 1–15.

Rogers, Nini. "A Changing Presence: The Irish in the Caribbean in the Seventeenth and Eighteenth Centuries." In *Caribbean Irish Connections: Interdisciplinary Perspectives,* edited by Alison Donnell, Maria McGarrity, and Evelyn O'Callaghan, 17–32. Kingston, Jamaica: University of the West Indies Press, 2015.

Roitman, Jessica Vance. "Creating Confusion in the Colonies: Jews, Citizenship, and the Dutch and British Atlantics." *Itinerario* 36, no. 2 (2012): 55–90.

Romney, Susanah Shaw. "'If at First You Fail . . .': New Amsterdam in the Context of Catastrophic Colonies." Paper presented at the Omohundro Institute of Early American History and Culture/Society of Early Americanists Conference, Loyola University (Chicago), June 2015.

———. *New Netherland Connections: Intimate Networks and Atlantic Ties in Seventeenth-Century America.* Chapel Hill: University of North Carolina Press, 2014.

Rönnbäck, Klas. "Power, Plenty, and Pressure Groups: A Comparative Study of British and Danish Colonialism in the West Indies and the Role of the State, 1768–1772." *Journal of Early American History* 1, no. 3 (2011): 215–40.

Roper, L. H. "Big Fish in a Bigger Transatlantic Pond: The Social and Political Leadership of Early Modern Anglo-American Colonies." In *Les élites européennes dans les colonies du débat du XVIe siècle au milieu du XXe siècle,* edited by C. Laux, F-J. Ruggiu, and P. Singaravelou, 141–66. Brussels: Peter Lang, 2009.

———. *Conceiving Carolina: Proprietors, Planters, and Plots, 1662–1729.* New York: Palgrave Macmillan, 2004.

———. *The English Empire in America, 1602–1658: Beyond Jamestown.* London: Pickering and Chatto, 2009.

———. "The Fall of New Netherland and Seventeenth-Century Anglo-American Imperial Formation, 1654–1676." *New England Quarterly* 87, no. 4 (2014): 666–708.

———. "The 1701 'Act for the Better Ordering of Slaves': Reconsidering the History of Slavery in Proprietary South Carolina." *William and Mary Quarterly,* 3rd ser., 64 (April 2007): 395–418.

Roper, L. H., and Bertrand Van Ruymbeke, eds. *Constructing Early Modern Empires: Proprietary Ventures in the Atlantic World, 1500–1750.* Leiden, the Netherlands: Brill, 2007.

Routledge, F. J., ed. *Calendar of the Clarendon State Papers Preserved in the Bodleian Library.* 5 vols. Oxford, U.K.: Clarendon Press, 1970.

Rupert, Linda M. *Creolization and Contraband: Curacao in the Early Modern Atlantic World.* Athens: University of Georgia Press, 2012.

Rushforth, Brett. *Bonds of Alliance: Indigenous and Atlantic Slaveries in New France.* Chapel Hill: University of North Carolina Press, 2012.

Sainsbury, Ethel Bruce. *A Calendar of the Court Minutes of the East India Company, 1660–1663.* Oxford, U.K.: Clarendon Press, 1922.

Sainton, Jean-Pierre. *Histoire et Civilisation de la Caraibe.* Vol. 1, *Le Temps des Genèses; Des Origines à 1685.* Paris: Éditions Maisonneuve et Larose, 2004.

Samuel, Edgar. "Antonio Rodrigues Robles, c. 1620–1688." *Jewish Historical Studies* 37 (2001): 113–15.

Sanchez, Jean-Pierre, ed. *Dans le sillage de Colomb. L'Europe du Ponant et la découverte du Nouveau Monde (1450–1650), Actes du Colloque International, Université Rennes 2, 5, 6 et 7 mai 1992.* Rennes, France: Presses Universitaires de Rennes, 1995.

Sandford, Robert. "A Relation of a Voyage on the Coast of the Province of Carolina, 1666." In *Narratives of Early Carolina, 1650–1708,* edited by Alexander S. Salley, Jr., 75–108. 1911. Reprint, New York: Barnes and Noble, 1967.

———. *Suriname Justice.* London, 1662.

Satchell, Veront M. *Hope Transformed: A Historical Sketch of the Hope Landscape, St. Andrew, Jamaica, 1660–1960.* Kingston, Jamaica: University of the West Indies Press, 2012.

Sauer, Carl Ortwin. *The Early Spanish Main.* New York: Oxford University Press, 1966.

Saunders, William L., ed. *The Colonial Records of North Carolina.* 10 vols. Raleigh, N.C.: Josephus Daniels, 1886–1890.

Schalkwijk, J. Marten, *The Colonial State in the Caribbean: Structural Analysis and Changing Elite Networks in Suriname, 1650–1920.* The Hague: Amrit, 2011.

Schiltkamp, J. A. "On Common Ground: Legislation, Government, Jurisprudence and Law in the Dutch West Indian Colonies: The Order of Government of 1629." *De Halve Maen* 70, no. 4 (1997): 73–80.

Schiltkamp, J. A., and J. Th. de Smidt, eds. *West Indische Plakaatboek: Plakaten, Ordonnantiën en andere wetten, uitgevaardign in Surinamee 1, 1667–1761.* Amsterdam: S. Emmering, 1973.

Schmidt, Benjamin. *Innocence Abroad: The Dutch Imagination and the New World, 1570–1670.* Cambridge, U.K.: Cambridge University Press, 2001.

———. Introduction. *The Discovery of Guiana by Sir Walter Ralegh with Related Documents,* edited by Schmidt, 1–44. Boston: Bedford/St. Martin's, 2008.

Schmitt, Eberhard. "The Brandenburg Overseas Trading Companies in the 17th Century." In *Companies and Trade,* edited by Leonard Blussé and Femme Gaastra, 159–76. Leiden, the Netherlands: Brill, 1981.

Schwartz, Stuart B. "Looking for a New Brazil: Crisis and Rebirth in the Atlantic World after the Fall of Pernambuco." In *The Legacy of Dutch Brazil,* edited by Michiel van Groesen, 41–58. New York: Cambridge University Press, 2014.

———. *Sugar Plantations in the Formation of Brazilian Society.* New York: Cambridge University Press, 1985.

Scott, Rebecca J., and Jean M. Hébrard. *Freedom Papers: An Atlantic Odyssey in the Age of Emancipation.* Cambridge, Mass.: Harvard University Press, 2012.

Sebro, Louise. "Freedom, Autonomy, and Independence: African Caribbean Performances of the Exceptional in St. Thomas, the Danish West Indies in the Middle of the 18th

Century." In *Ports of Globalisation, Places of Creolisation: Nordic Possessions in the Atlantic World during the Era of the Slave Trade,* edited by Holger Weiss, 218–44. Leiden, the Netherlands: Brill, 2015.

———. "The 1733 Slave Revolt on the Island of St. John: Continuity and Change from Africa to the Americas." In *Scandinavian Colonialism and the Rise of Modernity: Small Time Agents in a Global Arena,* edited by Magdalena Naum and Jonas M. Nordin, 261–74. New York: Springer, 2013.

Shaw, Jenny. *Everyday Life in the English Caribbean: Irish, Africans, and the Construction of Difference.* Athens: University of Georgia Press, 2013.

Sheridan, Richard B. "Eric Williams and Capitalism and Slavery: A Biographical and Historiographical Essay." In *British Capitalism and Caribbean Slavery: The Legacy of Eric Williams,* edited by Barbara L. Solow and Stanley L. Engerman, 317–45. New York: Cambridge University Press, 1987.

———. *Sugar and Slavery: An Economic History of the British West Indies, 1623–1775.* Baltimore: Johns Hopkins University Press, 1974.

Shoemaker, Nancy. "A Typology of Colonialism." *Perspectives on History* 53, no. 7 (2015): https://www.historians.org/publications-and-directories/perspectives-on-history/october -2015/a-typology-of-colonialism.

Sieveking, Heinrich. "Die Glückstädter Guineafahrt im 17. Jahrhundert. Ein Stück deutscher Kolonialgeschichte." *Vierteljahrschrift für Sozial und Wirtscahftsgeschichte* 30 (1937): 19–71.

Sloan, Kim, ed. *A New World: England's First View of America.* London: British Museum Press, 2007.

Sloane, Hans. *A Voyage to the Islands of Madeira, Barbados, Nieves, S. Christopher and Jamaica, with the Natural History of the Herbs and Trees, Four-footed Beasts, Fishes, Birds, Insects, Reptiles, &c. of the Last of Those Islands.* 2 vols. London, 1707–1725.

Smith, Adam. *An Inquiry into the Nature and Causes of the Wealth of Nations.* Edited by R. H. Campbell and A. S. Skinner. 2 vols. Oxford, U.K.: Oxford University Press, 1976.

Smith, Geoffrey. "Royalists in Exile: The Experience of Daniel O'Neill." In *Royalists and Royalism during the Interregnum,* edited by Jason McElligott and David L. Smith, 106–28. Manchester, U.K.: Manchester University Press, 2010.

Smith, John. *The True Travels, Adventures, And Observations Of Captaine John Smith.* London, 1630.

Smith, S. D. *Slavery, Family, and Gentry Capitalism in the British Atlantic: The World of the Lascelles, 1648–1834.* Cambridge, U.K.: Cambridge University Press, 2006.

Snyder, Amanda J. "Pirates, Exiles, and Empire." Ph.D. diss., Florida International University, 2013.

Solow, Barbara, and Stanley L. Engerman. "British Capitalism and Caribbean Slavery: The Legacy of Eric Williams; An Introduction." In *British Capitalism and Caribbean Slavery: The Legacy of Eric Williams,* edited by Solow and Engerman, 1–23. New York: Cambridge University Press, 1987.

Sooman, Imbi, Jesma McFarlane, Valdis Tēraudkalns, and Stefan Donecker. "From the Port of Ventspils to Great Courland Bay: The Couronian Colony on Tobago in Past and Present." *Journal of Baltic Studies* 44, no. 4 (2013): 503–26.

Spieler, Miranda Frances. *Empire and Underworld: Captivity in French Guiana.* Cambridge, Mass.: Harvard University Press, 2012.

Spurr, John. "Shaftesbury and the Politics of Religion." In *Anthony Ashley Cooper, First Earl of Shaftesbury, 1621–1683,* edited by John Spurr, 127–52. Farnham, U.K.: Ashgate, 2011.

Stavans, Ilan. *The Scroll and the Cross: 1,000 Years of Jewish-Hispanic Literature.* New York: Routledge, 2003.

Stein, Tristan. "Tangier in the Restoration Empire." *Historical Journal* 54, no. 4 (2011): 985–1011.

Stick, David. *Roanoke Island: The Beginnings of English America.* Chapel Hill: University of North Carolina Press, 1983.

Stiefel, Barry L. *Jewish Sanctuary in the Atlantic World: A Social and Architectural History.* Columbia: University of South Carolina Press, 2014.

Stow, John. *Survey of the Citties of London and Westminster.* London, 1598.

Stubbs, Henry. *The Indian Nectar, Or a Discourse Concerning Chocolata.* London, 1662.

Stradling, R. A. *The Armada of Flanders: Spanish Maritime Policy and European War, 1568– 1668.* Cambridge, U.K.: Cambridge University Press, 1992.

———. *Philip IV and the Government of Spain, 1621–1665.* New York: Cambridge University Press, 1988.

Symcox, Geoffrey. *The Crisis of the French Sea Power, 1688–1697 from the "Guerre d'Escadre" to the "Guerre de Course."* The Hague: M. Nijhoff, 1974.

Taylor, S. A. G. *The Western Design: An Account of Cromwell's Expedition to the Caribbean.* Kingston: Institute of Jamaica and Jamaica Historical Society, 1965.

Taylor, S. A. G., and David Buisseret. "Juan de Bolas and His Pelinco." *Caribbean Quarterly* 24, nos. 1, 2 (1978): 1–7.

Ten Hoorn, Jan Claesz. *Pertinente Beschrijvinge van Guyana Gelegen aen de vaste Kust van America . . . Hier is bygevoeght Der Participanten uytschot ende profijten, die daer uyt volgen staen. Also oock de conditien van . . . de Staten van Hollandt . . . voor die gene die nae Guyana begeeren te varen.* Amsterdam, 1676.

Ternaux-Compans, H. *Notice historique sur la Guyana française.* Paris: Firman Didot frères, 1843.

Terrell, Michelle M. *The Jewish Community of Early Colonial Nevis: A Historical Archaeological Study.* Gainesville: University Press of Florida, 2005.

Thibault de Chanvalon, Jean-Baptiste. *Voyage à la Martinique, contenant diverses Observations sur la Physique, l'Histoire Naturelle, l'Agriculture, les Moeurs, & les Usages de cette Isle, faites en 1751 & dans les années suivantes.* Paris, 1763.

Thornton, A. P. *West-India Policy under the Restoration.* Oxford, U.K.: Oxford University Press, 1956.

Thorpe, Francis N. *The Federal and State Constitutions, Colonial Charters, and Other Organic Laws of the States, Territories, and Colonies Now or Heretofore Forming the United States of America.* Vol. 5. Washington, D.C.: Government Printing Office, 1909.

Todd, Janet. *The Secret Life of Aphra Behn.* New Brunswick: Rutgers University Press, 1996.

United States Commission on the Boundary between Venezuela and British Guiana. *Report and Accompanying Papers of the Commission Appointed by the President of the United States "To Investigate and Report Upon the True Divisional Line between the Republic of Venezuela and British Guiana."* 2 vols. Washington: Government Printing Office, 1897.

Van Alphen, G. *Jan Reeps en zijn onbekende kolonisatiepoging in Zuid-Amerika 1692.* Assen, the Netherlands: Van Gorcum, 1960.

Van der Meiden, G. W. *Betwist bestuur: een eeuw strijd om de macht in Suriname 1651–1753.* Amsterdam: De Bataafsche Leeuw, 1987.

Van der Oest, E. W. "The Forgotten Colonies of Essequibo and Demerara, 1700–1814." In *Riches from Atlantic Commerce: Dutch Transatlantic Trade and Shipping, 1585–1817,* edited by Johannes Postma and Victor Enthoven, 325–61. Leiden, the Netherlands: Brill, 2003.

Van der Woude, Elisabeth. *Memorije van 't geen bij mijn tijt is vorgevallen soo in hollant als op ander plaetsen.* Noord-Hollands Archief, Haarlem, the Netherlands, 142 Collectie Semeijns de Vries van Doesburgh, 816.

Van Meeteren, E. *Historie der Nederlandschen ende haerder naburen oorlogen ende geschiedenissen.* The Hague, 1614.

Van Rees, O. *Geschiedenis der staathuishoudkunde in Nederland tot het einde der achttiende eeuw.* Vol. 2. Utrecht, the Netherlands: Kemick en Zoon, 1868.

Venning, Timothy. *Cromwellian Foreign Policy.* London: Macmillan, 1995.

Vernooij, Joop. "Godt niet meer Engels maer geheel Zeeuws. Jan Basseliers, kerk en slavernij." In *Zeeland. T'dschrift van het Koninkl'k Zeeuwsch Genootschap der Wetenschappen* 14, no. 1 (2005): 3–12.

Verrand, Laurence. *La Vie quotidienne des Indiens Caraïbes aux Petites Antilles (XVIIème siècle).* Paris: Karthala, 2001.

Viage, y sucesso de los carauelones, galeoncetes de la guarda de Cartagena de las Indias, y su costa.: Y la grandiosa vitoria que han tenido contra los costarios piratas y aquel mar, este año 1621. los qales en el hazian grandes robos, y por esto cessauan las contrataciones, con gran daño de las costas y vezinos de tierrafirme. Barcelona, 1621.

Villiers, Patrick. *Marine royale, corsaires et trafic dans l'Atlantique de Louis XIV à Louis XVI.* Dunkirk: Société Dunkerquoise d'Histoire et d'Archéologie, 1991.

Villiers, Patrick, and Pascal Cullerrier. "Du système des classes à l'inscription maritime, le recrutement des marines français de Louis XIV à 1952." *Revue Historique des Armées* 2, no. 147 (1982): 44–53.

Virol, Michèle. *Vauban: de la gloire du roi au service de l'Etat.* Paris: Vallon, 2003.

Visconsi, Elliott. "A Degenerate Race: English Barbarism in Aphra Behn's 'Oroonoko' and 'the Window Ranter.'" *ELH* 69, no. 3 (2002): 673–701.

Wall, Robert E. *Massachusetts Bay: The Crucial Decade, 1640–1650.* New Haven: Yale University Press, 1972.

Wallace, Vickie. "A List of Participants in the Roanoke Voyages." *Fort Raleigh National Historic Site.* http://www.nps.gov/fora/forteachers/a-list-of-participants-in-the-roanoke-voyages.htm.

Warren, George. *An Impartial Description of Suriname upon the Continent of Guiana in America with a History of Several Strange Beasts, Birds, Fishes, Serpents.* London, 1667.

Warsh, Molly. "Enslaved Pearl Divers in the Sixteenth Century Caribbean." *Slavery and Abolition* 31, no. 3 (2010): 345–62.

Watts, Arthur P. *Une Histoire des Colonies Anglaises aux Antilles (de 1649 à 1660).* Paris: Presses Universitaires de France, 1924.

Watts, David. *The West Indies: Patterns of Development, Culture and Environmental Change since 1492.* Cambridge, U.K.: Cambridge University Press, 1987.

Webb, Stephen Saunders. *The Governors-General: The English Army and the Definition of the Empire, 1569–1681.* Chapel Hill: University of North Carolina Press, 1979.

Westergaard, Waldemar. *The Danish West Indies under Company Rule, 1671–1754.* New York: Macmillan, 1917.

Weterings, Tom. "Rampjaar aan de Rivier: Zeeuws Suriname in brieven van kolonisten, December 1671-September 1672." M.A. thesis, University of Amsterdam, 2009.

———. "Should We Stay or Should We Go? Being on Opposing Sides after a Colonial Takeover." *Journal of Early American History* 4, no. 2 (2014): 130–48.

———. "Zeeuws Suriname, 1667–1683." *OSO, Tijdschrift voor Surinamistiek* 30, no. 2 (2011): 338–55.

Whitehead, Neil L. "Carib Ethnic Soldiering in Venezuela, the Guianas, and the Antilles, 1492–1820." *Ethnohistory* 37, no. 4 (1990): 357–85.

———, ed. *The Discoverie of the Large, Rich, and Bewtiful Empyre of Guiana by Sir Walter Ralegh.* Norman: University of Oklahoma Press, 1998.

————. "Native Peoples Confront Colonial Regimes in Northeastern South America (c.1500–1900)." In *The Cambridge History of the Native Peoples of the Americas*, vol. 3, *South America*, part 2, edited by Frank Salomon and Stuart Schwartz, 382–442. Cambridge, U.K.: Cambridge University Press, 1999.

Whitson, Agnes M. *The Constitutional Development of Jamaica, 1660 to 1729*. Manchester, U.K.: Manchester University Press, 1929.

Wilensky, M. "The Royalist Position Concerning the Readmission of Jews to England." *Jewish Quarterly Review*, n.s., 41, no. 4 (1951): 397–409.

Williams, Eric. *Capitalism and Slavery*. Chapel Hill: University of North Carolina Press, 1944.

Williamson, James A. *English Colonies in Guiana and on the Amazon, 1604–1668*. Oxford, U.K.: Oxford University Press, 1923.

Wilson, Samuel M. "Surviving European Conquest in the Caribbean." *Revista de Arqueologia Americana* 12 (January 1997): 141–60.

Wolinetz, Gary K. "New Jersey Slavery and the Law." *Rutgers Law Review* 50 (1998): 2227–58.

Wood, Laurie M. "Archipelago of Justice: Law in France's Early Modern Empire." Book manuscript in progress.

Wood, Peter H. *Black Majority: Negroes in Colonial South Carolina from 1670 through the Stono Rebellion*. New York: W. W. Norton, 1974.

Wright, Irene A. *Documents Concerning English Voyages to the Spanish Main, 1569–1580*. London: Hakluyt Society, 1932.

————. *Spanish Documents Concerning English Voyages to the Caribbean, 1527–1568*. London: Hakluyt Society, 1929.

————. "The Spanish Resistance to the English Occupation of Jamaica, 1655–1660." *Transactions of the Royal Historical Society*, 4th ser., 13 (1930): 117–47.

Zacek, Natalie. *Settler Society in the English Leeward Islands, 1670–1776*. Cambridge, U.K.: Cambridge University Press, 2010.

Zahedieh, Nuala, *The Capital and the Colonies: London and the Atlantic Economy, 1660–1700*. Cambridge, U.K.: Cambridge University Press, 2010.

————. "Trade, Plunder, and the Economic Development in Early English Jamaica, 1655–89." *Economic History Review*, 2nd ser., 39, no. 2 (1986): 205–22.

————. "'The Wickedest City in the World': Port Royal, Commercial Hub of the Seventeenth century Caribbean." In *Working Slavery, Pricing Freedom: Perspectives from the Caribbean, Africa and the African Diaspora*, edited by Verene Shepherd, 29–47. Kingston, Jamaica: Ian Randle, 2002.

Zijlstra, Suze. "Anglo-Dutch Suriname: Ethnic Interaction and Colonial Transition in the Caribbean, 1651–1682." Ph.D. diss., University of Amsterdam, 2015.

————. "Competing for European Settlers: Local Loyalties of Colonial Governments in Suriname and Jamaica, 1660–1680." *Journal of Early American History* 4, no. 2 (2014): 149–66.

————. "Om te sien of ick een wijf kan krijge." M.A. thesis, University of Amsterdam 2009.

Zook, George Frederick. "The Company of Royal Adventurers Trading into Africa." Ph.D. diss., Cornell University, 1919.

Contributors

CAROLYN ARENA earned her Ph.D. in International and Global History at Columbia University in 2017. She is a scholar of the indigenous Caribbean and of English and Dutch colonial expansion in the Atlantic. She is currently revising her dissertation as a book manuscript to be entitled "Caribana," which conceptualizes indigenous space in the Caribbean as both a site of resistance to colonization and the enslavement of Native peoples, at the Omohundro Institute of Early American History and Culture in Williamsburg, Virginia, where she is 2017–19 OEIAHC-National Endowment for the Humanities Postdoctoral Fellow. Her research has been funded through FLAS, the Folger Shakespeare Library, and a Fulbright Fellowship to the Netherlands, where she was a guest researcher at the University of Amsterdam.

SARAH BARBER is a senior lecturer in history at Lancaster University. Her focus in recent years has been on the ways in which reconstructing the manuscript sources for the Anglophone Caribbean in the long seventeenth century revise our traditional picture of the Torrid Zone. She has discussed issues of content and curation in various articles and in the first full-length treatment, *The Disputatious Caribbean: The West Indies in the Seventeenth Century* (Palgrave, 2014). Her next contribution will be an edition of manuscript sources dealing with the greater Caribbean in the period, drawn from the United States, Caribbean and Europe, to be published within the British Academy Records of Social and Economic History Series. Her current thinking is about a trans-locational exploration of planting as a means to define English people's relationship with the land, of which this study of indigenous people, plants, and Anglophone claims to Native right forms an exploratory part.

ERIK GØBEL, born 1949, is a historian and a senior researcher at the Danish National Archives. He has published extensively in Danish, especially on economic and social history. He is an expert on maritime history and the history of Denmark's former colonies in Asia, Africa, and America. His books in English include *A Guide to Sources for the History of the Danish West Indies (U. S. Virgin Islands), 1671–1917* (2002) and *The Danish Slave Trade and its Abolition* (Brill, 2016). His personal website is http://pure-01.kb.dk/portal/da/persons/erik -goebel(a48d55ef-8129–457c-97ab-fb052bb1f274).html.

TESSA MURPHY is assistant professor of early American history at Syracuse University. Her research, which focuses on early America and the colonial Caribbean, has been supported by organizations including the Social Sciences and Humanities Research Council of Canada, France's *Institut National d'Études Démographiques*, the Quinn Foundation, and the John Carter Brown Library.

JAMES ROBERTSON is professor of history in the Department of History and Archaeology at the University of the West Indies, Mona, where has taught since 1995. Before then he taught at Washington University, St. Louis, and Beloit College. His *Gone is the Ancient Glory! Spanish Town, Jamaica, 1535–2000* was published in 2005 by Ian Randle in Kingston. He is currently working on the Western Design and its consequences. A fellow of the Royal Historical Society, he is president of the Archaeological Society of Jamaica, vice-president of the Jamaican Historical Society, and, since December 2015, editor of the *Jamaican Historical Review.*

JESSICA VANCE ROITMAN is assistant professor at the University of Leiden's Institute of History and a researcher at the Royal Netherlands Institute of Southeast Asian and Caribbean Studies (KITLV), working on Caribbean History. Roitman received her B.A. in religion at Maryville College *(magna cum laude)*, an M.A. in Latin American studies from Vanderbilt University *(magna cum laude)*, and a Ph.D. in history from the University of Leiden in 2009 with a dissertation on intercultural trade and the Sephardim in the early seventeenth century. She was a fellow at the Katz Center for Advanced Judaic Studies at the University of Pennsylvania and the recipient of a Dutch Research Council–funded postdoctoral fellowship at Birkbeck College, University of London. Roitman has worked on diverse topics including intercultural trade, networks and network failure, comparative migration histories, the construction of identities and ethnicities, trans-nationality, conflict resolution, cross-cultural encounters, and the dynamics of colonial lawmaking.

L. H. ROPER is professor of history at the State University of New York—New Paltz and co-general editor of the *Journal of Early American History.* He is the author of *Advancing Empire: English Interests and Overseas Expansion: 1613–1688* (Cambridge University Press, 2017); *Conceiving Carolina: Proprietors, Planters, and Plots* (Palgrave Macmillan, 2004); and *The English Empire in America, 1602–1658: Beyond Jamestown* (Pickering and Chatto, 2009), co-editor (with Bertrand Van Ruymbeke) of *Constructing Early Modern Empires: Proprietary Ventures in the Atlantic World, 1500–1750* (Brill, 2007) and *The Worlds of the Seventeenth-Century Hudson Valley* with Jaap Jacobs (SUNY Press, 2014) as well as articles and essays on the seventeenth-century English Empire.

AMANDA J. SNYDER is lecturer in the Department of History at the University of Central Florida. She has worked at various archives in England and Spain, and has served as an Ahmanson-Getty Fellow with UCLA's Center for 17th- and 18th-Century Studies, as well as a postdoctoral associate for Florida International University's Writing in History Program. She is currently working on a manuscript tentatively titled "Pirates, Exiles, and Empire: Criminality and Identity in the Atlantic World." She teaches courses on Atlantic Empires, Constructing Identity in the New World, and Frontiers and Borderlands in the Atlantic World and Colonial Americas.

BARRY L. STIEFEL is an associate professor in the Historic Preservation and Community Planning program at the College of Charleston. He completed his Ph.D. in historic preservation from Tulane University, where he developed an interest in the preservation of Atlantic World heritages. Stiefel has published numerous articles and books, including *Jewish Sanctuary in the Atlantic World: A Social and Architectural History* (University of South Carolina Press, 2014), which was the recipient of the Hines Prize from the Carolina Lowcountry and Atlantic World Program.

GIOVANNI VENEGONI received his Ph.D. from the University of Bologna (Italy) and Paris-Sorbonne University (France), where he studied the evolution of balances of power and informal relationships in the population of Saint-Domingue. He then moved to Geneva, where he investigated customer behaviors and informal markets. He is now senior researcher and projects coordinator at the Milan Center for Food Law and Policy. His research interests include informal groups and their role in shaping society.

Contributors

TOM WETERINGS studied medieval and early modern history at Leiden University and editing at the University of Amsterdam, attaining his master's degrees in 2007 and 2009, respectively. His thesis on letters from early Dutch settlers in Suriname won the Flemish-Dutch Award for Text Edition in 2009. He has worked on Dutch texts from all over the world, including from New Netherland, and has published on Caribbean and Dutch history. He currently works for an academic publisher and as an independent researcher.

LAURIE M. WOOD is a historian of the early modern world, and her research focuses on law and Francophone history in comparative and global perspectives. She is currently assistant professor of history at Florida State University, where she teaches courses in Atlantic, Indian Ocean, and world history that bring together the early modern and twenty-first-century worlds. She holds a doctorate in history from the University of Texas at Austin and was the 2013–14 Law and Society Postdoctoral Fellow at the University of Wisconsin Law School.

SUZE ZIJLSTRA was appointed assistant professor of maritime history at Leiden University in 2016, after concluding a year as postdoctoral researcher at Georgetown University, where she focused on Anglo-Dutch colonialism in a global context. She received her Ph.D. at the University of Amsterdam in 2015, where she wrote a dissertation on interethnic encounters in seventeenth-century Suriname. She obtained her B.A. in history and religious studies at the same university, as well as a research M.A. in history. In 2010 she completed an M.A. in the Dutch Golden Age at University College London. She has received various scholarships for her studies and her postdoctoral work.

Index

Abrabenel, Rachel, wife of Rabbi Menasseh ben Israel, 169

Acadia, 138

Albemarle, George Monck, first Duke of, Carolina proprietor, 176, 181, 183

al-Nazir, Zidan, Sultan of Morocco, 164

Amazon River, 2, 34, 62, 63, 83. *See also* Guiana

Amsterdam: support of for colonization, 65; tobacco trade and, 34

Andrews, Richard Mowery, historian, 152

Antigua: incorporation of into Leeward Islands, 53; founding of English colony, 2, 20; relocation of Suriname planters to, 79–80; support of colonists for Charles II, 102–3. *See also* Kalinago; Second Anglo-Dutch War; servants; Sir William Stapleton; tobacco; Philip Warner

Antonelli, Juan Baptista, Spanish engineer, 100–101

Apricius, Johannes, Dutch cleric and colonizer, 64, 68, 74

Arawak (Indian nation), 4, 32; comparisons of by Europeans with Carib, 18; relations of with Carib, 42; relations of with Dutch, 40–41; relations of with English, 42

Arencibia, Juan de, Spanish military officer, 101

Arff, Nicolai Jansen, Danish slave trader, 121

Armada de la Guardia de la carrera de las Indias, 97, 99

Arnett, John, Barbados merchant, 36

Ashley, Lord, first Earl of Shaftesbury, Anthony Ashley Cooper, Carolina proprietor, 171, 176, 181, 182, 185, 186

Assier, Jean, Martinique councilor, 157

Atkins, Sir Jonathan, governor of Barbados, 53–54, 56

Auger, Charles, governor of Saint-Domingue, 137

Austen, Rebeccah, Suriname settler, 36

Avilés, Ménez de, Spanish admiral, 95

Ayscue, Sir George, and subjugation of Barbados and Virginia by, 35, 103, 184

Bacon, Francis, 157

Bailyn, Bernard, historian, 67, 70

Balboa, Vasco Nuñez de, Spanish explorer, 94

Bannister, James, 7, 80–82; success of family of in Jamaica, 117. *See also* Suriname; Zeeland

Barbados, 2, 3, 8, 9; Dutch trade with, 34–36; English territorial expansion in America and, 177–78, 180; founding of, 20, 48; importance of in seventeenth-century English Empire, 177; Indian trade and, 34, 35–36, 42–43; Jews in, 11–13; 36, 110, 168, 170–74; as model of Caribbean plantation society, 13; Native relations with, 4, 34, 54; piracy and, 98; population of, 12, 36; slavery in, 13, 35–36, 177–78; support of colonists for Charles II, 102–4; Suriname and, 35–36, 44, 71–72, 78–80, 83, 89, 184. *See also* Carib; Carolina; cotton; First Anglo-Dutch War; Guiana; indigo; Jamaica; servants; sugar; tobacco; transatlantic slave trade; Western Design

Barrington, Colonel Francis, Jamaica colonist, 108–9

Barrios, Daniel Levi de, Dutch-Jewish poet, 172

Baruch, Isaac Motes, Jewish merchant in Jamaica, 173

Batts, Nathaniel, Carolina settler, 179

Beaumont, Phillipe, missionary, 26, 27

Behn, Aphra: as Royalist spy, 31–32, 35, 40; as Suriname colonist, 31, 37–39. *See also* Oroonoko

Index

Index

Heijer den, Henk, historian, 67
Heins, Christopher, governor of St. Thomas, 125
Heinsius, Julius, Governor of Suriname, 44–45
Hélin, Jacques, French chronicler, 140
Henri IV, king of France, 1
Hilton, Captain William, explorer of Carolina coast, 180
Hispaniola, 1; connection of with Jamaica, 101–2, 104; enslavement of Natives in, 17; pirates and, 114, 145. *See also flibustiers;* Kalinago; Bartolomé de las Casas; Peace of Ryswick; Saint-Domingue; Western Design
Hondius, Jodocus, Dutch cartographer, 63
Hoüel, Charles, governor of Guadeloupe, 25–26
Hughes, Derek, literary scholar, 32
Huguenots: in Carolina, 183, 185; in Saint-Domingue, 10, 136; in Suriname, 87
Hulme, Peter, literary scholar, 18
hurricanes, 47, 48, 183
Hussey, Martin, Martinique official, 159–60
Hussey, Walter, Guadeloupe colonist, 159–60
Hyde, Lawrence, Suriname proprietor, 78

indigo: cultivation of in Barbados, 34; in Guiana, 63; in Jamaica, 113, 114; in Saint-Domingue, 141; in St. John, 122; in St. Thomas, 119
Ireland, 102, 108
Irish, 46; in Jamaica, 107; in Montserrat, 56; in Saint-Domingue, 10, 136, 159; in Suriname, 70
Israel, Rabbi Menasseh ben, 12, 169. *See also* Jews
Iversen, Jørgen, governor of St. Thomas, 119–21, 125

Jackson, William, English privateer, 9
Jamaica, 5–6; architecture of, 105, 112–13, 117; Church of England in, 117; coffee houses in, 111; earthquake of 1692 in, 116, 173; ecology of, 112–16; and English operations against Suriname, 83, 84; government of as English colony, 109, 116–17; hunting in, 8, 98, 110, 114; Jews and, 11, 109–10, 168–74; loss of and

decline of Spanish Empire, 7, 104, 106; mines and, 7, 115; pirates and, 94–98, 109, 110, 114, 137–38, 141; possibility of return to Spain of, 105–6, 109; Quakers in, 110; recruitment of settlers to, 107, 109–10, 171; relations of with Saint-Domingue, 10, 116, 136, 141; relocation of English Suriname colonists to, 88, 117; rice cultivation in, 8, 116; slavery in, 95, 105, 110, 114–16; smuggling in, 105, 109; as Spanish colony, 1, 94–102, 110–13; in Spanish historiography, 92, 94. *See also* cocoa; cotton; Cuba; Hispaniola; indigo; servants; sugar; Taíno; tamarind; tobacco; turtles; War of the League of Augsburg; Western Design
James I, king of England, naval policy of, 93–94
James II, king of England, 77
Jamestown, 166, 179
Jardif, François, pirate, 138
Jardin, Jean, translator, 25–26
Jeaffreson, John, St. Christopher's planter, 47, 50–51
Jews: and admission into Danish Empire, 167–68; and anti-Semitism, 168, 173–74; in Madras (Chennai), 172; readmission into England, 12, 168–75; situation of in Western Europe, 162–65, 174; support of for Western Design, 12, 168–69. *See also* Barbados; Berbice; Bermuda; Carolina; Cayenne; *conversos;* Curacao; Dutch Republic; Dutch West India Company; Essequibo; Guadeloupe; Jamaica; Louisiana; Martinique; Nevis; New Holland; St. Christopher's; Saint-Domingue; St. Eustatius; sugar; Suriname
Jews Relief Act (1858), 174
Johnson, Charles, pirate and chronicler, 140
Johnson, Edward, St. Christopher's settler, 50–51
Johnson, Sir Nathaniel, governor of the Leeward Islands and South Carolina, 178, 186
Joziau, Grandval Pierre, Martinique colonizer, 155

Kalinago (Indian nation): European characterizations of, 18, 21–23, 47; enslavement of by Spanish, 18; relations

Index

St. Thomas: Dutch presence in, 9, 119; establishment of Danish colony at, 9, 119; failure of initial Danish colony at, 119; Free Coloreds in, 127–28; government of, 120–22, 125, 127; and intercolonial trade, 120–21, 128–29; piracy and, 121; population of, 119; religion in, 125; slavery in, 119–20, 127–28; topography of, 118. *See also* cotton; indigo; ginger; Moravians; Puerto Rico; Saint-Domingue; servants; sugar; tobacco

St. Vincent and colonization of by Kalinago, 4, 19, 22–29. *See also* Guiana; Maroons

Saltonstall, Captain Charles, English mariner, 48

Salvador, Francis, Jewish planter in South Carolina, 175

Sandford, Robert, Suriname planter and Carolina colonizer, 184

Schimmelmann, Ernst, Danish finance minister, 129

Scot, William, English regicide and Suriname settler, 40

Scotland, 55, 107, 179. *See also* Jamaica, Stuarts Town

Scott, Major John, English chronicler and military commander, 40

Second Anglo-Dutch War (1665–67), 6, 12; and Antigua, 52; and Essequibo, 34, 40; and Montserrat, 52; and St. Christopher's, 52; and Suriname, 31–32, 41–42, 74, 78, 184. *See also* East Indies

servants: in Antigua, 54, 55; in Barbados, 177; in Carolina, 177, 178, 183, 185; in Cayenne, 61; in Jamaica, 108, 110, 114; in Martinique, 152; in St.   Christopher's, 56–57; in Saint-Domingue, 152; in St. Thomas, 125; in Suriname, 38, 44, 71, 89

Sharp, Benjamin, pirate, 121

Sheridan, Richard, historian, 3

slavery: as defining element in Caribbean historiography, 2–3. *See also* Barbados; Carolina; Grenada; Guadeloupe; Jamaica; Martinique; Maroons; St. Croix; Saint-Domingue; St. John; St. Thomas; Suriname

Sloane, Sir Hans, and observations of concerning Jamaica, 116

Smith, Adam, and views on Danish West Indies, 129–30

Smith, Captain John, English colonizer, 47

Smith, Erik Nielsen, Danish colonizer, 118–19

Smith, William, English mariner, 47, 50

Societiët van Suriname (Suriname Society), 65

Southwell, Sir Robert, English official, 56

Spanish Armada, 99, 102, 166

Stapleton, Sir William, governor of the Leeward Islands, 5, 53, 54–56

Stuarts Town, Scottish colony in Carolina, 186

sugar: cultivation of in Barbados, 36, 168, 177; in Cuba, 74; in Danish West Indies, 118, 126, 129; as defining element in Caribbean historiography, 2–3, 13; in Guiana, 63, 65; in Jamaica, 8, 74, 101, 105, 108, 110–14, 137; Jewish planters of, 167, 171–72; in Martinique, 74; in Nevis, 174; in New Holland, 36, 72, 168; in St. Croix, 118, 121, 124, 128; in Saint-Domingue, 10, 136, 137, 141, 153, 154, 157; in St. John, 122–23; in St. Thomas, 9, 119–21; in Suriname, 6, 37, 41, 42, 43, 62, 63, 65–66, 71–74, 78, 80, 84–85, 90, 171

Superior Council of Colonies (French), 157

Suriname: Dutch settlement of, 62, 86–88, 90; Dutch takeover of, 2, 6, 76, 79–81; English settlement of, 6, 35, 70, 71–73, 78, 91, 177; and expansion of European territorial interests, 7, 12, 177, 180; French settlement of, 69–70; French threat to, 77, 86–91; in eighteenth century, 91; Indian slave trade in, 37–38; Jews in, 11, 36, 40, 41, 66, 73, 76, 82, 83, 86, 88, 171–73; population of, 82, 84, 86, 88; slavery in, 6, 31, 34, 36–45, 69, 71, 74, 76, 78, 82, 84, 89, 90, 91. *See also* Arawak; Barbados; *bokkenruylers;* Carib; dyewood; English Civil Wars; First Anglo-Dutch War; Huguenots; Irish; Jamaica; New Holland; *Oronooko;* Second Anglo-Dutch War; servants; sugar; Third Anglo-Dutch War; tobacco; transatlantic slave trade; Walloons; Zeeland